RANGER DAWN

The Stackpole Military History Series

THE AMERICAN CIVIL WAR
Cavalry Raids of the Civil War
Ghost, Thunderbolt, and Wizard
Pickett's Charge
Witness to Gettysburg

WORLD WAR I
Doughboy War

WORLD WAR II
After D-Day
Armor Battles of the Waffen-SS, 1943–45
Armoured Guardsmen
Army of the West
Australian Commandos
The B-24 in China
Backwater War
The Battle of Sicily
Battle of the Bulge, Vol. 1
Battle of the Bulge, Vol. 2
Beyond the Beachhead
Beyond Stalingrad
The Brandenburger Commandos
The Brigade
Bringing the Thunder
The Canadian Army and the Normandy Campaign
Coast Watching in World War II
Colossal Cracks
A Dangerous Assignment
D-Day Deception
D-Day to Berlin
Destination Normandy
Dive Bomber!
A Drop Too Many
Eagles of the Third Reich
Eastern Front Combat
Exit Rommel
Fist from the Sky
Flying American Combat Aircraft of World War II
Forging the Thunderbolt
Fortress France
The German Defeat in the East, 1944–45
German Order of Battle, Vol. 1
German Order of Battle, Vol. 2
German Order of Battle, Vol. 3
The Germans in Normandy
Germany's Panzer Arm in World War II
GI Ingenuity
Goodwood
The Great Ships
Grenadiers
Hitler's Nemesis
Infantry Aces
Iron Arm
Iron Knights
Kampfgruppe Peiper at the Battle of the Bulge
The Key to the Bulge
Kursk
Luftwaffe Aces
Luftwaffe Fighter Ace
Massacre at Tobruk
Mechanized Juggernaut or Military Anachronism?
Messerschmitts over Sicily
Michael Wittmann, Vol. 1
Michael Wittmann, Vol. 2
Mountain Warriors
The Nazi Rocketeers
No Holding Back
On the Canal
Operation Mercury
Packs On!
Panzer Aces
Panzer Aces II
Panzer Commanders of the Western Front
Panzer Gunner
The Panzer Legions
Panzers in Normandy
Panzers in Winter
The Path to Blitzkrieg
Penalty Strike
Red Road from Stalingrad
Red Star under the Baltic
Retreat to the Reich
Rommel's Desert Commanders
Rommel's Desert War
Rommel's Lieutenants
The Savage Sky
The Siegfried Line
A Soldier in the Cockpit
Soviet Blitzkrieg
Stalin's Keys to Victory
Surviving Bataan and Beyond
T-34 in Action
Tank Tactics
Tigers in the Mud
Triumphant Fox
The 12th SS, Vol. 1
The 12th SS, Vol. 2
Twilight of the Gods
The War against Rommel's Supply Lines
War in the Aegean
Wolfpack Warriors
Zhukov at the Oder

THE COLD WAR / VIETNAM
Cyclops in the Jungle
Expendable Warriors
Flying American Combat Aircraft: The Cold War
Here There Are Tigers
Land with No Sun
Phantom Reflections
Street without Joy
Through the Valley

WARS OF THE MIDDLE EAST
Never-Ending Conflict

GENERAL MILITARY HISTORY
Carriers in Combat
Cavalry from Hoof to Track
Desert Battles
Guerrilla Warfare
Ranger Dawn
Sieges

RANGER DAWN

The American Ranger from the
Colonial Era to the Mexican War

Col. Robert W. Black

STACKPOLE
BOOKS

Copyright © 2009 by Robert W. Black

Published in 2009 by
STACKPOLE BOOKS
5067 Ritter Road
Mechanicsburg, PA 17055
www.stackpolebooks.com

All rights reserved, including the right to reproduce this book or portions thereof in any form or by any means, electronic or mechanical, including photocopying, recording, or by any information storage and retrieval system, without permission in writing from the publisher. All inquiries should be addressed to Stackpole Books.

Cover design by Tracy Patterson

Printed in the United States of America

10 9 8 7 6 5 4 3 2 1

FIRST EDITION

Library of Congress Cataloging-in-Publication Data

Black, Robert W.
  Ranger dawn : the American ranger from the colonial era to the Mexican War / Robert W. Black.
    p. cm. — (Stackpole military history series)
  Includes bibliographical references and index.
  ISBN 978-0-8117-3600-8
  1. United States. Army—Commando troops—History—18th century. 2. United States. Army—Commando troops—History—19th century. 3. United States—History—Revolution, 1775–1783—Commando operations. 4. Mexican War, 1846–1848—Commando operations. 5. Special forces (Military science)—United States—History—18th century. 6. Special forces (Military science)—United States—History—19th century. I. Title.
  UA34.R36B53 2009
  356'.167097309034—dc22
                           2008045324

To Tim Todish and Gary Zaboly,
superb historians who were born too late to be members of Rogers's Rangers
but have worked with diligence to make up for the error in timing

A RANGER PRAYER

Oh, Lord, we are about to join battle with vastly superior numbers of the enemy, and heavenly Father, we would like for you to be on our side and help us; but if you can't do it, for Christ's sake don't go over to the enemy, but just lie low and keep dark, and you'll see one of the damndest fights you ever saw in all your born days. Amen.

—Jack Hays, Texas Rangers

Contents

Preface viii

Chapter 1   Genesis of the Ranger. 1
Chapter 2   Early Indian Wars 9
Chapter 3   Old Fights, New World 22
Chapter 4   The French and Indian War, 1754–63. 38
Chapter 5   The River and the Lakes. 78
Chapter 6   Pontiac's War, 1763. 88
Chapter 7   Rangers in the Revolution 99
Chapter 8   Citizen-Soldiers. 108
Chapter 9   War in the North. 110
Chapter 10 To Boston and Beyond 131
Chapter 11 George Rogers Clark Captures the West 170
Chapter 12 Blood on the Border. 190
Chapter 13 War in the South. 196
Chapter 14 Turning the Tide. 216
Chapter 15 Post-Revolution Fights and the War of 1812 251
Chapter 16 The Birth of Texas 270
Chapter 17 The Triangle of War 275
Chapter 18 Texas Independence. 286
Chapter 19 Ranger Jack Hays and the Colts. 297
Chapter 20 Manifest Destiny 310
Chapter 21 Peace and War. 324

Appendix A: Robert Rogers's Rules for Rangers, 1757. . . . 336
*Appendix B: John Stark's Commission in the Rangers,
    July 23, 1756.* 341
Notes 342
Bibliography. 348
Index. 352

Preface

On the morning of March 22, 1622, the winds of spring caressed the fields and cabins of Berkeley Plantation in tidewater Virginia. The day held promise. The time for planting was at hand, and the men and women of the fledgling community were eager to start their work. The crude and scattered homes of several hundred people were an outpost far distant from the world across the ocean which the adults had known. Many children had no memory of the Old World; they had been born in America. Those who would survive the hardships of the frontier were destined to become a new breed.

There was much to look forward to that spring. Problems with the Indians had given way to a time of peace, even friendship, with the Powhatan tribes. Indians were welcomed into cabins, sometimes even eating with the colonists and staying overnight. Trade was extensive, benefitting both sides. A few Indians had mentioned that there was anger among the tribes at the perceived loss of land, but the settlers felt that they had justly paid or traded for the space they occupied and had treated the Indians with kindness. When a large party of Indians appeared, some men hurried forward to greet them, eager to see what items would be available for trade. Shouts of welcome turned to cries of fear, then screams of agony, as the Indians fell upon the colonists with war clubs, hatchets, and scalping knives. A merciless tide swept through the cabins of Berkeley Plantation, butchering men, women, and children. The community was not prepared for war, and hundreds died. The longest American war had begun, a war that would last 268 years. It was a war that would give rise to a unique breed of American warrior, one combining the best fighting qualities of the Indians and the Europeans. These men would be known as Rangers.

CHAPTER 1

Genesis of the Ranger

In 1598, a new name entered general usage, a name full of hope for those who had suffered under the yoke of repression in Europe. It was a name that promised opportunity and challenge. The name originated from that of Italian navigator Amerigo Vespucci, who made several trips to the New World. The accounts of his journeys were published by the German geographer Martin Waldseemuller, who suggested the new lands be called *America*.

In 1607, after a century of voyages of exploration and failed attempts to start permanent settlements, people came from Britain to settle on the coast of modern-day Virginia at a place they called Jamestown. Thirteen years later, the small ship *Mayflower* brought the Pilgrims to a new life at Plymouth, Massachusetts. Both colonies would experience difficulties with the local inhabitants and the mother country. Initially, these settlers thought of themselves as English, but when they left the Old World, they were often referred to as Americans, American Britons, provincials, or colonists. Separation from England by trackless ocean, self-interest, and a drifting fog of communication began to give rise to a new identity. Though the ties to the Old World were initially strong, each succeeding generation saw an increasing number of men and women who rejected control from overseas and thought of themselves as American rather than English.

These first Americans brought to North America the military experiences of Europe. The bloody religious wars had left Europe drained. War had become the practice of aristocratic professional officers far removed from the mercenaries and cast-offs of society who filled the ranks. The officer corps of the nations of Europe codified the rules of war as though it were a sporting contest. It was difficult to replace trained, experienced soldiers; therefore, maneuver was preferable to battles of attrition. In 1697, Daniel Defoe commented that it was "frequent to have armies of fifty thousand men of a side stand at bay within view of one another and spend a whole campaign in dodging, or, as it is genteelly called, observing one another, and then march off into winter quarters."

European armies had limited experience in irregular warfare and primarily fought in set-piece fashion. Each army marched and countermarched seeking advantage. This was done in good weather on broad, open fields that could accommodate large numbers of closely assembled men. Raids and ambushes—as well as most kinds of innovation—were exceptions that were frowned upon by many commanders. These were the military weaknesses the first Americans brought from Europe. There were strengths as well. The typical newcomer was accustomed to discipline and possessed firearms and steel blades.

To those who had been reared in the long-established towns, cultivated fields, and comparatively short distances of Europe, North America was terrifying in its raw immensity, its great distances, and its varied terrain. The forests were gigantic, at places impenetrable, with towering trees whose trunks often measured fifty inches across. There were pine forests and birch, maple, oak, and elm. Their interlocking leafy crowns shut out the sunlight and created a dark and foreboding wilderness. Bear, bison, wolf, and panther roamed the land. Rattlesnakes were so numerous that they became a factor in some military operations, and mosquitoes were so prevalent that in one instance an Indian tribe sentenced a man to death by tying him naked to a stake among the swarming insects.

The new Americans found themselves fenced into the Atlantic coast by the southwest-to-northeast barrier formed by the Appalachian, Adirondack, Green, and White Mountains. Rivers formed vital pathways from the coast to the foot of the mountains—the Savannah, Santee, Peedee, Cape Fear, Roanoke, James, Susquehanna, and Mohawk. Only the Mohawk offered a river, portage, and lake route to the interior beyond the mountains. From north to south, the mighty Hudson River offered Indians and whites a highway to war. Lake George and Lake Champlain were militarily significant. Lake Champlain linked with the Richelieu River, which in turn joined the St. Lawrence at the heart of New France. When the Hudson turned west, it led to access to Lake Ontario. Frontier travel by land was slow and hazardous. Large loads and heavy armaments could best be transported by water.

The nations of Europe looked to the New World as a prize to be quickly seized and exploited. The land and waters were rich in fur and fish, and the forest yielded timber for shipbuilding. The English, French, Dutch, Swedes, and Spanish staked out claims and struggled against each other. Rival English colonies fought over territorial claims. They all had to contend with the native inhabitants. The Indian tribes who had risen to supremacy in centuries of tribal warfare now stood in the way of a more powerful force. The newcomers believed in their natural superiority and were determined to prevail.

The forebears of the American Indians had come from Asia, arriving in North America by way of a land bridge across the Bering Strait. Though estimates vary, it is likely their arrival occurred between 50,000 and 10,000 BC. When the first European colonists arrived, there were probably about 1,150,000 Indians living north of Mexico. Approximately 220,000 of these lived along the east coast areas that would become known as British America. Tribes in the southeast included the Cherokee, Catawba, Creek, and Seminole. In the north were the Abenaki, Pequot, Sauk, Fox, Shawnee, Chippewa, and Delaware. The Spartans of North America were the Iroquois, a five-nation confederation so unique that its organization was studied by the framers of the U.S. Constitution. The Iroquois originally consisted of the Oneidas, Mohawks, Cayugas, Onondagas, and Senecas. In 1713, the Tuscaroras, who had been depleted by wars in North Carolina, received permission from the colonies and the Iroquois to migrate north. They passed through Pennsylvania and in 1722 became the sixth nation of the Iroquois Confederacy, which dominated the north. From their home in present-day New York state, their war canoes roamed the great rivers. Iroquois warriors ranged from Canada to the Carolinas and from the east coast to the western plains. They understood, spoke of, and practiced control "by right of conquest."[1]

The conquered were not permitted to make war without the approval of the Iroquois. They were allowed to sit at the council fires but without a voice. To the Iroquois, the defeated were "women." They had headmen—called "half-kings"—to oversee the activities of subject tribes. So great was Iroquois power that aged chiefs were sent alone to collect tribute and to start or end conflicts between other tribes. Lesser nations trembled before these ancients. They destroyed the Huron, Eries, and Andastes, crushed the Wyandots, and forced the Delaware to their knees.

In present-day Virginia, on the western side of the Chesapeake Bay, nine Algonquian tribes formed the Powhatan alliance. Their territory extended from the Chesapeake to the falls of the Rappahannock River and from the south side of the James River north to the Rappahannock. Unknowingly, the first English settlers took up residence in the heart of Powhatan territory. Farther south, the Creek Confederation was a powerful force. Like the Iroquois, the Creeks were highly developed politically and militarily.

The Indian was a hunter, and war was a natural part of his life. Indian tactics were adapted to the environment. He shunned pitched battles and fighting in the open. A favorite tactic was the raid. Small parties, often of no more than four men, would travel great distances, patiently reconnoiter, and lie in wait until the moment came to strike. In letters written in 1609–10, Capt. John Smith described Indian tactics: "They never fight in open fields but always amonge reede or behind trees takinge ther oportunitie to shoot at ther enimies till they can nock another arrow they make the trees the defense."[2] Absorbing his environment, the Indian became one with it. He used the hunter's skills, took advantage of cover and concealment to close with his enemy and made the most of his primitive armament of bow and arrow, club, spear, and knife. Success meant killing the enemy while taking as few casualties as possible.

Bravery in battle was the mark of a man. The Indian warrior fought to exterminate, capture, or enslave. Torture of the captured was entertainment. Many Indian tribes tore the hair from the heads of their slain enemies as proof of the kill and symbols of their prowess. By 1637, Europeans were rewarding Indians for the scalps of other Indians and, after 1688, for the scalps of other Europeans.[3] On occasion, prisoners were adopted into the tribe, sometimes to replace Indians killed in battle. Those adopted were treated with an affection that often produced lifelong bonds.

It was an age of cruelty. The European settlers came from countries where men were flogged, disfigured, or tortured by the powerful. A ruthless class system held men and women in bondage, and a totalitarian religion brooked no deviation in faith. Those convicted

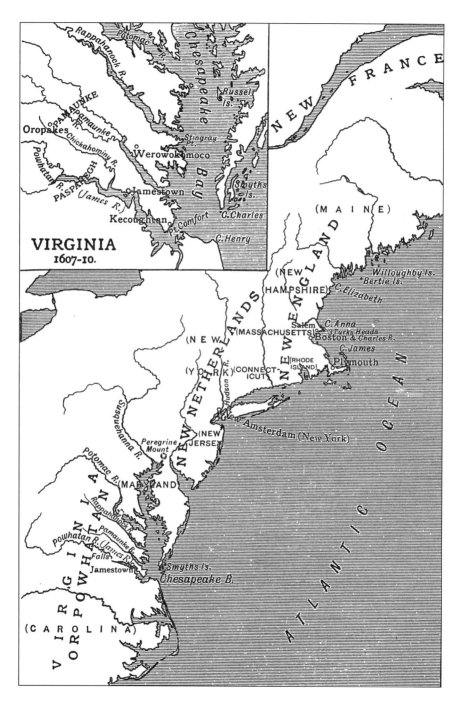

North America in the 1600s

of heresy were tortured or burned at the stake. Whatever rights and freedoms that existed were for the rich. Slavery was not determined by color of skin—all races held slaves. The poor were prey. In Europe, a starving man who stole a loaf of bread would be fortunate to escape mutilation or death and instead be sent to a distant colony into indentured servitude that many would never escape. Regardless of ethnic background or place of birth, inhuman treatment was routine for most people.

Distrust accompanied the meeting of colonists and Indians. There were desperate fights followed by uneasy peace, but they soon found use for each other. The white settlers needed the food that only the Indians could supply, and the Indians wanted the steel tools and weapons of the whites. The new arrivals were not in sufficient numbers for total war and sought accommodation as well as land. The Indians were not accustomed to the concept of private ownership of land, and their experience could not prepare them for the tide of land-hungry humanity that boiled out of Europe.

Terror was ubiquitous on the American frontier. It is difficult to conceive of the constant fear in which the settlers lived. No man can be consantly vigilant. A farmer plowing his field or tending his crops might stray too far by himself or be caught without his weapon close at hand. Thousands of people died in the horror of Indian raids. Survivors developed a hatred so deep that generations would hold to Gen. Phil Sheridan's bloody belief that "the only good Indians I ever saw were dead."[4]

Based on the English Muster Law of 1572, units of citizen-soldiers were formed to be used in emergencies. They were known as militia. As the threat of Indian attack was always present, American militia knew the bloody price of unpreparedness. If manpower was available, some worked the fields while others stood guard. Gradually, they improved their training and preparation. In the more populated areas, men gathered their families and built forts. In times of danger, they hid behind their palisades, venturing forth only in large parties or when the need for food drove them to take chances. On the frontier, warm weather was a time of fear. Only in the dead of winter was there a reduction in the Indian menace. In the late fall, the colonists would harvest their crops, then hope and pray for bad weather. As so often happens in the north after the winter cold had set in, there would be several weeks of sudden warming, bright days, and pleasant temperatures. The Indians seized upon this time to conduct deadly raids. Thus the term "Indian summer" was born.

Penned in small and crowded forts, desperate men tired of defensive life began to seek ways to provide early warning of Indian attacks and a more rapid response. The more daring of them sought ways to take the war to the enemy, burn his dwellings, destroy his crops and livestock, and kill him and his family. Torture, scalping, murder, and enslavement would be practiced by both sides. This would be total war, with extinction its goal.

Putting aside their useless European tactics, some colonists began to study the ways of the Indian. The new Americans developed survival techniques, woodcraft, knowledge of the terrain, and cross-country movement. They learned the advantages of an active defense and offensive action that included reconnaissance, raiding, and ambushing. This native knowledge blended with the better discipline and improved weaponry of Europe. The princes of the Old World had taken strong measures to keep the population unarmed. In the New World, every male child (and many females) quickly learned how to handle firearms. The importance of having the means to protect oneself became ingrained in the American character.

Conflict with the Indians came early in both Virginia and New England as colonists ranged outward for exploration and defensive or offensive operations. The earliest mention of Ranger operations comes from Capt. John Smith, who served in both Virginia and New England. Writing in 1622 about his earlier conflicts in Virginia, Smith recorded, "When I had ten men able to go abroad, our common wealth was very strong: with such a number I ranged that unknown country 14 weeks." Of his experience in New England, Smith wrote, "To range this country of New England, I had but eight, as is said, and amongst their brute conditions I met many of their encounters, and without any hurt, God be thanked."[5] Smith also wrote of Virginia Gov. Sir George Yearly, who participated in ranging operations. Smith wanted the Virginia Company to provide 100 soldiers and 30 sailors for use only "in ranging the countries."[6]

In 1622, after the Berkeley Plantation massacre of the whites in Virginia, grim-faced men went forth to search out the Indian enemy. They were militia—citizen-soldiers—but they were learning to blend the methods of Indian and European warfare. These men did not have standardized uniforms or equipment; they were not an army. They were men fighting a very personal battle for their homes and families. Informal killers, they expected and gave no mercy. As they went in search of the enemy, the words *range, ranging,* and *Ranger* were frequently used. In 1637, John Winthrop, writing to Gov. William Bradford of an action in the Pequot War, tells of parties of men "dividing themselves and ranging up & down."

The American Ranger had been born.

CHAPTER 2

Early Indian Wars

In seventeenth-century America, conflict between the colonists and the Indian began early and grew quickly. The Indian wars opened with the Berkeley Plantation Massacre in 1622 and continued with Virginia's battles with the Powhatan and Susquehannock Indians. New England experienced the Pequot War (1636–37) and King Philip's War (1675–76). From Maine to Florida, the battle was joined as Indian and white fought each other while also fighting members of their own races. This period was the cauldron of war in which the American Ranger was born.

Conflict existed from the earliest meeting between colonist and Indian. On April 26, 1607, after a four-month voyage, the three little ships of the Jamestown settlers entered the Chesapeake Bay. A landing party sent ashore near Cape Henry was promptly attacked. Thereafter, English suspicions were high. The Indians were friendly one day and would attack the settlers the next. Smith and other leaders forced the Indians to trade. When opposed, they attacked the Indians late in the growing season, destroying the Indian food supply too late for another crop to be planted. Cruelty by both Indian and colonist was routine and built to a repetitious cycle of violence.

Jamestown settler Capt. George Percy was brother to the Earl of Northumberland. In August 1610, Percy was ordered to lead a punitive expedition against the Paspehegh Indian village. Percy attacked the town with seventy men, killing sixteen Indians and putting the rest to flight. The Paspehegh queen and her two children were taken prisoner. Percy described the aftermath as follows:

> My Lieftenanntt bringeinge wth him the Quene and her Children and one Indyann prisoners for the wch I taxed him becawse he had Spared them his Answer was thatt haveinge them now in my Custodie I mighte doe wth them what I

pleased. Upon the same I cawsed the Indians heade to be cutte of. And then disposed my flyles Apointeinge my Sowldiers to burne their howses, and to cutt downe their Corne groweinge aboutt the Towne, And after we marched wth the queen to our Boates ageine, where beinge noe soener well shipped my sowldiers did begin to murmur because the quene and her Children were spared. So upon a councell beinge called itt was Agreed upon to put the Children to deathe the wch was effected by Throweinge them overboard and shoteinge owtt their Braynes in the water.[1]

The queen was later killed. Far away in England, there were complaints about these actions, but the men on the scene felt that anything that would contribute to the ruin of the Indian was just. The period 1609–14 is considered the First Anglo-Powhatan War.[2]

Of the original 900 settlers, all but 150 had quickly died from starvation and disease, but more settlers arrived. Fifteen years after the founding, the colony was well rooted, though the task of making it grow was arduous. Each day was a challenge of survival. Plantations were established along the Powhatan (James) River. Men, women, and children were early to work in the tobacco fields. Europe had developed an addiction for the smoking weed, and good profits could be made. Relations with the Indians were uneasy, but peaceful. The Powhatans now consisted of thirty-two tribes scattered across 200 villages. Peace with these Indians was largely through efforts of an astute Indian leader named Wahunsonacock, the man colonists called King Powhatan.

Around 1618, Wahunsonacock died and was replaced by his brother Opechancanough. The new chief had a broader appreciation of the impact the new arrivals were having on his land and people. He felt the Indians were mistreated, and while talking peace, Opechancanough sought an opportune time to attack the settlers. The English settlers provided him with the flame of his torch when they executed an Indian who they believed murdered a white trader.

The promise of spring was in the Virginia air at dawn on the morning of March 22, 1622, when the warriors of the Powhatan Confederacy came down with fury on the tidewater plantations. Some friendly Indians tried to warn the settlers, but the attack was well disguised. Edward Waterhouse, who was a Virginia official at the time, wrote that at the time of the attack the settlers houses were open to the Indians, who dined at their tables and commonly lodged in their bed chambers. On the morning of the attack, the Indians came as though to trade. They soon commenced to kill 347 men, women, and children. Terror was soon replaced with rage in the hearts of the survivors. Edward Waterhouse wrote, "Our hands, which before were tied with gentleness and fair usage, are now set at liberty by the treacherous violence of the savages . . . so that we, who hitherto have had possession of no more ground than their waste and our purchase at a valuable consideration to their contentment gained, may now by right of war, and the law of nations invade the country and destroy them who sought to destroy us."[3] The war to the death had begun.

The second war between the Virginia colonists and the Powhatans raged from 1622 to 1632. The killing of an Indian became generally accepted as a noble act. By right of conquest, all Indian lands could be seized. Armed bands began to range the tidewater area destroying Indian villages, burning and uprooting their crops, and slaying any Indian who crossed their paths. The war saw victories on both sides. The Indians ambushed and raided the colonists and killed male prisoners. They kept any women they captured. Fearing an ambush if they attempted rescue, the colonists proposed an end to all fighting if the women were returned. The Indians did this, but at the 1623 truce talk, they were served poisoned wine. As they writhed in pain, 200 Indians were killed; another 50 were hunted down. In 1625, the colonists destroyed the Indian village of Pamunkey, killing more than a thousand Indians.

In 1644, the third war erupted. After a rough truce, the Indians suddenly attacked and killed 500 settlers.

In 1646, after twenty-four years of fear and struggle, the aging and nearly blind Openchancanough was captured, publicly displayed, and shot dead. The intervening years saw the destruction of his people as the dogs of war had been unleashed. As other Indians took up the hatchet, they found that some men among the settlers would hunt as they hunted and kill as they killed. In war, men learn from their enemies. In tactics, the Ranger had become a "white Indian" able to exchange blow for blow.

The Indian would have been disadvantaged in weaponry had it not been for greed. Profit, regardless of cost, was foremost in the mind of some settlers. From their entry in the New World, the Dutch had provided weapons as items of trade. In New England, Thomas Morton sold his countrymen for profit by providing firearms and steel hatchets to Indians in return for furs.[4] His business prospered, and Morton's action inspired other traders to do the same. Thousands of colonists would die because of the avarice of these men.

In 1633, conflict erupted in the north. Capt. John Stone, Col. Walter Norton, and others took a small ship up the Connecticut River, presumably to trade. The crew was overpowered by Indians. Colonel Norton fought a valiant fight from the cookhouse until fire exploded his store of gunpowder and left him blinded and defenseless before the tomahawk. Captain Stone was struck in the head while in his cabin and pulled a cover over his face so that he would not see his death blow.[5] An expedition to punish the culprits executed two Indians who were alleged to have been involved.

In the Connecticut and Mystic River Valleys, the Pequot Indians were finding themselves squeezed between growing settlements of English and Dutch. The Narragansett Indians were also deemed a threat. The Pequots were Algonquin, a proud, warlike people whose dances and ceremonies were filled with shouts and songs of their bravery. Long the dominant force in the area, their numbers were reduced by smallpox contracted from European settlers and internal warfare. In 1631, the tribe split. The Pequot, who favored the Dutch, were under the leadership of a Sachem named Sassacus. A second group of Pequot discarded the old tribal name and called themselves Mohegan. Under the leadership of a Sachem named Uncas, the Mohegan supported the English.

When, in 1636, John Oldham was murdered and his boat seized by Indians, the colonists sought revenge. Massachusetts Bay Colony sent John Endicott and a force of ninety men to raid the Indians, primarily Narragansetts who lived on Block Island. Endicott's men burned the Indians out and killed every male Indian they encountered. The force then went after the Pequots, killed one Indian, and burned villages.

The Pequots struck back with a series of raids. At Fort Saybrook, where the Connecticut River flows into Long Island Sound, they harassed the settlers throughout the winter of 1636–37. They struck with fury at individual cabins and isolated homes. In the spring of 1637, they killed nine colonists at Wethersfield along the Connecticut River.

Again the colonists attacked. Capt. John Mason from Hartford led a force of eighty white men and Mohegan Indian allies. Mason sailed down river to Fort Saybrook, where he was joined by Capt. John Underhill and men from Massachusetts Bay Colony. At Fort Saybrook, the campaign strategy was resolved.

The Pequot lands and their two major villages lay between the colonists' settlements on the Connecticut River and the Narragansett Bay area where the Indians of the same name held sway. Taking advantage of Indian animosities, Mason sailed his force along the coast, bypassing Pequot lands. In the Narragansett area, he recruited Indian allies, then moved cross-country to strike a main Pequot village in a surprise attack. In stealthy night movement, the attackers surrounded the Pequots at a place on the Mystic River near today's location of the picturesque town of Stonington.

At dawn on May 25, 1637, with the Indian allies hanging back, the colonists attacked the stockaded village through the open gates at each side. Confusion reigned. Pequots and colonists fought hand to hand; other Pequots concealed themselves inside their wigwams and used their bows and arrows through openings with telling effect. The colonists brought fire from Indian habitations, setting the other Indian habitations ablaze. A strong wind spread the fire rapidly. Amid roaring flames, battle cries, and screams, 700 Pequot Indians were killed. Governor Bradford's *History of Plimouth Plantation* describes the attack: "It was a fearful sight to see them thus frying in ye fyer and ye streams of blood quenching ye same and horrible was ye stinch & sente ther of."

Any Pequots who escaped the flames found their Narrangansett and Mohegan enemies waiting, mocking them with Pequot songs and battle cries, before closing for the kill. As many as a thousand Pequots may have died. Two colonists were killed.

The remaining Pequot warriors, about 300 in number, hurried to the scene of the battle and tried to attack Mason's force on a narrow neck of land as the victors marched to the coast. When they saw the size of the force opposing them, these Pequots held back. Simultaneously, Mason was deserted by his Indian allies. Both sides backed away.

The hunt was on for the surviving Pequots and their sachem, Sassacus. In July 1637, near present-day New Haven, Mason and his men used a captured Indian to locate the Pequots. They were found in a small village by a thick shrubbed, boggy swamp about a mile in circumference. Sassacus and about twenty of his men slipped away, hoping to find sanctuary with the Mohawks, but these Indians cut off his head. About 80 male Pequots and 200 women and children hid in the swamp. Ninety colonists surrounded the swamp and moved inward. Lieutenant Davenporte and twelve men moved prematurely and found themselves stuck in deep mud under a hail of Pequot arrows. Davenporte and another man were wounded.

Throughout the day and night, the Pequots were herded into an ever more confined area. Stuck in mud, fighting fiercely at close range the Indians tried to break out. It was over by dawn. Nine Indian bodies were found in the swamp; others later perished of their wounds. Some surviving Pequots were given to Indian allies to do with as they chose. Some males were sold into slavery in Bermuda; females were made slaves in the colonies. The Pequots were nearly obliterated. Conflict was not limited to settler fighting Indian.

The men and women who struggled in the raw newness of seventeenth-century America were a hardy, courageous breed. The crossing of the Atlantic was itself a major challenge. Those who came to the New World carried in their breasts hope and determination; they also carried the hatreds and prejudices of the Old World.

From 1635 to 1644, the mostly Protestant Virginia and the mostly Catholic Maryland quarreled over land and religion. In the Chesapeake Bay, Kent Island was the scene of confrontation. The island had been included in the tract of land granted Maryland, but the Virginians did not retire with grace. Capt. William Claiborne, a member of the Virginia Council, set up a fort, trading post, and tobacco plantation on the island. The island was clearly in the Maryland grant to Lord Baltimore, but Claiborne refused to accept direction from Baltimore. In 1634 and 1635, Claiborne hired Edward Backler to be a "Rainger." Backler had experience with Indians, reporting in 1634, "This yeare we were much hindered and molested by Indians falling out with us and killing our men and by the Marylanders hindering our trade. We made our effort strong etc."[6]

In 1644, Claiborne seized Kent Island outright. In the same year, the primarily Catholic community of St. Mary's was occupied by a force led by a Protestant trader. A governor-to-governor appeal resulted in the settlement being restored to Maryland. The crown ruled against Claiborne, and he lost Kent Island. Ranger Backler lost his job.

Indian tribes waged war against each other. There was considerable profit to be made from trading beaver pelts. Indian tribes found this trade with the white man greatly enhanced their lives and soon became dependent upon it. Toward the middle of the century, the powerful Iroquois, seeing their supply of beaver diminishing, began to attack their neighbors and seize their trapping areas. Beginning in 1649 with an invasion of Huron lands to the north, the Iroquois struck outward to all points of the white man's compass. They attacked the Ottawas, Miamis, Illinois, Delaware, Susquehannocks, Potowamis, Nipissings, and Mohegans. Raiding and scalp-taking between Indian tribes were constant during the last half of the century.

In New England, the peaceful years that followed the Pequot War were a boon to the colonists and disaster for the Indians. While the colonists grew to number 50,000, the Indians were reduced by flight and disease from 140,000 to 10,000. As the colonies grew, the pressures on the Indian increased. There was frequent conflict over land, money, services, and treatment. The resentment of the New England grouping of Algonquin Indians called Wampanoag was deeply felt in the heart of their leader, a chief named Metacom and called Philip or King Philip by the colonists. These Indians lived in southern Massachusetts—including Cape Cod, Nantucket, and Vineyard Island—and parts of Rhode Island. The colonists believed that the seeds of the Great Indian War of 1675–76 were sown at the time of the defeat of the Pequots in 1637. During that war, the Narragansetts and the Mohegans had been allied with the colonists. The Narragansetts believed they did not receive a proper division of the Pequot spoils and vented their anger on the Mohegans. In 1645, the colonists felt they had to intervene to protect the Mohegans. Philip's Wampanoags were allies of the Narrangansetts. He was a leader of exceptional ability who had a list of grievances, including the belief that his brother had died at the hands of the white man. He set about to organize an alliance of Indian tribes that would act in concerted fashion to drive the colonists away.

Philip's efforts did not go unnoticed. The colonists sent out their Rangers to reconnoiter and provide early warning. The commander of one group of Rangers was Capt. Thomas Willet, a man of many parts. Though of English descent, Willet was probably born in Holland circa 1607–11. In 1629, Willet sailed from Gravesend en route to Plymouth Colony. On arrival, he became a trader and married into an influential family. In 1647–48, he was appointed captain of the Plymouth county militia. His relations with the Dutch leaders of New Amsterdam were excellent, and he is credited with being the man who talked Peter Stuyvesant into surrendering the Dutch settlement. With English ascendency, it was proclaimed on June 12, 1665, that the newly acquired territory renamed New York should have a municipal government, including a mayor. Ranger Capt. Thomas Willet thus became the first mayor of New York City. Willet served several terms as mayor and traveled back and forth between New York and Plymouth Colony. A deposition of a man named Hugh Cole taken at Plymouth Colony on March 8, 1670, recorded: "And some few days after I came from Mount Hope, I, with several others, saw one of Captain Willet's Rangers coming on horseback, who told us that King Philip was marching up the neck with about three score men."[7]

In 1661, the colonists received intelligence that Philip planned to attack the town of Taunton. Philip was sent for and came to parley with his armed warriors. He was not ready for war, and when the colonists surprised him with what they knew, he professed peaceful intent and allowed seventy firearms to be confiscated. This loss was difficult for the Indians to replace.

Willet was on good terms with Philip, and their mutual respect might have prevented the forthcoming war, but Willet died in August 1664. Philip believed a Christian Indian named John Sassamon had betrayed him. Sassamon was soon found murdered. On circumstantial evidence, three Indians close to Philip were arrested, tried, and executed. The Indians were outraged, and Philip could not hold them in check until his plan was fully implemented. Roving bands of Indians began to harass and attack the settlements.

The colonists continued organizing their defenses and dispatching parties of Rangers to search out the Indians. One of these was under the command of Benjamin Church, a thirty-six-year-old man of physical prowess and aggressive disposition. He was the first white man to build in an area that he described as "full of Indians." This close contact served him well as he understood Indian methods of

Col. Benjamin Church.

warfare and established friends among the Indians who would later serve as scouts and warriors in his forces.

Church sought out men who were experienced woodsmen. He was a relentless hunter who promptly carried the war to the Indians by using ambush and night attacks. His opponent, Philip, tried to enlist the aid of other Indian tribes and was partially successful. The colonists, under Gen. Josiah Winslow, were mustering the New England colonies and doing well recruiting among friendly Indian tribes. A force of 1,000 armed colonists supported by Indian allies was raised to combat the estimated 2,000 warriors at Philip's command.

Each side hunted the other in small but bloody fights. The fighting was at close quarters without mercy. Male prisoners were often tomahawked. Beheading and dismembering by both sides were commonplace. The communities of Middleborough and Dearborn were destroyed by Indians and hundreds of homes burned throughout the countryside. Church, with 20 men, held off a force of 300 Indians until he could escape by boat. In an act of bravado, he alone returned to shore to secure his hat and sword and came away safe. Later, in a night raid, he and his men surprised 18 sleeping Indians and captured them. Other parties of Rangers struck an Indian village, burned 150 dwellings, killed seven, and took eight prisoners.

Near Dartmouth, Church's Rangers captured 160 Indians. It was the Indian custom to torture and kill prisoners for amusement or to adopt them into the tribe. As the white settler came from a profit-minded society, Indian prisoners, particularly women and children, were frequently sold as slaves. Church recruited from his prisoners, giving them the choice of death, slavery, or service under his command as soldiers. This was effective recruiting, and some of Philip's warriors became Church's best scouts. In addition to his lieutenant, Jabez Howland, Church had a close friendship with two famed Indian scouts he called "Little Eyes" and "Lightfoot." Both Indian and white Rangers were devoted to Church and formed a personal guard to protect their audacious commander. Church said that these men were ready to "pilot him to any place where the Indians dwelt or haunted though their own fathers or nearest relations should be among them."

To thwart Church's patrols, Philip and the rest of his warriors kept on the move. Terror stalked the land as the sound of Indian war cries heralded death and destruction throughout the farms and hamlets of New England. The Arosaguntacook, Kennebec, Nipmuck, Saco, and Wawenoc Indians had entered the war on the side of Philip. They were decimating the whites, but the spoils from their raids were not sufficient to support them. Food shortages forced Philip's warriors to adopt a defensive strategy. This enabled the settlers to pinpoint their location. A battle was fought in July 1675 near Pocasset swamp with the colonists and their Indian allies winning. Action continued through the fall. More and more, Philip found the hand of other Indian tribes turned against him. His old enemies the Iroquois kept him penned in against the superior weaponry of the colonists.

Church's written orders usually began with the admonition that the command must pray daily and read the Bible. Somewhere in the orders would be a desire for as many captives as possible. Church had an advantage many commanders would envy. His orders from Winslow allowed Church maximum latitude to "discover, pursue, fight, destroy or subdue our Indian enemies."[8]

On November 19, 1675, Indian scouts for John Winslow located the main fort of the Narragansett Indians near South Kingston, Rhode Island. This was a fortified, elevated mound deep in a swamp. Winslow committed other units to make the initial attack. Church followed in with thirty Rangers. At the passage of the fort, he saw the

Early Indian Wars 19

bodies of other captains and their men. Seeing Captain Gardner, Church approached him, but as they prepared to talk, Gardner was shot through the head and died. Winslow and his men routed the Indians and began killing the wounded. While other colonists remained, Church immediately led his men in pursuit of the fleeing Indians. Church wanted information on Philip and was in hot pursuit of an Indian who turned to surrender. Before Church could question him, the Ranger behind Church killed the Indian. Behind them, they heard shouting in Indian tongue. A large number of Indians had joined the battle and were hurrying toward the fort. Church quietly moved his men in behind the Indians, concealing his Rangers behind a pile of brush. Church was uncertain which side these Indians were supporting. Church told his men to wait to see if the Indians fired on the fort. As the Indians rose to deliver a volley at the colonists, Church's Rangers fired into their backs, breaking their attack. Most of the surviving Indian warriors fled. About a dozen warriors took refuge in a hovel that appeared to be a corn crib. In attempting to root them out, Church was struck with three bullets. His men wanted to carry him away, but Church would not leave the scene of action. Winslow's troops were burning all buildings. Church had seen that they contained a large food supply needed by the army in the winter. Though seriously wounded, he attempted to stop the rash destruction, but he could not. Winslow's men burned food and shelter they would need greatly. In the months to come, some of their own wounded died as a result. The colonists lost 86 killed, including 6 captains, and 150 wounded. Between 300 and 350 Indians were killed and an equal amount wounded.

Desperate, Philip tried to recruit Mohawk Indians to fight against the colonists. When the Mohawks refused, Philip had some of his men ambush and kill some Mohawks, blaming it on the whites. One of the Mohawks survived to tell the truth of the occurrence. Philip had only added to the list of his enemies.

In May 1676, the colonists won again near Deerfield, and in August 1676, Philip was brought to bay. Recovered from his wounds, Church learned that Philip was on Great Hope Neck. The Great Swamp Fight, as the battle would become known, was fought at the Assowamsett Swamp on August 12, 1676. Using information supplied by his Rangers and Indian scouts, Church found Philip's hiding place.

Church frequently used the tactic of driving the Indians before him into an ambush. As Philip fled, he ran into the fire of one of Church's waiting Indians and was shot dead in the muck of a swamp. At the close of the fight, Church and his men dragged Philip's body through the mud to dry ground. Savoring his moment of victory. Church told his men that Philip had caused many an Englishman's body to lie unburied and none of Philip's bones would be buried. Church said that Philip had been a big man and many had been afraid of him, but as big as he was, Church "would now chop his arse for him."[9] Using his hatchet, Church cut off Philip's head and right hand and gave them to the Indian who killed Philip. The Indian was overjoyed as he could show his trophies to colonists for money. Philip's body was quartered. The war now became a gradual wearing down of the Indians until February 1678, when winter and starvation dealt the final blow.

In terms of percentage of population, King Philip's War was one the most destructive wars Americans have ever fought. More than 2,500 colonists—one out of every sixteen men of military age of the white population in New England—were killed, and 40 percent of the Indian population was either killed or fled.[10] Twelve New England towns were burned, and 50 percent of the remaining communities suffered damage.[11] The New England colonies had suffered greatly in loss of life and fortune. Many did not see the Indian as a fellow human being. Though steeped in Christian religious beliefs, the victors saw the enemy as subhuman and were not merciful to the captured Indians. Philip's wife and son were among those sold into slavery in the Caribbean; other Indians, including some that were promised amnesty, ended their lives as slaves in Spain.

In 1676, at the close of King Philip's War, the colonists imposed restrictions on New England Indians in essence requiring them to live on a reservation. Angered at the loss of both land and freedom, some displaced Indian tribes moved north into French Canada. From 1689 to 1697, Britain and France would fight what was known in Europe as the War of the League of Augsburg. The war soon reached the forests of New England, where it would become known as King William's War. Large raiding parties of French and Indians attacked settlements in the area of present-day Maine and Massachusetts. Families were slaughtered, communities decimated.

Church was promoted to major and commanded a force of 1,200 colonists and 300 Indians who hunted the perpetrators. The companies within the Rangers were a mixture of colonists and Indians, thus combining the advantages of both groups. Church said his Indians could track anything. Early on, Church made the acquaintance of a superb fighter named Capt. John Gorham, who was a waterman from Barnstable, Massachusetts. Church insisted that his command be supplied with some fifty whaleboats, which Gorham manned and equipped. Supported by larger, cannon-equipped vessels, Church and Gorham ranged the coast. When Church was promoted to colonel, John Gorham became a lieutenant colonel and Church's second in command.

Benjamin Church was a towering figure on the early frontier. Like every other early American Ranger who wished to keep his hair, he learned to combine Indian tactics with European discipline and weaponry. Some eighty years before Robert Rogers wrote his ranging rules, Church was writing of the importance of not traveling the same route twice. On at least one occasion, this knowledge saved Church and his command. He wrote that Indians had taught him to move with his men spread out rather then in a body as the English did. The Indians said that they always "took care not to come too thick together. But the English always kept in a heap together: that it was as easy to hit them as to hit a house."[12] Church wrote that he separated captives and questioned them individually so they could not fabricate stories. Church understood mobility and the importance of reconnaissance. He attacked at night, with his men crawling on their bellies until close to the enemy, then rising with a shout to attack. Church's lessons would serve the Rangers well in the years ahead.

CHAPTER 3

Old Fights, New World

The long-established animosities between England and France continued in the New World. The constant bickering, bushwhacking, and battles between them were rapidly drawing to a showdown. By the 1600s, both countries were keenly aware of the wealth available in North America. Tall trees, so important as the raw material for wooden navies, were readily available. There was tobacco and land, and the northern seas swarmed with cod, a fish that was vital as a food for the masses of Europe. The trade in fur was a key industry to France.

The French seaman Jacques Cartier made his first exploration of northern lands in 1534. Meeting some Iroquois Indians, he misunderstood an Indian word that probably referred to corn fields. Cartier understood the word as "Canada" and so named the land. Consumed by rivalry with Spain and internal civil and religious conflict, France lost an opportunity that likely would have made French the dominant language of North America. French Huguenots (i.e., Protestants) anxious to escape religious persecution offered to settle in the New World but remain loyal to France. Had the offer been accepted, France would have put down deep roots in North America. To Catholic France, the notion of allowing Protestant beliefs to spread was unacceptable. Only Catholics would be allowed in New France, which would be built on a foundation of the Catholic faith. The church, largely through the Jesuits, played a major role in determining French affairs in the New World. Their missionaries were active among the Indians. In France, thousands of Huguenots were butchered. Some fled to England and its colonies. In the New World, their descendants would include Paul Revere and Francis Marion. Lord John Ligonier, the overall commander of the British Army during the French and Indian War, was a displaced French Huguenot.

The French were active but never truly grasped the concept of settling the New World, building homes, raising crops, and expanding across lands far larger than their home country. More than the English, the French saw America as a source of wealth for the homeland. As traders, they traveled the rivers and streams that were the natural highways into the interior of the land. They married Indians. Many were adventurous French-Canadians who were unable to gain the required licenses. Though they operated outside French law, they were loyal to their motherland and became skilled woodsmen known as *coureurs de bois*. Advantageous to the French was their position in the north, where the great St. Lawrence led from the Atlantic Ocean and, with the Ottawa River, formed a water highway to the Great Lakes and the Ohio and Mississippi Rivers. The French could pass behind the Appalachian and Adirondack Mountains. The interior of the continent was open to them.

As the French did not seek to heavily populate the land or drive the original inhabitants from it, their relations with the Indians were good with one significant exception. In 1609, Samuel Champlain and a few French accompanied Algonquin Indians in a battle against the powerful Iroquois about a quarter of a mile from the present reconstruction of Fort Ticonderoga. The Iroquois had not previously encountered musket fire, and fearing the new weaponry, they fled. But their hatred remained and thereafter followed the French. The French allied themselves with the Huron tribe, whom they used as middlemen in the fur trade with western Indians. The Iroquois were actively engaged in fur trading with the Dutch and later the English. Resenting the competition, the Iroquois destroyed the Huron tribe, slaughtered the Jesuit missionaries, and threatened to wipe out New France. It took 1,000 French regulars to hold the Iroquois at bay. This was accomplished by 1701.

The English came to stay and reap the harvest for the benefit of the homeland. Their intent was to settle the land, peacefully if possible but by force of arms if necessary. They tended to put down roots along the seacoast, establish bases of supply, and move remorselessly inland. Both England and France brought their centuries-old hatred of each other to the New World. Both nations encouraged Indians to raid and kill. The Indians were able to bargain their services for the best offer.

By the close of the seventeenth century, the colonial powers England, France, and Spain were beginning a series of wars to establish the dimensions of their empires. A war was scarcely ended when a new one began. The fighting between Europeans wreaked havoc in the New World, where each side used Indian allies to conduct bloody raids. There was no peace, only an imperfect, frequently broken truce. One after another, wars came: Queen Anne's War (1702–13), the War of Jenkins' Ear (1739–43), King George's War (1744–48), and the French and Indian War (1754–63). Interspersed were wars with Indian tribes: with the Tuscaroras (1711–13), the Yamasee (1715–28), the Chickasaw (1720–63), the Fox (1720–35), the Natchez (1729–30), the Cherokee (1760–61), and Pontiac's War (1763–64). In these wars, the American Ranger was in the forefront of frontier defense. From the 1600s to Braddock's expedition in 1755, the colony of Virginia had employed forty-eight Ranger units, Maryland twenty-five, Massachusetts thirty-one, and Georgia eighteen. Rangers were found in all the North American colonies, including Nova Scotia.

By the mid 1700s, the English were a force to be reckoned with. A million and a half English settlers were in North America while the French could muster less than 100,000, most of whom were in northeast Canada. While not all the British colonies to the south had an interest in the competition over furs and fish, Massachusetts alone had more people than New France and also had a strong commercial interest.

The English were pushing inland from the Atlantic coast. In order to contain them, the French built a line of forts extending from Fort Niagara in the north down the Ohio Valley to New Orleans. As the English were absorbing Indian land and driving the tribes before them, the French found willing allies among the red men. The principal Indian force to remain allied with the English was the powerful Iroquois Confederacy. In time, they became adept at allowing both English and French to bid for their support.

The Ranger provisions passed by the Virginia legislature had been put into practice though modified. The base-of-operation forts proposed by Gov. William Berkeley had proven too expensive to maintain. In 1679, in the thirty-first year of the reign of Charles II of England, the counties on the eastern and western shore of the Chesapeake were authorized to recruit "souldiers to be Rangers for the security of their respective counties according to such order and direction as shall be agreed upon and made by their militia officers."[1] From 1683, some Rangers stayed at plantations, alternating their ranging activities with work in the fields.

In 1691, an act was passed in Virginia for "a certain number of Rangers [to be] kept under constant pay . . . at ye heads of their great Rivers from whence they are in danger of Incursions by land, who are at all times to give notice of any vestages they discover of ye Enemy & are strong enough to fall upon and defeat any Ordinary gang of Indians."[2] The dawn of the eighteenth century saw the Ranger concept become widely accepted. Skilled and determined frontiersmen were patrolling between the Indian lands and the settlements and, when required, carrying the war to the enemy. Maryland, which had employed Rangers for half a century, was sending out patrols in the area of present-day Baltimore and Washington.

From 1702 to 1713, Queen Anne's War (known as the War of Spanish Succession in Europe) occupied the colonists' attention with English settlers fighting French and Spanish. In 1703, John Gorham's Rangers were conducting amphibious operations against the Indians. They would land on remote areas of the coast and strike inland to destroy villages.[3]

The Tuscarora Indians lived in eastern North Carolina in the vicinity of present-day New Bern. On September 22, 1711, Tuscarora Indians raided the settlements and butchered 200 settlers, putting captives to horrible torture. Relations had been peaceful, and the colonists were unprepared for the attack. The settlers got help from Virginia and South Carolina and turned on the Indians with fury. In 1712, North Carolina began to employ Rangers to give early warning and provide for frontier offensive operations. In the battles that followed, the Tuscarora Indians were badly beaten. The survivors were forced to flee north to New York state, where they joined their distant relatives of the Iroquois Confederacy as the sixth nation.

The Treaty of Utrecht (1713) ended Queen Anne's War, but the difference was scarcely noticeable on the American frontier. By 1715, the whites of South Carolina were in a fight for survival. The Yamassee and lower Creek Indians forced settlers to flee from the land west of Savannah. It quickly became evident that fixed forts would not protect their interests. Ranger companies were established that covered the frontier from bases on the Ashepoo, Edisto, and Santee Rivers. In 1716, the combined strength of the settlers and the Cherokee Indians forced the Yamassee and their allies into Florida.

Rangers were also used in exploration. In 1716, Governor Spotswood of Virginia led sixty-three men and seventy-four horses westward to map routes to and through the Blue Ridge Mountains. Included in this number were two companies of Rangers, each consisting of six men and an officer, plus four Meherrin Indians. The party followed the trace of the James River and traveled more than 440 miles into the unknown. Governor Spotswood then turned back. The journal of a member of the expedition reports that "we parted with the Rangers who were to go farther on."[4] These Rangers were likely from the settlements of German immigrants in the region.

On the St. George River in Maine, in 1723, Tarratine Indians ambushed Capt. Josiah Winslow and sixteen of his men who where returning from scouting and were traveling in two whale boats. Suddenly, Winslow's men found themselves surrounded by Indian canoes. The fight was bloody and desperate, ending with the killing of Winslow and all the white men with him. Through this and other ambush-and-raid tactics, the Indians captured twenty-two boats which they used in amphibious raids on the coasts and to capture and loot vessels on the open water. Killing unneeded crew, they would keep the captain and some members of the crew alive to navigate and sail the vessel. Boats of various sizes were captured, including a large armed schooner that enabled the Indians to carry the war to sea and create terror among all those who sailed the coast. In 1724, the Abenaki sought to destroy the fort along the St. George's River. In this action, they used fire ships loaded with combustibles. They maneuvered the flaming vessels close to the blockhouse, and only heroic effort at staving off the fire saved the fort.

In a desperate ship-to-ship fight, the Indian sailors shot out the rigging of a New Hampshire schooner and wounded one of its principal officers. A small fleet with experienced British naval officers was dispatched to hunt out the Indian navy, but the Indians had tired of war on the water. They abandoned their vessels and returned to the forests.[5] During the years from 1721 to 1724, Capt. Jeremiah Moulton led several companies of Rangers in raids against the Abenaki Indians at Norridgewock, Maine, along the Kennebec River. Moulton had reason to hate Indians. As a child, he had watched them kill and scalp his parents and ran in terror to escape them.[6] The Abenaki had kept the settlers in a state of constant fear. The Indian attacks were sudden and terrifying. They ambushed the solitary traveler and killed the farmer, striking without warning as the plow reached the end of the field.

A source of Indian encouragement was Sebastian Rale, who came to America in 1689 as a thirty-two-year-old French Jesuit missionary. The hatreds of Europe that were transported to the New World were not limited to desire for territory. Religious intolerance crossed the ocean, and French missionaries used their influence with their Indian converts not only as agents of their church but of the French government. In times of war between the English and French, the colonists on the frontier lived in terror of French, supported Indian raids, and those who could often fled the area. When unsupported by the French, Indian raids diminished, and settlers would begin to flow back into the dangerous lands. Burned-out settlements were rebuilt, and in isolated cabins throughout the countryside, families staked their fortunes and their lives on the uneasy peace.

The arrival of Rale coincided with a French decision to support Indian attacks on the settlements. The zealous Rale would be in the forefront of French instigation of the Abenaki Indians. He devoted most of his time to the Abenaki at Norridgewock along the Kennebec River. This was in southern Maine, an advanced post of New France. There, Rale worked hard to learn the Algonquin language of the Abenaki, gain their trust, and convert them to his religious beliefs. When this was done, Rale whipped a flame of Indian rage against the Protestant colonists, whom he deemed heretics. Guns and powder, food and clothing were supplied by the French, with Rale controlling supplies and sitting in Indian counsel as advisor. Along the southward trails went painted warriors lusting for scalps and blood. The tomahawk and scalping knife fell with fury as Rale's raiders brought grief to many a family. Desperate fights for life occurred miles from assistance. On occasion, women whose husbands were away from home hunting for game found themselves fighting for their lives. In one cabin, women donned hats worn by men to make the Indians think the men were at home. The women maintained a strong enough fire to keep off their attackers. One woman shot an Indian as he lowered himself through a hole he had chopped in her roof. To protect against additional raids in Maine, a 1,000-man force was to be raised; of these, 100 men were to be stationed at York.

On August 19, 1724, Ranger Capt. Johnson Harmon led a Ranger force against Rale and his Abenaki at Norridgewock. There were 208 Rangers in the party divided into four companies. Harmon led one company and Jeremiah Moulton another. The third and fourth companies were led by Capt. Lewis Bane and Captain Bourn. Johnson Harmon had overall command.[7] Each of these men had established reputations as Indian fighters. Harmon was a skilled woodsman who had led a party of Rangers in silent movement upon an Indian war party that had fallen asleep without posting guard. Harmon's Rangers crept close to the twenty Indians who were at rest. Picking their individual targets, the Rangers killed most of them with the first volley.

The attack on Norridgewock was one of the most daring raids of the eighteenth-century Ranger experience. Accompanied by three Mohawk Indians, the Rangers departed Fort Richmond in seventeen whale boats. For nine days, they worked their way northward along the Kennebec River. At Teuconick Falls, they left the boats under a guard of forty men and proceeded overland toward the objective. En route, they encountered two Indian women who proved to be the daughter and wife of the Indian chief Bomarzeen. The Rangers shot the daughter and put Bomarzeen's wife through a brutal interrogation that provided useful information. On the twelfth day of the mission, they arrived at Norridgewock at about 3 P.M. In the northeast, many Indian settlements were protected by stockades, but the Abenaki at Norridgewock had felt themselves secure and left their cabins unprotected by fortifications. Johnson saw smoke in the direction of the mouth of the Sandy River. Reasoning the Indians might be working their corn fields, Harmon divided his force and, with about eighty Rangers, moved northward to destroy these Indians and their crops.

Ninety Rangers under Jeremiah Moulton were closing on the town when an Indian warrior stepped from a bark house and saw them. The Indian gave a whoop of warning and reached for his weapons. As the Rangers came on, about sixty Indian warriors took up position and began firing. Moulton knew that the surprised Indians would not maintain an accurate or disciplined fire and ordered his Rangers to hold their fire The Indians fired first, but their shooting was erratic. At pistol range, the Rangers delivered a telling fire and charged. Some Indians fired again, but all quickly fled, hoping to escape by canoe. The flight was futile; the Rangers were so close upon them that the Indians could not use paddles, and many were shot down in the canoes. The river was approximately sixty feet wide with a maximum depth of six feet.

Many Indians attempted to wade or swim the river. Some Rangers killed them by firing from the near bank while others carrying pent-up years of rage pursued the Indians into and through the water to the far bank. Many of the Rangers had lost family members to the Indians, and no mercy was shown regardless of sex or age.

Moulton wanted Rale alive, but fire was still coming from some of the Indian dwellings, and Rale had no intention of surrendering. He was firing at Rangers who had not followed the Indians that fled to the river. Rale wounded a Ranger. Shortly afterward, Lt. Benjamin Jaques beat in the door of the dwelling and found Rale reloading. Jaques later claimed he asked Rale to surrender, and Rale replied that he would neither give nor take quarter. Jaques then shot Rale through the head, killing him. An Indian chief named Mogg wounded Lieutenant Dimmuck and killed one of Moulton's Indians named Jeremy Queach. The Rangers stormed the bark house, and Queach's brother killed Mogg, whose wife and two children were also cut down.

As darkness closed in, the Rangers destroyed the Indian corn and collected twenty-five muskets and pistols, three barrels of gunpowder, and a variety of spoils including kettles and blankets. Posting a strong guard, they spent the night in the village, then at dawn's light counted the bodies of Rale and twenty-six others and took the scalps of any who had not had their hair lifted during the battle. Among the dead were top warriors of the Abenaki at Norridgewock, including chiefs Bomarzeen, Mogg, Carabassett, and Wissememet. One woman and three children were taken captive. Concerned about the security of their boats, the Rangers then left the area. One man, a Mohawk Indian named Christian, returned to the scene of the battle and burned Rale's church and Indian dwellings.

In French Canada, Rale was mourned as a martyr. In Maine, his death was seen as the end of a devil who had instigated the murder or captivity of hundreds. Rale's papers taken during the raid showed his aim. He was a powerful presence whose fury toward what he perceived as the heretic English unleashed the Abenaki warriors as terror from the forests. After Moulton's attack, Norridgewock was no longer a viable settlement for the Abenaki. As the seventeenth century ended, the Indians withdrew northward to settle at Becancour and St. Francis. They continued to raid elsewhere, but the battle at Norridgewock quieted the Indians and ended French influence along the Kennebec River.

Though Moulton and his men had done the fighting, Harmon had held overall command and was promoted. Moulton took this in good grace. He was a true Ranger, a citizen-soldier, a warrior-diplomat, aggressive and courageous in battle, In peace, his treatment of the Indians was humane and fair.

The great fights of the Rangers have often been small-unit affairs the French called *la petite guerre*. These were desperate struggles far from assistance by friendly forces. They were times when men pitted themselves against the terrain and the enemy, knowing that failure offered little or no chance of survival. Such was the experience of Ranger John Lovewell in 1725.

After the battle at Norridgewock, one group of Abenaki called the Sokokis began to retire northward. One band that remained stayed near what is now Fryeburg, Maine. These Indians were known as the Pequawkets and were led by a famed war chief named Paugus. Farther south, at the Massachusetts–New Hampshire town of Dunstable, lived John Lovewell, a woodsman in his thirties whose father had been at the Great Swamp Fight against the Narragansett. In 1724, Dunstable came under Indian attack. Two men were taken prisoner, and ten others went in pursuit. As so often happened on the frontier, these men were ambushed, and most were killed. Men of the Dunstable area applied to the Massachusetts government for authority to go kill their enemies. Approval followed, but little money was granted for the task. Large rewards were promised for the scalp of any male Indian deemed of sufficient age to fight.[8]

John Lovewell desired to take revenge on the Indians and organized a ranging party of thirty men to go killing. They brought back a captive and one scalp which was worth $500. Success helped recruiting, and Ranger Lovewell was soon back in the forest leading eighty-seven Rangers on snow shoes through the dense woods. They searched for Indian raiding parties, finding them first and then waiting until the Indians were asleep to close upon the Indian camp site and kill. Ten more scalps were brought home, and Lovewell's name became well known on the frontier. On April 15, 1725, Captain Lovewell again went raiding, this time at the head of forty-five Rangers. Included in this number were an audacious junior officer named Seth Wyman and Jonathan Frye, a twenty-one-year-old warrior-chaplain who was as quick to kill as pray.

The objective was the Pequawket village about two miles from from present-day Fryeburg. It was a hard journey, and several men were injured or became ill and were forced to turn back or wait along the route. On the night of May 7, 1725, Lovewell and thirty-three Rangers took position, concealed by trees near the northeast shore of what is now Lovewell's Pond. The Indians were close by, and throughout the hours of darkness, the Rangers heard movement in the woods about them.

In the morning, Chaplain Frye was leading a prayer when they heard a gunshot and, dropping their packs, went to the sound of the gun. They could see an Indian who was apparently shooting at ducks. Lovewell was suspicious of an ambush and queried his men, who were determined to close with the enemy. As they continued, they encountered an Indian at close range whose musket was loaded with scattershot instead of ball. The Indian fired first, and the scattering of shot wounded several Rangers, including Captain Lovewell, who was at the head of his men. Ranger Wyman immediately killed the Indian, who was then scalped by Chaplain Frye.

With the Indians now aroused, the Rangers fell back upon the place they had left their packs. This was an error. The Indians had been wary of an attack, and their scouts under war chiefs Paugus and Wahwa had located the abandoned packs. An ambush awaited the Rangers, who were assisting Lovewell and another Ranger named Whiting. The infuriated Indians fired once, then charged the Rangers, and a fierce hand-to-hand fight began. Lovewell was struck again, but kept fighting as his life ebbed away to death. The next two senior Ranger officers were badly wounded, and eight Rangers were killed, but young Seth Wyman was equal to the task of leadership. The surviving Rangers kept up the fire and retreated to the edge of the pond. This prevented them from being surrounded by the superior numbers of the Indians who took up firing positions and commenced a galling fire. The fight began in mid-morning, and throughout the long daylight hours, both Rangers and Indians fought from behind trees and deadfall while they called encouragement to their comrades and shouted their war cries. At one point, the Indians ceased their fire for a war council. While they were thus occupied, Ranger Wyman crawled to an advantageous position and shot Paugus dead.

The Rangers were now in desperate straits, outnumbered and far from any assistance. They could fight only until darkness and then try to break free. Only nine unhurt Rangers remained, with most of the others dead or so badly wounded that escape was doubtful. Knowing that he would die, the wounded Lt. Jonathan Robbins asked the other Rangers to leave him but to first load his gun as he had the strength to kill one more Indian. It was after midnight that those Rangers began to break contact and evade the enemy that surrounded them. Four of the wounded, including Chaplain Frye, could not continue and told the others to go on. The surviving Rangers split up into small parties to better escape pursuit. Some of these men were never heard from again. The twenty-one-year-old fighting chaplain died trying to escape capture. Eleven Rangers, including the courageous Seth Wyman, were able to elude the Indians and come home. Indian casualties are not known. Some of their survivors fled to St. Francis, and those who remained made no future attempts to raid the settlements.

In 1739, England declared a war on Spain that was to last until 1743. Smuggling was rampant in the Caribbean, and both Spain and England had agreed they could search each other's merchant ships in that area. An English merchant captain and smuggler named Robert Jenkins was caught, and the Spanish punished him by cutting off one of his ears. Jenkins carried his loose ear for seven years until he had an opportunity to tell his story in England and, assisted by the government, make his treatment and that of other English sailors a national outrage. Thus, the fight known by the strange name of the War of Jenkins's Ear began. The roots of the war were disagreement over Florida boundaries, Spanish mistreatment of British sailors, and disputes over rights of commerce. Ranger units were once again committed to battle.

John Oglethorpe was an army officer and a member of the British Parliament. Oglethorpe cared about the poor. This was unusual for the time as many in England felt that to give help to the less fortunate would encourage poor people to breed more poor people. Oglethorpe was also disturbed by a system that put people who could not pay their bills in debtors prison. He was a strong supporter of the navy and of overseas trade. With nineteen associates, Oglethorpe was given a charter in the area between the Altamaha and the Savannah Rivers. Oglethorpe founded the city of Savannah in 1733 and offered it as an outlet to those in distressed circumstances.

Primarily concerned about Spanish attacks from Florida, Oglethorpe made peace with the Creek Indians and began building forts along the southern frontier, the most notable of which was Fort Frederika on St. Simon's Island. The Spanish were alarmed by this incursion, and the uneasy peace was barely maintained. Oglethorpe employed Rangers in boats to patrol the rivers and provide early warning to his settlement. When the War of Jenkins's Ear began, Oglethorpe promptly went on the offensive.

He captured two small forts on the St. John's River and hindered Spanish communication with St. Augustine. In 1740, Oglethorpe led 1,800 men, including 400 Rangers, in an attack on St. Augustine. He planned to block the approaches to St. Augustine from the sea with warships that would shell the town while he attacked from the landward side. The waters were shallow, and his ships could not give fire support. The result was a month-long siege that Oglethorpe could not continue. On July 10, 1740, he began his withdrawal. In May 1742, the Spanish determined to eliminate Oglethorpe's stronghold and sent a fleet and 3,000 troops to attack Fort Fredericka. Oglethorpe had 650 men, including Indians, but he went on the offensive and killed more than 100 of the Spanish advance party. Oglethorpe's men continued in the attack and clashed with 300 Spanish under Captain Barba. The Spaniards fought bravely and repulsed Oglethorpe's troops except for a platoon of Scottish Highlanders and a company of Rangers, who bypassed the Spanish and found their camp.

They waited patiently until the Spanish returned to their camp, put down their weapons, and began to rest. The Rangers and Highlanders then attacked with fury, killing Captain Barba and 167 Spanish and taking 20 men prisoner.[9]

Oglethorpe cleverly played off of the Ranger success by allowing a false letter to fall into the hands of the Spanish commander. Believing that a large British force was close at hand, the Spanish withdrew, leaving a large amount of weapons and materiel behind them. The colony of Georgia was saved. Oglethorpe had also used mounted Rangers. He praised them in a letter to the Duke of Newcastle, writing, "They not only carry advices through these vast Forests & swim Rivers, but in Action, by taking the enemy in flank or Rear, do great service . . . They are also of great Service in watching the Sea Coasts, since they can swiftly move from one Place to another."[10] In 1746, Georgia Ranger strength was 122 men and 15 officers.

The War of Jenkins's Ear was not concluded when King George's War—known in Europe as the War of Austrian Succession—began. In 1743, France and Spain joined forces against England. The primary conflict was in Europe, but from 1743 to 1748, the British and French settlers, each aided by Indian allies, fought along the northern frontier. Two brothers, John and Joseph Gorham, would perform remarkable service as Ranger leaders during King George's War. John Gorham (1709–51) was a native-born American from Barnstable, Massachusetts.[11] He traded along the New England coast and voyaged to England, gaining seagoing experience that would prove valuable in warfare that was to come.

In 1744, the French and their Indian allies, the Micmac and the Malicete, swept across Nova Scotia, leaving only the capital of the province, Annapolis Royal, under the English flag. English Gov. Paul Mascarene had only 100 regulars and 100 newly arrived provincials to defend an unfinished fort. Mascarene appealed to Massachusetts Governor Shirley for assistance. The reinforcements sent to Annapolis Royal (Port Royal) were led by John Gorham and his "Indian Rangers of the Deep Woods"—primarily Mohawk Indians. Gorham's Rangers were trained to be equally at home in the forests and at sea.

Gorham began to employ amphibious warfare against the French. Using two armed sloops that he owned, he took his Rangers on a series of raids, swooping in from the sea to attack the villages of the Indian allies of the French. So audacious were his raids that this small Ranger force changed the balance of power in Nova Scotia. Soon after the Rangers' arrival, the French force withdrew to their powerful base at Louisbourg. Soon John Gorham returned to New England to recruit a second company of Rangers. The campaign to capture Louisbourg was underway. John Gorham was promoted to lieutenant colonel of the 7th Massachusetts Regiment, which was commanded by his father, Shubael Gorham.

The great stone fortress of Louisbourg on Cape Breton Island was constructed in 1720. The linchpin of the French presence in North America, Louisbourg was to the French in America what Gibralter has been to the British in the Mediterranean. Louisbourg was a key fortress that secured the St. Lawrence approaches to the rich interior lands. Gov. William Shirley of Massachusetts became convinced that Louisbourg could be successfully attacked by colonial forces supported by the British navy. Shirley appointed William Pepperell, a merchant who was a colonel in the militia, to command the land forces. On March 25, 1745, New Englanders, assisted by a British fleet under Sir Peter Warren, sailed from Boston to capture the French jewel in their New World crown.

Pepperell had mustered 4,300 militia from Massachusetts, Maine, New York, New Hampshire, and Rhode Island. The security of the frontier was left to thirteen Ranger companies who operated from patrol bases that included fortified farm houses. The French had 560 soldiers, 1,500 militia, and 100 cannon. Warren's fleet included one sixty-gun and three forty-gun warships. Save for some daring and unsuccessful attempts to seize a critical French battery, the action at Louisbourg was primarily an artillery fight. Pepperrell reported firing 9,000 cannon balls and 600 bombs. Warren's ships picked off French supply vessels and captured several French warships, but the fierce fighting on land was done by the colonists.

On April 30, Ranger John Gorham used his landing craft skill to take troops ashore at Garabus Bay by whaleboat. On May 23, he was involved in another amphibious assault. These actions were done under fire with considerable skill. Claiming they were short of food and gunpowder and without hope of reinforcement, the French surrendered on June 16, 1745. The great victory at Louisbourg was primarily the work of the colonists. The French would surrender only to regular force officers, so Warren got the honor. The prize money on items captured was split between the British crown and the British navy. Pepperrell was the first American to be made a baronet, but the men under him got nothing. At the Treaty of Aix-la-Chapelle on October 18, 1748, the English gave Louisbourg back to the French. There was rage in America at this injustice, and men who had proved they could fight and win began to talk of independence. John Gorham returned to Annapolis Royal. His younger brother, the twenty-one-year-old Lt. Joseph Gorham, accompanied him.

In June 1746, Capt. David Ladd of Exeter led a company of Rangers to patrol the frontier of New Hampshire. Ladd was an experienced woodsman. Another was Capt. John Goffe, who led a scouting party in winter that lasted 106 days. These men were well known in their time and contributed to the future reputation of the American Rangers through valiant service and because of a man they trained. In the ranks of Ladd's Rangers was a fifteen-year-old warrior named Robert Rogers.[12] Both Robert Rogers and his friend John Stark learned the art of Indian warfare under David Ladd and John Goffe.

Shubael Gorham died of disease, and John Gorham succeeded to his father's post as colonel of the 7th Massachusetts Regiment. In April 1747, John Gorham went to London to present the plan the governors and their advisors had drawn to remove the French from Nova Scotia. While there, he was granted a king's commission, and his Ranger company, which was now mainly white, was enlarged to nearly 100 men and became part of the royal forces in Nova Scotia. This made Gorham's men the first Rangers to be part of the regular establishment. The 1749 title of Gorham's Rangers was His Majesty's First Independent Company of American Rangers.

From 1747 to 1749, Gorham's Rangers were the primary defense of Nova Scotia. They continued to specialize in amphibious operations, using two armed sloops to carry them on their raids. In a September 11, 1747, letter from the Duke of Bedford to the Duke of Newcastle, Bedford wrote, "I hope your Grace will think proper to give all due encouragement to Capt Gorham, whose Service now with his body of Rangers, is more than ever absolutely necessary for the immediate preservation of the Province of Nova Scotia."

The British government was now committed to settling Nova Scotia with Englishmen. Col. (later Gen.) Edward Cornwallis arrived to bring this to pass. Cornwallis initially did not like John Gorham and his men. The new commander formed two new Ranger companies (which would be disbanded in 1751), one under Capt. Francis Bartelo and a company of "English" Rangers under Capt. William Clapham. Despite the additions, it was primarily Gorham's Rangers who carried the war to the enemy. In March 1750, in a nasty wilderness fight along the St. Croix River, Gorham's Rangers—supported by a company of royal troops, one of Rangers and another of light artillery—smashed a strong force of French and Indians.

This was followed by another success in April 1750. The Isthmus of Chignecto is the land bridge between present-day New Brunswick and Nova Scotia. In the mid eighteenth century, the Missaquash River crossed the area and separated the French and the English forces. This is the area of the Bay of Fundy with tides of great dimension. Here at Chignecto in September 1750, Ranger John Gorham led his men in an amphibious assault, leaping from armed vessels and charging across the beach into battle. The fighting was vicious, but the Rangers won the day. Desperate battles continued for months with heavy losses on both sides. Rangers would go into the deep woods and never return, or they would come back carrying the bloody scalps of their enemies. In 1751, after seven years of battle, the Rangers prevailed. They kept the French from winning Nova Scotia.

In 1751, John Gorham sailed to London to sell ship masts to the Royal Navy. He contracted smallpox while there and died during the month of December. John Gorham's younger brother Joseph was now experienced as a recruiter and leader. On his brother's death, Joseph Gorham assumed command of the Rangers. He was a successful commander, leading his Rangers in General Amherst's July 1758 recapture of Louisbourg. Six Ranger companies were with General Wolfe in the capture of Quebec. One of these was directly commanded by Joseph Gorham. In 1761, Gorham was commissioned a major in the regular establishment of the British Army. In 1762, Gorham and his Rangers participated in the British expedition to seize Havana. In 1763, his Ranger unit was disbanded. In later life, Ranger Joseph Gorham would serve as the lieutenant governor of Newfoundland. He died around 1790.

CHAPTER 4

The French and Indian War, 1754–63

The rivalry between England and France spread worldwide. In North America, the showdown between the two powers came in the years between 1754 and 1763. Called the Seven Years' War in Europe, in America it would be known as the French and Indian War. It opened with a brisk little fight near present-day Uniontown in western Pennsylvania and ended with the signing of a peace treaty in Paris in 1763. This war determined that English law and language and the Protestant faith would be the primary shaping forces in eighteenth century North America. It set a man named George Washington and those who took pride in being Americans on the road to destiny. Command of British forces in North America was difficult and brought most men who held it despair or death. One after another they came: William Shirley, 1741–54; Edward Braddock, 1754–55; Shirley again, 1755–56; Lord Loudoun (John Campbell), 1756–58; James Abercromby, 1758–59; and Jeffrey Amherst, 1759–63.

By the mid 1700s, the control of key waterways was of strategic importance in determining whether the English or the French would control North America. The French presence on the St. Lawrence River allowed them to penetrate deep into the continent. From the St. Lawrence, other waterways allowed the French to move west and south and frustrate English interests. A natural corridor was formed southward from the St. Lawrence to the Richelieu River to Lake Champlain to Lake St. Sacrement (Lake George) and to the Hudson River. To protect their interests, the French built Fort St. Frederic (Crown Point) and Fort Carillon (Fort Ticonderoga).

Lake Champlain is a 110-mile-long lake that at its widest is twelve miles and narrows to less than a third of a mile. Here in 1731, the French began construction of Fort Frederic, a stone fort that mounted sixty-two guns. They claimed the right to do this on the basis of the 1609 discovery of the lake by Samuel Champlain. The English also claimed the lake based upon their friendly relationship with the Iroquois. These nations had fought for generations for control of this area against the Algonquins and their supporters.

South of Lake Champlain in the Adirondack Mountains lay Lake St. Sacrement (Lake George), a primarily spring-fed lake thirty-two miles long north to south with a maximum depth of 200 feet. In 1755, the French began construction of another fort at the southern end of Lake Champlain set high on a rocky overlook; its guns controlled the southern tip of Lake Champlain and the northern outlet of Lake St. Sacrement. This stone fort, often called "the key to the continent", was located a days' march or about 16 miles from Fort St. Frederic. The intent was that the two French forts could support each other.

South and west in the triangle where the Allegheny and Monongahela Rivers meet to form the mighty Ohio is today the spot where the great city of Pittsburgh, Pennsylvania, stands. In 1754, it was wilderness surrounded by these vital and strategic waterways. To control that junction of rivers, both the French and English sent construction parties. The English arrived first, but were driven off by a stronger French force. The French then built a fort at the apex of the triangle and named it Fort Duquesne.

Robert Dinwiddie, lieutenant governor of Virginia, sent 800 men under Col. Joshua Fry to dislodge the French. Fry's budding career ended when he fell from his horse and died as a result. He was succeeded by his second in command, the ambitious twenty-two-year-old lieutenant colonel of the Virginia Provincial Regiment, George Washington. Fifty miles before reaching Fort Dusquene, Washington learned of a small party of French camped nearby. In an early-morning raid, Washington led forty Virginians in a surprise attack. The leader of these French, Ensign Coulon de Jumonville, and nine of his force were killed, with the remainder taken prisoner. Washington then withdrew and built a poorly positioned fort named Necessity. The French launched an attacking force that greatly outnumbered Washington's men. After a spirited fight, Washington surrendered. Though they were required to give up their artillery, Washington and his men were released. This occurred only after Washington signed a document in French that included an admission that he was an assassin. He may not have understood what he was signing, but his signature would haunt his reputation for years. Captured with Washington were men who would share other adventures with him, including Lt. George Mercer, Lt. Thomas Waggoner, Captain Hogg, and Captain Stephens. The Chavalier William La Peyroney had been forced to flee France as he was a Protestant. When the French required hostages, the dashing young Capt. Robert Stobo and Captain Van Braam, who spoke French, agreed to serve and departed for Fort Duquesne.

On April 14, 1755, Gen. Edward Braddock arrived to take charge of the British fortunes. A proud, brave, stiff-necked man who had served only three years of his four decades of army service out of England, Braddock was determined to remove French influence in America. Braddock's orders called for attacks on four key French bastions: Fort Beausejour in Nova Scotia, Crown Point on Lake Champlain, Niagara in New York, and Fort Duquesne at the site of present-day Pittsburgh. Braddock would command the attack on Fort Duquesne. Regular army Col. Robert Monckton and colonial Col. John Winslow would lead the attack on Fort Beausjour on the Isthmus of Chignecto, a land bridge between Nova Scotia and New Brunswick. (The French built the star-shaped Fort Beausjour in 1751 to protect the interior from British attacks from Nova Scotia.) English Gov. William Shirley of Massachusetts was a devoted man but not a soldier; nonetheless, he was appointed major general and assigned the mission of capturing Fort Niagara. Command of the attack on Crown Point was assigned to trader William Johnson, a man who had no military experience but great influence with the Indians. Johnson was appointed colonel of the Six Nations, which greatly facilitated trading relationship with the Indians. Despite his lack of military training, Johnson could read a map better then General Braddock. Johnson, with Shirley's support, encouraged Braddock to forego an attack on Fort Duquesne. Both these civilians believed the conquest of Niagara would shut off a northern French route of supply and forts in the interior close to Canada would wither.[1]

Edward Braddock was a product of his time and class. He disliked colonials and had little understanding of Indians or Indian warfare. He was a man of courage but was rigid and inflexible. No matter how reasonable Braddock felt the advice was to attack Niagara, he had orders to attack Fort Duquesne.

Few commanders have had more detailed knowledge of their objective. Braddock had a detailed map of the French fort that included numbers and locations of artillery and powder storage. With this valuable information, Braddock could tell that Fort Duquesne was not completed. The map had been prepared at Fort Duquesne by Capt. Robert Stobo, the hostage taken at the French capture of Washington at Fort Necessity. Stobo had managed to get the map carried back to Virginia by a friendly Mohawk Indian.[2]

On June 19, 1755, after a two-week siege, Fort Beausejour was taken by Col. Robert Monckton and Col. John Winslow with a force of about 2,000 men. Jealous that success by the governor of Massachusetts might harm their interests, New York's acting governor, De Lancey, did what he could to discredit Shirley. When Shirley learned that the French had been able to penetrate an English sea blockade and bring strong reinforcements to Niagara, he postponed his attack.

As his force gathered, tradition has it that Braddock was offered the services of the legendary Pennsylvania Ranger Captain Jack. So little is known of this man that he is a shadow on the page of Ranger history. It was said he was a frontiersman who lived with his small family far from settlements along the Juniata River. He fed his family by hunting and fishing and one day returned to find his cabin burned and his wife and two children murdered by Indians. From that point in his life, this experienced woodsman lived with the single purpose of killing the red man. He was seldom in the settlements. He roamed the forest in search of Indians, sleeping in caves or the rotted hollows of trees. He was a giant of a man and a relentless, merciless killer. Far from assistance, he once fought a lonely and ferocious hand-to-hand battle with four Indians, killing three and badly wounding the fourth with his knife. Though bleeding from numerous wounds, Jack made it to the settlements for care and was soon back on his quest.

With the extermination of Indians as his goal, Captain Jack raised a company of Rangers and trained them in his knowledge. When his deeds came to the attention of Governor Hamilton of Pennsylvania, his band was given official sanction. Knowing the conquest of Fort Duquesne was vital to security of the Pennsylvania frontier, Jack offered his services to Braddock, but British regimen and discipline were not compatible with frontier knowledge and independence. Braddock's coldness angered Jack and his woodsmen, and they left.[3]

There was opportunity to engage friendly Indians for the expedition. They could have been useful in scouting. Some historians claim Braddock's treatment of them was high-handed. Others dispute this. He did have a low regard for Indians, but his problem may have been women. The skilled frontier trader George Croghan had brought in nearly 100 Iroquois Indian men who brought their women. The Indian women and Braddock's officers and men made camp life hum. When ordered from camp, the women went to a nearby grove of trees, and the men followed. Soon the Indians were requested to send their women home. When they did, the Indian warriors went with them. The net result was that only eight Indians accompanied the expedition.

Braddock's force of 2,500 regulars included the 44th and 48th Regiments of Maryland and Virginia. The regulars were unfamiliar with war as fought in America, and most of the colonists were inexperienced men. Though Braddock had lost Captain Jack and his Pennsylvanians, eight companies of Rangers were included in the expedition. Captain Dobb brought 100 Rangers from North Carolina. All other companies had 50 men. These were Virginia Rangers under Captains Hogg, Stephen, Waggoner, Cook, Dobbs, and La Peyroney and Maryland Rangers commanded by Captain Dagworthy. Peter Hogg's company would be left at Will's Creek, but the remaining seven companies made the march.

Braddock had no experience in forest warfare or confidence in colonials, so the Rangers were inefficiently used. Initially, instead of scouting to the front and flanks, they were assigned to march in the column, with Captain Cook's company being toward the rear, just to the front of the women and rear guard. The army marched from Alexandria, Virginia, on April 20, 1755, and arrived at Fort Cumberland, Maryland, on May 10.

The fort was located on high ground where Wills Creek and the Potomac River meet. No colonial was permitted to hold rank higher than captain, so George Washington, in order to further his study of the art of war and his military ambition, had chosen to participate as a volunteer member of Braddock's staff without pay. Washington felt the French and Indian resistance would be in the north against Governor Shirley. His overconfidence would soon be shattered.

The French and Indian War, 1754–63 43

The French and Indian War

Artillery was needed since the objective of the campaign was a fortified position, and this required transport. A horse needed a minimum of eight gallons of water per day and between twenty-eight and thirty-two pounds of fodder. The horses could not subsist off what they found along the way. All this had to be hauled by wagon. Benjamin Franklin played a major role in getting 150 to 200 wagons for the expedition. The drivers included Daniel Boone and Daniel Morgan. From Fort Cumberland, a new road had to be built, and about 600 men went forward with axes and spades. The road would be a stump-filled wilderness track twelve feet wide. There were shortages of horses, so wagons were brought forward in increments, drivers being responsible for more then one wagon. Horses had to be unhitched and wagons lowered down steep hills by rope and pulley. The army then marched by stages, taking ten days to cover thirty miles and reach Little Meadows. A decision was made to press ahead with a lighter force and leave Dunbar to follow as soon as he could with the wagons. Indians allied to the French lurked in the woods and killed stragglers. Washington was ill and complained that his servant John Alton was also sick. He remained for some days with Dunbar. He would not be able to rejoin the army until it was near the east side of the Monongahela River about twelve miles from Fort Duquesne.

On July 9, 1755, security was sent to the other side of the river and the crossing was made unopposed. Considerable sign of Indian presence was visible. The army proceeded on the left bank of the Monogahela to Turtle Creek. In order to get in position to attack Fort Duquesne, it was again necessary to cross the river. The river crossings were shallow and had not been contested. Close to his goal and feeling confident, Braddock made the second crossing much like a parade. Drums and fifes were played, and colors were opened to the breeze. It was a sight George Washington would never forget. When Braddock split his army, his advance force consisted of 1,400 men. In command of Braddock's 300-man point was Lt. Col. Thomas Gage, the second son of a family best known for a tradition of supporting the losing side. Gage had fought at the battles of Fontenoy and Culloden and in the low countries. He had come to America with his regiment in the fall of 1754 and would become one of the most controversial British officers in North America. Though this was Gage's first significant experience in battles involving American Rangers, he would have many contacts with them in the years ahead. Behind Gage was a working party of 200 men to hew out the road.

Captain Contrecoeur commanded Fort Duquesne and was well aware of the oncoming enemy. Though he doubted that he had the strength to hold his post, Contrecoeur had been sending frequent scouts and Indian raiding parties, but their minimal success only confirmed his fears. He had hoped that the Shawnee and Delaware Indians would join him, but they were waiting and watching to see who won. The Indians he had were Missisauga Algonquins, who lived between Lake Erie and Lake Huron near Detroit. With Contrecoeur was the forty-five-year-old Daniel Lienard, Beujeau, Dumas, and de

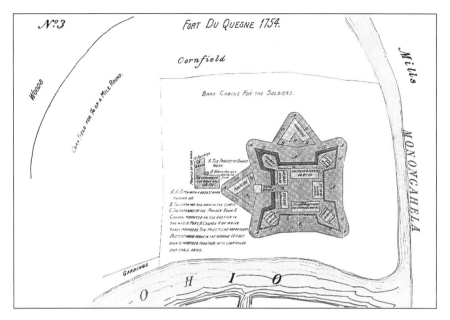

Fort Duquesne

Lignery. Beujeau was Contrecoeur's replacement but had not yet taken command. Also in the fort were two capable woodsman who could rival the best on the frontier. One was a twenty-six-year-old named Charles Langlade. The son of a French father and Ottawa mother, Langlade had great influence with the Indians. With Langlade was his friend De St. Luc. To contest Braddock's advance, the French officers decided to attempt an ambush. Depending on the source, the credit for the plan goes to Contrecoeur, Beujeau, or Langlade. There is no doubt that it was Beaujeu who led a force of 35 French officers, 72 French troops, 146 experienced Canadian woodsmen, and 637 Indians sent out from Fort Duquesne. The size of the French force was observed and counted by a young prisoner and future Ranger.

Manhood came early on the frontier, and many cases were recorded of young boys killing Indians or escaping from captivity and finding their way through many miles of deep forests to return to the settlements. Some would then be killed in later raids by the Indians. One of those taken prisoner was an eighteen-year-old named James Smith. He was a rarity on the frontier, a youth with a good cabin education who could read, write, do sums, and also had knowledge of the forest. Smith had been part of group working on a forest road near

Bedford when taken captive by the Indians. He was marched to Fort Duquesne, then forced to run the gauntlet. Smith probably would have been killed, but a French officer rescued him from the Indians. He was awaiting whatever fate would befall him when a runner brought news of Braddock's location. The information created a great stir. Smith was recovering from his beating, and hobbling with the aid of a staff, he positioned himself on the wall. At the gate, the French and Indians were drawing powder, ball, and flints. They soon left the fort to attack the approaching force. Smith estimated there to be about 400 French and Indians, thought that number small for the task, and hoped they would be whipped.[4]

Nine miles from the fort, the ground along the river was wet and soft. Seeking firmer footing, Gage's advance party led the column toward higher ground, then turned to guide on the river. The ground was less open at the higher elevation with thickets of underbrush and briars. Washouts created depressions ranging from gullies to ravines. These ran from high ground to low, and some following the path of least resistance were parallel to the line of march. These depressions offered protective cover and had the natural concealment of brush and vines.

Beaujeu did not have time to establish an ambush, but as the two forces met, he signaled his men to envelop the English flanks. They began to deliver a heavy volume of fire while taking advantage of the terrain. Beaujeu was stripped to the waist, painted like an Indian, and wearing only a gorget, a half-moon shaped metal pendant on his chest. The last symbol of a knight's armor, it was worn as a pendant on an officer's breast as token of authority. A burst of fire from the advance party killed Beaujeu, but Capt. Jean Daniel Dumas took command and kept up a galling fire on the British.

Gage's troops recoiled on the working party, and both fell back onto the main body in a contagious panic. The main body had been hastening forward, and continuity was lost as advancing and retreating British units collided. The wagons with the column also continued forward and added to the confusion. The Rangers hurried to cover and returned fire. British officers were unaccustomed to war as fought in America and forced their men to stand upright in cleared areas. Some officers beat at the Rangers and their own men with their swords, trying to force them to stand in formation in the open. With men being shot down around them, unable to see enemy formations and terrorized by the cries of wounded being tortured and scalped, small groups of Braddock's men began to withdraw. The rivulet of fear became a stream, then a torrent, as men broke and ran. The courageous Braddock was mortally wounded as he mounted a fifth horse, having had four shot out from under him.

The Rangers knew the futility of fighting European-style in the forest. They employed the same tactic as the enemy and fought from behind cover. Braddock and other British officers saw this as cowardice and ordered the Rangers to stand in ranks in the open to fight. Captain Waggoner moved his Rangers to higher ground, took position behind a fallen tree, and began a withering fire on the Indians. They were soon driving the Indians in that sector back. Seeing the clouds of gun smoke, the confused British regulars fired into the backs of Waggoner's men, wounding or killing two thirds of the Rangers.[5]

The confused British also fired at each other and into La Peyroney's Ranger company. In a letter after the battle, Washington reported to Governor Dinwiddie that "Captain Peronney [sic] and all his officers down to a Corporal were killed." Washington was furious at the regulars, calling them "cowardly dogs." He felt that two thirds of the killed and wounded came from panicked British troops firing on their own people.[6] William La Peyroney's untimely death ended a career of promise.

Nearly 1,000 British and colonials were slain; 63 of 86 officers were killed. Braddock was buried in his road, and wagons rolled over the site to conceal the location of his grave. Fewer than 60 of the French and Indians were casualties. The victors fell upon the wounded, slaughtering them under the tomahawk, scalping the living and the dead. Thirty men and women were taken prisoner. A dozen of these had their faces painted black to signify they were selected for torture. At Fort Duquesne, young James Smith saw the prisoners brought in and watched while the first of them underwent slow burning while tied to a stake. Smith could not bear watching more than one death, but the savagery continued. Heated ramrods and red-hot musket barrels were thrust into eyes and genitals, flesh was pierced with pointed sticks, ears and fingers were severed. A fortunate few were taken to Canada to trade to the French for supplies. Some prisoners were slaughtered and eaten on the route north.

Young George Washington drew lessons from this fight, but not those that would be of benefit on the frontier. He saw the battle lost not because of the tactics of the British, but as a breakdown in discipline. It would shape his future thinking about war.

Despite this terrible defeat, the British still had sufficient force to take Fort Duquesne. The French and Indians did not follow their fleeing foe across the river to the second British camp. Still, the mindless fear that infected those with Braddock also reached the camp of Col. Thomas Dunbar with the baggage train. Wagoners cut their traces and fled. Dunbar could think of nothing but retreat and gave orders to destroy the equipment and spike the guns, then marched away as quickly as possible. Dunbar now had but one objective: get to Philadelphia and go into winter quarters—in August.

Governor Dinwiddie, George Washington, and others pleaded with Dunbar not to leave the frontier unprotected. Governor Morris of Pennsylvania wrote from Philadelphia to the new commander: "It appears . . . extraordinary to me and everybody here that the Colonel should have any thoughts of coming to this town at this season and leaving the back inhabitants of this and neighboring provinces exposed to the incursions of the Indians, etc."[7] It was obvious to all except Dunbar that the withdrawal of the troops would leave the frontier completely exposed to Indian attack. Dunbar would not be dissuaded. He paused briefly at Fort Cumberland, and leaving 400 wounded, he continued to hurry eastward to safety.

At Fort Duquesne, the French had awaited the next attack with apprehension. When it did not come, they remained on the defensive, giving the Indians encouragement and material support. The Indians knew the frontier lay open, and Braddock's road became a pathway for Indian attack. Now that they saw a clear winner, the Shawnee and Delaware raised the hatchet. In the fall and winter of 1755–56, a torrent of terror spread across the Virginia and Pennsylvania frontiers. Over 700 men, women, and children were made captive or died shrieking under the tomahawk, their hair torn from them in grisly trophy. The French paid for these scalps and were delighted to buy even though the wily Indians had learned to make one scalp into two or three. Lines of whimpering prisoners were hurried through the forests, knowing that Indian anger or caprice would bring the tomahawk. Those with faces darkened with charcoal prayed for such a fate but struggled on with the terrible knowledge that they had been chosen for slow and horrible death.

The advantage of surprise was practically always with the Indians. War parties of several hundred Indians would descend upon a settlement, but unless attacking a fort, they tended to do their bloody work in small bands. In an undated letter of the period, Maj. James Burd wrote that the Indians would come within striking range of a dispersed settlement and then camp in difficult terrain, an area seldom frequented. From there, they would send out scouting parties of one or two men who would creep close to a house or a cluster of houses. For several days, these scouts would remain concealed, observing how many men and women were in each house and the daily routine. When they returned to the camp with information, leaders would assign two to five warriors to attack each house. They would then move at night, with each small group of warriors taking up position for an attack at first light. Burd wrote that the Indians, using this tactic, "seldom fail to kill, and make prisoners of the whole family." Having achieved their objective, the Indians would promptly take their prisoners (often heavily laden with plunder) and scalps and reassemble at their camp. An immediate and rapid march of twenty-four hours or more would be accomplished by the full body to clear the area. Effort to assemble men and pursue the raiders took some time. Burd wrote that the Indians would likely have an eight- to ten-hour start. Those in pursuit had to be very careful as the Indians usually established an ambush on their trail.[8]

Burd recommended that the same tactics be employed against the Indian villages. He wanted well-trained men with long enlistments to perform the work. He also recommended that as most of their work would be done in summer, the clothing and blankets of these Rangers should be green to assist in concealing them from the Indians.

Braddock's defeat was followed by Johnson's attack on Crown Point. William Johnson was one of the most intriguing men of the colonial period. Born in difficult circumstances in County Meath, Ireland, Johnson found a broad horizon for his talents when employed by his rich and powerful uncle, Sir Peter Warren, to manage this famous sea captain's frontier affairs. William Johnson became a trader equally at home in the drawing room or the forest. From his stone headquarters called Mount Johnson on the Mohawk River, he treated the Indians fairly, lived with them, and learned from them.

With his sudden promotion to colonel, Johnson found himself in the administrative nightmare of assembling men from New Hampshire, Connecticut, Rhode Island, and New York, each of which had its own priorities. He also had to convince his unreliable Mohawk friends and their allies to take up the hatchet against the French. Aware of Johnson's lack of military experience, Braddock had sent him Capt. William Eyre, a superb officer of the 44th Regiment who was a trained artilleryman and understood engineering and the general workings of an army.

On Braddock's death, Shirley became commander in chief, and Johnson found himself promoted from trader to colonel and then to major general in breathtaking advancement. The newly minted Major General Johnson painted his face and danced a Mohawk war dance to encourage his Indian brothers. Albany was the assembly point of what was to be a force of nearly 4,000 colonials and all the Indians he could muster. From there, in early August 1775, Johnson dispatched Phinehas Lyman, a capable officer, to build a fort by the Hudson River at the south end of the portage between the Hudson and Lake St. Sacrement. This crude but strong fortification was initially called Fort Lyman. Johnson would later name it Fort Edward in honor of the powerful Duke of York. The fort was not complete, so Johnson bypassed it to move north, leaving Colonel Blanchard and 500 men of the New Hampshire regiment to complete construction.

On August 28, 1755, Johnson marched to the head of Lake St. Sacrement. Politically astute, Johnson renamed the body of water Lake George to honor his king and establish the king's authority over the lake. Now Johnson set about constructing another fort, which he named Fort William Henry after the Duke of Gloucester, grandson of King George II and the brother of George III. Fort William Henry initially consisted of four bastions made of pine logs banked with sand and surrounded by a deep ditch. This fort was fourteen miles from Fort Lyman. Like the French, Johnson was conscious of mutually supporting defense.

While his political mapmaking would please his masters, Johnson had also established a critical link of forts that combined the Hudson River with a portage to Lake George, which provided access to Lake Champlain and the heart of New France in Canada. This route would be a path to death or glory for many American Rangers.

The French had taken letters and documents from Braddock's dead that revealed the English strategy, including the planned attack on Fort Frederic (Crown Point).[9] French reconnaissance patrols had gone as far as the Hudson and were tracking Johnson's movements. The Marquis de Vaudreuil had become French governor of Canada and had been planning an attack on the English settlement at Oswego, New York. Now he ordered the military commander Baron Dieskau down Lake Champlain. Dieskau had several battalions of regulars that had recently arrived from France and was eager to deal with the rabble of colonials.

Dieskau's Abenaki Indian scouts brought in a prisoner who, under threat of Indian torture, revealed that the 500 men who were building Fort Lyman were camped beside the unfinished fort. The courageous prisoner, no doubt misleading Dieskau, told the Frenchman that Johnson's main body had retreated to Albany. Dieskau, with a force of over 3,000, saw the opportunity to fall upon and destroy the smaller force of English and moved to the attack, unknowingly bypassing Johnson's force at Lake George.

Johnson's Mohawks found trails of the French movement. A brave messenger named Adams volunteered to carry a warning to Lyman but was ambushed and killed by Abenaki. Some fearful men who had fled Johnson's camp were taken captive, and Dieskau learned the truth about Johnson's location and forces. After much persuasive argument with his reluctant Indian allies, the confident Dieskau moved to attack Johnson. Meanwhile, Johnson, not knowing Dieskau's numbers, had determined to send a force of 1,000 to assist Fort Lyman. The old Mohawk chief Hendrick, who was a friend of Johnson's, determined to participate in the attack though he complained the force was too small.

It was around 8 A.M. on September 8, 1755, that Col. Ephraim Williams and Chief Hendrick began to lead the relief column toward Fort Lyman. Dieskau's French, Canadians, and Indians were also on the move. The two columns seemed destined to find themselves in the unplanned collision known as a meeting engagement. The situation changed when Dieskau's scouts captured a prisoner who said Johnson's men were coming. Dieskau quickly arranged an ambush and waited for the unwary provincials who were moving without front or flank security forces. Dieskau posted the Canadians and Indians on the flanks of the road and his regulars in the center. The colonists walked into the ambush that became known as "the bloody morning scout" and were shot down. Chief Hendrick and the commander of the provincials, Col. Ephraim Williams, were among those killed. The survivors fled back along the road to tumble with fear into a hastily arranged defense line established by Johnson and his officers.

The emboldened Dieskau pressed on toward Johnson's camp. Dieskau was under the mistaken impression that Johnson did not have cannon. Johnson had three in the line sweeping the road and another providing flanking fire. The Abenaki Indians had resisted attacking the smaller group at Fort Lyman because they thought the English there had cannon. Now faced with the big guns of Johnson, the Indians quickly lost heart for the battle. Dieskau attacked both the left and the right of Johnson's line in a savage battle with roaring waves of musketry and clouds of black powder smoke. Though not experienced in military matters, Johnson had made good dispositions and fought well until wounded in the thigh. After some time, his leg stiffened sufficiently to retire him to his tent, where he would remain for the rest of the battle.

The conduct of the fight now fell to Col. Phineas Lyman, who fought gamely for four hours. Dieskau was hit twice, first in the leg and then as he was being treated, in the thigh and knee. Many of Dieskau's Canadians and Indians quickly tired of the fight. They retreated back down the road and occupied themselves robbing and scalping the dead from the morning's fight, after which they pulled away and rested by a pond in the forest.

Things were not going well for Dieskau and his French. The colonists sensed the turning of the tide of battle and began to pour over their log fortifications and assault the French. The battle became a rout, and as his troops fled, the wounded Dieskau was captured.

A woods-experienced ranging party from Fort Lyman under McGinnis and Folsom came upon the Canadians and Indians resting by the water. Though outnumbered, they attacked. McGinnis was killed, but the ground was littered with the enemy dead. They were unceremoniously dumped into the pool which still carries the name Bloody Pond.

The casualties were about equal, roughly 250 on each side, but the French had lost their commander and most of their regular officers. The battle had begun well but ended badly for them, and withdrawal to the Ticonderoga Peninsula was their only option. Johnson had 500 men who had not been engaged, and the opportunity to go on the offensive was at hand. A rapid advance could have snared the French boats and struck at Carillon before the French could recover. Confusion, jealousy, in-fighting between the forces of the colonials, and the departure of the Mohawks cost the English a golden opportunity.

It was a time of stalemate. Still, the French had withdrawn, and a much-needed victory could be proclaimed. Hungry for good news that would fade the stain of Braddock's disaster, King George II declared William Johnson a baronet, and Parliament awarded him 5,000 pounds and 50,000 acres of land. Johnson occupied himself with improving the defenses of Fort William Henry. With the loss of his Mohawk scouts, Johnson began to search for volunteers who would go in harm's way to scout the enemy positions and conduct the ambush and the raid. He found them in Robert Rogers, John Stark, and Israel Putnam.

As junior leaders in his ranks, Johnson had men whose names would ring in American history. Robert Rogers would become the best known of American Rangers. Israel Putnam, a private in a Connecticut regiment, would become a captain of Connecticut Rangers and the first major general of the American army. John Stark would be critical to the success of Rogers Rangers and one of the greatest of American heroes of the Revolutionary War. Though he is less well known, no war seemed complete without the presence of Seth Pomeroy, who always marched to the sound of the guns. In the painted line of Indians was a young warrior who would one day cast a long shadow. His name was Joseph Brant.

Robert Rogers would become one of the most dynamic and tragic men of eighteenth-century America. Rogers was born on November 18, 1731, in the small village of Methun in Massachusetts Bay Colony.

He had six brothers and four sisters and was the fifth child. Rogers's parents were Scotch-Irish Presbyterians. Seeking land of his own, Robert's father, James, moved the family in 1739 to a place called the Great Meadow, a lonely frontier area near present-day Concord, New Hampshire. Here, with some neighbors, they began the arduous task of creating farms. By the standards of the time, the Rogers family lived a middle-class existence, including providing the children a basic education of reading, writing, and arithmetic.

Most Indians had left the area from the pressure of the whites. Some tribes, including the Abenaki, had gone north to Canada. Near the St. Lawrence River, the Abenaki had settled in a village they called Odanak (the French and British usually called the settlement St. Francis). The fury of the Abenaki was kept alive by French rhetoric and weapons of war.

Indian raids in the Rogers's area were frequent and devastating. Though the family escaped before an Indian war party arrived, the family's home was burned by Indians. Military knowledge is gained by training and experience. At age fourteen, Rogers began to participate in scouting missions against the Indians, learning woodcraft from the many experienced Rangers in the area, including Daniel Ladd, Ebenezer Eastman, and John Goffe. He was an observant youth with a quick mind and eagerness for knowledge. His military service was frequent. He went exploring in Indian territory and could be frequently found talking to those who went in the path of danger. Rogers was building a vast store of knowledge on the enemy and the terrain.

Rogers formed a friendship with another youth, a keen woodsman named John Stark. Destined to become an authentic American hero, Stark would be far more significant to the founding of the United States than Robert Rogers. As a young man, Stark had been captured by the Abenaki Indians. Forced to run the gauntlet carrying only a ceremonial pole, John Stark charged the line of Indians, belaboring them with the pole. When they set him to hoe corn, he chopped the corn and preserved the weeds, complaining that he was a warrior and would not do squaw's work. His courage saved him from torture and death. The admiring Indians adopted him into the tribe and treated him with kindness. He was later ransomed.

The French and Indian War, 1754–63

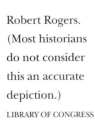
Robert Rogers. (Most historians do not consider this an accurate depiction.)
LIBRARY OF CONGRESS

Unsuited to the farm, Robert Rogers and his younger brother Richard became involved in a circumstance that led to a charge of intentionally passing counterfeit money. Dealing in do-it-yourself money was not frowned upon by many on the frontier. They saw it as a means of equalizing wealth. The law did not share that view. Conviction of counterfeiting carried the death penalty, and Rogers sweated at the thought of a rope around his neck. Rogers's trial for counterfeiting has been dismissed by some of his biographers as a youthful error, but it was not. That the charge was serious is demonstrated by the court's composition, four justices of the peace—an unusual happening for the time. Included in the justices were Col. Joseph Blanchard and Maj. John Goffe, military leaders of the area. Rogers was in trouble, but war was at hand, and Massachusetts and New Hampshire were looking for men to fight. This gave Rogers a way to escape punishment.

In February 1755, Gov. William Shirley of Massachusetts was mustering a regiment to remove the French from the Bay of Fundy. Now twenty-four years old, Rogers was ready to lead and offered to raise a company. He proved himself a successful recruiter, bringing in twenty-four men who volunteered to serve under him. With the blessing of Gov. Benning Wentworth of New Hampshire, Rogers broke his

John Stark.
NATIONAL ARCHIVES

agreement with Shirley and signed on for the New Hampshire Regiment. Rogers continued recruiting and brought in nearly sixty men. Robert Rogers was appointed captain of the First Company of Blanchard's regiment. John Stark became lieutenant of the company.

On the Crown Point expedition, Rogers met William Johnson. Though later life would bring great enmity between the two men, the immediate effect was to establish an operational rapport that would greatly benefit the English cause. Johnson's Indians had a habit of going home. Hampered by the fog of war, Johnson badly needed information. He turned to Rogers to provide the required intelligence. With a small party of men, Rogers conducted a long-range reconnaissance patrol, one of many that were to follow.

Rogers's courage was immediately evident. He performed both reconnaissance and combat patrols. He moved among the French forts and studied their positions. He captured and brought back prisoners for interrogation. Especially daring was his willingness to overcome the obvious hazards and engage the enemy deep in his own territory. His ambush of a canoe-borne party of Indians on Lake George was the talk of the English camp. Many scouting parties were terrified of the Indians and turned for home without contact. Rogers pressed on deep into enemy lands. Johnson came to rely upon him for badly needed intelligence. He brilliantly performed his mission from Governor Shirley to "distress the French and their allies by sacking, burning, and destroying."

When the campaign ended, English spirits were low. The only rays of sunshine in the gloomy gray skies of incompetence and defeat were Johnson's victory at Lake George and Robert Rogers and his Rangers. In an age when armies left the field during winter, Rogers and his men went forth in snow and freezing cold. Using ice skates and snow shoes, they prowled the frozen lakes and waters on long-range reconnaissance patrols and raids. They scouted French and Indian encampments and captured prisoners. Parties of unwary French suddenly found themselves being ambushed, their cattle slaughtered, and their critically needed winter supplies burned.

In newspapers, in taverns, and around campfires, Rogers and his Rangers were mentioned frequently and with admiration bordering on awe. In 1755, Robert Rogers was an unknown; five years later, he was a hero known on both sides of the Atlantic. William Shirley was in Massachusetts Bay as governor and commander in chief of the British Army in North America. Shirley was quick to grasp the potential of the Rangers and wanted a force to be employed around the contested areas of Lake Champlain and Lake George. Shirley contemplated a Ranger force that would combine the missions of scouting, reconnaissance, and raiding. He wrote in a letter to Henry Fox, "It is absolutely necessary for his Majesty's Sevice, that one Company at least of Rangers should be constantly employ'd in differant Parties upon Lake George and Lake Iroquois [Champlain], and the wood Creek and Lands adjacent."[10]

A Ranger whom Rogers and Stark came to know well was a Connecticut man named Israel Putnam. In 1755, Putnam was thirty-seven years old, the father of five children, and a lieutenant in a Connecticut regiment. Though illiterate, he was a successful farmer near Brooklyn, Connecticut. He gave this up and left home and family because he could not resist the call to battle. Putnam was not a member of Rogers's Rangers but frequently went on scout with him and in time would have his own company of Connecticut Rangers. On October 26, 1755, Rogers, Putnam, and two other Rangers were lying in ambush near Fort St. Frederick (Crown Point). A careless Frenchmen came out of the fort without a musket. When the Frenchman was within ten yards of them, Rogers jumped from cover and demanded that the man surrender. He refused, called for help, and attempted to stab Rogers with a knife. Rogers and the French soldier struggled until Putnam came up and struck the French soldier on the head with the butt of his musket. They then killed and scalped the man. This action took place within 350 yards of the French bastion and in plain sight of members of the garrison. Putnam was out again with Rogers on November 4 in a party of thirty men and four boats, each equipped with two wall-pieces, scatter guns of the period. Rogers, half the men, and two boats stayed on the water while Putnam commanded the men on land. When attacked by Indians in canoes, Rogers let them come close enough to use his superior firepower, then lured them into the fire of Putnam's guns.

On May 24, 1756, Governor Shirley commissioned Robert Rogers to be captain of "an independent company of Rangers." The sixty-seven-man unit of volunteer woodsmen would have four officers and three sergeants. Until his death, Richard Rogers, Robert's brother, would be second in command, with John Stark next in seniority. The early Rangers of the seventeenth century had been militia organizations. Rogers's company was at least an unofficial part of the regular army.

Shirley had replaced Braddock in command. In July 1756, John Campbell, the fourth Earl of Loudoun, replaced Shirley. Loudoun was a man of good ideas seldom fulfilled. Despite this, he had an understanding of the importance of using Rangers. British soldiers were reluctant to go on winter reconnaissance. In an August 20, 1756, letter to the Duke of Cumberland, Loudoun wrote, "From the Indians you will see we have no support; some Rangers I shall be obliged to keep all the Winter, till I can make some of our own people fit for that service. When I arrived I found that there was a disposition in the soldiers, to go out with the Indians and Rangers, and that some of them were then out. I shall encourage it all I can."[11]

Loudoun's admiration for Rangers did not lessen; in a letter to Cumberland begun in November and completed in December 1756, he observed, "It is impossible for an Army to Act in this Country, without Rangers; and there ought to be a considerable body of them, and the breeding them up to that, will be a great advantage to the country, for they will be able to deal with the Indians in their own way; and

Israel Putnam.
NATIONAL ARCHIVES

from all I can see, are much stronger and hardier fellows than the Indians."[12]

The need for Rangers brought about a continuing recruitment that would swell the ranks. Another Ranger company was formed to be commanded by Richard Rogers. Companies were formed in Boston to be commanded by Captains Hobbs and Speakman.[13] In addition to Rogers's corps of Rangers, numerous provincial Ranger companies were formed.

In Pennsylvania, the government—and therefore the response to Indian attack—was controlled by Quaker legislators. Safe in Philadelphia and well-populated areas, they tended to blame the horrors of frontier life on the Scotch-Irish who had moved there. They would do little to provide for defense. Governor Morris and Benjamin Franklin spoke for a policy of taking the offensive against the Indian. In January 1756, at a council in Carlisle, Governor Morris was informed that a friendly Indian reported 100 white captives were being held at an Indian town named Kittanning. This was west of the Allegheny Mountains beside the Allegheny River about forty miles north of French-held Fort Duquesne. At Kittanning lived two famed Delaware war chiefs, one named Shingas and the other Captain Jacobs. They had led or participated in a number of raids in Pennsylvania.

With the backing of Morris and Franklin, it was determined to raid the Indian settlement. Command was assigned to John Armstrong of Carlisle, Pennsylvania. He had recently lost his younger brother Lt. Edward Armstrong, who had fought valiantly at the fall of Fort Granville on the Juniata River in August. Armstrong set out with 300 men on horseback to attack Kittanning. Thinking they were about six miles from their objective, the Ranger scouts reported a small Indian hunting party of about three men near a fire. Concerned that one of the hunters might escape to give warning, Armstrong left a small number of men under Lieutenant Hogg to keep the Indians under observation and to attack them at first light.

He dismounted the rest of his men and took a circuitous route to approach the town. This was off the track known by the guide, and time was lost in an exhausting approach over rough terrain. In the darkness, Indian drums and the shouts of the warriors at dance guided Armstrong and his men. The night was warm, and as the dancing ended, many Indians chose to sleep outside their dwellings. Some of them bedded down in a cornfield and built small fires to keep off the gnats. A skilled Ranger by the name of Baker kept Armstrong informed of Indian activities, and as the night wore on, Indian fires began to be extinguished.

Armstrong saw that with many of the Indians sleeping in the open, their response would be quicker. He divided his force into two parties—one to attack the town from higher ground and one to sweep the cornfield into the Indian cabins. The attack began at first light and met strong resistance. The Indians had their women and children flee to the woods, but most of the men chose to stay and fight. Shingas was away at Fort Duquesne. Captain Jacobs barricaded himself in a cabin, and he and his men killed some of the Rangers and wounded others. Armstrong was shot in the shoulder. Unable to take the fortified cabins, Armstrong ordered them set on fire.

As the fire took hold of Jacobs's cabin, two Indian men and a woman tried to break free. These were shot down. Jacobs tried to jump from the cabin loft but was shot and killed. About thirty houses were burned, some of them exploding as stored gunpowder was ignited. Body parts were blown high in the air.

While Armstrong's wound was being bandaged, he received a report that there were Indians on the other side of the river who appeared in position to cut off the raiding party. Released prisoners told Armstrong that French and Indians had been there the day previous and a scouting party of twenty-four had been sent forward to begin planning an attack on a frontier fort. Armstrong recognized that the fire his scouts had said was for a hunting party was likely this force. Hogg and his men would be outnumbered.

They had planned to burn the Indian corn, but Armstrong made the decision to withdraw before that was done. Some Indians fired at them from along the flanks as the column withdrew. As Armstrong had feared, Lieutenant Hogg had unknowingly attacked a much stronger force. Hogg was shot three times. Badly wounded, Hogg lived to tell Armstrong that some of his men had run from the Indians. Armstrong was also concerned about a small group of men under the wounded Captain Mercer who, without orders, had left the battlefield earlier. Mercer got back, but some of his men were not heard of again. Armstrong estimated thirty to forty of the enemy killed at a loss of seventeen of his own men. Eleven prisoners were rescued, but four of these were with Mercer's party and were recaptured.

Tactically, the raid achieved little, the best benefit being that it made the Indians aware that they too were vulnerable. They had to give more thought to the defense of their villages. Indian raids continued, and Quaker control of the Pennsylvania legislature dictated a defensive mentality. Across the frontier, the Indian depredations continued. Most Ranger operations consisted of patrolling, providing early warning, and conducting ambushes.

In time, Rogers would draft rules of ranging, but no rule fits all circumstances, as Rogers recognized. On January 21, 1757, Rogers, Stark, and Speakman, along with approximately seventy other Rangers, were on patrol beside Lake George when they saw a French supply sled on the ice. Rogers sent Stark and twenty men after them. With Stark en route, Rogers saw ten more sleds coming and tried to call off Stark, but it was too late. The occupants of follow-on sleds saw Stark take their comrades and began to flee. Rogers captured some, but he knew others escaped to warn the French. His prisoners told him that the French

Joseph Brant.
NATIONAL ARCHIVES

and Indians in the area vastly outnumbered the Rangers. Rogers withdrew but violated his own procedures by returning to the same camp he had occupied the night before. It was raining, and he wanted to dry off the muskets with fires he had built at the last camp. The wet-wood smoke from fires in territory inhabited by the enemy would not be conducive to secrecy or security. While the Rangers were fireside, the French and Indians, who were in the same rain, bypassed and took up ambush positions. Without fires, they kept sufficient weapons and powder dry to be prepared for action.

In his journal, Rogers describes his men as moving single file, with himself and Lieutenant Kennedy in the lead. Single-file movement does not provide flank security. As senior officer, Rogers was acting as point man, a task better assigned to one of his best Rangers. On this occasion, Rogers led his men into an ambush. At five yards, the French and Indians opened fire. Rogers received a slight head wound, and Kennedy was killed. John Stark was toward the rear of the Ranger column. Occupying a hill, Stark and his men poured a hot fire on the enemy, providing the wounded Rogers and the surviving Rangers a rally point. In his journal, Rogers claimed he returned to the hill occupied by Stark, provided flank security, and was again wounded by being shot through the wrist. French attempts to flank the position were defeated, and at night, the Rangers slipped away.

The next morning, Stark, Ranger Thomas Burnside, and an unidentified Ranger volunteered to leave the wounded Rogers and the other Rangers to bring help. These were incredibly hardy men. Despite the exhaustion of battle and the difficult night withdrawal, Stark and his two companions traveled over thirty miles through snow and ice to arrange for sleds to bring Rogers and his men to safety. Rogers's wounds were serious enough to warrant his going to Albany to recover. Fourteen Rangers lost their their lives in this fight. Six Rangers were wounded, and six had the unhappy fate of being taken prisoner by the French and Indians. A Ranger named Schute later said that Rogers had told his men that the French would not dare to follow him. Ranger Stilson Eastman credited Stark with saving the command. In his journal, Rogers estimated the enemy force at 250 and made the unrealistic claim that 116 of the enemy had been killed. Though he would not laud Stark in a journal designed to report on himself, Rogers was grateful to his friend. Stark was given command of the deceased Speakman's company. This was one of many occasions that they would support each other. Later, when Stark was recovering from smallpox, his lieutenant, Jonathan Brewer, tried to usurp his command and put him under arrest. Rogers backed Stark, and Brewer was reprimanded.

In Britain, a new star had risen. William Pitt was a great orator projecting a great ego. Not given to self doubt, Pitt knew where he wanted to take his country. He intended to project British power overseas and defeat the French in North America. He had entered parliament in 1735 and been appointed to and dismissed from a number of positions. Pitt's words were like nails, and his voice was the hammer. Though he did not like Pitt, King George II appointed him as leader of commons and secretary of state. Regretting his action the king promptly fired Pitt, but the abrasive Pitt was much needed and was soon recalled. In June 1757, as prime minister, Pitt was given control of military and foreign affairs. Though he angered many, Pitt was the leadership England needed to beat the French.

Though his vision was worldwide, Pitt's plan for North America consisted of seizing the linchpins of French power in the New World. He would capture Louisbourg, sealing off the St. Lawrence River approach to the French capital of Quebec. He would further isolate Quebec by taking Fort Ticonderoga. These captures would strangle the French in Canada and lead to the eventual fall of Quebec. Fort Duquesne, the objective of Braddock's ill-fated expedition, was back on the planning board. Pitt wanted to capture this French-held doorway to the Ohio country. Lord Louden was recalled to England, and the ponderous Maj. Gen. James Abercromby was appointed commander in chief in North America.

Lord Jeffery Amherst would be given the mission to seize Louisbourg. With him went a red-haired young brigadier general named James Wolfe. Called "Aunt Abby" by his troops, the ineffective Abercrombie was assigned the mission of taking Fort Carillon (Ticonderoga). He had with him one of the brightest and best of the British officers, Brig. Lord Howe. Pitt ordered Brig. Gen. John Forbes to seize Fort Duquesne. Forbes was born in Scotland and, with Howe and Wolf, ranked among the most efficient of the young British brigadiers. Forbes also seemed to have a good opinion of Robert Rogers. On hearing a false report that Rogers was mortally wounded, Forbes wrote, "I shall be very sorry if it proves true, as I take him to good a man in his way to be easily spared at present."[14]

A few senior British officers admired the Rangers and set about to learn from them. The gallant Lord George Howe participated in operations with Rangers. He was believed to be the only British officer above the rank of captain who would do so. Howe saw the possibility of training British troops as light infantry using Ranger tactics and, in 1758, set about organizing such units. Howe was killed in action and his loss greatly mourned. Many British officers shared the view of General Wolfe, who thought Americans were "contemptible cowardly dogs."

The British regulars found American Rangers useful in war but were not about to let them into the inner circle of the army. An early foe of Rogers was Col. William Haviland of the 27th Regiment. If not guilty of treachery, this officer certainly exercised poor judgement. Rogers and Haviland had quarreled frequently while the Rangers were camped on a Hudson River island known as Rogers's Island. This island was beside Haviland's post of Fort Edward. In the harsh discipline of the times, two Rangers had been tied to a six-foot whipping post and flogged for stealing British rum. Other Rangers chopped down the whipping post and set out to rescue their comrades. Ranger officers broke up the fracas, but Haviland used a ruse to get the two unfortunates into his guardhouse. Haviland and Rogers quarreled over this and other matters, with Haviland stating that "it would be better [if] they were all gone than have such a riotous sort of people." To the British, the Rangers cutting down the whipping post showed a lack of discipline, and some historians have accepted that view. Haviland next sent provincial Capt. Israel Putnam and his Connecticut ranging company on a scout, but through design or carelessness, he announced that on Putnam's return, Rogers would lead 400 men on another expedition. The news was certain to reach the enemy.

It was the afternoon of March 10, 1758, when Rogers, with a force reduced by Haviland to 181 officers and enlisted men, marched out from Fort Edward, heading north. The Rangers moved with their accustomed caution, ghosting through the night with scouts out, halting before first light, maintaining good security. Travel was most rapid on the lake where the Rangers could use their skates, but there was a strong concern that the skillful French and their Indian allies might have an ambush waiting. Given Haviland's action, they expected the French and Indians would be hunting for them. It was decided to leave the lake and travel inland, passing behind a screen of mountains. On March 13, the weather was cold and the snow as deep as a man's waist when the Rangers strapped on snowshoes and began the march. The advance party reported a possible enemy encampment ahead, but further reconnaissance turned up only patches in the snow. To the right of the Rangers was a steep mountain with a frozen stream at its base which offered itself as a natural roadway for the traveler. The advance party was under the command of Captain Bulkeley, with Rogers traveling with the main body. Bulkeley sent back word that a large party of French and Indians were traveling toward them on the frozen stream. The Rangers moved rapidly into position setting up an ambush for the unsuspecting enemy.

The enemy force, consisting of about 100 Indians and a few French, was heavily bundled against the cold. Holding their fire, the Rangers waited quietly, letting the enemy walk fully into the trap. The harsh blast of Rogers's musket rent the air. Immediately, the other Rangers opened fire with telling effect. The authoritative crash of gunfire was interspersed with Ranger shouts and Indian whoops. Rogers estimated that over forty of the enemy died at the first volley.[15] Capt. Charles Bulkeley's men tried to cut off the enemy retreat, but the French and Indians were heading pellmell for the rear and broke through. Eager for the kill, the Rangers rushed after them.

Suddenly, a scythe-like volley of musketry cut through the charging Rangers. The French and Indians ambushed by the Rangers were only the advance party for a force of 600 that was closing fast and spoiling for a fight.

Ranger casualties were immediate and heavy. Bulkeley and about fifty of his men went down. The triumphant French and Indians were on them immediately with war whoop and scalping knife while others charged after the Rangers and a large party circled to the rear of Rogers's men. The Rangers fought a desperate delaying action, fighting from behind snow-covered rocks and trees. Clouds of powder smoke rolled over the battlefield as men screamed, cursed, and died. The Rangers fought to secure high ground to the left and right of their center position. The fighting was hand-to-hand with the late afternoon sun glinting along the honed edge of tomahawks until the cold metal shine was dulled by blood.

Around dark, the enemy broke through Rogers's defenses in the center. On the right, Lieutenant Phillips and a party of eighteen Rangers were surrounded by 300 enemy and surrendered to promises of humane treatment. They were tied to trees, tortured, and hacked to pieces with knives and tomahawks. Delay and defense turned into a rout as Rogers's men fired and ran for their lives. Rogers barely escaped.

The Rangers who were captured were tortured by having lighted slivers of pine thrust into their flesh, then hacked to pieces with knives and tomahawks. Death came hard and slow. After a difficult escape and journey, the surviving Rangers regrouped at a rally point and made their way back to Fort Edward. The journey home was an ordeal for wounded, suffering men in cold and gray weather that seemed to mock their ordeal. Rogers was the last to come in. The fight would be called the Battle of the Snowshoes. It was a licking.

The Rangers lost 127 of 181 men. Many of those who returned were wounded, some seriously.

Amherst moved on Louisbourg with 4,000 troops and 2,600 sailors. On June 8, the first landing was attempted. A French ambush took a heavy toll, but Amherst's men pressed on and gained the shore. When heavy cannon could be mounted, they began to knock down the walls, and on July 26, 1758, Louisbourg surrendered for the second time.

The next effort was that of Abercromby against Ticonderoga. A great fleet consisting of some 136 whale boats, 900 bateau, canoes, and flatboats with artillery sailed north on the waters of Lake George. The army consisted of 5,900 colonial militia and 6,300 British regulars. This powerful force far exceeded the 3,500 men the French General Montcalm could muster. Though fewer in number than the British, the French had too many men to maintain and fight from within the walls of their fort. Masters of the art of entrenchment, the French constructed an exterior defensive wall made of logs.

Pierced with firing ports and done in an irregular line to permit enfilade fire, it was a position that would withstand any attack not supported by artillery. Save for a small reserve within the fort, Montcalm positioned his men along this line. To the front, he posted a picket of Indians and Canadian woodsmen.

Abercromby landed his troops in a cove near the French fort during the night of July 5–6. A scouting party was sent forward that included the Rangers. Montcalm had sent out a probing force, and a bloody meeting engagement was the result. Both sides took heavy casualties, but the British got the worst of it. Lord Howe was killed, and the aggressive spirit of the British command perished with him. Col. Thomas Gage was now second in command. On the seventh, Abercromby attacked the French line with the Rangers leading the way. Following were the regulars advancing in individual columns and not supporting each other. The well-protected French smashed this attack and the five more that followed. The attacking force was thrashed, with 1,600 men as casualties. The French lost a quarter of that number. Abercromby's great waterborne force returned to their boats and, against the wishes of many, sailed away. Montcalm had little time to celebrate. He soon heard that Amherst had taken Louisbourg.

He knew he had to abandon this post to the British and move north to protect Quebec.

British General Forbes would in large part have to depend on the colonies of Pennsylvania, Maryland, and Virginia for the force to move west toward Ohio. Forbes was wiser than Braddock and leaned heavily on the advice of John Armstrong and George Washington. He could also count on the Swiss mercenary Lt. Col. Henri Bouquet. Rangers played a major role in this operation. For example, in the Pennsylvania forces, nearly all the commanders and subordinate officers were "experienced woodsmen and Indian fighters."[16]

As Braddock's old road was now overgrown and forty miles longer, Forbes decided to take a route through Pennsylvania. Col. George Washington and his fellow Virginian Col. James Byrd saw a threat to Virginia's interests in this. Washington complained that by his reckoning, there was only nineteen miles' difference, but his efforts to dissuade Forbes were to no avail. Forbes felt Washington was putting the interest of Virginia above that of the expedition. He was not impressed by Washington's understanding of the difficulties they faced.

Forbes was a true soldier of his king. Though in such ill health that he had to be carried in a litter, he pursued his mission. He was prudent. In place of a headlong dash through the wilderness, he proceeded in stages. He had a solid base of supply at Carlisle and built well-staffed forts and blockhouses along the way. He made certain that a strong logistical tail supported his effort. Forbes's orders were to begin his expedition by May 1, 1758.

Forbes paid attention to detail, nearly driving Col. John Armstrong to distraction with his pestering, but it was in a good cause. Bouquet was well in advance, building the road with Indian and Ranger scouts protecting the column. Forbes made Indian alliances, even bringing some Cherokee and Catawba from the south. These were enemies of the Shawnee and Delaware aligned with the French.

A Highland officer named Major Grant badgered Bouquet to allow him to lead a detachment forward against Fort Duquesne. Bouquet made a rare bad judgment and agreed. With 37 officers and 850 men, Grant made a series of tactical blunders, including playing bagpipes that alerted his enemy. The British were surrounded and several hundred slaughtered. Major Grant, 4 officers, and 100 men were taken prisoner. Many of these faced torture and burning. Eager to show their success, the Indians took their plunder and captives and departed for their home villages. Despite this victory, the French saw that they could not defeat the powerful force that was coming.

Washington was ranging out with scouting parties and got into a firefight with the Indians on November 12. He took three prisoners, one of which was a white Indian captive named Johnson. Captain Mercer of Virgina heard the firing and hurried to the scene with reinforcements. The two parties of Virginians mistook each other for the enemy, and one officer and thirteen men were killed by their own people. Washington showed great personal courage in walking among the men, striking the musket barrels to have the men cease fire.

The prisoner Johnson told Forbes that French volunteers from Canada and Louisiana had deserted. The Indians had gone home, and the French were low on supplies. This information caused Forbes to press onward.

On November 24, when twelve miles from Fort Duquesne, an Indian said the fort was being burned and the French were leaving. A detachment was sent forward to put out the fires. The next day, Forbes took Fort Duquesne. He promptly renamed it Fort Pitt. It would have to be completely rebuilt. The most dramatic sight was the scalped heads and bloody kilts of the Scottish Highlanders. They had been set on poles.

The army set about building what would be a great fort, the key to the interior of America and the birth of the great city of Pittsburgh. Forbes's Indians were fickle friends. They took all the presents they could get, added whatever they could steal, and went south. Along the way, they raided their allies' frontier settlements. Forbes had given his all. He made it back to Philadelphia but died there on March 11, 1759.

Prime Minister William Pitt ordered a two-pronged attack. Amherst would erase the disaster Abercromby had suffered at Fort Carillon (Ticonderoga). Amherst was ordered to move by way of the Champlain Valley against Fort Carillon, then north to Fort Frederic (Crown Point). Another force under General Wolfe would sail up the St. Lawrence River and attack Quebec.

Amherst was a prudent commander. While building his army, he gathered information on the enemy. Escorted by Rogers's Rangers, a British officer of engineers made a perilous journey into French lines.

While some Rangers seized prisoners, others escorted the engineer, a Lieutenant Brehm, along the log wall the French had so successfully defended against Abercromby. By midyear, Amherst had brought together a force of 10,000 troops about equally divided in number between regulars and colonists. He also had detailed knowledge of the French works and knew that he outnumbered the French about five to one and the French were lacking in food and basic military supplies.

In July, Amherst moved on Fort Carillon. The French force was so weak that Amherst was able to occupy their log wall and use it as a position to direct cannon fire against the fort. After four days of artillery fire and counterfire, the French saw that they could not sustain the position and, on July 26, withdrew, blowing up the fort behind them. Amherst took Fort Carillon, renamed it Ticonderoga and proceeded to rebuild it. The French knew they could not hold Fort Frederic either, and on July 31, they destroyed it and withdrew north. Amherst followed and began to rebuild this fort as well. He named it Crown Point. In addition to construction of forts, he was occupied with building cannon-carrying vessels that could defeat those the French had on Lake Champlain.

Rogers was about to conduct a daring military operation that would live in history. Amherst was anxious to know how General Wolfe's assault on Quebec was proceeding and sent two regular officers, Captain Kennedy and Lieutenant Hamilton, to Quebec to check Wolfe's situation. The cover plan was that the two men were carrying peace offerings to the Indians they would have to pass through. The Indians were not taken in by this ruse. The two officers were captured by the Abenaki, who encamped along the St. Francis River. This fierce band had for many years raided the settlements, tortured, murdered, and stretched the hair of their victims from their lodge poles.

Had Kennedy and Hamilton been Americans, it is unlikely action would have been taken, but they were British regulars. Amherst, who was xenophobic to his core, was determined to take action. On September 13, 1759, Amherst sent written orders to Rogers: "You are this night to set out with detachment as ordered yesterday." The orders directed Rogers to go attack the enemy's settlements on the south side of the St. Lawrence river and, while being careful of the women and children, "take your revenge." For security purposes, the published orders would differ from those Rogers received privately. He knew he was to proceed directly to St. Francis.[17] The route of march challenged the skill of the woodsmen. From Crown Point, the Rangers had to travel over 150 miles of uncharted enemy territory. Lakes were controlled by heavily armed French vessels, and French forts dotted the area, their garrisons in excellent position to block the attack or cut off the withdrawal.

Rogers began to organize a force of select men. Stark did not go on this mission. He had previously been sent with 200 Rangers to cut a road to the post known as Number 4. That the objective was the Abenaki camp at St. Francis was known to only a few. The rest of the men were told they were going to a place Rogers called "Suagothel." As darkness fell on the night of September 13, 1759, Robert Rogers and 200 Rangers stepped into whaleboats and embarked northward on Lake Champlain. They rowed by night, quietly listening for the sound of block and tackle or the grumbling of the watch on some French ship. At dawn, they went ashore, hid the boats, and reconnoitered the lake shore. Sickness struck, and there was a gunpowder explosion and an accidental firing of a weapon that injured men. Within six days of departure, thirty-one men had to be returned to Crown Point.

Rogers pressed on in rain and fog. The Ranger boats quietly rowed past the heavily armed French guard ships on Lake Champlain. Though they passed the lake's narrow choke point, they knew the threat of discovery was ever-present and bent their backs to the oars. At the north end of the lake, Rogers found a short stretch of dry ground suitable for landing. Rogers had the boats drawn inland and well concealed. Two Indians were left to keep watch over this vital means of escape. On September 23, the Rangers headed north overland.

Two days later, the trail-weary boat guards caught up with the fast-moving Rangers. A large force of French and Indians had found the hiding place of the boats, burned them, and were in hot pursuit. Rogers knew the enemy would know the approximate size of his force by the simple expedient of counting the boats. While the French did not know his objective, the alarm would be raised and the hunters turned out.

Returning by way of Lake Champlain was not an option. Ranger officers discussed the alternatives and decided that after the Indian village was raided, they would head overland to the southeast, guiding on the St. Francis River to its forks. They planned to follow the southern fork of the St. Francis, then continue south past Lake Memphremagog into the valley of the Passumpic River and into the Connecticut River region. Rogers dispatched a small party to return to General Amherst, tell him of the plan, and request that supplies be sent up the Connecticut. He knew that the odds were against the Rangers making the rendevous, but if they did, resupply would be vital.

Of immediate importance was to avoid the pursuing enemy. Rogers knew the most difficult terrain offered the best chance of avoiding contact. The thick-forested swamps offered a route that even skilled Indian trackers would have difficulty following. For nine days, Rogers led his men through a world of muck, water, and swarming insects. The men and their equipment were constantly wet, their skin wrinkled and cracked; hardened men shivered. They gave up slapping at insects and let them feed. Fires could not be risked. Boughs of spruce tied together were the only bed and a precarious one indeed. A startled cry, a splash, and hearty curses were heard in the night. From dawn to dusk, they marched, always on short rations of the dried corn and beef that was the trail ration of the age.

When they broke free of the swamp, another obstacle loomed large before them. The Rangers were on the west bank of the cold, swift-moving St. Francis River. The enemy camp was on the east side. The water was about five feet deep and boiling with the force of its flow. Stepping off the bank, Rogers anchored himself by placing his arm around a tree and called for the next man. One by one, the tallest men stepped into the torrent, made their way along the line, and grasped the hand of the last man. When the human chain reached the other bank, men carrying the Ranger muskets stepped into the water on the upstream side of the line and began to make their way across. Men went down, some muskets were lost, but none of the Rangers drowned. Wet and cold, they made the far shore and concealed themselves while wringing out wet clothes and checking that powder was dry.

Fifteen miles downstream lay the objective, the village that housed Abenaki Indians, a tribe renowned for their cruelty. Many of the Rangers had personal reasons for wanting revenge. Late on the afternoon of October 5, three miles from his objective, Rogers climbed a tree and looked upon the curling columns of smoke rising from the Abenaki cook fires. As night fell, Rogers and two officers made their careful way forward, reconnoitered, and watched the unsuspecting Indians in leaping, whirling dance.

The approach had taken twenty-two days. Because men had been sent back to Crown Point because of injuries and illness, there were 142 Rangers left to make the attack. Several hours before dawn, they moved to a final assembly area 1,500 yards short of the village, dropped packs and blankets, and made a final check of weapons while getting the last briefing from their officers. When all was in readiness, they moved quietly to surround the town. One hundred Rangers were to be employed on the attack on Indian huts; the remainder would block the potential escape route along the St. Francis River. In the shadowy predawn gloom, Rogers led his men stealthily forward while the Indians slept.

Suddenly, the Ranger yell split the morning quiet. Muskets roared; tomahawks, knives, and bayonets flashed downward into startled flesh. The Indians were drowsy from the previous night's revelry. Many were killed in their blankets. Some Indians fought back, trying to shoot from the windows and doors of their huts. Flame put a quick and terrifying end to these efforts. One after another, the Rangers torched the Indian dwellings. Not only men but Indian women and children died. The sight of blond, red, and brown haired scalps—many of them small—hanging from lodge poles brought on a blood lust for revenge that the Rangers satisfied.

Some Indians tried to escape by the river, leaping into canoes. The blocking force shot them down, knifed and scalped them in the canoes or in the water, staining the waters of the St. Francis red. The Jesuit missionary Robaud was captured and roped like an animal. This was a slaughter. Several hundred Indians were dead, a sufficient number to cow the Abenaki. Captain Ogden of the Rangers was seriously wounded. Six Rangers were lightly wounded and one Stockbridge Indian killed. Five captives were released and a score of Indian women and children spared.

Rogers questioned the survivors and learned that the French and Indians were out in strength. A force twice the size of that of the Rangers was nearby. Filling their packs with corn from the village, the

Rangers took five captives and moved off, the wounded Ogden staggering along behind. There were 110 miles of wilderness between them and the area of Lake Memphremagog.

Eight days of cross-country, foul-weather movement left them exhausted. The Indian corn was gone, and game seemed to have disappeared from the mountains. Men lived on leaves and mushrooms. Near the lake, they decided to split up into small parties and search for food. The parties set off in various directions. Split into small groups, they were much more susceptible to enemy attack. Ensign Avery's party lost seven men. Lieutenant Dunbar, Lieutenant Turner, and ten Rangers were killed. Some who were captured were taken back to the Abenaki village and horribly tortured and killed.

The surviving parties pressed on, each enduring its own hell. Starvation brought madness. Men insane with hunger babbled and tried to eat their own excrement. They ate tree bark, leather, even pack straps and cartouche boxes. Some found dead bodies in a stream and, without waiting for fire, ate the cold flesh.

Rogers had asked the relief force to meet him at Wells River. A party under Lieutenant Stevens had made the trip, but stopped short when rapids blocked his path. Daily patrols had failed to make contact with Rogers, so Stevens left the meeting area. Even Rogers lost heart when he received no response to his calls and musket shots. Deep despair settled on the men. Rogers was the essence of a leader and was soon in control of himself. Shucking off his gloom, he decided to leave the main body behind and press on to obtain supplies. Equally astounding was the incredible hardiness of Ranger Captain Ogden. This seriously wounded man had kept pace under the most arduous conditions and grown stronger every day. Now Rogers and Ogden built a raft, and with another Ranger and an Indian boy, they began a trip down the foaming river heading for the fort known as Number 4.

The rapids beat at them, tossing them about like a cork in a maelstrom. Near White River Falls, they barely escaped with their lives and made shore. The raft soon broke apart. Downstream, they salvaged what they could, rebuilt the raft, and continued on. On October 31, 1759, they landed near Number 4. Provisions were immediately sent to the starving Rangers at Wells River. Rogers had told the men he would have food back to then within ten days. He kept his promise.

Critical to British aims was the seizure of Quebec. The Quebec plateau is a natural fortress, its high, steep cliffs falling to the St. Lawrence River below. Atop it, and ringed about by miles of earthworks, the stone-topped citadel perched like an eagle surveying its domain. Wolfe was thirty-two, a major general sick in body but not in spirit. He sailed from recently captured Louisbourg on June 4, 1759. With him was a powerful fleet and an army of 8,000 men. Six companies of American Rangers were included in his force.

Wolfe was a good soldier and a hidebound professional of the European school. He did not like Rangers, whom he called "the worst soldiers in the universe." Wolfe then made good use of them. Arriving at Quebec, Wolfe decided to camp on the Ile d'Orleans, which was out of artillery range of Quebec and offered security for his force. Forty Rangers landed on the island and made the reconnaissance to be certain it was clear of the French. Wolfe then landed his main body. On the opposite shore from Quebec was a projection of land then called Cape Levi, and not far from that was Pointe des Peres. These sites offered excellent artillery positions to fire on Quebec. Rangers, supported by light infantry, made the attack and seized this critical terrain. Wolfe now had much of the city of Quebec under his guns. Fires of the twenty-two warships of his supporting fleet could be supplimented and his ships could better pass under the French cannon to take important firing position above the town.

The Rangers began to roam the shores of the St. Lawrence. Nine of Gorham's Rangers were ambushed, killed, and scalped by Indians. Other Rangers had killed some captive children whom they were bringing in, but claimed were crying and giving away their position to the Indians. British Colonel Fraser attributed it to "that cowardice and barbarity which seems so natural to a native of America, whether of Indian or European extraction."[18] Wolfe next attempted to put ashore a force of regulars on the northern shore of the St. Lawrence. The attack would be made between the town and Montmorencey Cataract. It was a rather desperate effort for a soldier with Wolfe's reputation. A beach covered by French artillery had to be crossed to get to a cliff that no one was sure how to climb. The predictable result was that the British took over 400 casualties without a single Frenchman being hurt. Wolfe was always at the scene of action. A cannon ball smashed the walking stick he carried in his hand, and he was repeatedly hit by splinters. He had to watch his best regulars flee for their lives, leaving their wounded to the scalping knife.

The French sent 400 Indians through the woods to attack Wolfe's flanks. While in the woods, the Indians found the Rangers waiting for them. The tribesmen were beaten back with heavy loss.

A sudden, heavy rain wet the powder of both sides. Wolfe felt he had been ill supported by the navy and said so. When Admiral Saunders complained of the criticism, Wolfe said he still felt that way but would withdraw the remarks. He said the blame was his and wrote, "A man sees his errors often too late to remedy."[19]

Wolfe's fame now eclipses the fact that he next blamed his regulars for failing him. This angered the ranks, who said that his generalship was as bad as his health. Wolfe's health was very bad and so was that of many of his troops. Sickness had incapacitated half of his army. Meanwhile, the Rangers were passing through the countryside taking or destroying the crops the French in Quebec needed to supply their garrison.

At midnight on September 13, 1759, troops began to load into whaleboats equipped with muffled oars. Two hours later, the attack began. It was facilitated by a Highland officer who spoke fluent French. He answered the queries of French sentinels, enabling Wolfe, though very ill to lead his men ashore. At the top of the 250-foot cliff the French guards were scattered. By 6 A.M., the English were formed in ordered ranks on the Plains of Abraham. Wolfe was now in his element. What followed was a traditional European battle fought on an American battlefield.

The French under General Montcalm marched in formation six deep; they paused periodically and began firing at 150 yards. This was beyond the range of a musket. They continued forward until they were within 40 yards of each other. The British were in two ranks and spaced. They took the French fire until close range, then with concerted volley smashed them. The British advanced to about 20 yards and fired another volley. The French tried but could not gain superiority of fire. Their best effort was from Canadians and Indians firing from the flanks. When the British charged with the bayonet, the rout was on. Both Montcalm and Wolfe were hit and would die of their wounds.

History rightfully records that the battle was won on the Plains of Abraham and accords Wolfe well-earned honors. What the British found when they entered Quebec was a starving population. The Ranger operations in preventing relief and capturing and destroying food had greatly weakened the French will to fight.

CHAPTER 5

The River and the Lakes

In February 1757, John Stark's company of approximately sixty Rangers was at Fort William Henry at the south end of Lake George. Located fourteen miles from Fort Edward on the Hudson, these two outposts were the most northern of the British garrisons. Some forty miles to the north was the French Fort Carillon. (The site was originally named Ticonderoga by Indians, and the British adopted that name.) Stark had sent several officers on recruiting service.

The Fort William Henry regular army force consisted of Irish troops under Major Eyre. Total effective strength of the garrison was 346 men with another 128 sick or wounded. March 17 was St. Patrick's Day, and the Irish celebrated with heavy drinking. Stark, to the disappointment and anger of his men, would not allow them to participate. Ranger patrols continued to be maintained, and they found evidence that the enemy was coming.

Looking to surprise Fort William Henry, the French governor, the Marquis de Vaudreuil, sent out his brother Rigaud with a force of 1,600 French, Canadians, and Indians. This French force came down from Canada, well prepared and protected from the cold with blankets and bearskins. They moved beside the ice of Lake Champlain and paused at Fort Carillon for two weeks to build several hundred scaling ladders. Marching along Lake George, they closed on the fort on the evening of the eighteenth. Historians agree the Irish soldiers had been drinking heavily. There is dispute over whether they were still drunk, hungover, or sober. As the Irish have been known to fight well under any of these circumstances, the argument is academic. No one disputes that the Rangers were alert and the garrison under Major Eyre and Capt. John Stark responded well. Crossing the ice of Lake George with 1,600 men and 300 ladders could not be accomplished in absolute quiet by the French and Indians. An alert sentry sounded the alarm.

The approach of the enemy was sobering for the small garrison. Surrender to a force containing Indians often meant a slow and painful death. Sick men clutched weapons and crawled to the ramparts. As the enemy moved approximately twenty-five yards from the fort, they were met with a blast of cannon and musketry. The French and Indians surrounded the fort and kept a heavy fire of musketry on it, but they had no cannon. Again attempting to reach the walls, they were hit again with heavy fire and withdrew. Stark led a few Rangers in a reconnaissance of the enemy positions. Around noon on the twentieth, the French and Indians moved into the open but stayed out of range. They showed their superior numbers and sent Chevalier Le Mercier to seek the surrender. Major Eyre, Captain Stark, and their officers heard the generous French terms and rejected them.

That night, French and Indians fired the outbuildings of the fort, storehouses, hospital, Ranger huts, and saw mill, with sparks endangering the fort. Snow began to fall and the French lay in camp throughout the day and the next night, the snow reaching a depth of three feet. When the snow stopped, the French again attempted to use fire. Twenty French volunteers set ablaze a sloop and some storehouses and attempted to burn the whaleboats. John Stark left the fort with a party of Rangers and took the French under fire. Five Frenchmen were wounded or killed.

Recognizing that they could not take the fort, the French and Indians chopped holes in the ice and slid their dead into the waters. They then began the long trek back to Canada. In this action, John Stark was struck by what was apparently a spent bullet. It did not break the skin. It was the only occasion an enemy bullet would ever touch John Stark.

For Robert Rogers, recruiting and training went forward. The regular British establishement could not overcome their distrust of Americans. The captain-general of the British Army, the Duke of Cumberland, urged that regulars be trained to officer Ranger units. Lord Loudoun sent fifty-six volunteers, most of whom were regulars, to be trained as Rangers. Rogers put these men through their paces by taking them on training missions. They scouted the woods of Rogers's Island, learned woodcraft and land navigation, and practiced the raid, ambush, attack, and withdrawal. To become efficient, they practiced the art of their calling under the whiplash of criticism from experienced Rangers. The experiment of the cadet company was not long lived. To the disappointment of the men involved, it was dissolved on November 8, 1757. Thereafter, some young volunteers trained with the Rangers but on an informal basis.

With success, more Ranger companies were added. Though not all active at the same time, Rogers's force would come to number seventeen companies. Some men were loosely recruited. Loudoun panned some of the Ranger units as composed of "Irish, sailors and Spaniards."

Lord Loudoun asked Rogers to put his practices on paper. Rogers was a man who studied warfare in the practical frontier fashion. He was intelligent and reasonably educated for his time. It is unlikely that he read Ranger Capt. Benjamin Church's rules and many military books before sitting down to draft his famous rules for Rangers to observe. What Rogers wrote was the knowledge of the frontier. It was personal experience handed down around the campfire. These were the rules of survival. Many of the twenty-eight rules are eternal military truths.

Some British officers saw merit in Ranger tactics, but not in Rangers. Thomas Gage, who had lead the advance party in Braddock's 1755 defeat, felt it would be better to have Rangers under the command of line officers. Lieutenant Colonel Gage had taken command of the 44th Foot following the death of Col. Peter Halkett. In time, Gage believed that Ranger units should be abolished and replaced by British troops trained in forest warfare and organized as light infantry. The proposal naturally included that he was best suited to be given command of the new organization. Gage facilitated approval of his recommendation by offering to raise the new command at his own expense. British leadership did not doubt Thomas Gage's courage or his willingness to learn. Loudoun reported Gage participating in winter actions—an unusual action for an officer of Gage's rank. His seniors felt he was an honest man and dedicated soldier of his king. Gage did not like Rogers, but his dislike was based on scorn of a colonial rather than jealousy. The careers of senior British officers were not threatened by colonials. Gage was in the class system, and Rogers was not. Thomas Gage thought that Rogers was an upstart bumpkin who did not have the character to rise in command and responsibility.

The light infantry was a worthy experiment. American woodsmen were recruited to become the 80th Regiment, the first light infantry in the British Army. Gage was promoted colonel, and the concept of light infantry spread in spite of British eighteenth-century tactics designed for European conflict that did not fit the American frontier. Gage got his command and promotion and still did not like Rangers. He wrote Col. Frederick Haldimand that Ranger officers had no rank in the army.

Rogers's Rangers went on to other successes. They participated in the Louisbourg campaign, the siege at Fort William Henry, and the attacks on Ticonderoga and Montreal, to name a few. When victory came, the Rangers were not a part of regular forces, and the companies were disbanded. Despite the defeat of the French, it seemed possible that their western posts might continue to hold out. It was Robert Rogers who was selected to accept the surrender of the French holdings along the Great Lakes, including Detroit and Michilimackinac. Rogers was delighted by the prospect as he had no permanent rank and was as temporary as his units. The debts incurred in the service loomed large, and the west seemed the place for a man to make his fortune. The surrender of the French installations and the treaties with their former Indian allies were accomplished during severe winter conditions that tested even Rogers's ability as a woodsman. He succeeded, however, and returned to New York.

Financial disaster struck. Rogers had believed the British government would pay for the goods and services of the men who served as Rangers. To his dismay, account after account was turned down. Sued by his own men, hounded by creditors, his pleas ignored by the men who instructed him to raise the Ranger companies, Rogers was a worried man. After much wrangling, he found it necessary to accept a settlement of his account that left him in debt.

He tried land speculation and came into conflict with Sir William Johnson, his former senior officer. Johnson now saw Rogers as a potential rival and thwarted Rogers's efforts to carve out a land empire. After a trip to England, Rogers married Elizabeth "Betsy" Browne, whose minister father performed the service. Rogers then caught a trooper (i.e., a troopship) on the tide and sailed to the Carolinas, where he met Gov. Arthur Dobbs of North Carolina. Here he became interested in Dobbs's dream of finding a Northwest Passage, an Atlantic-to-Pacific water route for shipping. The summer heat and swarms of mosquitoes of the Carolinas were an experience Rogers found tedious. He returned to New York to face an even greater heat from the swarms of creditors who were waiting on the dock. Rogers sold his South Carolina commission and bought a position as a captain in the New York Independents. He was constantly unsuccessfully searching for ways to get out of debt. He sought to have his company assigned to a western post in order that he might trade for furs. This request was denied. Soon even his father-in-law was suing him. Betsy supported Robert against her father.

Rogers returned east and sailed to England in hopes of finding something that would relieve his desperate financial condition. Gage tried to stop Rogers's army pay by claiming the Ranger was a volunteer.

In London, Rogers decided to enter the literary world, publishing two books that he hoped would earn money and attract the attention of those in government. *Journals of Major Robert Rogers* and *A Concise Account of North America* received acclaim. In the latter work, Rogers wrote of the possibility of a Northwest Passage. His writings put forth a plan of exploration to determine if it existed. Certainly, he hoped to lead the expedition and thereby gain employment and possibly wealth. The trade advantages offered huge rewards, but the English treasury was low and his proposal got a lukewarm reception. The best Rogers could achieve was to be appointed commandant of the western post of Michilimackinac. This could serve as a jumping-off point for his Northwest Passage search.

With joy in his heart, Rogers sailed for America. The joy soon turned to bitterness. Old foes in high positions conspired to thwart him. Whatever Johnson's feelings may have been toward Rogers in their early relationship, it was clear that anyone who opened northwest America would become a wealthy and powerful man and a competitor. The former subordinate must be brought to heel. Gage's dislike of Rogers abetted Sir William Johnson's efforts. Both powerful men worked to limit Rogers's authority and scoff at his accomplishments. When directed to review Rogers's claims for payment, Gage began and ended with the view that Rogers deserved nothing. Johnson and Gage issued contradictory orders to Rogers. No matter what course of action he took, he would be in violation of someone's instruction.

At the far north of the peninsula separating Lake Michigan and Lake Huron was the small stockade and trading post known as Michilimackinac. Rogers had barely arrived when he appointed a surveyor to begin mapping western lands. A party under Capt. James Tute was assembled to begin the search to determine if a Northwest Passage existed. The expedition would cost money that Rogers thought would be forthcoming. Throughout his active years, Rogers displayed trust in his government. He tended to act on promises thinking they would support him. When they did not, he was left with the bills.

Rogers got on well with both the Indians and the traders, but the men in high places were steadily building a wall around him. Captain Tute's party returned without success, and the dream of a Northwest Passage would remain a dream. His enemies began to concoct a story that Rogers was a traitor. Those who bore him ill will found this a juicy tale to spread.

In 1767, under orders from General Gage, Rogers was arrested and charged with high treason. Both he and his wife were cut off from contact with friends. Elizabeth was treated with contempt, even pushed about. Rogers was put in irons. The man who had once been lionized by the press now became a subject of mockery and disdain. In this time of trouble, it was the Indians who loyally supported the man who had been such an effective leader against them. Still in irons, under the cruelest of treatment, Rogers was taken to Fort Niagara, then to Montreal for trial. Elizabeth was supportive and carrying his child.

Rumor, malicious gossip, and personal hatred were not a substitute for evidence at a court-martial. Witness after witness for the prosecution was unable to provide proof that Rogers conspired to deliver the west to the French. Rogers handled his own defense and tore the prosecution argument to shreds. After all his suffering, the verdict was not guilty.

General Gage took his time about letting Rogers out of jail. Though found not guilty in late October 1768, it would be June 1769 before Rogers was set free. His innocence, however, did not allay the suspicions or hatreds, and Rogers would not be reinstated to his position. Without funds, hounded by American creditors, Robert Rogers, now the father of a newborn son, sailed to England. He tried to get his back pay, was thrown into debtors prison, wrote petitions, and on release pleaded his case in every manner possible. The pay he was due was never granted in full, and Rogers was always short of funds and in debt. He tried again to raise the hope of a Northwest Passage, but that was turned down. After six years of effort, he was granted the retired pay of a major and money for passage home. At forty-three, Robert Rogers was destitute, a man without a future.

Rogers had lost contact with America and was buried in his own financial woes. He did not see that seeds sewn in the colonial wars were now bearing fruit. Men who had learned to conduct their affairs and defend their homes and families questioned why they should be ruled by a distant sovereign who had little understanding or sympathy for their problems. A revolution was beginning.

Had he been loyal to the land of his birth and his friends, Rogers would have cut his ties with the British as John Stark did. Rogers did not, and desperate for money, he tried to sell himself to the highest bidder. By siding with the crown, Robert Rogers lost the opportunity to be a founding father of a new nation. His friend John Stark would become an American hero. Israel Putnam was not a member of Rogers's Rangers, but he had accompanied them on expeditions and knew the Rangers well; Putnam would fight for independence, as would Moses Hazen, Edmund Munroe, and other Rangers.

John Cuneo and other biographers have sought to excuse Rogers for fighting with the British against his birthplace and his comrades. Some believe Washington treated Rogers unfairly. But Washington had reason to suspect Robert Rogers. He was a British officer on half pay, and his stated interest in finding a Northwest Passage would not have been funded by the fledgling Congress. It needed British support. Rogers's travels were to areas that did not fit his stated purpose, and he was corresponding with British officials. Washington wrote a letter to John Hancock, the president of Congress, on June 27, 1776:

> Sir: Upon information that Major Rogers was travelling thro' the Country under suspicious circumstances, I thought it necessary to have him secured. I therefore sent after him. He was taken at South Amboy and brought up to New York. Upon examination, he informed me, that he came from New

Hampshire, the Country of his usual abode and pretended he was destined for Philadelphia on business with Congress when he left his family. As by his own confession he had crossed the Hudson's River at New Windsor and was taken so far out of his proper and direct rout to Philadelphia, this consideration added to the length of Time he had taken to perform his journey; his being found in so suspicious a place as Amboy; his unnecessary stay there on pretence of getting some baggage from New York and an expectation of receiving money from a person here of bad Character and in no circumstances to furnish him out of his Stock; the Major's reputation and his being a half pay Officer increased my Jealousies about him.[1]

Suspicious, Washington sent Rogers and an officer escort onward to Philadelphia, where Rogers claimed he had a secret offer to make to Congress, stating that if Congress rejected this, he would seek leave to go to Great Britain and assignment in the East Indies. Congress resolved on July 6 "that Major Rogers be sent to New Hampshire, to be disposed of as the government of the State shall judge best."[2]

Rogers offered his services to both sides, hoping to make the best arrangements for himself. The result was that he was not trusted by either the Americans, who turned down his offer of service, or the British, who accepted with reservation.

In 1776, the British gave Rogers authority to raise and command a body of Loyalists who would be known as the Queen's American Rangers. This collection of uprooted farmers, malcontent city dwellers, crooks, and self-seekers was nothing like the skilled men who formed the original Rogers's Rangers, but Rogers's name struck fear. The people of New England were familiar with his fighting prowess, and when they learned Rogers was headquartered on Long Island, they were concerned that their houses would soon be ablaze.

Rogers had a sloop that figured in an unhappy circumstance of American Ranger history. Rogers arrived in New York with a prisoner in tow, a man who was an officer in Knowlton's Rangers. Whether he had made the capture or merely provided transport is unknown, but the prisoner whom Rogers turned over to the British was Nathan Hale.

An early fight with American forces was indecisive but served to deepen the breech between Rogers and the regular officers of the British Army. Fighting against his countrymen brought no glory. Rogers was removed from command and retired as a lieutenant colonel. His native New Hampshire banned his return. Elizabeth divorced him, and the debts remained. Rogers began to drink heavily. A ship he was sailing on was captured by the Americans, and he was confined in prison. When freed, he returned to London, where he passed his remaining days in drunkenness and debtor's prison. Sick and alone, he died on May 18, 1795. He was buried in London.

The life of Robert Rogers is a tragedy. He was the best of men and the worst of men. He was not the founder of the American Rangers, but it would be difficult to find a man who more encompassed the skill and daring spirit of the American Ranger. Rogers was a desperate man, seeking acceptance, recognition, and success in a system of which he could not be a part. He was an outsider, giving his all to the British class system that ignored or despised him.

Rogers is not an American hero. He did far less for the cause of American freedom than Benedict Arnold, who is reviled as a traitor. The British do not glorify Robert Rogers in their history or even remember him as a man who fought against American independence. His name was in danger of being buried in the trash heap of history. Rogers was wise enough to recognize that there are other paths besides the warpath. It was the pen that came to the rescue of this redoubtable warrior. The publication of his journals proved that the written word had longer life than the tomahawk. Like most journals, his were written in a manner to extol his personal reputation.

There is historical debate over who actually recounted Rogers's exploits. Some historians credit his secretary, Nathanial Potter, a graduate of Princeton, with the actual writing of the journals. While that issue is debatable, what put Rogers on the path to modern recognition is confirmed. Rogers's writings captured the imagination of famed historian Francis Parkman, who praised Rogers in his work *Montcalm and Wolfe.* That book later became a primary reference for a masterpiece of historical fiction, Kenneth Roberts's 1936 *Northwest Passage,* which featured Rogers's raid on the Abenaki Indians. In 1940, the book was made into a film of the same name starring Spencer Tracy. Like the book, the film was a great success, and by

1941, many Americans knew the word "Ranger" and had some understanding of its military context. In December of that year, the United States officially entered World War II. When searching for a name for an elite American unit being trained by British Commandos, Brig. Gen. Lucian Truscott decided to call them Rangers. Truscott was from Texas, and no one knows if he was thinking of Rogers's Rangers or the Texas Rangers. Either would have been a worthy inspiration.

The experience of Robert Rogers with the regular British forces and the ill treatment he received at the hands of the professional British officer corps go beyond the experience of a single man. In colonial times, Americans were treated by the British as much-needed allies in war but as socially and militarily unacceptable in peace. Ranger units were temporary. They were outsiders. This hide-bound thinking dominated the approach of British (and later American) officers to the concept of Ranger units and tactics. Useful in war, the Rangers were quickly disbanded in peace. This process would continue well into the twentieth century. In order to beat the system, the Rangers would have to become the system.

CHAPTER 6

Pontiac's War, 1763

For 200 years, the French had been present in the New World and exerted a powerful influence on the American Indians, forming alliances with them, supplying them, leading them in battle against the English, and converting them to Catholicism. With Wolfe's victory at Quebec, the English became the masters of North America. The French turned away from their former allies, and shock waves reverberated among the Indian villages. They knew the victors were colonizers who would take their land.

In this time of Indian despair, fundamentalism took root; prophets came forth and preached a return to the basic forms of Indian life. A wandering Delaware mystic named Neolin urged his brothers to turn their backs on the steel culture and return to that of the stone.

All the French forts in the New World now belonged to Britain. In September 1760, Lord Jeffery Amherst sent Maj. Robert Rogers to take a detachment of Rangers and occupy western posts including Detroit and Michillimackinac. In early November, Rogers and 200 Rangers were en route to their destination, traveling by whaleboat along the southern shore of Lake Erie. In his 1765 book, *A Concise Account of North America*, without giving the date or location of the meeting, Rogers would claim he was met by Pontiac, an adopted Catawba captive who had grown up to be a powerful chief of the Ottawa. At this time, Pontiac was about fifty years old, had long been a close friend of the French, and likely fought with them in the 1755 defeat of Edward Braddock. Though claiming the land was his, Pontiac allowed Rogers and his men to pass. The Indians watched in disbelief as the French garrisons surrendered. The Indians were accustomed to generous gifts and much-needed supplies from the French. It was Amherst's policy to not make presents to the Indians. The English would not treat the Indian with the kindness they had received from the French.

Pontiac's War, 1763

With the French defeated, the British disbanded colonial defenses and rested. Amherst informed Colonel Bouquet that "the post of Fort Pitt, or any of the others commanded by officers can certainly never be in danger from such a wretched enemy."

Pontiac saw a horde of settlers coming to take Indian land. He saw unscrupulous traders who cheated the Indian and were not prosecuted. He saw his old enemies, the British, now threatening the existence of the Indian. French traders and disgruntled former soldiers told him the French would return. Pontiac was a powerful orator whose eloquence was an amalgam of truth and mysticism. As 1763 opened, the Indians learned that the French king had given the English king all the Indian land. The Indians had not been consulted in this transaction.

The disgruntled tribes listened as Pontiac spoke of the Indians rising as one to repel the invaders. The Indian had no written language, but belts of wampum told of events that were a reliable record of history and their plans. These were pieces of periwinkle, hard clams, and whelk rubbed on stone until round and smooth. They were then strung together with their color and pictorial arrangements depicting the desired message. War belts were carried from tribe to tribe, and tomahawks and scalping knives were sharpened. Over the winter of 1762–63, the cold wind carried the word that the Indians would attack. Those on the frontier heard the warnings, but in the comfort and safety of the eastern cities, those in power ignored them. The frontier forts were so stripped of men that most did not have the garrison strength to maintain outposts or properly man the walls of forts.

Pontiac began his war with an attempt to take Detroit. The garrison was warned, and the attempt failed. With 900 warriors at his command, but no artillery, Pontiac laid siege. He successfully ambushed supply columns, some of whom did know that war had begun. Indians to the east took up the hatchet. Of the 120 Indian traders on the frontier, only a few escaped death. One after the other, the frontier forts began to fall.

Fort Sandusky was taken on May 16, Fort St. Joseph on May 25, Fort Miami on May 27, Fort Ouiatenon on June 1, and Fort Michilimackinac on June 2. The garrison was forced out of Fort Edward Augustus. Fort Venango was taken on June 16, and its commander, Lieutenant Gordon, was captured and tortured for three days before he died. Fort Le Boeuf fell on June 18, and Fort Presque Isle followed on June 20. George Crogham, who ranged the frontier, later estimated that 2,000 whites were killed in Indian attacks across frontier. Fort Pitt, Fort Ligonier, and Fort Bedford received warning in time to repel attacks, but they remained under Indian pressure.

Though Pontiac could control the approach to Detroit by land, the post could also be reached by water. On July 29, an English relief force of 260 men landed at Detroit. It was under the command of Capt. James Dalyell, the aristocratic aide to Lord Amherst. Accompanying Dalyell was Ranger Robert Rogers.

The post commander, Major Gladwin, was delighted to see the reinforcement but was taken aback when the ambitious Dalyell decided to lead a force out to attack the Indians. Dalyell had his way and took 270 men in search of Pontiac. He did not make use of Rogers's experience and left the Ranger with the main body of troops. Pontiac was quick to take advantage of this rash act. His Indians ambushed the column, killing Dalyell and sixty other officers and men. The Indians cut out Dalyell's heart.

Rogers organized a rear guard of two officers and thirty-two men. He fought a skillful rear-guard action, driving Indians from a waterside house and fortifying it with beaver skins and boards. For two hours, they held off Indian attacks. Being close to water saved them. A boat with a small cannon came up and showered the Indians with shot. Rogers and his party were able to reach the fort in safety.

Meanwhile, the Delaware, Huron, Mingo, and Shawnee Indians in the east had continued their wave of terror. Tiny Shippensburg at the eastern foot of the Alleghenies in Pennsylvania found more than 700 terrified refugees crowded in cellars and stables. Carlisle was once again crowded with those who fled before the knife. Bypassing this strongpoint, the Indians raided eastward over the Susquehanna River.

Paxtang is just east of what is now Harrisburg, Pennsylvania. In this area lived the Reverend John Elder. He was the highly respected pastor of the Paxton Presbyterian Church. Elder was a fighting preacher who organized and commanded the Paxtang Rangers, which consisted of several companies of horse-mounted riflemen. These men scouted from the Susquehanna River through Lancaster to Berks County. Elder's congregation came to his sermons carrying rifles. He kept two loaded rifles on the desk he used as an altar. These precautions foiled an Indian plan to kill him and his followers while they prayed.

Elder's Rangers were concerned about a group of Christian Indians called Moravians. They had not openly joined in Pontiac's initial raids. As hostiles showed no mercy to Christian Indians, efforts were made to protect the Moravians. They were settled in a community at Conestoga. Reports were being received that the Moravian Indians were not what they seemed. Colonel Armstrong's Rangers reported meeting some of them in battle at a place called Muncy Hills. In early September 1763, some of Elder's Rangers were scouting in Berks County when they had a fight with Indians they claimed were Moravians. In October, several families were murdered, and the Moravian Indians were blamed.

John Elder, John Harris, and other frontier leaders wrote to Governor Penn, telling him of the fear people felt and the anger that was building. They asked that the Indians be removed. The governor responded that his government had pledged protection for these Indians and he would not remove them without adequate cause.

Under pressure from his men, Elder agreed to the arrest of several Moravians who were suspected of murder. He sent Rangers under the command of Capt. Lazarus Stewart to make the arrest. Stewart and his men claimed the Indians came out to meet them with tomahawks raised for battle. True or not, these Indians were slaughtered. Stewart and his men were now out of control. Other Moravians were in Lancaster, and fifty Rangers rode there and killed them. Elder had tried to stop them, blocking the road with his horse and pleading with them as their minister. Matthew Smith had pointed his rifle at Reverend Elder, and they rode on. At Lancaster, a company of Highlanders would not interfere to stop the killing. The colony of Pennsylvania was in an uproar. Those on the frontier had suffered the tomahawk and scalping knife and hated all Indians. The government of Pennsylvania was not a representative body. Quakers in the three eastern counties and Philadelphia controlled the government. They would not approve expenditures for frontier defense. They denounced the Paxtang Rangers as murderers. German settlers of central Pennsylvania took the scalped and tortured bodies of their dead and laid them before the Quaker government, but no funds for defense were forthcoming.

The remaining Moravians were hurried to Philadelphia. The city was terrified that the Rangers might come and attack the citizens, and indeed the frontiersmen planned to. Artillery was put in position; outposts manned the roads. Militia companies hurriedly trained to defend the city; even Quakers took up arms.

The cause was pitting Presbyterian against Quaker, frontiersman against those who led a protected life. As the Paxtang Rangers began their march, fear gnawed at Philadelphia. It was believed there were 1,500 Rangers coming and at least 3,500 men of the outlying districts would rise to join them. It was decided to send someone out to meet them. A minister named Brycelius accepted the mission.

Brycelius met the Rangers at Germantown. There were about 250 of them, but they expected their total would soon be 3,000. The Rangers said they were not coming to harm Philadelphia or its inhabitants. They intended to take these Indians out of Pennsylvania and to present the grievances of the frontier to those who lived in safety. Brycelius told them of the city's plan to fight, and the Rangers laughed at the thought of armed Quakers. He had more success telling them that it was wiser to send an unarmed delegation to present their views.

To a degree, that view prevailed. The Rangers would not give up their weapons. Matthew Smith and a delegation of thirty Rangers rode into a city that was armed to the teeth, knew little of weapons, and felt the desperation of terror. The Rangers were allowed to visit the Indians but did not find those they sought. There was belief that the Quakers had taken some away to safety. Matthew Smith and Gibson put the complaints of the frontier before the assembly, including lack of representation in the government, an uncaring attitude about the suffering of those on the frontier, and expenditures for defense. They argued against the practice of sending trading goods that were war material to the Indians and did not want Indians living in the inhabited parts of Pennsylvania while at war with other Indians.

No redress was promised. The Ranger leaders went home angered. None were ever convicted in the killing of the Moravian Indians. The Quakers had no intention of giving up power and tried stalling legislation, hoping the problem would die on the vine. It did not. This was the beginning of the end for Quaker power in Pennsylvania. The frontier demand for political representation and security would not be denied.

In western Pennsylvania, Fort Bedford, Fort Ligonier, and Fort Pitt held out. Bedford had strong defenses and was less exposed. Commanded by Capt. Lewis Ourry, it had a garrison of six men and a corporal, but frontier militia and reinforcements brought that number to 155. Bedford was not attacked, and Ourry had difficulty getting men to stay. They wanted to go back to see if their farms still existed. When parties went out, they were ambushed.

In the third week of June, Ligonier was subject to Indian probes. Leaving the fort was an invitation to be tomahawked. Indian ambush prevented communication to and from Fort Pitt. This westernmost Pennsylvania fort was under frequent harassment but was well stocked with supplies. Some 550 men, women, and children were crowded into the enclosure.

The Indians and the garrison commander, Capt. Simon Ecuyer, sought to bluff each other by yelling solicitous messages back and forth. Both sides said that large forces were coming. Little Turtle, the Delaware chief, called to Ecuyer that the Six Nations were coming and that all those in Fort Pitt should leave while the Delaware could protect them. Ecuyer was the better liar. He told Little Turtle that three large forces were en route totaling 6,000 men. These included Catawba and Cherokee enemies of the Delaware and Shawnee. Ecuyer begged Little Turtle to save his people while he could. In a masterstroke of guile, he added the request that no other Indians be told so that they would escape punishment. The Indians and the whites were determined to kill each other, and the means did not matter. To demonstrate that he was well supplied and to destroy his enemy, Ecuyer sent presents to the Indians. Discussions included sending blankets that came from the smallpox hospital in the fort. It is unproven if that occurred, but it was not long before a plague began to ravage the tribes.

Their ruse having failed, the Shawnee and the Delaware attacked Fort Pitt on July 28. It was a persistent attack that continued over a four-day period. Fire arrows were shot into the fort, but these were extinguished. Ecuyer was wounded in the leg by an arrow but still held command. Then, on August 1, 1763, the Indians vanished. From the walls of Fort Pitt, Ecuyer looked at the green forest that cloaked the Indians and wondered why. The answer lay to the east.

Amherst had a wife in England who was becoming mentally ill. He had been looking forward to going home. Now he had a war on his hands. Shocked and angered at the Indian attack, Amherst had hastily rounded up whatever force he could muster. He ordered that no Indian prisoners be taken and opened discussion on the use of using dogs and small-pox to kill the Indians. Amherst directed Col. Henri Bouquet, the commander of the Royal American Regiment, to relieve Fort Pitt. Bouquet set about assembling his small force at Carlisle. The British Army in North America had been reduced in strength after the French and Indian War and had taken heavy casualties from combat and disease in Caribbean campaigns. Amherst had sent Bouquet a force of 460 men, including companies of the 42nd (Black Watch), the 77th Highlanders, and the 60th Regiment (Royal Americans). On July 18, these men marched from Carlisle and arrived at Fort Bedford on the twenty-fifth.

En route, Bouquet observed that "the Highlanders lose themselves in the Woods as soon as they get out of the road, and cannot on that Account be employed as Flankers."[1] Regulars assigned as scouts and flankers were being waylaid and killed by the Indians. At Bedford, Bouquet was joined by thirty Rangers, all of whom were experienced woodsmen. Fourteen of these had come from Fort Cumberland and were under the command of Capt. Lemuel Barrett.[2] Bouquet needed these Rangers but was short of some supplies and ordered that they should not be issued meat.

Bouquet reached Ligonier on August 2 and rested his troops for two days. They had marched nearly 200 miles. The journey was arduous and the column slowed by the need to carry relief supplies by wagon. At Ligonier, about forty miles from Fort Pitt, Bouquet unloaded his wagons. He left supplies and loaded what he was taking, including bags of flour, onto the backs of 340 pack horses. On August 4, he resumed march. Indian scouts had long been aware of Bouquet's approach. No doubt remembering the fate of General Braddock's much larger expedition, the Delaware, Mingo, and Shawnee moved to ambush the approaching column.

By 1 P.M. on August 5, Bouquet's men had already marched seventeen arduous miles for the day. He intended to halt about a mile farther on at Bushy Run. There he would rest his men, fill canteens, and water his horses. He then intended to make a night march over Turtle Creek, a place Bouquet described as "a very dangerous Defile of several miles, commanded by high and craggy hills." The Indians did not intend to let him get to water. A mile short of Bushy Run, the Ranger scouts and following members of Bouquet's advance guard came under attack. Bouquet committed two light infantry companies of the Black Watch. Initially, his troops had success, but just as they had with Braddock, the Indians flowed around the sides of his column. On a rise of ground called Edge Hill, Bouquet formed a perimeter defense and prepared to fight it out. Surrounded, tired from a long march, and with little water, the defenders were in desperate straits. The battle continued until darkness, seven hours of hell during which heavy fire from concealed Indians took a steady toll on Bouquet's force. During the night, Bouquet constructed a breastwork of flour bags within the perimeter that would shelter his wounded and issued instructions for the next day.

At first light on August 6, the Indians commenced shouting and shrieking war cries around the perimeter. They followed this with heavy fire and efforts to penetrate the perimeter. Bouquet later wrote Amherst that the men were distressed by "a total want of water, much more intolerable then the enemy's fire."

The need to protect the supplies they carried to Fort Pitt hindered the defense. Many horses were killed or captured by the Indians. The terrified pack train drivers tried to hide in the bushes and ignored orders.

Seeking a decisive stroke, Bouquet used a tactic employed in the Battle of Hastings in 1066. He feigned a retreat into a second perimeter to lure the Indians into an open killing ground. Two light infantry companies under Major Campbell were ordered to pull back within the perimeter. The units to either side of the gap had a few men fill in the gap and withdraw, creating the illusion that they were covering a retreat. The Indians began to come from around the perimeter to pour into this opening.

Another light infantry company and one of the grenadiers under Captain Bassett were brought off line into the perimeter and took up the fire. As this occurred, Major Campbell moved his men into a concealed position on the right flank of the Indians. The Rangers were the extreme right flank element of this attack. Once in position, Campbell delivered a volley into the side of the oncoming Indians and attacked. The Indians returned fire on Campbell's men, but light infantry and Ranger attacks came on. At that moment, Bouquet sent

Captain Bassett's two light infantry companies forward. The Indians did not have time to reload before they were hit by the fire of this reinforcement. Then all four companies continued the attack with the bayonet. As the Indians broke and ran across the front of the second perimeter, Bouquet moved grenadiers forward to fire into the Indian flank. Those Indians who survived ran for their lives. The Rangers involved in this action took the opportunity to lift some Indian hair.

The need to carry wounded and the loss of many pack horses forced Bouquet to destroy the supplies he was carrying. The weary column marched on for a few hours, then paused to make camp. The Indians made an effort to attack again, but their hearts were not in it, and the attack was beaten off. Bouquet took time to write a report of the actions to Jeffrey Amherst. His words were more of survival than victory: "I hope we shall be no more disturbed, for, if we have another action, we shall hardly be able to carry our wounded." Bouquet reported to Amherst that he had fifty killed, sixty wounded, and five missing.

Lt. Joseph Randell of the Rangers was among the dead. Bouquet noted that other Rangers had also been killed but did not give the number. Amherst would not have cared. With typical British Army disdain for Americans, he wrote Bouquet that he had "a very poor opinion of them."

Four days were required to cover the twenty-five miles to Fort Pitt. The beleaguered garrison was on the verge of starvation and was overjoyed at the sight of Bouquet's men. In the Indian camps, the wailing for the dead was accompanied by a howling hunger for revenge. War parties again went forth in search of scalps, but they could not take the forts, and soon the deadly scourge of smallpox was among them.

The help Pontiac expected from the French did not materialize. Without this assistance, he could not take Detroit. By October, the disillusioned followers of Pontiac were drifting away. With his dream shattered, Pontiac went back to the forest.

Peace did not come to the frontier. Determined bands of Indians continued to strike without warning. The hatred of those on the frontier for the Indians was extending to the British. Those who lived in danger felt that insufficient effort was being made for defense. The Delaware and Shawnee launched a major attack on Fort Augusta at present-day Sunbury, Pennsylvania.

At Carlisle, Col. John Armstrong raised a force of 300 Rangers and militia from the frontier in the area of Bedford, Carlisle, and Shippensburg. Armstrong moved to attack the Indian settlements, but they had been forewarned and had vanished. The colonials burned Indian dwellings and destroyed crops, but the Indians chose not to fight them.[3]

Once again, the frontier was in turmoil. Fear prevented trade between settlements, and crops went unplanted. The danger of attack was ever present. There were taxes to be paid, and distrusting the British commanders, Americans encouraged British soldiers to desert. Several hundred did and, in their own minds, became Americans.

Again the Rangers were the mainstay of frontier defense. In 1755, the young captive James Smith had watched Braddock's soldier burned at the stake. In 1760, Smith escaped. In the summer of 1764, a schoolmaster and ten of his students were murdered and scalped while at their lessons near Greencastle in Franklin County, Pennsylvania. James Smith was now wise in the ways of Indian life and was burning with the desire to revenge his captivity. Smith formed a company of volunteer Ranger riflemen. On their expeditions against the Indians, Smith and his men painted their faces in black and red. Because of this habit, Smith's Ranger company became known as the Black Boys. Smith despised the practice of trading with the Indians, which he thought gave them the means to kill the settlers. He sought to stop this trade.

Bouquet was not finished with the Indians. In August 1764, he assembled 1,500 men at Carlisle and marched them by stages to Fort Pitt and then into the Ohio country. Many of the men were from Pennsylvania and Virginia. He came with the air of a conqueror, telling the Indians that if they did not cease their raids, he would destroy them and their villages. Bouquet gave the Indians twelve days to turn over all their white captives and provide them with clothes, food, and horses. By November 9, 206 had been returned, including 32 males and 58 women and children from Virginia and 49 males and 67 women and children from Pennsylvania.[5] After a long march, the captives were brought to Carlisle. There hundreds of families who had lost loved ones in Indian raids were gathered in hope and prayer.

While its formal conclusion would come in July 1766, Pontiac's War was at an end by December 1764. Pontiac would be murdered by an Indian assassin at Cahokia, Illinois, in April 1769. Bouquet was promoted to brigadier general and assigned to a southern command. While at Fort George at Pensacola, Florida, he contracted yellow fever and died at age forty-seven in September 1765; the Spanish captured and destroyed the fort in 1781, holding it until 1821, when they ceded it to the United States.

Despite the peace, those who lived on the frontier did not trust the Indians. Traders, assisted by British authorities, promptly resumed sending pack trains of material to the Indians in exchange for furs. It was a lucrative business for those who were not on the frontier. In 1765, when they learned that traders were planning to legally take supplies to the Indians, Ranger James Smith and his men determined to stop the convoy. After a brief shoot-out, the Rangers stopped the wagon train and found that it included powder, tomahawks, and scalping knives. They burned the wagons. Lieutenant Grant of the Highlanders commanded at Fort Loudoun. He took captive and disarmed some of the Rangers at the fort and threatened to take them to the Carlisle jail. Smith and his Rangers swept into Fort Loudoun and released the prisoners. Some days later, Smith and his men kidnapped Lieutenant Grant and would not let him go until he returned the Ranger weapons.

This was the first British fort taken by Americans. There was a great uproar in the government. General Gage and Governor Penn were angry about the disruption of trade and what they felt was the insolence of Smith and his Rangers. Smith was arrested and brought to trial, but no frontier jury would convict him. Smith became a force in frontier politics, a lawyer, and a businessman. He would raise troops in the Revolutionary War.

CHAPTER 7

Rangers in the Revolution

The seeds of the American Revolution were sewn in the French and Indian War and the subsequent Pontiac's War. Britain had invested large sums in defending its American possession and felt that the cost of such defense should be shared by those who were defended, so it levied taxes on items needed by the colonies. The colonists were not consulted and resented what they considered "taxation without representation." Moreover, Britain saw the colonies as a source of raw materials for the homeland and a captive market for finished goods made in Britain. Though moderate in comparison with many other nations, the British political system was based on birth and privilege; those who lived in America were in large part considered low class, a mongrel colonial race of Dutch, Swedes, Scots, Irish, Germans, and the refuse of English prisons, incapable of governing themselves.

Blinded by arrogance, the British could not see that America was a growing force. There were eight million people in Britain, but by 1774, the population of the thirteen American colonies exceeded two million.[1] The British regular army dated from Cromwell's New Model Army of 1645. This was an army of compulsion in which the number of recruits was closely approximated by the number of their guards.[2] The recruitment, mistreatment, and depredations of the regular army engendered a revulsion that immigrants carried to the New World and would imprint itself on the American psyche. Regulars are prone to look down their noses at citizen-soldiers. The arrogance of many British officers and officials enraged Americans. In the French and Indian War, American frontiersmen felt they made major contributions to the war only to be treated unjustly. A British lieutenant in regular service who had no experience and purchased his commission could order around an America major of militia who had earned his rank by merit. Americans recognized that on many battlefields where Indians were involved, few British officers could adjust from the folly of using Old World tactics in the New World.

Armed forces were not novel in the New World. The 1640 militia laws of Plymouth Colony decreed "that the inhabitants of every Towne within the government fitt and able to beare armes, be traynedat least six tymes in the yeare." Militia forces had existed in New England for over a century. The conflicts between Britain and France and the scalping cry of Indians had created a climate of military skill and preparedness. The British view of American fighting men as "rabble in arms" was wide of the the mark. Each community had its share of experienced leaders. Men in the New World lived with military preparation. Though they lacked uniforms, Americans were armed and capable.

Americans tried to achieve equal treatment, and some British politicians supported them, but the class system was deeply imbedded in England, and both sides were losing their patience. In May 1774, the British governor of Virginia, Lord Dunmore, tired of arguing with colonials, dissolved the Virginia House of Burgesses. Unable to find a redress of their grievances, eighty-nine of these men met in Williamsburg, Virginia, to seek solutions. Committees of correspondence were established with the other twelve colonies and a recommendation went forth to form a congress to coordinate views. The idea of separation from the mother country and its ruler was a new and untested concept that would grow until the Declaration of Independence in July 1776.

Many in America did not want to leave the English fold. Many of these were people of property who were doing well under the existing system. Some were also angry at the king but would not participate in what they saw as treason. Some men who fought for King George III were sons of men who thirty-one years prior at Culloden Moor had fought against his father, King George II. In America, rational disagreement became rage, even insanity. A Tory was defined as "a thing whose head is in England . . . body . . . in America, and its neck ought to be stretched." Both sides confiscated property, drove neighbors from their homes, and committed depredations on people they knew well. When neighbors and families split allegiance, the savagery of civil war became the norm. This was American against American. Prisoners were butchered by both sides; wives were raped and watched their husbands hung; children saw their fathers murdered before their eyes.

To a much greater degree than the American Civil War, the Revolutionary War was brother against brother and neighbor against neighbor. A claim often attributed to John Adams estimated that at least a third of the colonists favored allegiance to the king. Modern studies indicate the number of Loyalists, as they called themselves, or Tories, as their opponents called them, comprised approximately 20 percent of the population of white Americans.

The British seldom made good usage of the Loyalist Americans. Time and again, the British had Washington's unprofessional army ripe for defeat only to dally away their opportunities. British generals had a prime fighting force available in Loyalists who had lost their homes and suffered indignities. With few exceptions, British generals did not use this resource and left men anxious for battle as rear-area guards. When the war began, the British Army had 45,123 soldiers throughout its empire. Six years later, as the fighting in America drew to a close, Britain had 87,000 British and German troops in America and the West Indies.[3] In 1783, approximately ninety-eight Loyalist regiments were disbanded by the British and their men offered land in Canada. As many as 80,000 Americans who supported the king were unable to, or would not, continue living in the new United States.[4] At war's end, 35,000 New York City residents fled to safety in Canada. This exodus created animosities that lasted for generations and did much to prevent the uniting of the North American continent under one flag.

By the Revolutionary War, the concepts of the American Ranger were a century and a half old. They had been learned by thousands of men who survived the terror of the frontier. Few, if any, of these men had studied the writings of Church or Rogers. Many of the best woodsmen could not read or write. It was the Indian—the enemy—that was the great teacher. Most Rangers had learned by the hard path of experience. Many died, but those who could adapt best survived and developed into a breed of unique men. The product of his time, the Ranger had proved his versatility in battle. In the war for American Independence, more than 100 units were designated as Rangers. Men who had learned the fighting trade as Rangers provided battlefield leadership that gave their countrymen hope. John Stark at Bunker Hill and Bennington, Daniel Morgan at Saratoga and Cowpens, and George Rogers Clark in the west are examples of Ranger leadership that contributed to American independence.

In this war, the American Ranger would face his old adversary, the Indian; his neighbor who supported the king; German soldiers; and his onetime ally and countryman, the British soldier. The opposition was formidable. The British Army was a trained and disciplined force that at the time of the American Revolution was fighting on every inhabited continent of the world. Nearly half of the British Army—forty-five infantry regiments and two cavalry regiments—would be employed in the attempt to crush the American rebels.

The primary force of the British was the regiments of foot. A regiment normally consisted of ten battalion companies, two of which were designated flank companies. One of these—positioned on the right of the line in parades—was the grenadiers, the tallest and strongest men committed to deal the decisive blow. The other flank company was the light company, which was used to develop the battle, perform scouting and reconnaissance, and spearhead attacks. For close-in fighting, they used hatchets. Flank companies were frequently combined to form ad hoc battalions of light infantry or grenadiers or work in conjunction with each other.

The British foot soldier carried a .75-caliber, fifteen-pound flintlock known as the Brown Bess and at least thirty rounds of ammunition. The English musket was most effective at a range below seventy-five yards. Volley fire was preferred. At the end of the foot soldier's weapon was a foot-long bayonet that he used effectively. The tactics of British infantry were to march in formation as close as possible to the enemy, point weapons in his direction, fire a massed volley, and then close with the bayonet.

The grandfather of King George III of England, George Guelph, was a prince of Hanover in Germany. He became king of England because his maternal descent included the English-ruling Stuart line that died out in England. The family still retained its rule of the German state of Hanover and had treaties with other German states that allowed George III to buy their support. Twenty-seven German regiments were sent to fight against the Americans. To combat the American frontiersmen who comprised the Rangers, units of *jaegers* ("hunters") were formed. They were not effective as the American wilderness baffled them. In addition, the German gunsmiths who had become Americans had produced a better weapon—the Pennsylvania Long Rifle—than was being made in Germany.

The desire of the British to crush the American rebellion did not stop with hiring Germans. Though it did not come to pass, efforts were made to hire Russian troops to fight the Americans. Lord Dartmouth wrote a letter to General Howe on September 5, 1775, telling him that Catherine the Great, Empress of Russia, had been approached to provide troops against the Americans and that she had "given the most ample Assurances, of letting us have any number of infantry that may be wanted."[5]

Also fighting with the British were a wide variety of American Loyalist Ranger units. These included the Florida Rangers, the King's Rangers, the Queen's Rangers, the Queen's Loyal Rangers, and the Loyal American Rangers. Most British Ranger units, including the unusual all-black Jamaica Rangers from the Caribbean, were not significant. Robert Rogers raised and initially commanded the Queen's Rangers for nine months in 1776 and 1777. Rogers raised the 250-man King's Rangers in Nova Scotia in 1777. These were not the skilled woodsmen he once led, and Rogers was not the man he had been. He was on a slide to the gutter and did not command for long. The most effective Ranger units supporting the British included John Butler's Rangers, who were responsible for the Wyoming Valley Massacre. He was the father of another Tory Ranger leader, Walter Butler, who carried out the Cherry Valley Massacre. Both of these events were devastating raids that were part of the border war between Canada and New York.

In 1775, passions were high, and mobs, self-styled as "Sons of Liberty," roamed the east coast, tarring and feathering those who showed any support for the king. A wealthy young Savannah planter named Thomas Brown mocked those who were opposed to the king's actions. He was brutalized, tarred, and feathered, then put in a cart and towed about. Finally, he was forced to recant. At his first opportunity, Brown fled to British security. He formed a group of raiders known as the Florida Rangers (or King's Rangers) and operated over the Georgia border. His revenge was considerable.

The best of these Tory Rangers took time to eliminate. Walter Butler's Rangers continued to raid along the northern New York border until Butler was killed and scalped in October 1781. Thomas Brown and his men were captured by American Rangers Harry Lee, Andrew Pickens, and Elijah Clarke at the fall of Fort Cornwallis on June 4,

1781. John Simcoe was the most effective leader of the Queen's Rangers. Simcoe and his men raided in Pennsylvania, Virginia, and the Carolinas until they surrendered at Yorktown.

While American males between eighteen and forty-five or fifty had long been required to be part of local defense organizations, older men up to age seventy were also organized into reserve units that could be called upon. While some of these organizations were indifferently led, they also featured men who had long experience at war. Their ability to communicate through riders, church bells and musket fire created a rapid reaction ability that was a model of efficiency. The British understood the value of intelligence and so did the Americans. Each side had agents deeply embedded in the others camp. A weakness of American militia was that the men were often unpaid volunteers who had families to feed. Men often served or went home based on the seasons of planting and harvesting.

On Friday, June 2, 1775, the Continental Congress convened in Philadelphia. The next day, the Congress established a committee to borrow money to buy gunpowder for the Continental Army, which it had not yet voted to approve. They had still not voted to accept the troops at Boston under Artemus Ward when, on June 14, the Congress resolved that "six Companies [three were later added] of expert Riflemen be immediately raised in Pennsylvania, two in Maryland and two in Virginia." These soldiers were to be enlisted in the American Continental Army for a period of one year. They were to join the army of several colonies at Boston to be employed as light infantry under the command of the chief officer in that army.

The United States Army dates its birth as June 14, 1775. Many historians, including those of the U.S. Army, believe that Congress took control of or "adopted" the Boston army on or before the fourteenth. This is an assumption. Despite extensive documentation, there is nothing that shows Congress voted to take control of the Boston army at this time. Revolutionary War historian Christopher Ward wrote that the vote would not occur until July 25, 1776.[6] Another historian gives secrecy as one reason that no record exists but agrees that on June 14, "the record indicates only that Congress undertook to raise ten companies of riflemen."[7]

The Second Continental Congress was not a secretive body. They had already taken sufficient action to put their necks in a noose.

They had voted for powder for an army on June 3 and voted to raise troops on the fourteenth. Until valid documentation is produced that shows Congress resolved to accept the Boston army on or before June 14, 1775, all that can be proven is that frontier Rangers were the first Continental soldiers established by Congress.

By December 1775, Congress had raised a Continental Army consisting of forty-nine battalions (also called regiments).[8] Several Ranger units were organized as or accepted into the Continental service. Whitcomb's Rangers is an example of the former and Bedel's Corps of Rangers the latter. Initially, most enlistments in the Continentals were for six months. Col. Hugh Stephenson's Maryland and Virginia riflemen/Rangers was the first unit to be enlisted for three years. At the onset of the war, the thirteen colonies had a free adult male population of nearly 400,000; of these, 87,000 were between the ages of twenty-one and twenty-five and 190,000 were between the ages of twenty-five and forty-four.[9]

The citizen-soldier militia was critical to battlefield success. The strength of the Continental Army varied greatly throughout the war. Estimates for the Continental line units prepared by General Knox, Washington's first secretary of war, show 27,443 for 1775, rising to a high of 46,891 in 1776, and declining to a low of 13,292 in 1781.

At the beginning of the Revolutionary War, the Americans had among their ranks the finest irregular fighting force in the world. Early in the war, American commanders tried to fight a European army with militia forces using European tactics. That did not work. As the war progressed, Continental officers emulated the British and sought to develop a European-style army with European-style discipline, including flogging. Washington, Greene, and others tended to denigrate the militia. Anxious to promote a regular service, they did not distinguish between those militia units who fought well and those who did not or investigate the reasons for success or failure. Despite a Ranger militia performance that was critical to his success at Cowpens, Dan Morgan, then a regular officer, did not even include them in his troop strength or casualties reports. To be killed or maimed as a citizen-soldier did not count. The regulars tended to ignore their failures. It was American regulars that the British slaughtered at Paoli and Waxhaws.

Whether they became regulars or not, American Rangers were sons of the frontier. The rifle, the tomahawk, and hunting-scalping knife were a daily part of the life of a frontier boy. Hunting kept the family supplied with meat. If he lived near a fort, at age twelve he was expected to take his place at a loophole. He probably could not read or write. If he read, it was primarily the Bible or other religious tracts. His school was the outdoors, and he was taught the ways of the forest by more experienced men. He learned land navigation and survival and self-sufficiency. He learned well or died under an Indian scalping knife. With his one-pound tomahawk, he could build a shelter or split a skull. As developed by gunsmiths in Pennsylvania, his rifle was a work of art. The spiral groove of the rifle bore added range and accuracy. The Ranger rifle could routinely kill at twice the effective range of the British musket. George Merchant, a Ranger captured on Benedict Arnold's expedition to Quebec, was taken to England, where he astounded the British with his marksmanship. Col. George Hanger, onetime second in command to the British raider Banastre Tarleton, saw the rifle from the viewpoint of both an expert on weaponry and a target. Hanger believed that on a still day, an American rifleman could hit him at 300 yards.[10]

In the Revolutionary War, the terms Ranger, riflemen, borderers, frontiersmen, over-mountain men, and shirt men were used interchangeably. Uncertain how to deal with them, historians have often called them partisans or guerrillas. They would be used as scouts, ambushers, and raiders. They would serve as spearheads and as light infantry. Such units usually drew their name from their commanders. With few exceptions, they were militia in the sense that they were citizen-soldiers who served in time of emergency. Many were untrained and had little to offer but patriotism. In the Revolutionary War, some Ranger units used muskets, but most were riflemen. Though in many battles, the bayonet was equally or more decisive, the Ranger's long rifle was the most highly touted weapon of the war. It had the ability to kill at long range.

Lancaster County, Pennsylvania, was the birthplace of the long rifle, which would also become known as the Pennsylvania or Kentucky rifle. The first rifles were made by Martin Meylan, who established his gun shop at Lancaster in 1719. Before King George's War began in 1744, Philip LeFevre and Matthew Roesser were also in the business, and by the time of the Revolutionary War, there were more than forty Lancaster gunsmiths making rifles. They would continue making them until 1884.[11]

The rifle was individually crafted, not mass produced. Overall length might range from fifty to sixty inches. It fired a ball normally .55 to .60 caliber, depending on the wishes of the customer. Some rifles were made double-barreled.

The ability of Rangers to kill at distances far beyond the British capability in large measure dictated their tactics. The weakness of the rifle was that it took more time to load and was not equipped with a bayonet. As the 1776 Battle of Long Island proved, the British learned to fix bayonets and charge, accepting some losses while closing on the Rangers with cold steel before they could reload. The Americans began to counter by stationing musket- and bayonet-equipped light infantry units behind the Rangers. Concentrating on killing officers as the British charged, the Rangers would then withdraw behind the light infantry, who would fight the leader-depleted red coats musket-to-musket, bayonet-to-bayonet. In the summer of 1777, Dearborn's 300-man light infantry battalion was attached to Morgan's Rangers in this fashion.

CHAPTER 8

Citizen-Soldiers

During the Revolutionary War, both the Continental Congress and the various colonies raised Ranger units. These American Rangers played a significant role in major battles, such as Saratoga and Cowpens. Their participation in the second front of this war has been largely unrecorded. While the battles known to history were being fought, the mountains, forests, and swamps of the vast frontier were the scene of a multitude of small-unit actions. Ambush and murder were routine as neighbor fought neighbor, and the dreaded Indian raids fell upon the isolated settlements.

Georgia and Pennsylvania were among the colonies who unsuccessfully tried to use a militia of farmers to fend off Indian attacks. Referring to such militia, one Pennsylvania observer wrote, "Not one fourth part of them are fit to go against the Indians or can be of the least use as Rangers, neither being acquainted with the woods or the proper use of the gun."

In the French and Indian War and the Revolution, Pennsylvania alone had about 200 forts. Throughout the Revolutionary War, an estimated 3,500 men served as Pennsylvania Rangers. For example, Capt. Jacob White served periodically in six-month enlistments from 1777 to 1780. He wrote that once a week he would "range out and return, watching for the Indians and giving notice to the frontier settlers of their approach." The work was hard, dangerous, and unsupported. Captain Phillips and eleven of his Pennsylvania Rangers were captured, tortured horribly, and killed by Indians. Capt. Thomas Robinson's company was left unsupplied, operating with little in the way of clothing or ammunition and less than a pound of meat a week. Despite the hardships, locally raised Ranger units were the prime means of preserving the frontier, and some of these were absorbed into the regular establishment.

While some units achieved fame, others are little known. On January 11, 1777, under orders from General Washington, the organization of Col. Nathaniel Gist's Ranger corps began. Initially, this unit consisted of four companies, two from Maryland and two from Virginia; additional units were later added. This unit included Indians. Gist was a Virginian with long experience with the Cherokee tribe, whom the Americans had defeated in 1776. Gist succeeded in obtaining seventeen Indian scouts. The Congress considered raising Ranger companies of Christian Mohegan and Stockbridge Indians as Rangers but abandoned the plan.

The Bedford County Rangers were three companies raised to defend the Pennsylvania frontier in 1778. Their initial company commanders were Captains Black, Cluggage, and McDonald. New Hampshire formed three companies of Rangers in 1775 under Col. Thomas Bedel. They served under General Schuyler, operating in Canada. The New York Rangers consisted of four companies raised in 1778. Three of these apparently served within the borders of New York only. The North Carolina Rangers were horsemen, sometimes called light horse units. There were three troops, each consisting of three officers and thirty men. At various times, bodies of Rangers, called partisan corps, were raised for reconnaissance and raiding. Armand's, Lee's, and Pulaski's Legions fall in this category. On June 24, 1781, Washington requested six rifle companies of fifty men and three officers each from Pennsylvania. These units are believed to have served under Major Parr. They distinguished themselves at the Battle of Yorktown.

The 1st South Carolina Regiment of 1775 included two regiments (battalions actually) of line infantry and one of Rangers. They fought well at Charleston. The 3rd South Carolina was a mounted Ranger unit under Lt. Col. William Thompson (not to be confused with Ranger Col. William Thompson of Pennsylvania). In 1776, the rifle companies of Maryland and Virginia were formed into a regiment commanded by Col. Hugh Stephenson. This unit and Knowlton's Rangers were among those captured by the British when a traitor brought about the fall of Fort Washington on November 16, 1776.

CHAPTER 9

War in the North

The theater where the American Revolution began was in and around Boston, Massachusetts. There in 1761, James Otis, a thirty-five-year-old American lawyer who loved Britain, was so outraged by British conduct that he made a mesmerizing speech. John Adams, who was present, would write, "American Independence was then and there born."[1] The fury of Americans found tongue in the passion of Samuel Adams and John Hancock. In the years that followed, British political leadership alternated between grudging concession and dictatorial crackdowns. To be a British soldier in America during this period was to live in an atmosphere of hatred. Living under harsh discipline and ordered to enforce an oppressive political policy without harming life or property, the British soldier in America was an unhappy and angry trooper.

Boston was the headquarters of the commander of the British Army, Thomas Gage. In 1774, Robert Rogers, who was deeply in debt, had scarcely disturbed his old adversary by filing a lawsuit against him just as Gage was leaving for America. The suit was dropped, and Rogers went to debtors prison and later begged Gage's forgiveness. Whatever Rogers's successes in the French and Indian War, by 1775 there was no contest between them. Gage had the power of a lieutenant general in command of all he surveyed. His Achilles heel was that he married an American woman who was most likely an American sympathizer and possibly an American spy. Gage was a tight-fisted disciplinarian who felt he was a fair and reasonable man. He could not understand why the Americans did not see him as reasonable and became increasingly intolerant of American complaints and actions. If the Americans had Gage's wife as a spy, Gage had Benjamin Church, the namesake and grandson of the famed Ranger who fought in King Philip's War. Church posed as an American patriot and sat in council with Adams, Hancock, Warren, and Revere, then reported to Gage.

Later in the war, Church, the Boston-born, Harvard-educated spy, was exposed, jailed, and exported to the West Indies. On the way there, Church and his ship were lost at sea, and he drowned.

Large crowds of threatening Americans frequently thwarted British plans. Some Americans were killed by frightened soldiers. In a prearranged demonstration organized by Sam Adams, sixty tons of British tea were peaceably dumped in Boston Harbor. The Americans had taken muskets, cannon, and powder from provincial powder houses and stored these war materials in scattered locations about the countryside. Gage often knew where the material was put, but by the time his troops got there, the weapons and powder had been moved or his men faced an overwhelming number of Americans. Wisely, he was reluctant to use force, but nothing he did seemed to please these colonists.

Incensed that American riders were giving early warning, Gage dispatched a number of patrols to restrict American road movement when he moved his forces. In great secrecy, he ordered Lt. Col. Francis Smith of the 10th Foot, with Marine Maj. John Pitcairn as second in command, to make a night march with 900 light infantry, grenadiers, and Loyalist guides about twenty miles via Lexington to Concord, Massachusetts. Gage's orders to Smith read that he was to "seize and destroy all the Artillery and Ammunition, provisions, tents and all other military supplies you can find."

Boston and Charlestown, which lay on the opposite side of the Charles River, were peninsulas shaped somewhat like pears hanging from stems. The British had the option of taking the land route by way of the mile-long Boston neck or row across the river to the Charlestown. They chose the water, using boats from British warships in the harbor. Troop activity, soldier gossip, and a careless daytime assembling of boats by the navy contributed to American awareness, but inside information, possibly from Mrs. Gates, confirmed the planned movement. The Americans were reasonably certain that munitions at Concord were the British objective, but the capture of Sam Adams and John Hancock, who were in Lexington, was another possibility. The countryside needed to be alerted.

In the darkness of April 18, 1775, Joseph Warren, who would die in the battle incorrectly known as Bunker Hill, dispatched rider William Dawes overland by the Boston Neck to Lexington. Warren also instructed silversmith and experienced patriot courier, Paul Revere, to alert the countryside. Young Tom Newman, janitor of the Anglican Christ Church, and vestryman John Pulling displayed the prearranged lights of two lanterns high in the church tower to warn the people across the river in Charlestown that the British would cross the Charles River. Charlestown leaders immediately dispatched warning riders. Paul Revere was taken over the Charles River by boat and given a fast horse, and he rode for Lexington. The routes of Revere and Dawes caused them to meet before Lexington. Together, they warned Adams and Hancock.

As the Lexington Company began to turn out, Dawes and Revere rode for Concord. En route, they met the skilled horseman Samuel Prescott returning from courting a girl. When the three riders were stopped by a British patrol, Revere was captured, but Dawes and Prescott escaped. It was the gallant Prescott who took the warning to Concord. Later in the war, he would be one of more than 7,000 Americans who died in the hellish confinement of a British prison ship.

Like the outgoing ripples when a stone is tossed in a pond, many riders carried the message. They did not say, "The British are coming!" but called, "The regulars are out!" Thundering through the night, they rode through a night pierced by the ringing of church bells, warning shots from muskets, and the hurried voices of thousands of Americans as they began to assemble. This was not an authoritative system. In many cases, the men quickly discussed and debated what action should be taken. The decision was for action.

At about five o'clock on the morning of April 19, 1775, at Lexington, Massachusetts, forty to seventy Americans of the Lexington Company stood in formation as the advance guard of over 600 British regulars under Major Pitcairn marched toward them. The Americans had elected forty-six-year-old John Parker as captain of the Lexington contingent. The 1893 genealogy and biographical notes of the Parker family written by Captain Parker's grandson claims that John Parker was possibly a member of Rogers's Rangers in the French and Indian War, but no confirming evidence has been found. On the field was Ranger Edmund Munro, who was sergeant major of Rogers's Rangers from 1758 to 1760 and was promoted to the twenty-sixth ensign in Rogers's Rangers. Munro would rise in rank to captain, distinguish himself at Bennington and Saratoga, and die at age forty-three when struck by a cannon ball at the Battle of Monmouth.

As the British approached, tradition has it that Captain Parker issued the command, "Stand your ground. Don't fire unless fired upon. But if they mean to have a war, let it begin here!" The depositions of several of his men do not record this statement, however.

Six companies—about 240 men—of British light infantry moved forward and formed on line within 100 steps of the Americans. Knowing his men would be uselessly sacrificed, Parker ordered his men to keep their weapons but disperse. Major Pitcairn was determined that the Americans must give up their weapons. The dispute of who fired first that day has never been resolved, but it would have been madness for the outgunned, outnumbered Americans to have done so. The pent-up anger of the British soldiers exploded as they disregarded their orders and swept forward firing and thrusting with their bayonets. Eight Americans were killed, including the wounded Jonas Parker, who died skewered with a British bayonet, and Robert Munroe, the ensign of the Lexington Company. Ten Americans were wounded. No British were killed, and only one soldier was wounded. The British light infantry gave the traditional three cheers of victory and marched on for Concord. The Americans were left with the horror and anger of what had happened. Men had been killed under the eyes of their wives and children. Mortally wounded Jonathan Harrington crawled to his doorstep and died at the feet of his wife.

The firing at Lexington carried on the wind, and American horsemen spurred to spread the news. In the early-morning sunlight, the Redcoats marched in ordered ranks to Concord. Around Concord were elements of two patriot regiments under the command of the sixty-four-year-old Col. James Barrett of Concord. With about 150 men assembled, the Americans marched on the road to meet the British. Fortunately, they caught sight of the quarter mile of glistening British bayonets before a meeting engagement occurred. Recognizing that they did not have sufficient numbers, the Americans waited until the British were 550 yards away, then faced about, and preceding the British, they marched back to Concord with fifes and drums playing. At Concord, they joined the older men who were guarding the town. Then, deciding they must await more reinforcements, the Americans marched out of Concord, crossed the North Bridge, and occupied a hill north of town from which they could observe the British actions.

On Colonel Smith's orders, the British occupied the town and began their search. The grenadiers remained in the town, but six companies of light infantry were sent to the North Bridge—three to guard it and three to cross and proceed to James Barrett's house, where colonist arms were stored. While the British search was underway, more Americans joined Barrett's force, which now totaled 500. When the British began to burn the small amount of supplies they found, Barrett, Maj. John Buttrick of Col. Abijah Pierce's Minuteman regiment, and other officers stood looking at the rising smoke and discussing their options. Hot with emotion, Lt. Joseph Hosner asked, "Colonel Barrett, will you let them burn the town down?"[2]

Hosner's words sparked action. Barrett ordered weapons loaded but cautioned the men not to fire first. The Americans moved down the hill in column formation with fifes playing. At the sight of them, the British moved back across the bridge and began attempting to tear up the planks. The bridge was the product of American labor, and the bottled-up anger of the Americans exploded. Barrett turned to his men and asked if they agreed that the British should be driven from the bridge. The men agreed. In column formation, they moved in an ordered and disciplined formation that surprised the British. The approximately 150 men of the light infantry companies fell back across the bridge and formed in rank to deliver fire. A panicked British soldier fired on the Americans, followed by other fire from his comrades. The fire was erratic and mostly high, but two Americans were killed and four wounded. As the firing continued, the Americans closed to within fifty yards of the British, and Major Buttrick gave the command to fire. Ten British were wounded, four of them officers, and three privates were killed. The incredulous Americans watched as British regulars broke and ran before them.

Now uncertainty set in. The British had retreated, and no one had considered what to do next. Some men wandered about; some went home while others waited, muskets in hand. The three companies of light infantry that had marched beyond the bridge came back over it. They passed under the musket muzzles of the Americans, who, without a command to engage, stood in silence and watched.

Historians tend to fault Colonel Smith for being slow as he made preparations to care for his British wounded and readied his command for the march back to Boston. Smith was a careful commander and calm was needed. On the road by the bridge, a young American walked to a wounded British soldier and struck him in the head with his hatchet. The British light infantry was armed with hatchets, used them in battle, and were hardly blameless at killing wounded men in this and other wars. The sight of one of their own being so treated created a torrent of fear and rage in them.

An uneasy quiet reigned as the British force began to withdraw on the road toward Lexington. They could see swarms of Americans on a high ridge line to the north as the companies from other communities arrived. Men from Concord took an overland route that put them beside Smith's route of withdrawal. Colonel Smith sent men to protect his flanks, and the first mile passed without incident. Soon the column arrived at Meriam's Corner, a critical road junction. The ridge line fell sharply to the road here, and the flanking light infantry rejoined the column. A bridge over a small stream needed to be crossed; it was here the British would begin seventeen miles of hell.

Some 1,000 Americans under combat-experienced leaders had taken position in and behind buildings, trees, and stone walls. Again, a single shot initiated an exchange that clearly favored the Americans. Two British soldiers were killed and at least another eight wounded. The British hurried on, with Smith putting out flank security when terrain permitted. The Americans ran alongside the column, using their knowledge of the terrain to avoid British bayonets and taking shots when they could. Messengers went ahead, alerting other units to close on the road. Another mile passed, and at Brook's Hill, the Americans engaged again. More British soldiers fell. Smith's men ran a gauntlet of fire as they encountered repeated ambush to the front and were struck in the flanks and rear. At a spot known as the Bloody Curve, thirty British soldiers were killed or wounded. The American fire beat heavily on Smith's officers, most of whom were wounded or killed. British noncommissioned officers took command and led their men bravely. American marksmen took their toll. William Thorning of Lincoln took position behind a boulder and killed two British soldiers.

As they neared Lexington, Smith's men were mauled in an ambush by Capt. John Parker's Lexington Company. Taking their revenge for the killing of their townsmen, Parker's men wounded Colonel Smith, shooting him from the saddle. The British were stalled until Major Pitcairn rode forward and put them in the attack. Pitcairn was thrown as his horse was wounded. The horse ran into the American positions, carrying away Pitcairn's pistols. The British were desperate, discipline was breaking down, and more Americans were crowding in upon them. Surrender seemed the only alternative to death.

From the front of the battered column came a sudden cheer. The lead elements had seen the Redcoats of a brigade-size British force drawn up on the high ground east of Lexington Common. The dark mouths of cannon spat flame as Smith's men, shaking with relief, hurried to the seeming security of British arms. Had it not been for this relief, Smith's force would have been captured or killed.

The relief force was under the leadership of Brig. Hugh Percy, Thomas Gage's second in command and an English nobleman of enormous wealth. The thirty-two-year-old Percy was a superb soldier, trained since the age of sixteen, and had experienced the wars of Europe. He commanded the 111th Regiment as a lieutenant colonel in the Battles of Bergen and Minden. His wealth, his experience, and his personality made him an officer without peer in the British service. In an age where British officers looked down upon their men and drove them with the discipline of the lash, Hugh Percy got down off his horse and marched with his footsore soldiers. He had paid to bring their wives with them when they were ordered to America. When husbands were killed, Percy paid the widows' passages home and gave them money to sustain themselves and their children in England.

Gage had ordered Percy's Brigade—three superb regiments of infantry and a battalion of marines—to be ready to march. But the orders to march went astray, with the result that Percy was not informed until a horseback messenger from the desperate Colonel Smith arrived at Gage's headquarters. Percy marched shortly before 9 A.M. He was nearing Lexington when he heard the sounds of battle and deployed his brigade on line.

Taken under cannon fire, the Americans dispersed, with a number creeping close enough to gall the British with fire. The vaunted discipline of the British was not holding for Smith or Percy. The maddened troops frequently broke ranks to pursue Americans, but more Americans were arriving in the battle area, and they grew increasingly bold. Percy rested his men, knowing he must now run the gauntlet. With Smith's troops, he had about 1,900 men. Strong columns were positioned on the flanks and considerable firepower at the rear. The wounded and prisoners were in the center, and in the front was a small force to clear the road.

The Americans were now under the command of Brig. William Heath, a militia general who was a student of war. Heath had many combat-experienced leaders and men with him. They fought an intelligent battle, employing Ranger tactics and, when it suited them, the massed formations Europeans favored. At Menotomy, the British troops were fired on from houses. Smashing down the doors, they killed the inhabitants and began looting, burning buildings, and killing their prisoners. The Americans were infuriated by this and pressed home their attack. There was little quarter given on either side. Percy wrote, "We retired for 15 miles under an incessant fire, which like a moving circle surrounded and followed us wherever we went." Some of the Americans used horses in dragoon fashion, dismounting to fight, riding ahead of the enemy, and dismounting to fight again.

Eight miles from Boston, Percy's column was low on ammunition. At Cambridge, there was a critical bridge that the Americans controlled. They meant to hit the British hard there. Percy briefly confused the Americans by taking another road to Charlestown, but they quickly were after him. All the elements were present for a disaster for the British Army. Inexplicably, American Col. Timothy Pickering's brigade from Salem and Marblehead allowed the British to pass. Percy's weary men stumbled into Charlestown. Out of 1,900 men engaged, the British regulars had lost 273. The remarkable notification system of the American militia had brought 3,500 men to the battlefield, of which 95 were lost.[3] Thousands more Americans were hurrying toward Boston. These totaled nearly 50 regiments. They would pen the British in.

The long and difficult learning process of the American Ranger had borne fruit. His attitude about American fighting ability shaken, Lord Percy would write, "Whoever looks upon them as an irregular mob will find himself very much mistaken. They have men among them who know very well what they are about having been employed as Rangers against the Indians and Canadians, and this country being much covered with wood and hilly, is very advantageous for their method of fighting."[4]

The highlands of New York, New Hampshire, and present-day Vermont were ablaze with patriotic fervor. With Ethan Allen as their leader, an organization known as the Green Mountain Rangers (also called the Green Mountain Boys) was formed. This force originally consisted of New Hampshire men who had been having brutal fights with New Yorkers over land now in Vermont. Independently, Ethan Allen and another audacious American leader named Benedict Arnold saw the value of seizing Fort Ticonderoga and its much-needed cannon. Near White Creek (now Salem), New York, a meeting was held between American patriots from Connecticut, New Hampshire, and New York. Its purpose was to make plans to seize British positions at Ticonderoga and Skenesborough (Whitehall).

The Hudson River, Lake George, and Lake Champlain were highways of water in the 1700s. The old forts of the French and Indian War

Benedict Arnold.
LIBRARY OF CONGRESS

still guarded these shores. Though thinly manned, they contained cannon, small arms, and powder desperately needed by the patriots. Fort Ticonderoga controlled the narrow water connection between Lake George and Lake Champlain. Skenesboro was the site of an important iron forge and home of wealthy Tory Philip Skene, who was royal judge of Charlotte County and governor of Fort Ticonderoga.

The Connecticut men wanted Benedict Arnold of Connecticut to command the operation. Ethan Allen of New Hampshire wanted command. The New Yorkers wanted anyone but the violent Allen, whom they despised. In compromise, the patriots decided that Ethan Allen, accompanied by the energetic Benedict Arnold, would attack Fort Ticonderoga. The New York Rangers would be under the command of Capt. John Barnes, who moved first. Planning to attack by night, Barnes and his Rangers approached Skenesboro on May 9, 1775. The Rangers were seen by an alert outpost who fired a warning shot. Barnes's Rangers hurried their approach, but a second warning shot enabled the Loyalist Skene to escape. Though they lost their man, Barnes's Rangers captured the shipyard and iron foundry and the corpse of Skene's wife, who had died some time before. The Americans said she had left a daily sum of money to her husband for each day he would keep her body above ground. The Tories claimed that Skene intended to ship the corpse back to England. She had been placed in a lead-sheeted wooden coffin in a small room. Barnes's Rangers took the coffin apart, dumped the late Mrs. Skene, and melted down the lead from her coffin for bullets.

John Barnes and his New York Rangers are little known to history, but they annoyed the British greatly throughout the New York campaigns. British General Burgoyne complained about them in letters back to England. At the end of the Revolutionary War, Ranger Barnes followed the frontier to Pennsylvania and on to Ohio.

The following day, it was Fort Ticonderoga's turn for capture. Coming in by boat and then foot at night, the Green Mountain Boys under Ethan Allen captured the fort on Lake Champlain on May 10, 1775. Allen startled a rudely awakened British officer by yelling, "Come out of there, you dammed old rat!" Arnold was with Allen at Ticonderoga, then led a contingent to seize St. Johns. Another force of Rangers under Seth Warner captured Crown Point on May 12.

On June 23, 1775, the Congress authorized Allen's and Warner's Rangers to be part of a separate army under General Schuyler. A battalion was created, and Seth Warner won election as commander over Ethan Allen. Formed of Rangers from the woodlands of New York and present-day Vermont, they became Colonel Warner's Continental Regiment. After suffering heavy loss in the winter Canadian campaign of 1776–76, they distinguished themselves at the Battle of Bennington.

In June 1775, about 7,000 British under General Gage occupied the Massachusetts town of Boston. It was an uneasy occupation, supported by the guns of British warships. For two months, a congregation of 15,000 armed and angry colonists had penned them on the peninsula. The Americans were a loose lot of Rangers, farmers, tradesmen, and sailors. Massachusetts, Connecticut, Rhode Island, and New Hampshire each contributed men, but there was no central leadership or control. Americans had never had the opportunity to command such large numbers and consequently had no understanding of the logistics required. Anger was a poor substitute for ammunition, food, water, and tools needed for entrenching.

Across the water from Boston, the Charles and Mystic Rivers flowed into Boston Harbor. There, the Charlestown neck, a ten-yard-wide strip of land, led to a triangular-shaped peninsula. About a mile wide at its base and primarily of grassland, the peninsula contained the village of Charlestown and two hills. Bunker Hill had an elevation of 110 feet. To its south slightly lower was the Breed's Hill. Both hills overlooked Boston and its harbor. If the Americans moved cannon into these positions, they would control access to Boston from the sea. British warships could not elevate their guns sufficiently to bring fire on the hills.

The respected Col. William Prescott of Massachusetts was ordered to occupy Bunker Hill. Disregarding, or ignorant of, the fact that they could be literally cut off at the Charlestown Neck, the Americans moved on the night of June 16 to take the high ground. A forceful voice in this effort was Israel Putnam, who never met a war he did not fight. Putnam had been a scout for William Johnson and later commanded a Connecticut Ranger company in the French and Indian War. Putnam was built like a broad stump and as deeply rooted in his opinions. No one doubted his courage. Despite his lack of formal

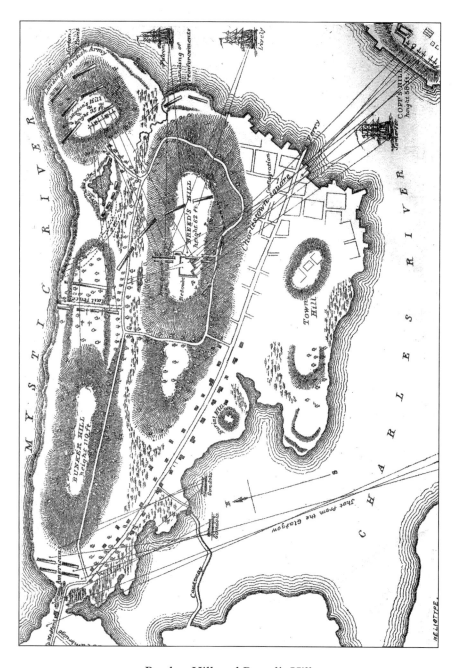

Bunker Hill and Breed's Hill

schooling, Putnam had vision and would pen words some would consider prophetic. In a letter written on August 11, 1774, to Sam Adams, Putnam wrote of America, "Here we have an unbounded, fertile country worth contending for with blood . . . To us, ere long, Britain's glory will be transferred, where it will shine with accumulated brilliancy."

Putnam, who was fifty-seven when the war began, had the most military experience and such force of personality that he exercised considerable influence on the battle that would follow. "Old Put" would be made a major general in the Continental Army. Though his heart and will were mighty, he was not skilled in the employment of large bodies of men. In 1779, he suffered a stroke and was retired. He died in 1790. Accompanying Putnam were 200 men, most of whom were from Connecticut. Many of these had frontier warfare experience. They were commanded by Capt. Thomas Knowlton, a skilled fighter who had participated in the bloody Cuban campaign of August 1762. He would later form and lead one of the most distinguished Revolutionary War Ranger units.

On reaching Bunker Hill, Colonel Prescott, General Putnam, and the engineer Colonel Gridley disagreed over the location of their emplacements. Most historians believe it was Israel Putnam who successfully argued that Breed's Hill was the best terrain to fight from. Prescott agreed, provided the higher Bunker Hill was also fortified. By midnight, the Americans were digging in on Breed's Hill. Below them, unsuspecting British sentries paced the decks of their warships, calling out, "All's well."

When the sun came up, the British found themselves challenged by threatening earthworks. Each side of the American position was about forty yards in length, and the earthen wall was about six feet high. The British were unaware that the earthworks had a weakness. Constructed in darkness, they had a berm that made the few American cannon in the redoubt fire high.

Standing on Breed's Hill, Prescott looked over his dispositions. He was on a sixty-five-foot-high hill. To his left and right was steep ground. To his left flank at a lower elevation and slightly to his rear was a rail fence that led from the base of the hill to a narrow beach on the Mystic River. To his left rear was the 110-foot Bunker Hill and behind that the ten-yard-wide Charlestown Neck. To his right and lower was the village of Charlestown. To his front, the ground sloped away to the thirty-five-foot- high Moulton's Hill and Moulton's Point, a shore line suitable for landings. On three sides were the waters of the Mystic River and Boston Harbor. On these waters to his south and west, British warships swung at anchor. To better protect the redoubt and his left flank, Prescott had his men begin work on a breastwork that would extend to his left in the general direction of the rail fence.

At dawn, the crew of the HMS *Lively*, which had twenty guns, saw the redoubt and opened fire. Soon the rest of the British ships began shelling the Americans with more than sixty cannon. The British warships could not elevate their guns sufficiently and the heavy fire was largely wasted. Colonel Prescott leaped to the top of the berm and calmly walked along it while thousands of onlookers in Boston cheered his courage. The men in the redoubt were mostly militia and little inspired by Prescott. They were tired from digging, there was little water or food, and there was not much powder. Prescott sent for resupply, but it did not come. Putnam asked for more troops, but they did not arrive. On the mainland, General Ward, who was in overall command, thought it probable that the British would cut off the Americans from behind or launch a mainland attack. When the battle began, Ward tried to reinforce, but badly needed ammunition was not provided in time. Putnam raged as he rode to and fro trying to get men and supplies forward. Later, the old warrior would apologize to his church for the profanity he used that day,

Gen. Thomas Gage, who distrusted and derided Americans and their Rangers in the French and Indian War, was now commanding the British forces. Gage called a council of war that included Generals Howe, Clinton, and Pigot. Henry Clinton pointed out that the entire American position was risky. If the British chose to control the narrow neck of land behind the Americans, they could trap them. Striking from the rear would allow taking the high ground of Bunker Hill and thus dominating the lower Breed's Hill. General Gage differed, observing that the Americans had forces on the mainland that could attack the British from the rear. The council decided they must attack the American position on Breed's Hill. Landing at Moulton's Point, they could hold the Americans on the hill by the nose with a frontal assault while sending forces along the beach to kick them in the rear with a flanking attack. There was a low regard of American fighting ability. Gage felt certain British bayonets would put this rabble to flight.

Seeing that cannon fire was ineffective, General Gage ordered General Howe and his disciplined regulars to conduct an over-water landing at Moulton's Point out of range of American fire. Hours dragged by as this was effected. After seeing American dispositions, Howe sent for reinforcements. He then formed his men into three lines.

Howe's final plan was based on maneuver. The elite light infantry of the 23rd Royal Welsh Fusiliers would move along the beach, while the grenadiers would attack the rail fence. These troops were expected to flank the redoubt, take position to attack its rear, and cut off the American retreat. The flanking movement would be complemented by a frontal demonstration on the redoubt. This was intended to hold the Americans on Breed's Hill in position while the flanking attack cut them off. The frontal effort would be with the 5th, 38th, 52nd, and 47th Regiments and Marines. Howe formed these troops in three lines. The first was light infantry, followed by grenadiers and the battalion companies. The frontal effort would be under the command of Brigadier Pigot. Howe's right was to be supported by eight small field pieces. Through error or sabotage, these guns were supplied with the wrong ammunition and therefore not a factor until the last stages of the battle.

Meanwhile, the Americans had been active and three Ranger leaders were in the forefront. Putnam was everywhere on the field, often with Prescott in building the works of Breed's Hill, then supervising preparation and occupying a supporting position on Bunker Hill.

Putnam rode to Breed's Hill and asked Prescott for the entrenching tools to dig in on Bunker Hill. Prescott objected; he had not brought any men to carry them. Prescott believed that Putnam would have no trouble getting volunteers to carry tools to the rear. He also believed the men who carried them would not return. He was correct on both counts. Capt. Ebenezer Bancroft, who was there, describes the scene thus: "Putnam, rode up to us at the fort and says 'My lads, these tools must be carried back' and turned and rode away. An order was never obeyed with more readiness. From every part of the line volunteers ran, and some picked up one, some two shovels, mattocks &c., and hurried over the hill."[5] Putnam wrongly expected every man to have the same fighting spirit he had and did not supervise their return. Thus, the American position was weakened.

When it appeared the British would attack the left flank, Ranger Thomas Knowlton and his men were sent to hold position behind the rail fence. The position was critical and undermanned when the third Ranger appeared on the scene. Ranger John Stark, now a colonel, had brought his regiment to the neck of land only to find two regiments who would not cross the field of fire. Stark asked them to step aside and marched his men through cannon fire, crossing the neck and moving toward Bunker Hill. The British cannon fire was not effective, but it was frightening. When Captain Dearborn suggested they run through the fire, Stark observed that "one fresh man is worth ten in battle" and continued walking. Now, newly arrived on Breed's Hill with his New Hampshire frontiersmen, Colonel Stark saw the weak point in the American line and on his own initiative led them into position with Tom Knowlton along the fence. The sixteen-year-old Caleb Stark, who was about to fight his first battle, said that at his father's side were Rangers of his company in the French and Indian War. One of these men was Maj. Andrew McClary, a blue-eyed giant of six feet, six inches who had done Ranger duty with Goffe, Rogers, and Stark. When he left his wife and seven children to fight the British, Andrew McClary had vowed to "kill one of the Devils before he came home." Among those at the rail fence was Ranger Seth Pomeroy, now sixty-nine years old. He had been in every war he could find for thirty-two years. Pomeroy carried the musket he had used at Louisbourg in 1745 and could still use it well. When Putnam saw his old comrade, he shouted, "My God! Pomeroy, you here! A cannon-shot would waken you out of your grave."[6]

As John Stark looked over the terrain, he reasoned that the British might attack along the narrow beach and attempt to turn the American position on Breed's Hill. Stark placed Capt. John Moor and his sixty men in position on the beach. He set these men to collecting stones from the beach and pasture walls to form a low wall, while other men reinforced the fence. Stark then moved forward at between fifty and eighty yards and put a stick in the ground. Returning to his men, he said, "Don't a man fire until the redcoats come up to that stick. If one of you fires till they reach that stick, I'll shoot him." The combat-experienced officers were cautioning their men to hold their fire until the enemy was close upon them. Tradition has it that Putnam told the Connecticut men, "Don't fire till you see the whites of their eyes."

It was nearly three o'clock in the afternoon of a cloudless day. From the rooftops of Boston, spectators watched as the redcoats formed and the sun gleamed on British metal. Quickly, Pigot's men came under fire from American snipers in the houses of Charleston. The British ships fired heated cannon balls into the town and set it ablaze. Howe began his attack with his men, moving in disciplined formations, carrying packs and full equipment, a weight estimated at 125 pounds. Seeking to flank the American earthworks on Breed's Hill, the British light infantry moved like a red tide against Rangers Stark and Knowlton at the beach wall and fence. The British attack broke and receded before a flaming wall of fire at close range. The light infantry of the Royal Welsh Fusiliers were slaughtered. A second British attack was shattered. Howe sent in two waves of his towering grenadiers. Both efforts met a devastating fire. The ground before Rangers Stark and Knowlton was littered with bodies. Ninety-six dead lay in front of John Moor's company. The British officers were a prime target. They were easily distinguished by sword belts, sashes, and a half-moon-shaped piece of metal called a gorget that hung on ribbons around their necks. General Howe marched with his men and by a miracle remained untouched. All the officers of his staff were wounded or killed.

Badly hurt by their efforts at the rail fence, the British feigned an attack on Stark and Knowlton to hold them in position while pressing their attack on the earthworks. Colonel Prescott was in command of 400 men, mostly from Massachusetts, in the redoubt. Prescott was a superb swordsman whose energy and courage were widely praised.

Rifles and muskets flamed, and British soldiers fell in ordered ranks with survivors retreating. One gallant American leaped up on the berm for a better view of the enemy. He was a skilled marksman. According to Lieutenant Clark, a British officer, this unknown American hero would fire and quickly be handed up another weapon. Clark said the American shot only at officers and wounded or killed twenty of them before he was himself killed by grenadiers of the Royal Welsh Fusiliers.

For the British, the desperation of this frontal attack was only matched by the courage of their officers and men. With every officer and noncommissioned officer shot down, a senior private took command of his few remaining comrades and continued the attack. In the American position, men poured out their last grains of powder and called in vain for more. As the American fire died, the British pressed home the attack. Unburdened by packs, with many shedding their heavy uniform coats and bayonets fixed, the British moved in a relentless column against the Americans. British artillery was now in action beating on the American ramparts.

One last volley from the Americans shattered the point of the British attack, but the following columns came on into the American position. A shower of stones came from the Americans; then the bayonets of the British were upon them. Out of ammunition, battling with stones and clubbed muskets, thirty Americans fought until they died under cold steel. Sword against bayonet, Colonel Prescott fought his way out of the redoubt, but Dr. Warren was killed.

Other Americans fled over Bunker Hill, crossed the Charlestown Neck, and established a new defensive position on the other side. Putnam tried to make a stand on Bunker Hill, exhorting men to fight, beating fleeing men with the flat of his sword, trying to rally reinforcements, and personally working to load powder in a cannon, only to find the cartridges were too large. Putnam's efforts were hindered by the cowardice of Col. Samuel Gerrish, who, having a regiment of militia on Bunker Hill, could have reinforced the redoubt. The fat colonel fell prone on the ground, crying out, "Retreat, retreat, or we shall all be cut off!" Other American units performed a fighting withdrawal. British officers said it was bravely and skillfully done.

At the rail fence and on the beach, Stark witnessed the British success at the redoubt. American marksmanship had cost the British dearly, but few Americans had bayonets. Without bayonets, unable to fire into mixed forces, Stark and Knowlton's men withdrew in good order. Maj. Andrew McClary had kept his vow and killed British soldiers but was himself killed in the action. The stock of Seth Pomeroy's musket had been shattered by a lead ball, but the old veteran left the field of fire walking backward with his face to his enemy.

In two hours of bloody action, the British had gained the field. The American felt they had lost. But soon the terrible cost to temporarily gain ground reverberated in both the colonies and England. Some 2,200 British officers and men had made the attack against approximately 1,500 Americans. Nearly 50 percent of the British were casualties—226 British soldiers were killed, including 27 officers, and 828 British soldiers and 70 officers were wounded, with many later perishing from these wounds. American losses were 140 killed, 271 wounded, and 30 taken prisoner.

The battle that would become incorrectly known as Bunker Hill was a spur to American self-confidence. It is often portrayed as a battle of American farmers and shopkeepers against British regulars. In actuality, Ranger leaders Stark, Putnam, Knowlton, and many Rangers under them had as much or more combat experience than the men they faced. These Americans knew weaponry and small-unit tactics well. What they and other American leaders of the period did not know was how to politically and operationally coordinate the efforts of the various colonies and the logistics of supporting military operations. There was no sense of unity as Americans. There were many who had long since ceased to think of themselves as British, but they did not all think of themselves as Americans. They were men of Massachusetts, Connecticut, or New Hampshire. They did not fight as a team. As with most military knowledge, the lessons to be learned would be written out in blood.

The Battle of Breed's Hill was a rude awakening for the British. General Gage tried to minimize the results, praising his troops and saying that nearly 100 Americans were buried and 30 wounded. The British press ripped into his account, pointing out that more men were lost in this battle than when the French Army was defeated at Quebec. Why did it cost more than 1,000 casualties to take a redoubt that had been thrown up in one night? The Americans were supposed to be cowardly. What had gone wrong? How many victories like this could Britain sustain?

War in the North

The American force surrounding Boston continued to grow. The first troops raised by Congress were the ten rifle companies authorized on June 14, 1775. They were Ranger frontiersmen trained in warfare with the Indians and commanded by Ranger officers. Promoted to colonel, William Thompson of Carlisle would head the six companies raised in Pennsylvania, which, with three additional companies, were combined to form William Thompson's Pennsylvania Rifle Regiment. Thompson had been on the Kittanning raid as one of Armstrong's Rangers and had been a leader in Elder's Paxtang Rangers. His last appointment had been as a captain of Pennsylvania Rangers. On January 1, 1776, this unit was redesignated the 1st Continental Regiment.

On June 15, 1775, Congress was discussing the need for a military commander. John Hancock wanted the job. George Washington had not spoken of his desire for the command but arrived at the gathering in full uniform. The Congress understood his unspoken message. John Adams stood to speak of the need for a "Commander in Chief of a Grand American Army." Adams praised his candidate, whom he did not name at first: "skill as an officer . . . independent fortune . . . great talents . . . universal character." Hancock was beaming until Adams said, "A gentleman from Virginia." Hancock's body recoiled, and his expression transformed to embarrassment and anger.[7] Washington immediately rose, hurried from the room, and disposed himself in the library. Despite regional rivalry, Adams knew that Virginia was vital to the cause and Washington was the most combat-experienced officer available. John Adams pressed for Washington's appointment, and when Thomas Johnson of Maryland formally proposed Washington, the vote was unanimous. On the way out to dinner, the members of Congress greeted George Washington as "general."

Congress also compiled a list of major generals and brigadier generals to serve under the new commander. Artemus Ward, who had the army at Boston, was selected as the senior major general, with Ranger Israel Putnam in fourth place. Ranger Seth Pomeroy was chosen as the senior brigadier general.

At the end of June, Washington joined his assorted colonial militia at Boston. What should have been a happy circumstance for Washington was a rude introduction to army command. Jealous men who felt that promotions should have gone to them filled the air with complaint and resignations. It was a long way from being an army, but these men had inflicted 1,327 casualties on the regulars of the best army in the world, and they had done it suffering but 536 of their own.

Washington knew the inherent problems of militia, included short-term enlistments, lack of standardization of equipment and training, and independent thought. He had populated areas to defend, and that could not be done with a guerrilla campaign. Washington needed to build an army that could fight toe-to-toe with the British regulars. That could not be done with ease or speed and would have to be accomplished while fighting. This meant American militia facing British and Hessian regulars and attempting to use the tactics of the regulars. The results were predictable. Washington was usually beaten, but he rose to fight again, and he was careful to save his army.

For 153 years since the Berkeley Plantation massacre, the colonists had fought against Indian warriors who verged on perfection in their conduct of the raid and ambush. One course of action open to Washington was to withdraw into the depths of America and fight a guerrilla war. This would draw the heavy laden Redcoats far from their line of supply. However, the new nation was still heavily dependent on foreign sources of supply, and the Royal Navy ruled the waves.

The Americans were in better shape on land than on sea. On December 13, 1775, Congress authorized the construction of thirteen frigates. Many did not get their anchors away before the British were on them. The fledgling American navy had its best success by employing hit-and-run Ranger tactics at sea. They had just the man and ship to lead the way. On the June 14, 1777, the Congress resolved that John Paul Jones would be appointed to command the ship *Ranger*. The eighteen-gun sloop *Ranger* was built at Portsmouth, New Hampshire, the home of many famed Rangers including Dan Ladd, John Goffe, Robert Rogers, and John Stark. Men involved in building the ship had served in or had knowledge of the Rangers. It had been planned to call the ship *Hampshire*, but it seemed more fitting to name her after men who went in harm's way.[8] The American Ranger would therefore gain fame on sea as well as land.

CHAPTER 10

To Boston and Beyond

Eager for battle, about 1,400 Ranger riflemen marched for Boston as soon as companies could be assembled. They traveled light, many wearing white or ash-colored hunting shirts, Indian leggings, and breech-clouts with thighs exposed for ease of running. On their feet were moccasins stuffed with moss or grass. The waist of their long shirt was secured by a belt that carried tomahawk and scalping knife. Disdaining swords, most of the officers also carried rifles. On their heads, they wore a round hat. Over the shoulder was suspended canteen, bullet pouch, and powder horn. On march, they frequently ate Rockahominy, ground Indian corn which, when added to water, swelled in the stomach and satisfied hunger. Among these men were the finest marksmen in the world.

In time, nine Pennsylvania companies of Ranger riflemen would assemble. A report from New York stated that between July 28 and August 2, six Pennsylvania companies—those of Chambers, Doudel, Hendricks, Lowden, Nagel, and Miller—passed through New Windsor a few miles north of West Point en route to Boston. The two Pennsylvania companies from Cumberland County were commanded by Capt. William Hendricks and Capt. James Chambers. From Lancaster came two companies commanded by Capt. James Ross and Capt. Matthew Smith.

Of the Ranger officers who survived, many would rise to positions of high authority in the Continental Army. One who exhibited brilliance but died young was twenty-one-year-old Capt. William Hendricks, who was born near Harrisburg, Pennsylvania. He commanded one of the two companies from Cumberland County. Leaving Carlisle, Pennsylvania, with ninety men on July 13, he arrived at Cambridge, near Boston, on August 9. Along the way, his company marched as much as twenty-nine miles a day.

The Virginia companies were commanded by Capt. Hugh Stephenson and Capt. Daniel Morgan. Later, when Morgan was captured at Quebec, Stephenson would command both the Maryland and Virginia Rangers. Stephenson and his men were captured while Nathanael Greene was learning to be a general and lost Fort Washington. When Stephenson was taken prisoner, Morgan, who had been exchanged, was available to form a new corps of Rangers. When Stephenson was later exchanged in this musical chairs game of prisoners, Washington ordered him to form a regiment of riflemen. Stephenson was in Virginia recruiting when he took ill and died in August 1776.

Hugh Stephenson was born at Berkeley in western Virginia. He was an experienced woodsman who had fought in Dunmore's War. He was senior in rank to Morgan. His Rangers were recruited from "the right bank of the Potomac." They were all skilled hunters who sported a bucktail on the side of their caps as a sign of their marksmanship. Stephenson and Morgan agreed to march their two companies to meet at Frederick Town and then proceed to Boston together. If the two companies arrived together, the attention would go to the senior captain. It is uncertain if this motivated Morgan to break his agreement. Without informing Stephenson, Morgan marched a day early and did not wait at Frederick. This made Morgan's company the first troops from south of the Potomac to arrive. Predictably, he got the adulation.[1]

The son of an iron master, Morgan was born on the Pennsylvania–New Jersey border during the winter of 1736. One of his extended relatives was Daniel Boone. As with most of his contemporaries, Morgan's education was minimal. Much of his youth was spent in the hard work of clearing land. His mother died, and the child grew up rustic and rude and unable to get along with his step-mother. At age seventeen, after a family argument, he turned his back on his family and took to the natural highways of the Cumberland and Shenandoah Valleys. He spent several weeks in Carlisle, then continued on to the area of present-day Charlestown, West Virginia. Morgan was now well on his way to achieving a height of six feet, two inches. His blue eyes flashed from under a high forehead and an over-size nose. His physique was imposing. He was a mouthy youth, quick to back up his opinion with ham-like fists.

In Virginia, he found hard employment clearing farmland of rocks, stumps, and trees. In time, he advanced, working in a sawmill and soon supervising the work of other men. The thirst for adventure was in him, and when offered the chance to be a teamster hauling supplies from Fredericksburg to the mountains, he took the job. By the time he was twenty, he owned his own team and wagon. In 1755, Morgan was hired as one of the wagoners in support of General Braddock's disastrous expedition to seize Fort Duquesne. He was not engaged in combat. After Braddock's defeat, Indian raids increased, and Morgan's mountain treks became more hazardous. He acquitted himself well in these skirmishes.

In 1756, while at Fort Chiswell on the frontier, Morgan felt the bite of British Army discipline when he was lashed. The most common version of the story is that a British lieutenant grew weary of Morgan's mouth and told him to be quiet. Words followed, and the officer struck him with the flat of his sword. Morgan used his fists on the man with telling affect. Quickly arrested, Morgan was summarily tried and sentenced to be lashed with a cat-o'-nine-tails. Such punishments were routine in the British Army of the period. Men were whipped through the regiment, tied to posts, and beaten before company after company for trivial offenses. Wiping the nose in ranks or looking angry at a noncommissioned officer could bring a severe beating. Commanding officers could administer punishment on the spot. Desertion or mutiny brought a death sentence.

After convalescence, Morgan resumed his wagoner's trade, but in the summer of 1757, he volunteered to be part of a fifty-man force sent to the relief of Edward's Fort, located twenty miles northwest of Winchester. The fort had recently lost most of its garrison to an Indian ambush. Within a short time of Morgan's arrival, the French and Indians attacked. The fight spanned several days and included an Indian incursion within the walls. The French and Indians were beaten off. During this fight, Morgan acquitted himself well. One source credits him with killing four Indians in four minutes with gun, knife, and bare hands.

Morgan's ability earned him an appointment as an ensign, the lowest commissioned rank in the Virginia militia. He served at Edward's Fort and other frontier posts, where he developed his military skills. Delivering dispatches to Winchester on horseback with an escort of two enlisted men, Morgan was ambushed in a narrow defile by Indians firing from rocks overhead. The two enlisted men were killed, and Morgan was desperately wounded, shot through the neck and jaw, destroying the teeth on the left side of his mouth. Clinging to the neck of his horse and pursued by an ambitious warrior, Morgan managed to make his way to Edward's Fort. At twenty-three, he was close to death. Given the medical practices of the time, it took a hardy constitution and six months for Morgan to recover.

Back on his feet, Morgan resumed his brawling ways, building a reputation that varied according to the observer. The years passed, the times were hard, and Dan Morgan was a hard man. He spent his time farming and fist-fighting. When Pontiac's War began in 1763, Morgan served for a time as a lieutenant in one of the frontier companies. Military fame did not come his way. He returned to his former pursuits and had minor but frequent brushes with the law, including breaking the peace, trespass, and assault and battery. In 1773, he married Abigail Curry, who, in the manner of her sex, set about remaking him. She gave him the rudiments of an education, kept him out of the taverns and brawls, and gave him two daughters to love. Morgan put down roots and, through hard work, began to acquire land.

In 1774, Pennsylvania and Virginia were quarreling over western land, with the Indians caught between. A scoundrel named Jacob Greathouse and his men murdered the brother, sister, and sister's child of the Mingo chief Logan. Now this great war chief, who had been a friend, vowed to kill ten whites for each of his slain family and began butchering settlers. John Connolly, the scheming agent of Lord Dunmore, the governor of Virginian, arbitrarily seized Fort Pitt (present-day Pittsburgh), renamed it Fort Dunmore, and started an Indian war to cover his activities.

Outraged by atrocities committed by the whites, the Shawnee Indians took up the hatchet. The Miami, Huron, and Ottawa tribes joined in, and the frontier was ablaze. Dunmore called out 3,000 Virginia militia. Among them was Capt. Dan Morgan, who had recruited a company of Rangers. As part of a larger force, Morgan's company moved to attack the Indian towns at the head of the Muskingham River. It was a war of ambush and raid, hard fought by men who were ill-supplied. On October 10, Dunmore's columns defeated the Indians in a major engagement at the mouth of the Kanawha River. The Indians sued for peace and tribes were required to send chiefs for negotiations; some did not. Dan Morgan, with 400 riflemen, was sent on a search-and-destroy operation through the ill-defended Indian towns. Dunmore's War was unjustified, but it had several effects. It opened the way for further white expansion, it reduced the ability of some Indian tribes to assist the British in the Revolutionary War, and it was a training ground for military leaders, including Dan Morgan and George Rogers Clark.

As they passed into New England en route to Boston, the Pennsylvania and Maryland Rangers met at Litchfield, Connecticut. Captain Price of the Maryland men had captured a Tory along the way, and Rangers amused themselves by tarring and feathering the poor wretch and drumming him out of camp.[2]

The companies arrived at Boston, cocky and proud, filled with the arrogance of young men who feel they can whip anyone and are eager to prove it. In camp, they demonstrated their marksmanship in competitions. Every man of one Ranger company demonstrated he could put shots through a seven-inch target at 250 yards.[3] One Ranger put eight shots in a row through a piece of wood five-by-seven inches at sixty yards. Their marksmanship demonstrations were halted when Washington learned he had only enough powder and ball for his army to allow nine shots per man. A report of the time states that "their shots have frequently proved fatal to British officers and soldiers who expose themselves to view even at more than double the distance of common musket shot."[4]

Capt. James Chambers wrote his wife that within an hour of arriving at Boston, his men were sniping at the British. After some days of action, Chambers wrote that the riflemen had killed forty-two British and taken thirty-eight prisoners, twelve of whom were Tories. Four of the British who were killed were captains, and one of these was the wealthy son of a lord.

Washington wanted a British prisoner. The mission was for a Ranger unit to move by night down to the Charlestown Neck pass through friendly lines then capture one or more British troops from works on Bunker Hill. The mission was assigned to Capt. Michael Doudel's company. Doudel led one party of thirty-nine men, and 1st Lt. Henry Miller led forty men in another. Nearing the British position, they divided, with Doudel going to the right and Miller to the left. Crawling on hands and knees, they passed to the rear of the British fortifications. As they moved into position to snatch a prisoner from the outposts, a unit of British troops came down off the hill to relieve their guards.

The Rangers laid prone, hoping to avoid discovery, but within twenty yards, the British saw them and fired. Doudel's men returned fire, killed five British, and took two prisoners. The British captured Ranger Walter Cruise, who would be a prisoner for seventeen months but return to become a captain in the 6th Pennsylvania Regiment.

Seeking to lure his foe into a frontal attack, Washington on August 26, 1775, challenged the British by moving approximately 2,000 men into position on Ploughed Hill, a knoll a few hundred yards from the British line. Moving into position at night, the troops dug entrenchments while the Rangers moved forward into concealed positions close to the British lines. The British formed as though to attack, but the lessons of the battle at Breed's Hill were upon them. They contented themselves with cannon fire from batteries on Bunker Hill and a warship and two floating batteries on the Mystic River. They killed several Americans and wounded a few more, but American artillery opened fire, sank one of the floating batteries, and quieted the other. In this action, Ranger William Simpson of Captain Smith's company from Lancaster, Pennsylvania, was wounded in the foot. In these times, amputation was the defense against gangrene. Simpson's leg was taken, but he died.

The Ranger camp was about 100 yards from the rest of the army. They were treated as elite troops and not required to participate in camp duty, as guards, or on work details. The fledgling American army patterned itself on that of the British and also used the whip to enforce discipline. This enraged the free spirits of the frontier, and they began to resist punishment. When a Ranger was brought to the post to be whipped, an observer noted, "It was with the utmost difficulty they were kept from rescuing him in the presence of all their officers. They openly dammed them and behaved with great insolence."

A unit frequently takes the personality of its commander. Captain Ross of one of the Pennsylvania Ranger companies decided something needed done at home and left camp without orders or farewell. This greatly angered General Washington. Then thirty-two of Ross's men decided to free one of their comrades from the guardhouse. The other Ranger companies refused to participate in this. Ross's men formed with loaded rifles to accomplish their goal. An angry Washington reinforced the guard with 500 men with loaded weapons and fixed bayonets.

On November 9, 1775, the British put a landing party ashore at Lechmere Point under cover of their guns on Breed's, Bunker. and Copp's Hills and from a British warship. At high tide, the point became an island. The Rangers were assigned the mission of routing the enemy. Storms were whipping the water, and the Rangers had to wade in water up to their armpits for a quarter mile to get to the island. Colonel Thompson led the attack. They made the crossing and engaged a British force that was firing from cover. Despite this, the Rangers drove the British from Lechmere Point at a cost of one man killed and three wounded. British losses were seventeen killed and one wounded.[5] Washington commended Thompson's men in General Orders on November 10.

Washington had built his military reputation on the frontier, and he understood Rangers and believed they could contribute to a plan he was considering: the invasion of Canada.

At the onset of the Revolutionary War, the British Empire reached from the Hudson Bay to the Gulf of Mexico. Four British possessions were in present-day Canada: Nova Scotia, Newfoundland, Quebec, and Rupert's Land. Only Quebec and Nova Scotia were significant, with Quebec being the key to the north. The thirteen colonies to the south saw Quebec as another colony occupied by British forces and worthy of adding to the revolutionary fold. While French Canada came under British rule in 1760, most of the citizens of Quebec remained French. In 1774, the British, angry at the thirteen southern colonies and hoping to bind the loyalty of their French subjects, passed a law that would reverberate through the centuries. The Quebec Act guaranteed the French citizens of Quebec that they would be allowed to retain their French language, French civil law, and Roman Catholic faith if they would be loyal to the British king. Monstrous in the eyes of the Americans was the arbitrary British extension of Quebec's border south to the Ohio River and restructuring of the lucrative fur trade to favor those in Quebec at the expense of the other colonies. The British hoped that as a result of these guarantees, they would block westward movement of the Americans and encourage the French citizens of Quebec to side with Britain. The Americans were furious, and this became one of the so-called Intolerable Acts that generated the Revolution. The French took the civil and religious guarantees and hold them to this day, but few would take up arms in support of the British against the Americans.

The Americans hoped the capture of Quebec would raise a rebellion against the British in the north and break their hold on the north. This was wishful thinking. The French in Quebec had no love for their English conquerors or the Americans who had helped in the destruction of New France. Nova Scotia was primarily inhabited by New Englanders who were generally sympathetic, but it was isolated geographically. Capturing Montreal and the city of Quebec would break the British hold on the north. Quebec City was a critical objective as it dominated the St. Lawrence River.

The American effort took the form of a two-pronged invasion. One force under the brilliant young Gen. Richard Montgomery would seize Montreal and prepare to continue the attack to Quebec City, and another column would come at Quebec from Boston.

To command the force moving from Boston, Washington chose a short, chunky, and immensely energetic young officer named Benedict Arnold. Aggressive and hungry for battle and promotion, Arnold had tried to wrest command of the Ticonderoga expedition from Ethan Allen. Failing that, he went along at Allen's side, then led another force to seize Fort St. John south of Montreal. He knew Quebec City, having traded there. Washington had a high regard for Arnold and told him, "It is not in the power of any man to command success; but you have done more—you have deserved it."

The force using the Boston-to-Quebec axis would proceed along the Chaudiere, Dead, and Kennebec Rivers, which Indian war parties had used. British and French commanders had considered it, but they had never used the treacherous terrain through the Maine wilderness.

Washington gave the newly promoted Colonel Arnold the pick of his 16,000-man army. The plan was to form an all-volunteer force of men who were experienced in woodcraft and boat handling. Arnold got five times the number of volunteers he wanted, many of whom lied about their ability because they wanted to get out of camp life at Boston. Questioning reduced the number to 750, to which the Rangers were added.

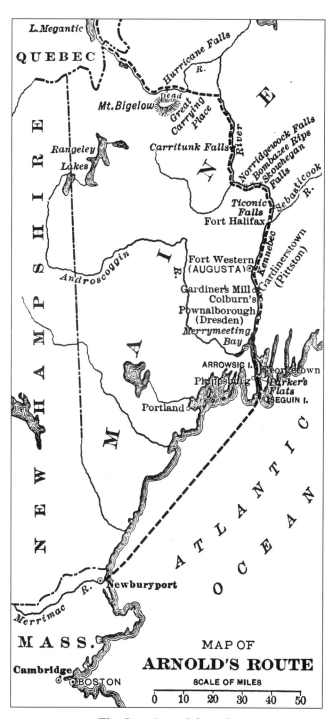

The Invasion of Canada

On September 12, 1775, Arnold led a force of 1,100 men (and two women who would not leave their husbands) northward. Counting on traveling much of the way by water, they carried bateaux. These were flat bottom boats, well suited to known waters, but difficult to carry in rugged terrain. They were also a major problem in the raging whitewater rapids the men would encounter. Experienced boatmen felt that canoes would have been better than the heavy bateaux, which were made of green wood and leaked.

Three Ranger companies were selected by lot and marched as units.[6] These were Capt. William Hendricks's and Capt. Matthew Smith's companies from Pennsylvania and Capt. Daniel Morgan's company from Virginia. The three Ranger companies served as scouts and security for the main body. They moved ahead, preventing ambush and determining the best route to be taken through trackless wilderness. They carried axes and cut the rough road for the main body. This winter march of nearly a thousand miles through unmapped wilderness was an epic of American military history.

Winter comes early in Maine. Those who were not chopping trees or scouting carried boats though terrible terrain, one day covering nearly twenty miles. Hendricks's journal recounts men moving in water up to their chins, swamps with mud to the knee, drenching rains, intense cold, and snow. There were three days of torrential rain. The Dead River rose eight feet above its banks and left men floundering in despair. Ranger John Henry of Smith's company was a volunteer, not on company rolls, drawing no recompense for his misery. Henry wrote he had half a biscuit and an inch of pork for a day's ration. They shot a moose but had not the time or the means to adequately prepare it, and many were sickened by the meat.

In these trying times, Lt. Archibald Steele proved himself to be a Ranger's Ranger. Steele was from near Harris Ferry (now Harrisburg), Pennsylvania. He was a skilled woodsman, ranging far ahead by canoe to determine where the rivers were suitable for passage and where there must be portage. Steele was also to make contact with Indians along the route and gain intelligence. Lieutenant Church also led a reconnaissance party, though closer to the main force.

Second in command to Arnold was Lt. Col. Christopher Greene, a distant relative of Nathaniel Greene and an able Rhode Island officer. Greene would distinguish himself throughout the war in a variety of difficult and unusual operations, including commanding a regiment of black troops. He would die fighting under Tory knives and bayonets at Croton River, New York.

Arnold put Greene in charge of his Ranger advance party and immediately found resistance. Morgan claimed the right to command the Rangers was his, that the rifle companies were raised before Green and other field-grade officers were commissioned. Though he had no authority to do so, he insisted that the Rangers would take orders only from Arnold. Morgan claimed that Washington had dictated this arrangement. Arnold wrote Washington, who in turn wrote a letter to Morgan, praising his dedication but telling him that he was wrong. "Every officer should command according to his rank."

The other Ranger captains supported Morgan in this affair, claiming they had been promised that no militia officer would be their commander, only another Ranger. Historians have often portrayed Morgan as the Ranger leader in this march. If Hendricks and Smith accepted Morgan's command, it was a very loose arrangement. Hendricks was slightly the senior officer, but he was only twenty-one years old. Simeon Thayer, who was on the march, described Hendricks as "tall, of a mild and beautiful countenance. His soul was animated by a genuine spark of heroism. He was active and energetic in the march through the wilderness and shared freely in the toils and privations of his men."[7] Morgan was thirty-nine and had seen more action. Smith was forty-one and hated Indians with a frontier passion. Smith had been a leader of the Paxtang Rangers, a man in the forefront of the Moravian Indian uproar in Pennsylvania.

Some reports indicate that Hendricks accepted Morgan's command, but Hendricks's journal makes no mention of it. When there was discontent about rations coming from Arnold, the three captains went to see their leader, not Morgan alone as a commander. During the march, Morgan accused a Ranger named Chamberlaine of firing his rifle against orders for silent movement. There was no proof against Chamberlaine, who denied it, but Morgan took a club-like piece of wood and prepared to beat a confession out of the man. Though Chamberlaine was not of his company, Captain Smith picked up another club and assured Morgan he would have to fight Smith before he would beat the man. Morgan did not choose to fight. During an incident over the portage of boats 100 miles from Quebec, Hendricks and Smith thought Morgan's plans unrealistic and ignored them.

The Rangers respected Arnold. He was a superb commander, more admired by the enlisted men than by officers who felt the lash of his tongue. Arnold had an unfortunate distrust of an Indian named Natanis, who proved to be a great friend to the expedition. At times when the column wondered about lost in land covered with water, an Indian would appear and guide them to dry land; these were from the band of Natanis. Conversely, Arnold was led to believe he could trust an Indian named Eneas, who was actually a spy for the British.

Hunting was poor and rations ran short. To break a leg was a death sentence, and men died of cold and hunger in those awful woods and raging rivers. Thayer describes going six miles through a swamp that had water frozen as thick as a pane of glass, when men broke through they were in mud to the calf. They forded a small river with ice-cold water to the armpits of an average-size man. They had to cross another on a narrow log, and men fell in. He wrote of starving men reduced to killing Dearborn's dog and eating it. Morgan and Smith nearly drowned when a bateau overturned in raging water. The two Ranger leaders lost all spare clothes and whatever money they did not have on them. The flooded woodlands trapped men and were difficult to navigate. A participant's journal records, "Morgan lost himself and found himself again. He lost his hatchet, found it, and lost it again—Amen."[8] Some 600 weary, starving men arrived near Quebec on November 8, the rest having fallen by the trail and left to make their way home. Smith had started with eighty woods-hardened men and arrived with sixty-five. Hendricks's journal records that a small stick on the trail would trip the strongest man.

Arnold obtained food from the French settlements, but there was not enough. Finally, on December 5, the Americans stood before Quebec emaciated but ready to fight. Located on a high point of land between the St. Lawrence and St. Charles Rivers, Quebec was a walled city of high and low levels, each capable of being independently defended. Short of food and ammunition, knowing they could not hold a long siege, the Americans planned their attack. Quebec must be taken before ice melted on the St. Lawrence and the British fleet brought reinforcements.

To get to Quebec, the ragged band had to cross a mile of water guarded by two British warships, the *Lizard* (twenty-six guns) and the *Hunter* (sixteen). These were supported by smaller armed vessels and boat patrols. The Americans procured canoes from the Indians, and on the night of November 13, they followed a storm, slipping past the British defenders. En route, the canoe carrying Ranger Lt. Archibald Steele sank. With no room in the other boats, Steele remained immersed in the cold waters clinging to the side of a canoe. On the other side, a fire was kindled, and he survived. In later years, the brave Arch Steele became a brigadier general.

The Americans landed in the same cove which sixteen years before had been used by British General Wolfe in the capture of French Quebec. Making their way up a narrow path, the Americans reached the Plains of Abraham. The garrison of Quebec had been reinforced with Canadians, sailors, marines, and every able-bodied man that Gov. Guy Carleton could muster. He now had 1,200 defenders, but the walls were long and his militia questionable.

Awaiting the arrival of Montgomery, Arnold made a brave show trying to talk Carleton into surrendering. The response was cannon balls. Word came that a large force of the British were coming to attack the Americans. This resulted in a twenty-mile march through miserable conditions, with Arnold's men taking up quarters in outlying houses. There was a two-week respite while hungry men feasted on local cattle and made new moccasins of their hides.

On December 2, Montgomery arrived. With him, he brought stores of winter clothing taken when he captured Montreal and light artillery. The Americans lacked the heavy guns needed to batter down Quebec's walls. They did not have the supplies to effect a long siege, and they knew that the April thaws would bring a British fleet coming in on the St. Lawrence. Smallpox began to rage in the camps and enlistments were expiring. A major strength of the British was the will of Guy Carleton. Montgomery sent Carleton a message asking for surrender; Carleton had it burned by a drummer boy, instructing the lad to use tongs rather than touch the paper. Other messages were scorned. Montgomery tried his artillery, but the guns of Quebec were heavier and of longer range. There was no choice for the Americans but to attempt direct assault. Montgomery, as senior officer, had chosen an attack on the lower town as he believed it to be weaker. Carleton knew the lower town was his weakest point, and he strongly fortified its approaches and those that led from the lower to the upper town.

Behind Quebec's walls, Carleton now had 1,800 men. Montgomery could muster 800 to make his attack. It was an assault born of desperation. The Americans had come far under enormous suffering.

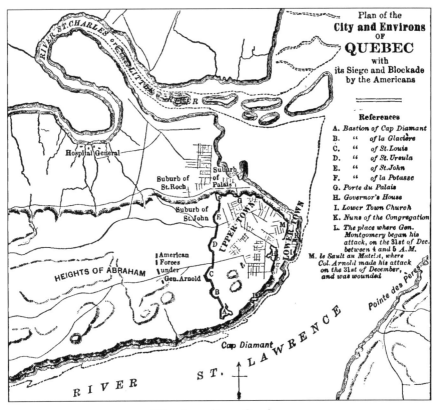

The Assault on Quebec

They were outnumbered, outgunned, and up against rested, well-fed troops in a strong defensive position. Men wrote last notes they hoped would be delivered to their loved ones. They also pinned notes to their caps that read "Liberty or Death."[9]

At 5 A.M. on December 31, the Americans attacked the lower town, with Montgomery's men coming from the south and Arnold from the north. They had waited for bad weather to conceal their movements. Now it was snowing heavily, and deep snow and ice hindered their ability to get over the walls. They bypassed an outpost without being detected but soon were forced to run a hail of fire from higher ground. Arnold was in the lead; the Rangers and some artillery men with a sled-mounted 6-pounder field piece behind him. A high barricade with two cannon blocked their way. One misfired, and the other got off one ineffective shot. Arnold led a headlong charge, telling the men to fire through the portholes. The British were returning fire, and Arnold was hit in the leg below the knee. Bleeding badly, he had to be evacuated. Morgan's company was the lead Ranger element. Smith's was next, but Captain Smith was not present, and the company was under Lieutenant Steele. Hendricks's company was third in the Ranger line of march.

Morgan put a scaling ladder against the barricade and led the way to the top. As soon as his head rose above the wall, he was fired on at such close range that his face had powder burns. A slug went through his cap; others clipped locks of his hair. Knocked off the ladder, Morgan went right back to it and led the men up and over the wall. He fell on a cannon and slid beneath it as British soldiers tried to bayonet him. The Rangers who followed drove the British into a house, where they surrendered.

Morgan then led the attack forward to Sault au Matelot, the avenue of approach to the lower town. Another barricade was seen 300 yards ahead. Behind it was a platform with cannon. A gate in the barricade was open. French Canadians were behind the barricade, calling friendly greetings to the Americans. Civilians were coming in numbers giving themselves up. Success seemed certain. Then indecision took a hand.

Coming through the snow and ice, the Rangers had traveled in single file, and most of them were still moving forward. Morgan did not have significant numbers. He later said that he went forward with an interpreter and found the firing had ceased and the way was open. Morgan then returned and called a council of war of the few officers who were with him. Morgan said he wanted to attack, but the other officers told him that they had arrived at the point where they were to meet Montgomery's men, that the number of prisoners was greater than their own, and that, if left behind, these prisoners could cut off the Rangers' way out.

It was dark, the storm was blowing hard, and they were in unfamiliar surroundings. Doubt gnawed at them. Morgan knew that when time permits, giving subordinates an opportunity to comment is worthwhile, but when a moment of opportunity comes, it is necessary that the leaders should lead and commanders should command. Councils of war seldom take offensive action. In this case, they recommended waiting for Montgomery. Morgan was now the leader and must have felt his failure in this instance. He later said, "I sacrificed my own opinion and lost the town."

Montgomery and his force would not arrive. Attacking a blockhouse with Aaron Burr and less than twenty men, he met a withering fire and was killed. Without him, his attack disintegrated. Morgan was unaware of this and waited until Captain Hendricks and his company and the New England militia came up. The men were at hand, but dawn was breaking, and on the British side, Carleton had not been idle. He sent Captain Laws and a body of men to attack Morgan's rear. Captain Macdougal was sent with more troops to support Laws and seize the first barricade the Americans had crossed. Major Nairne and Colonel Maclean moved to attack the Americans frontally.

Too late, the Americans pressed the attack. They moved forward and met a detachment of British under Lieutenant Anderson, who came through the barrier gate and called upon the Americans to surrender. Morgan shot him through the head, killing him, and the British withdrew. There was a pause in the action. The Americans closed and, using mounded snow as a base for ladders, attempted to get over. Carleton had positioned men in the houses who fired through the windows. Up the street, a double line of British troops with fixed bayonets blocked the way. The youthful Capt. William Hendricks was firing from a window when struck in the heart by a bullet. He fell across a bed and died. Lieutenant Steele had three fingers shot away and was out of action. The left side of Captain Lamb's face was torn off by canister. Rangers James Angles, John Campbell, Alexander Elliott, Dennis Kelly, Henry Miller, and Alexander Nelson were among those killed; many were wounded. There was a stone house at the end of the barricade. Seeing that its gable windows overlooked their objective, the Americans occupied the house, hoping to fire down on their enemies. The British under Major Nairne and Lieutenant Dembourges went in through the windows with bayonets fixed and drove the rifle-carrying Americans out.

Captain Law's troops closed on the rear of Morgan's men. Without bayonets, the Rangers were now faced with the malfunctioning of wet rifles. Where possible, they occupied houses along the street, fighting as best they could from the windows. Morgan fought with valor, leading by example. Hemmed in, he tried to get the men out of the houses, leading a fighting withdrawal, but few could follow. In the roar of battle, many could not hear him.

The Americans lost 48 killed, 34 wounded, and 372 captured, including Morgan. The British loss was one officer and five men killed. The wounded Arnold moved his survivors about a mile off, built defenses of ice blocks, and sent for reinforcements that did not come. In the spring, the arrival of a British fleet finished the plan. In an age of slow communication, it would be January 17 before General Washington learned of the disaster.

The previous November, while American Rangers were struggling through the New England forests en route to battle, an unusual visitor had come to Washington's camp. He was a retired half-pay British Army major wandering about, seemingly trying to secure and broker land grants. It was Robert Rogers, covering his time in debtors prison by the false claim he had been fighting for the Dey of Algiers. At Medford, Rogers met with his old friend John Stark. No record of the meeting survives. Stark's grandson, Caleb, claimed that Rogers sought to induce Stark to join the British cause, and Stark refused.

Washington was aware of the heavy suspicion of Rogers and felt there was just cause. He did not offer him a commission. Rogers's wife, Elizabeth, had strongly supported him throughout the years. Now she would have nothing to do with him. Elizabeth Rogers had learned something about her husband that she despised yet refused to reveal. She would have no further contact with him and later sought a divorce.

The Ranger riflemen had enlisted for a year. Washington was concerned about the loss of their services, and on April 22, 1776, he wrote the president of Congress, "The time for which the riflemen enlisted will expire on the 1st of July next, and as the loss of such a valuable and brave body of men will be of great injury to the service, I would submit to the consideration of Congress whether it would not be best to adopt some method to induce them to continue. They are, indeed a very useful corps; but I need not mention this as their importance is already well known to the Congress."

The 1st Continental Regiment (Regular Army) formed by the Congress to establish a national—as opposed to a state—loyalty would be largely drawn from the companies of riflemen in Thompson's Pennsylvania Rifle Battalion. The men of the 1st Continental would be armed with muskets. To a Ranger rifleman, fighting with a musket would be little different than fighting with a bow and arrow. Still, a number of these men stayed with Washington, some fighting for eight years. Others went home and sought frontier service in Ranger operations.

Some 140 men, mostly from Connecticut, volunteered to serve. Activated on August 26, 1776, this Ranger unit would be named for its initial commander, Lt. Col. Thomas Knowlton (1740–76). Knowlton was from Connecticut, dark-haired, and six feet tall with the physical grace of a natural athlete. He was highly respected by his fellow officers and his men. Knowlton had enlisted around the age of fifteen during the French and Indian War and was commissioned a lieutenant during that war, participating with Putnam in the siege of Havana in 1762. He had fought bravely at the battle of Breed's (Bunker) Hill.

On September 15, 1776, the Americans were poorly entrenched on Manhattan Island, looking with apprehension at five British warships and six transports that lay just off shore. At 10 A.M., the British under General Howe executed an amphibious assault at Kip's Bay, bringing 4,000 troops ashore by boat and covering the landing with an hour-long bombardment by eighty cannon. Terrified by the shelling and the sight of British bayonets coming ashore as close as forty yards, the Americans fled in panic. Generals Parson and Fellows tried to stem the flight. Washington came up, and by some accounts, he struck both enlisted men and officers trying to get them to stand, but the men were in the grip of fear. Some tried to surrender and were shot down or bayoneted by the Hessians.

With disaster at hand, Israel Putnam galloped south to alert the rest of the army and its artillery who were in danger of being cut off. Putnam's aide, Aaron Burr, knew the area. With Burr as guide, Putnam led the Americans' army out of the potential trap. While only a skirmish, the flight at Kip's Bay meant the loss of New York City was at hand. Of even greater consequence was the loss of morale. It was a dispirited American army that took up defensive positions on Harlem Heights. Officers and men did not have confidence in each other. There was doubt that this army would fight.

The Americans prepared three successive defensive lines that had the Hudson River on their right and the Harlem River on the left.

Some two miles distant were the British lines, located in the general vicinity of what is today Central Park. Washington did not know if Howe was preparing to continue the attack. Seeking information, Washington called on his Rangers. On September 16, in the faint predawn light, Knowlton led 120 Rangers forward. Their mission was to determine British intent and the location of their positions.

Knowlton's Rangers crossed a low-ground area called the Hollow Way, then moved to higher ground and through a woods. This put them in position close to the British left. Here, in advance of the main British line, they found two battalions of light infantry comprising about 400 men under General Leslie. Seeing the Americans, the British formed and moved to the attack. The Rangers assumed a defensive position behind a stone wall and opened a galling volley.

Troops of the 42nd Highlanders, the famed Black Watch, hurried to the action, threatening the American left. Knowlton had ten men down with wounds. The American Rangers had stood their ground against the larger force, delivering eight volleys into the British. With the threat to his flank, Knowlton now began to execute a skillful withdrawal. As the Americans withdrew, the British followed, coming into sight of the American lines and stopping on Vanderwater's Heights, high ground that overlooked the Hollow Way. British bugles began to sound, and a wave of anger surged among those Americans who knew the tune. Deriding the Americans, the British were playing the notes to signify the locating of the animal in a fox hunt.

Knowlton and his Rangers were regaining their lines, still full of fight and urging an attack. Washington saw the opportunity to hurt the exposed British force. He sent 150 volunteers of Gen. John Nixon's brigade under Lt. Col. Archibald Crary to make a demonstration in the British front. Knowlton moved again with his own Rangers and three riflemen from Ranger companies under the command of the valiant Maj. Andrew Leitch. Comprising 230 Americans, they began to circle around the British right to cut them off.

Drawn in by the deception, the British left their high ground positions and came down in the hollow to engage Crary and his volunteers. A hot, but long-range fire ensued. Guided by Col. Joseph Reed, who knew the area, the Rangers arrived on the British flank. By traveling only a few hundred yards farther, they would have cut off the enemy, but the sight of the hated Redcoats brought a lapse of discipline.

Someone called for fire, and Rangers shot into the enemy flank. Alarmed, the British promptly withdrew 200 yards and took position behind a rail fence. The Americans advanced, and the firing was heavy at forty yards' range.

Both sides brought up reinforcements. Washington threw in the disgraced regiment of Douglas but prudently added two pieces of artillery, more Virginia Rangers, nine companies of Beall's Maryland state troops, and Colonel Sargent's brigade from Massachusetts and Connecticut. The British now began to run. From the British side came reinforcements, panting from moving at the double quick for more than three miles. The 33rd Regiment, British and Hessian Grenadiers, and two pieces of artillery arrived, bringing the British total to 5,000 men.

For two hours, the battle raged. Major Leitch's body was brought back to the main line. He had been killed by three shots through the body. Shortly thereafter, the mortally wounded Tom Knowlton was brought in. Some expected that the loss of these leaders would cause the Americans to crack, but it did not happen. The captains and lieutenants took charge and kept fighting. Then the British began to withdraw. The Americans were in close pursuit, hustling the British through an orchard, a downslope and up a hill. The British were in flight, but more of their reserves were coming up fast. Washington had accomplished what he set out to do and did not want an open ground major battle. He sent orders forward for the Americans to return to their lines. With the sweet taste of victory in their mouths, it was difficult to bring them back, but they came cheering.

Harlem Heights was not a major battle. The British lost approximately 70 dead and 200 wounded, and the Americans lost 30 dead and 100 wounded. Despite this, Harlem Heights turned the American army around. In this war of many defeats, the sight of the enemy fleeing was a spur to morale. The Rangers had led the way in rejuvenating a fighting spirit in the army. Knowlton's Rangers were now led by Capt. Stephen Brown, who took command when Knowlton was killed. Brown would be followed by Maj. Andrew Colburn and Capt. Lemuel Holmes until November 16, 1776, when the unit was captured at the surrender of Fort Washington.

In the course of its brief existence, Knowlton's Rangers performed many roles, including scouting, raids, and light infantry. It also produced the authentic American hero, Nathan Hale.

Today, the spot where Third Avenue crosses 66th Street in New York City is thronged by people, few of whom know that they walk on hallowed ground. In 1776, this was the site of a British artillery park, part of a larger British camp. Here at eleven o'clock on September 22, the twenty-one-year-old Nathan Hale, a captain in Knowlton's Rangers, was executed by hanging.

Born in Coventry, Connecticut, June 6, 1755, Nathan Hale was part of a family of nine sons, six of whom fought in the Revolutionary War (three at Lexington). Educated at Yale, Nathan Hale became a school teacher at Haddam and New London. He was an attractive and passionate man devoutly committed to the cause of American independence. While at Yale, he probably read Addison's *Cato* and its line: "What pity is it that we can die but once to serve our country."

In July 1775, Hale was commissioned a first lieutenant and became a part of the Continental force that was holding Boston under siege. New Year's Day of 1776 saw his promotion to captain. Hale led his men on a daring raid to seize a sloop loaded with British supplies, taking it right from under the guns of the British warship *Asia*. His success led to his selection for a command in Knowlton's Rangers.

Washington was desperate for information and anxious to form an intelligence service. Both sides were employing spies. The Americans had recently hung a man named Hickey for spying for the British. The prospect of the noose was a great deterrent to those who were asked to go behind enemy lines.

Washington called for a volunteer from the Rangers to undertake a spying mission of British positions in New York. Knowlton presented the mission to his officers, but no one wanted the job. Lt. James Sprague summed up the general feeling when he said, "I am willing to go and fight them, but as for going among them and being taken and hung up like a dog, I will not do it." Knowlton made a second attempt, and Nathan Hale accepted. His friends tried to dissuade him, but Hale replied, "I wish to be useful and every kind of service necessary to the public good becomes honorable by being necessary."

Donning the garb he wore as a school teacher and carrying his Yale diploma as proof of his education, Hale left the American positions on Harlem Heights about September 12, 1776, to cross Long Island Sound by schooner to Huntington. Nine days were spent in travel and gathering information, some of which Hale unfortunately put in writing. On the twenty-first, while en route to return to friendly lines, Hale was captured. The story of his capture and who accomplished it varies. Robert Rogers may have played some role in his capture. British Capt. William Bamford of the 40th Foot made the following entry in his diary: "Nathan Hale, a Cap't in ye Rebel Army, & a spy was taken by Maj'r Rogers & this m'g hanged."

Questioned, Hale readily admitted he was an American officer in disguise. There was no trial. General Howe promptly ordered him hung. Denied a Bible and waiting for execution, Hale wrote letters to his brother Enoch and to Colonel Knowlton, who, unknown to Hale, was already dead. Hale's demeanor and courage impressed a British engineer officer, Captain Montresor. The Britisher later provided the details of Nathan Hale's courageous end, including the now famous statement, "I only regret that I have but one life to lose for my country." Hale's body was left hanging on display for several days. He was buried without ceremony in an unmarked grave, its location undetermined. Ten years went by, and his father, still stricken with grief, erected a simple headstone that included the words, "He resign'd his life a sacrifice to his country's liberty."

In October 1776, George Washington was using the lash and Rangers to keep his troops in line. His General Orders from Harlem Heights show Sgt. George Douglas received a reduction in grade and thirty-nine lashes for "embezzelling and selling provisions belonging to the company." It appears that Douglas also made some "mutinous speeches" and used disrespectful language regarding Washington and got another thirty-nine strokes for that. George Harris received thirty-nine lashes for desertion.[10]

The General Orders reflect that soldiers were straying from camp to go to Harlem and other places, often without taking weapons. Under orders from Washington, the Rangers had been returning the stragglers to their commanders. No action was being taken in the units. The October 8, 1776, orders directed that "no officer or soldier [Rangers excepted] go on any pretense beyond the lines without leave from himself [Washington], a Major General, the Brigadier of the day, or the Adjutant General, in writing." Stragglers were to be put under guard, tried by regimental courts-martial, and receive ten lashes immediately. The uniform condition of the army was evident in that the Rangers were to be identified by wearing "something white round their arms."[11] In November 1776, the fortunes of George Washington and the Continental Army were at a low ebb. His army had suffered a succession of defeats and was in desperate straits, and the enemy knew it. The English noted that dead Americans were without shoes, stockings, or blankets and confidently predicted the war would soon be over. Most of the Americans' enlistments would expire on December 1. Defeat is not a spur to reenlistment, and Washington was wrapped in gloom as many in his army left early. Certain of their prey, the British followed leisurely as Washington retreated through New Jersey and crossed the Delaware River. British General Cornwallis would have followed, but Washington had collected all the boats. In these desperate times when officers deserted to the British and politicians ran for cover, a volunteer named Tom Paine used a drumhead as a desk and wrote a small pamphlet called "The Crisis," which lit a fire in the American spirit. By Christmas, Washington had 6,000 men. They were cold, hungry, sick, and unfit for duty, but the British had gone into winter quarters. It was time to attack.

Across the river in Trenton were three regiments of Hessians, a few British dragoons, and six artillery pieces. Col. Johann Rall was in command. Scorning the Americans, Rall made no effort to entrench. Washington said dire necessity motivated his attack. On Christmas Eve in a night of rain, sleet, and snow, the Americans, many without shoes, boarded boats and crossed the Delaware in three places. One element would block enemy reinforcements, one would block the enemy escape route, and the third, the major force under Washington, would make the main attack. Light field pieces were brought to support the attack. Some 600 men of the approximately 1,900 who were to block any attack on Washington made the crossing. Cadwalder then had difficulty getting his artillery across. Despite a near mutiny from his men who wanted to fight, he took them back across the river.

In Trenton, the well-supplied Hessians were celebrating Christmas with food and drink. Rall was playing cards, and a note was delivered by a stranger. Without reading it, he put it in his pocket and played until bedtime.

The rain ruined powder charges for the muskets. Unable to fire, most Americans fixed bayonets. It was about 8:00 A.M. when the Hessian pickets saw the Americans upon them. The Americans charged, and the Germans retreated into Trenton. Rall was awakened and began to form his troops. The Americans enveloped the Germans and positioned their artillery to maximum effect. As the Hessians fell back before the artillery, the Americans struck them in the flank. On reaching the town, some Americans occupied the houses, dried their rifles and muskets, and made the streets uncomfortable for the Hessians. It continued to rain. In the streets when the two forces met, they battled with the bayonet.

Coming up from the south was General Sullivan's force, his advance guard under the command of Col. John Stark. With his usual audacity, Stark led a charge that drove in the Hessian pickets and fought his way into the lower part of Trenton. Capt. Eben Frye had Stark's lead company, and Frye had Sgt. Ephraim Stevens breaking down doors and bayoneting the Hessians inside. Sixteen of Frye's company ambushed and surprised a large number of Germans who, when they saw the ragged youths that had captured them, tried to regain their weapons. The rest of Captain Frye's company came up and completed the capture. Following Stark's men, Sullivan's main body came forward and routed a Hessian regiment. By nine o'clock, the battle was over. The Hessians had lost 22 killed, 98 wounded, and 948 captured, including 32 officers. Much-needed supplies were taken, including food and clothing, wagons, horses, muskets, and six cannon. Colonel Rall died of his wounds. The note found in his pocket read that the Americans were marching against him.

The Germans, who had been manning the river posts, quickly withdrew. Three Americans froze to death on the withdrawal, and more than 1,000 were too sick for duty on return to camp. Stark took the opportunity to ask his men to reenlist. He told them of all that had been sacrificed and asked them to reenlist for six weeks. These were men who had known suffering as few have known it, but not a man refused. Stark remained with Washington through the Battle of Princeton, and when the American army went into winter quarters and the enlistments of his men expired, Stark returned to New Hampshire and the business of recruiting another regiment.

When the British left Boston, Col. John Stark, with the 5th and 25th Regiments under his command, departed for New York to assist in developing its defenses. In May 1776, he took five regiments north through Albany to Canada to support an army that was unsuccessfully trying to secure Quebec. When Sullivan decided to attack Trios Rivieres, Stark protested. He knew the objective was on the opposite side of nearly ten miles of water controlled by British vessels. Sullivan went ahead with his plan, and the Americans were soundly defeated, with Gen. William Thompson taken prisoner.

Smallpox raged through the army. When withdrawal was necessary, it was Col. John Stark who commanded the rear guard. None of the Americans or their equipment was lost, and the pursuing British found nothing but burned buildings. Sullivan wanted to abandon Fort Ticonderoga, but Stark bluntly told his commander that the fort controlled a key approach and should not be abandoned. Sullivan and other commanders were finding that John Stark spoke his mind. Stark is reputed to have later told Washington that if he wanted to win, he had to get his men out from behind emplacements and get them to trust in their own weapons and courage. As an aggressive commander, Washington had no fault with that, but others did. Some generals and members of Congress thought that John Stark was insubordinate and too outspoken to be a general. This image would plague him throughout the war and hinder his advancement. Stark resigned and went home.

Now the British searched for one of their best officers to crush the Americans. British Gen. John Burgoyne had a flair for life. Though his family name was that of an obscure captain who gambled his way into debtors prison, young John was believed to be the bastard son of an English lord who took good care of John's mother and John. Being a bastard was not harmful if one had the right connections, which John had, along with looks, courage, and a flair for the dramatic—all useful tools for a soldier. He proved an innovative officer who had introduced light cavalry units to the British Army. Though he had little combat experience, he distinguished himself in limited fighting against the Spanish in Portugal. Unusual for his army at this time, he treated his men with kindness and earned the nickname Gentleman Johnnie. He was an enthusiastic but indifferent playwright and a gambler. Burgoyne had watched earlier actions in the war and returned to England to consult with King George and Lord Germain. He had a plan that would split the American colonies in two.

The Hudson River was the avenue of approach, and Albany was the key objective. Burgoyne would strike southward from Canada down the Hudson while Howe's army would attack north from New York. Barry St. Leger would move another column in from the northwest, all aiming at Albany on the Hudson. When the armies united,

New England would be cut off from the rest of the colonies, while the northern interior would strangle for want of supples. Travel overland posed enormous difficulty, but the Hudson River was a watery road that would allow heavy artillery and supplies to keep abreast.

In June 1777, Burgoyne began moving south from Canada toward Albany. His force consisted of 8,500 men, including British, German mercenaries, Tories, and a few Indians. A thousand camp followers tramped along. His land and ship artillery numbered 138 guns, and he had nearly thirty gunboats and bateaux to transport troops and supplies. Burgoyne's army moved in two columns, the right wing with 3,700 British and the left with more than 3,000 Germans. They were screened to the front by 700 Canadians, Tories, and Indians. The route of approach was generally down the west bank of the Hudson. Burgoyne's army was short of horses and transport. Ever the playwright, Burgoyne preceded his attack with a badly written document that told the Americans that he could turn several thousand Indians loose on them (though he had only 400). Meanwhile, he was telling his Indians to fight a sanitary war, killing only soldiers, not women, children, or the aged. The effect of his words was to anger the Americans, disaffect the Indians, and make him an object of ridicule among the British.

In August 1777, the drums of war rolled in the Mohawk Valley of New York. Americans were fighting a stubborn battle to hold Fort Stanwix against Barry St. Leger's British, Hessians, Tories, and Indians. A militia relief force under General Herkimer fought a desperate battle that was neighbor against neighbor, brother against brother. Both sides were so badly hurt that they withdrew.

As Burgoyne moved south, the Americans gave way before him. Along the upper Hudson River, Burgoyne decided to launch a raid to strip the countryside of supplies and badly needed horses. His force would be 800 primarily dismounted dragoons and grenadiers from Brunswick under Lt. Col. Frederich Baum. The Germans were disciplined soldiers, but their boots and sabers alone weighed more than a British soldier's heavy pack. The English and the Germans faced a great language barrier. Burgoyne wrote Baum a 2.5-page order that spelled out the route he was to take, what to do if he encountered resistance, and what he should bring back. Horses were in critical supply. Burgoyne wanted enough horses to mount Baum's troops and 1,300 extra for the needs of the rest of his army. Each of Baum's men was to carry bridles and tie ropes to lead ten horses. To the front and flanks of the raiders was a screen of British light infantry, Tories, and Indians. The Indians roamed to the front, killing any cattle they found. American farmers rounded up their livestock and fled. Baum wanted an independent command; he had difficulty understanding his commanders' orders, found them unreasonable, and at the last moment learned that his objective was changed.

Burgoyne had been told that the Americans had a large cache of supplies at the town of Bennington. Over the strenuous objections of Baum's commander, Baron von Ridesel, Burgoyne insisted Baum proceed to Bennington.

The land west of New Hampshire—the home of the Green Mountain Boys—had been claimed by that state and New York; in 1777, the area announced that it now belonged to Vermont. John Stark had left the army after the Battle of Princeton. He went home to recruit but became disgusted with the politics of the Congress and their inability or unwillingness to supply the fighting men. He was undoubtedly angry because while he was fighting and winning, those who were doing less were being promoted over him. Now Baum's raiders threatened Vermont and New Hampshire, and Stark could not sit by. John Langdon, the speaker of the General Court, had pledged all his worldly goods to raise an American force of 2,000 men. Most of them were farmer-militia, but among them were Capt. Ebenezer Allen's company from Herrick's Rangers.

Ethan Allen was now a prisoner of the British, and Col. Seth Warner had been made a Continental officer. The Council of Safety of Vermont had appointed Samuel Herrick of Bennington commandant of Vermont's Regiment of Rangers on July 15, 1777.[12] His men of Ebenezer Allen's Ranger company were scouting Baum's raiding force.

Eager for a fight, Stark took command of this small New England army. He did so, making it clear that he would take no orders from the Congress or the Continental Army. General Schuyler, whom Stark despised, ordered Stark to join him with his men. Stark refused, and proceedings were started against him by Congress.

As local militia moved to join him, Stark marched northwest to block Baum's approach. Four miles west of Bennington, the opposing forces sighted each other. With a river and a bridge between him and the Germans, Stark put his men in position to deny Bennington

Phillip Schuyler.
NATIONAL ARCHIVES

to Baum. Recognizing that he faced an increasing number of American muskets, the German commander dug his men in near the bridge and on a hill about half a mile distant. Stark decided to pin Baum on the hill and divided his force to surround the German positions. His plan was to hit the Germans from the rear and flanks and quickly follow with a decisive frontal attack. Samuel Herrick, with three companies of his Rangers, was now on the scene. Stark decided to send Colonel Nichols of New Hampshire with 200 men to attack Baum's left. This route was through heavy woods that would make observation by Baum difficult. Herrick's Rangers would approach from the right. His route required travel through open pastures and cornfields, bottom land beside the river. Herrick knew his men would be seen from Baum's position and decided on a ruse. He instructed his men to move in small groups to appear as scattered militia either trying to get home or coming to Baum's assistance.[13] On August 16, 1777, the battle began.

To suit their own purposes of revenge and loot, Skene and other Tories had incorrectly advised Baum that most of the locals favored the king. When the German officer saw men in rough garb coming into his rear and flanks, he thought they were supporting him. The Americans quickly disabused him by opening a hot fire. With the first part of his plan successful, John Stark leaped on his horse and rode

John Burgoyne.
NATIONAL ARCHIVES

to the front of his men. "There they are!" he cried, pointing at the enemy. "The British and the Tories. Tonight our flag flies over yonder hill or Molly Stark sleeps a widow."

The American attack routed their opponents at and around the bridge. Only the Germans dug in on the high ground held out. The battle for the hill was desperate. Stark, who had been in many engagements, said, "It lasted about two hours, and was the hottest engagement I have ever witnessed, resembling a continual clap of thunder." Creeping close and firing from behind rocks and trees, the Americans poured a heavy fire on the Germans, who responded with musketry and cannon fire. Nearly out of ammunition, Baum called on his men to draw their swords and cut their way out. Without bayonets, the Americans swarmed around them firing until Colonel Baum was mortally wounded. The Germans then surrendered.

Prior to the action, Baum, seeing that he was strongly opposed, had managed to send a courier to Burgoyne asking for reinforcements. Burgoyne sent Lieutenant Colonel Breyman with 642 men and two cannon. An advocate of precision formations, Breyman moved slowly, insisting that his men march in formation as he felt good soldiers should. This was fortunate for the Americans who were scattered, chasing fleeing Germans and taking weapons, equipment, and whatever loot they could find.

A series of skirmishes began between Americans and Breyman's advance guard. In timely fashion, Lt. Col. Samuel Safford arrived to assist Stark, bringing 200 Rangers and 130 Continentals. They moved forward and engaged Breyman. Stark gathered his force and joined the fight. The fight was vicious, with both sides trying flanking movements, then settling for a toe-to-toe slugging match. German artillery gave the Americans problems, but the Americans worked in close, killed the horses that drew the cannon, then picked off the gunners. Running low on ammunition, Breyman tried to retreat. The Americans had no shortage of ammunition and turned the German retreat into a rout. Breyman tried to surrender, having his drums sound a call for talks. The sound was not understood by the Americans, who continued killing Germans. Running, falling to their knees, and begging for mercy, the Germans lost all pretense of discipline. Only darkness saved those who did escape, including the wounded Colonel Breyman.

It was a stunning victory. At a loss of 30 killed and 40 wounded, John Stark's men had killed 207 Germans and captured 30 officers, more than 650 men, four cannons, and hundreds of muskets and swords. Singled out for special treatment were 152 Tories of the region. The housewives of Bennington took the cords from their beds. These were used to tie the Tories in pairs and lead them off behind horses.

Though small, the Battle of Bennington seriously weakened General Burgoyne's plans and set the stage for the American efforts at Saratoga. Congress forgot about efforts to discipline Ranger John Stark. They voted him thanks and made him a brigadier general.

Paroled and exchanged by his British captors, Morgan had returned to battle. With a stroke of a quill, he passed from captain to colonel, being commissioned colonel of the 11th Virginia Regiment on November 12, 1776. Recruiting 100 riflemen, Morgan headed for Morristown, New Jersey, to join the Continental Army. George Washington had a high regard for Morgan. In April 1777, Washington picked 500 riflemen from the various commands and placed them under Morgan's leadership. Morgan's second in command was Lt. Col. Richard "Dickie" Butler from Lancaster and Carlisle, Pennsylvania. Butler had been an officer with Colonel Bouquet in Pontiac's War. He was one of five warrior brothers known as the "fighting Butlers." Washington described Morgan's organization as "the corps of

Rangers, newly formed." Though frequently known as Morgan's Virginians, 337 of the 500 men were from Pennsylvania. They were superb fighters who had been recruited from the Cumberland Valley and the area of the west branch of the Susquehanna River. Many had seen service with the 1st and 8th Pennsylvania Regiments.[14]

Gen. Philip Schuyler, commander of the American forces facing Burgoyne, fought a delaying action while he sought reinforcements. In particular, Schuyler wanted Morgan's Rangers. Morgan and an estimated 330 Rangers were dispatched from Washington's army in New Jersey. The Rangers would be backed up by John Stark's former captain, Henry Dearborn. Under the command of Morgan, Dearborn would compliment the Rangers with 250 light infantry armed with muskets and the all-important bayonet. Also sent were several infantry brigades. Schuyler was from New York and distrusted by the New Englanders, so Washington sent two subordinate New England generals, the hard-fighting Benedict Arnold and Benjamin Lincoln. Though each retreat weakened their morale, the Americans were drawing Burgoyne farther from his base of supply. Not having sufficient boats to transport his entire force, Burgoyne sent his artillery and heavy stores by water on Lake George while marching his troops overland. The Americans had 1,000 men with axes obstructing his way by felling trees over trails and rolling boulders into streams.

On August 4, 1777, Congress replaced Schuyler with Gen. Horatio Gates, unjustly blaming Schuyler for the loss of Fort Ticonderoga and feeling pressure from New England. Gates had been born in England of working-class parentage. It was said he fought for the Americans because of his jealous hatred of the British class system, a system that looked with disdain on those considered low born. His reputation has few defenders and, among historians, borders on universal dislike.

Gates was not without his strengths. He understood public opinion and how to use it. When Burgoyne's Indians murdered and scalped young Jenny McCrea, the fiancée of a Tory officer, Gates wrote Burgoyne a letter accusing him of being responsible for such outrages by hiring the "savages of America." Burgoyne was hindered in taking action against the murderers, as his efforts to restrict their blood-letting angered them and caused them to drift away. As action approached, he had fewer than fifty Indians—insufficient to serve as his eyes and ears.

Horatio Gates.
NATIONAL ARCHIVES

Gates cleverly published his letter, and the subsequent anger at the McCrea atrocity brought a flood of armed militia to his army.

Often called the turning point of the war, the Battle of Saratoga was the Gettysburg of the Revolution. It was divided into two actions: Freeman's Farm on September 19 and Bemis Heights on October 7.

Shaking off an operational paralysis caused by Stark's victory at Bennington, Burgoyne resumed his offensive, but the delay had allowed American reinforcements to arrive. They had been digging for a week, and now an American army of 7,000 men was entrenched on high ground along the Hudson River, known as Bemis Heights. Remembering Breed's Hill, Gates was content to let the British take the offense.

Burgoyne moved to the attack in three columns. Burgoyne accompanied the center column of 1,100 men. An equal force under the astute German commander Riedesel moved on the left, and Gen. Simon Fraser was leading 2,200 on an envelopment on the right. Fraser was moving toward open farmland owned by a Loyalist who had fled north by the name of Freeman. The hope was that the Americans would come out and attack one of the columns and the others would then strike the Americans in the flank. Burgoyne's center column anticipated a link-up with Fraser. The morning fog lifted, and at eleven o'clock, the British began movement. The terrain was wooded and uneven. The separated British columns frequently lost contact with each other.

For three hours, Ranger scouts in treetops had observed the British movement and reported it, yet Gates did nothing. To the Americans, it was obvious that the British columns were so widely separated that they could not support each other. The aggressive Benedict Arnold was vehemently urging Gates to attack, but Gates would not. Arnold stormed and raged. At length, Gates agreed to send out Morgan's Rangers and Dearborn's light infantry with Arnold's division in support.

Morgan, moving behind his men and controlling them by the turkey calls used on the frontier, moved forward. Burgoyne's center column had come to Freeman's cabin when the Rangers took them under a devastating fire. All the officers in Burgoyne's advance guard were shot down, and many other soldiers of the advance guard fled. At this point, Morgan lost control of his men, who went into a headlong charge after the fleeing British. Stricken with panic, the Redcoats ran into their main body, causing great confusion, with British units firing at each other. Led by Lt. Col. Richard Butler and Major Morris, the jubilant Rangers plunged into Burgoyne's column, where the Rangers were met by volley fire and were hit in the flank by a Tory force. Morgan was in despair; he had lost control of his men and thought disaster was at hand. "I am ruined, by God," he told an officer. "My men are scattered, God knows where!" His fears were premature. Some of his officers and men had been killed, but the rest had taken cover, kept up the fire, and reassembled at the sound of his turkey call.

Burgoyne began to move forward, with the American Rangers executing a fighting withdrawal. Reaching the cleared land of Freeman's farm, Burgoyne found that the men of Morgan and Dearborn were in the woods on the other side. Seven American regiments had joined them, and Benedict Arnold was in command of this advance force. Both American and British sought to capitalize on their positions. For nearly four hours, a see-saw battle raged. As the British formations advanced across open ground for volley fire, the Americans shot them down and forced them back to their woods. As the Americans advanced, British artillery or volley fire hammered them. The Americans captured the British field pieces but could not use them since the gunners had taken away the slow matches with which the guns were fired. The British soon recaptured them. Some guns changed hands five times.

With Burgoyne's center column in desperate circumstance, the Germans under Riedesel came to their assistance with 500 men and two guns. Arnold had ridden back to the main line to get reinforcements from Gates, who, for his own reasons, kept him there. Thus, at this critical time, Arnold's battle skills were not where they were needed. Gates sent forward a brigade under Colonel Learned, but it was uncertain where it was going and made an ineffectual attack on Fraser's force.

Riedesel committed several companies to the American right flank and moved to join Burgoyne. The German drums sounding on their flank concerned the Americans. As evening came, they began to withdraw. Fraser was too distant to be a factor in this battle. Burgoyne had won the ground, but the price was high. He had 800 men engaged and lost 600. His 62nd Regiment began the fight with 350 men and came out of it with 60 effectives. Gates had let numerous opportunities slip. From Bemis Heights, the German flank and Burgoyne's lightly guarded supply train could be clearly seen. An aggressive commander would have seized these opportunities. Benedict Arnold wanted to attack, but the passive Gates would neither take nor allow the action. The Americans had 8 officers and 57 men killed; counting wounded and captured, a total of 319 Americans was removed from duty.

Burgoyne desired to attack promptly but listened to the advice of his subordinates. He was influenced by General Fraser, who felt the troops needed rest. Burgoyne dallied, giving his men time to relax and regroup while awaiting help from British General Clinton's force he thought was moving up the Hudson. Clinton had no orders from Howe to come to Burgoyne's assistance, only some vague conjectures. He had not heard from Howe for weeks. Clinton had made a raid up the Hudson and captured two American forts, but that was as far as he would go. Burgoyne's hope for assistance would not come. His attempts at reconnaissance were thwartedm and Ranger marksmen kept up a constant peppering of British positions. British nerves were frayed from the constant harassment. Rangers moved close to the British lines and, sniping from treetops, killed dozens of British. Other Americans scoured the countryside to deprive the British of food. Burgoyne's men were critically short on supplies, rations were drastically cut, and animals were starving. Desertions were rising. The Americans were growing in strength and were freshly resupplied. Both armies remained in position until October 7; this was far more detrimental to the British, who were operating over a 185 mile supply line and were exhausting food supplies which they could not replace. Still lacking information on the American positions, Burgoyne planned a reconnaissance in force with 2,100 men, including 1,500 regulars. Burgoyne hoped to learn if the American left could be successfully attacked. If the position was too strong, the British would retreat.

At about 10:30 on October 7, the British advanced in three columns with ten cannon. The British took up a position that allowed them some field-glass observation of the American lines while foragers worked a wheat field to provide desperately needed food for their animals. The ground to their front was open. There was little chance the Americans would attack over it into the cannon's mouth.

From Bemis Heights, the Americans could see opportunity developing. While the British front was cleared area, their flanks offered the cover of woods. Morgan proposed taking his Rangers to strike the British right flank. It was also decided to send Poor's brigade to hit Burgoyne's left. Poor's men of New York, New Hampshire, and Connecticut were first in position, and in mid-afternoon, they opened fire. The British were firing downhill and aiming high. When they attempted a bayonet charge, the Americans met them with a withering volley fire.

Meanwhile, Morgan's Rangers had hit the British right flank. Driving in the security, they struck the British light infantry under the command of Balcarres. The British tried to change front and use the bayonet, but the Americans had learned their lesson well. The British charge met Henry Dearborn's light infantry, who gave them volley fire and a return dose of the bayonet. The British were routed. A British officer attempting to spread Burgoyne's order to withdraw was wounded and captured, leaving the Germans unaware of the order.

Arnold, who had so disturbed Gates that he had been relieved, rode on his own into battle. Gates raged in futility and sent messengers attempting to call Arnold back.

Some historians believe Arnold saw British Gen. Simon Fraser gallantly rallying the British and told Morgan to dispose of him; others claim that Morgan acted on his own. It is certain that Morgan ordered several Ranger marksmen to concentrate their fire on Fraser. Rangers were firing from positions in treetops. With bullets clipping his uniform and saddle, Fraser knew he had been marked for death, but he would not shirk his duty. One of the snipers was Tim Murphy, a Pennsylvania Ranger who reportedly carried a double-barreled rifle.

Tim Murphy is generally credited with the shot that mortally wounded Fraser. He had been one of the Northumberland Rifle Company of Capt. John Lowden, who made the original march to Boston in 1775. Murphy was from the vicinity of present-day Sunbury, Pennsylvania. He had come to war with other noted frontier Rangers, including Peter Pence and Samuel Brady.

Col. Ebenezer Learned's crack Continental Brigade pitched into the fray, and the British were driven back to their main line. With many commanders, it would have been enough to drive them back, but Arnold was relentless. He galloped from point to point, his courage inspiring men to attack the British lines. He led an attack that opened the flank of the German position, then rounded up other troops and led them to drive out the Germans. When his men began to run, Bremann, the German commander, killed four of his own men with his saber. Angered by this, another of his men shot and killed him.

Burgoyne's army was defeated. Arnold was down, shot in the same leg that had taken a bullet at Quebec. To him belonged credit for the victory, but he would not get it. Horatio Gates, who sat in his trenches, received the laurels for the victory. Burgoyne attempted to withdraw, the American following and hemming him in on three sides. Burgoyne and his officers were discussing making a night withdrawal, but before it could begin, Ranger John Stark arrived on the battlefield. John Stark had an uncanny ability to be at the right place at the right time. With 1,100 men, John Stark closed the last route of escape for Burgoyne. The Americans closed in on the British and hammered them relentlessly. Desperate, Burgoyne sought terms of surrender.

Gates now compounded his inefficiency by allowing Burgoyne to persuade him that the British would surrender by "convention" rather than capitulation. Thus, the British were not prisoners of war, just men who agreed not to fight in North America. Gates and Burgoyne dined. Burgoyne's sword was returned by Gates with a promise to defend Burgoyne's reputation. The victorious Americans were to pay for the rations for the defeated British to wherever they were marching in order to take ship to England. Rations also ahd to be provided for the Canadians to return home. No American soldier was permitted to watch the British lay down their weapons. The Indians, so despised by the Americans, were allowed to walk by friends and relatives of their victims. Depending on the view of the audience, this surrender was the greatest comedy or tragedy that the would-be playwright John Burgoyne would ever stage.

At Saratoga, a British force of 306 officers and 5,422 men had been swept from the board. The army included two lieutenant generals, two major generals, and three brigadier generals. Great stores of equipment were seized, including 5,000 stands of arms and 30 cannon. It was a monumental victory. Throughout New York and New England, the British recoiled into safe haven.

Joseph Brant, a full-blooded Mohawk, was ravaging the nothern frontier at the head of 150 Indians and 300 Tories, striking when and where they wished. John Stark would twice command the Northern Department and seek to eliminate enemy actions. In 1778, Stark sought to protect the population of New York and New England and said a company of "good Rangers" could be more effective at the work than a regiment of militia against the Tories and Indians. He stressed the importance of raids, telling the New York Rangers to "go into the enemy's country and serve them as they have served you."

One of the most successful of Stark's Rangers was Maj. Benjamin Whitcomb. He was born in what is now Leominster, Massachusetts, on July 2, 1737. During the French and Indian War, he participated in Johnson's expedition against Crown Point, the Battle of Lake George in September of 1755, and the Amhearst expedition against Montreal. Ending the war as a lieutenant, Whitcomb married and, after several moves, settled in Vermont. In the Revolutionary War, he was a Ranger lieutenant in the terrain between Fort Ticonderoga and Montreal. A letter to Stark described Whitcomb as "an unlettered child of the woods." With all the forest skills of an Indian and a dauntless heart, Whitcomb proposed and carried out audacious patrols. Claiming he would bring back a British officer as prisoner, Whitcomb and one other man set out to move deep in enemy territory. In the forest, the other man disappeared. Whitcomb continued on. He moved down the west side of Lake Champlain, passed St. John's, and approached the stone fort of Chambly to the east of Montreal. Moving silently, Whitcomb passed the ring of sentry posts outside the fort. An alert sentry suspected movement and turned out the guard. Surrounded in a field of knee-high grass, Whitcomb covered himself with twigs and grass and remained motionless for a day while British troops searched within six feet of him and an officer almost rode over him. The British were cutting the grass and had come within twenty feet when they stopped for the night. Whitcomb crept away and took a position near the road from Chambly to St. John's, awaiting a chance to capture an officer. To his misfortune, British Brigadier General Gordon chose to take a morning ride. Dressed in the splendor of his uniform, mounted on a spirited horse, and accompanied by two of his officers, Gordon rode past Whitcomb. The horses were moving too fast for Whitcomb to make the capture. His shot hit Gordon under the right shoulder blade. Gordon wheeled and galloped for his fort but died soon after.

The British learned that Whitcomb had killed General Gordon and put a dead-or-alive reward of fifty guineas on his head, the highest reward offered during the war. Ordered by Gates to bring back a prisoner, Whitcomb promptly set out again. This time, he captured a British corporal and Alexander Saunders, a well-armed and powerful British quartermaster officer of the 29th Regiment. For his heroic feats, Whitcomb was promoted to captain-commandant and ordered to recruit two fifty-man Ranger companies. These were in the field by the spring of 1777 and struck hard at the Loyalists and Indians.

Some Tory units would disguise themselves as Indians and raid, loot, and murder in the settlements. Stark had no mercy on these people. He told his leaders: "If your scouts should be fortunate enough to fall in with any more of these painted scoundrels, I think it not worth the trouble to send them to me. Your wisdom and your scouts may direct you in that matter." Occasionally, Stark's men sent him battle trophies. A Ranger under Captain Long shot Tory leader Charles Smith and sent Smith's scalp to Stark.

Stark was one of thirteen general officers who tried and convicted British spy Maj. John Andre. Stark's grandson said that six voted for shooting and six for hanging. General Greene cast the deciding vote for hanging. In 1781, Stark, still a brigadier general, was asked by Washington to again command the Northern Department.

Toward the end of the Revolutionary War, Ranger John Stark was promoted to brevet major general. He was one of the forty-four officers invited by George Washington to be present at Fraunces Tavern in New York City for the commander's farewell. That touching ceremony also ended Stark's life as a soldier. In 1783, American officers of the Revolution founded the Society of the Cincinnati. It was an association named after the experience of the Roman Lucius Quintius Cincinnatus, who twice left his farm to save Rome and twice returned to it when the danger was passed. Stark would not join, preferring to put the associations of war behind him.

He returned to his farm and his sawmill. A valiant leader during the French and Indian War, an American with every breath he took, John Stark was a hero of the Battle of Bunker (Breed's) Hill, victor of Bennington, and a significant contributor to American success at Saratoga and Trenton.

John Stark's piercing blue eyes closed in death on May 8, 1822, at the age of ninety-three. He was a crusty, acerbic old warrior to the end. In 1809, he had been invited to attend a reunion of men who fought in the Battle of Bennington. Stark was ill at the time, but he sent a toast to his old comrades that became famous: "Live free or die. Death is not the worst of evils."

CHAPTER 11

George Rogers Clark Captures the West

The British victory in the French and Indian War and the subsequent rebellion of Americans against the British created a mix of loyalties and inevitable conflict in the west. The colonies from New York to Georgia contained less land than they do now as states. The Appalachian Mountains represented a line determined by the English in 1763 as the western boundary for settlement. Beyond these blue hills was Indian country, but the French traders had been there for generations and had small settlements. These were tolerated, as the Indians had developed a need for manufactured goods and the French did not seek to colonize. With the British victory, little changed. Though the British now ruled America and had plans for the future, they were busy elsewhere and exercised nominal control in the west. American-born French in the west were restless in compulsory service under the British flag. The Americans did not see the Appalachians as a barrier and ignored the royal decree as enterprising settlers pushed westward into Kentucky. The colonies were rivals long before they united, and most tried to expand their territory. An angry British parliament sought to punish the Americans for a variety of perceived transgressions by extending the border of Quebec south to the Ohio River, depriving Americans of much lucrative trade in furs. The power in this giant land from the Appalachians to the Mississippi and from the Great Lakes to the Gulf of Mexico was the Indians. The British unleashed these savage warriors in a wave of terror on the frontier by bribing them with supplies the Americans could not furnish. In the west, the British sought to contain, the Americans to expand, the Indians to keep their land, and the French to cut the best deal possible with the victor.

George Rogers Clark Captures the West

West of the Mississippi was the giant land called Louisiana, which stretched from Canada to the Gulf of Mexico. In 1762, by the Treaty of Fontainebleau, France had ceded this territory to Spain. Though Spanish power had declined, they had a headquarters at St. Louis from which they quietly looked for advantage. It was a situation ready for a man of audacity to capitalize on.

Such a man was found in George Rogers Clark. As a red-haired youth, he stood six feet tall. In the Revolutionary War, his shadow would encompass all the land from Kentucky to the Great Lakes and west to the Mississippi River.

Clark was born near the Blue Ridge Mountains, just east of Charlottesville, Virginia, on November 19, 1752. His birthplace was very close to that of Thomas Jefferson, and these two great men would come to know each other well. Clark came from a home of moderate means, and though his education was of the frontier, his thinking and expression was that of a leader of men. As a teenager, Clark learned the trade of surveyor, and at age nineteen, he went west. He survived by also becoming an accomplished woodsman.

Going west violated a British royal decree, but enterprising Americans, some boldly taking families with them, were eager to take the risks. They came by way of western Pennsylvania to present-day West Virginia or through the Cumberland Gap and along Daniel Boone's Wilderness Trail to the land called Kentucky. They moved west to this land of plenty, and many of them died from Indian attacks or fled eastward again. Only the strongest could endure.

Indian terror was ever present. The Shawnee were a southern tribe that migrated north, then had been driven from the Ohio and Cumberland Valleys by the Iroquois. After a time in western Pennsylvania, they occupied Kentucky and were allied to the Miami and Illinois. The Cherokee were one of the largest tribes. Their land encompassed Alabama, the Carolinas, Kentucky, Tennessee, and Georgia. The Chickasaw may have begun in Mexico, but they also claimed vast lands in the southeast. The Indian tribes formed alliances as they fought each other for control of the land. As individual tribes and in alliance, they fought the migration of the Americans to the west.

The fear of Indians was such that as the independence year of 1776 dawned, there were only 200 settlers living in Kentucky. They

George Rogers Clark's march against Vincennes.
NATIONAL ARCHIVES

were scattered among five settlements, one of which was Daniel Boone's holding at Boonesborough. Clark became a leader among these settlers. During Lord Dunmore's War, he commanded a militia company. After the Indians were beaten at the Battle of Point Pleasant, Clark had a role in arranging the treaty which opened the Ohio River to unmolested traffic. Despite the treaty, relations with the Indians were uncertain. Kentucky remained a difficult and dangerous place to live.

Clark knew that Kentucky needed the support of Virginia, and Virginia saw Kentucky as an expansion of its territory. Virginia had ousted the royal governor, the Earl of Dunmore. Patrick Henry now served as American governor, and Clark represented Kentucky's interest to him. The new western land was made a Virginia county on December 7, 1776. In return, Kentucky got 500 pounds of gunpowder without which the settlements could not have survived. The powder was to be provided from Fort Pitt.

The Indians learned of Clark's mission and pursued him as he floated the powder down the Ohio River. With the Indians closing in, Clark hid the gunpowder in several locations ashore. Clark and his party continued down river, then confused the Indians about the location of the powder by abandoning their boats. Tracked overland by Indian warriors, several of Clark's party were killed or captured, but the location of the powder was not revealed. Clark was unable to make a prompt return for the powder, as he was at a frontier post under heavy attack by Indians. A party of experienced Rangers went after the powder and were killed or captured by the Indians. A second group that included the frontier hero Simon Kenton retrieved the much-needed supplies.

As war raged in the east, Clark knew the Kentucky frontier must look to itself for protection. The linchpin of American defense in the west was at Fort Pitt, 300 miles away. There were 200 miles of mountain trail to Virginia and over 5,000 Indian warriors. The fierce Shawnee and Cherokee could interdict travel at any place en route. Indian attacks were frequent. By 1777, only the settlements at Boonesborough and Harrodsburg remained in Kentucky. George Rogers Clark and the few men and women of the Kentucky frontier made the perilous choice to fight, and the odds were not in their favor. Now a Virginia major and senior American officer in the area, Clark knew he did not have sufficient strength to defend. Undeterred by his difficulties, Clark conceived an audacious plan to attack.

Clark's English opponent was Lt. Gov. Henry Hamilton, who was headquartered at Detroit. Hamilton was of Scottish descent from an established family of means. He was commissioned in the 15th Foot at age twenty-one, came to America in 1758, and was wounded in the taking of the French fortress of Louisbourg. In 1760, he was taken prisoner by the French, who had to dress him in a French uniform to save him from the Indians. Hamilton watched others being tortured and knew full well what the Indians were capable of. He became lieutenant governor of Detroit on April 7, 1775.

Hamilton was intended to be one of four British lieutenant governors who would be stationed at Detroit, Vincennes, Kaskaskia, and Michilimackinac. For various reasons, the other three did not take their posts, and Hamilton inherited total responsibility with limited resources. That did not appear to be a problem as the English controlled Canada and the St. Lawrence seaway. By the Revolutionary

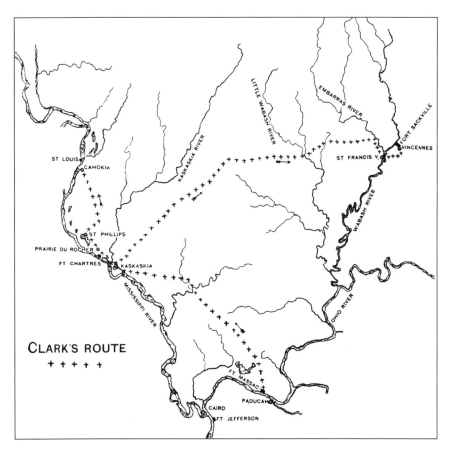

War, the Indian, were dependent on the whites for their new necessities of life. It was British policy to bribe the Indians with guns, powder, and supplies that the Americans could not furnish. A terror was unleashed on the American settlements that engendered a burning hatred. Hamilton was known as "the hair buyer." He would protest that he did not buy scalps, but the rewards he gave the Indians for scalps and captives amounted to a purchase of death.

Trying to make the best of his little force, Clark formed four small Ranger companies captained by Daniel Boone, Benjamin Logan, James Harrod, and John Todd. All of these men were experienced Indian fighters who could range the land. Clark dispatched Rangers Benjamin Linn and Samuel Moore to make a reconnaissance of the Illinois country.

Clark knew that from the early 1700s, the French had sought to control the Mississippi Valley and the tributaries that fed this great river. The mighty Ohio and the Illinois, Miami, Wabash, and White Rivers were water highways to the wealth of the interior. Rivalry between French factions had led to competing efforts to move south from Canada and the Great Lakes and north from Louisiana. The result was a French line of forts and settlements on the Mississippi that extended from Detroit to New Orleans. Though France had recently lost the New World, most of the French inhabitants of these posts remained behind, living under English rule. Detroit was the door to the northwest, critical for contact with western tribes and the trade in furs. From Detroit, the Maumee River trail and the Upper Wabash led to Vincennes on the Wabash River, 102 miles southwest of present-day Indianapolis; another extended to Kaskaskia and other French settlements on the Mississippi River south of St. Louis. These posts were in a strategic location for control of river traffic between Detroit and New Orleans.

In a courageous reconnaissance, Rangers Linn and Moore traveled hundreds of miles. They posed as wandering fur traders and trappers and moved among the small and scattered former French settlements of the frontier. Their report to Clark confirmed his opinion that it was better to attack than defend. Confident that the Americans had no army in the area, the British looked upon Kentucky as a plum to be picked at their time of choosing. The British forces primarily consisted of French militia headed by a former French officer, Phillipe de Rocheblave.

Though it was considerably farther west than Vincennes, Clark decided to make Kaskaskia his first objective. The capture of Kaskaskia would impress the Indians, and it was close to Spanish St. Louis, which would open the fur trade of the west to Virginia. Clark did not reveal his plans to anyone on the frontier. He left Harrodsburg on October 1, 1777, to travel to the Virginia capital of Williamsburg to present his plan to Patrick Henry. In an age when travel was time-consuming and difficult, Clark pursued his objective. During the next seventeen months, he would travel over 2,500 miles by foot, horse, and boat.

Patrick Henry shared Clark's plan with Thomas Jefferson and George Mason; all agreed to support the enterprise. Clark was provided with 1,200 pounds, commissioned a Virginia lieutenant colonel, and authorized to raise troops. He was provided with two sets of orders.

The public set was to defend Kentucky from Indian and British attack. The secret orders authorized him to attack British holdings in the northwest.

Clark believed that 500 men would be sufficient to achieve his goal, but he meant to attack no matter the size of his force. Virginia would only provide the funds to pay 350. A few could be found among the twenty more families who took the risk of coming to Kentucky. Among them was William Linn, the brother of Clark's Ranger scout. Recruiting was slow. Those with families found it difficult to leave them to face probable Indian attack alone. Raising 150 men for his enterprise, Clark established an assembly area at the falls (rapids) of the Ohio at present-day Louisville, Kentucky. Twenty families accompanied Clark to the falls and began to establish a settlement. To hinder desertion, Clark located his men on the seven-acre Corn Island in the Ohio River. Here they were to be joined by major reinforcements, but scarcely more than a company arrived.

At Corn Island, Clark revealed his plan to the men. When they heard his intention to attack British forts, fifty men waded the shallows and deserted. Instead of the 500 men he wanted, Clark had only 178 Rangers left. Fortunately, they were skilled frontiersmen, accustomed to hardship and dedicated to taking revenge for the British-inspired savagery of the Indians. Clark knew he had the best men possible for the job. His company commanders—Joseph Bowman, William Harrod, Leonard Helm, and John Montgomery—were experienced men of proven courage. With boats at hand, Clark and his men rode the rapids on June 24, 1778. It was a time of total eclipse of the sun, and Clark recognized that darkness would cover his movement. He proclaimed it as a good omen. They continued on to the mouth of the Tennessee River, where they met American buffalo hunters who were recruited at rifle point. Less than two weeks before, the hunters had been at Kaskaskia and knew the military situation there. They told Clark that only French militia were on hand, but he could expect a fight. The British had told the French that if the Americans ever came, it would be to slaughter, rape, and pillage their community. While there, William Linn arrived in a canoe. He made the perilous journey to bring Clark a letter from the commander at Fort Pitt stating that the French had entered the war on the side of the Americans.

Clark and his men had covered 425 miles in four days by boating the river. Continuing by water increased the likelihood of discovery, and surprise was critical. Clark opted to hide his boats near the ruins of an old French fort and cover the last 120 miles on foot through wilderness terrain. One of the buffalo hunters knew the country and was encouraged to serve as guide.

It was uncharted country of thick wood, swamps, and stretches of high grassland. The hunter, a man named Saunders, became disoriented and took wrong turns. The expedition was in a critical circumstance. Food was almost exhausted. Clark was not a man to cross, and he suspected Saunders of leading them astray. Clark made it clear he would kill Saunders if the hunter's memory did not rapidly improve. This inspiration was sufficient for the path to be found. They traveled six days, the last two without food, and reached the shore of the Kaskaskia River across from the settlement of the same name as night fell on July 4, 1778.

Searching the riverside, the Rangers found sufficient boats to ferry them across the river to the sleeping town. The gates of the fort stood open and unguarded. Commandant Rocheblave and his wife were rousted from bed by the towering Simon Fraser while the lady protested the intrusion of her chamber.

As the dawn broke, terrified French citizens looked out upon the rugged band of Rangers. A cordon had been thrown around the town to prevent escape. The fearful people allowed their imaginations to run wild regarding their fate. Their priest, Father Pierre Gibault, came to plead for his parishioners. They were willing to do anything, even be slaves, if they would be spared. Clark let the tension grow to a high peak, then expressed amazement at their fears. He told the priest that the Americans were their friends who had come to rescue them from an uncaring English rule. The Rangers were there to protect the townspeople, preserve their goods and property, and respect their religion. The townspeople went wild with joy, rushing about and hugging each other. When Clark broke the news that America and France were now allies, the people were beside themselves with joy and rushed to take the oath of allegiance that Clark required.

Not everyone was pleased. Commandant Rocheblave was vociferous and began a campaign of vilification against the Americans. Rocheblave was sent to Virginia under guard. His property was sold and the money distributed among the Rangers.

Clark mounted Bowman's Ranger company on horseback and sent it off to take the other French towns at Cahokia, Prairie du

Rocher, and St. Phillipe, all of which quickly supported the Americans. Father Pierre Gibault had become an ardent supporter of Clark. At Clark's behest, the priest and another man gathered letters of praise from the inhabitants of Kaskaskia and traveled to Vincennes. He returned to report that the people of Vincennes now supported Clark and the American flag flew over this important post. Clark dispatched Captain Helm to take command at Vincennes. What had been accomplished seemed beyond reason. The gigantic Illinois country had been taken by audacity, without a shot being fired.

Clark left Kaskaskia to travel fifty miles north to St. Louis to establish relations with the Spanish. He succeeded on several levels. He became friends with the Spanish lieutenant governor, Fernando DeLeyba, and some believe became even friendlier with the governor's beautiful sister.

A critical part of Ranger George Rogers Clark's success was that he understood the art of deception in war. Clark had doubts, but he kept them well hidden and let audacity carry him through. His demeanor and actions were such that he always projected an assurance that he was in control of events. He made his enemy worry.

At Cahokia, south of St. Louis, he met with an assemblage of Indians. Clark was so vastly outnumbered that he and all whites with him could have been easily slaughtered. The Indians respected courage. They practiced and enjoyed dramatic oratory and Clark gave it to them. Clark belittled Indian strength. He accused the chiefs of being nothing but hirelings of the British and said he did not care if they remained so. He was ready to fight them. Clark haughtily told the chiefs that he was a man and a warrior and he knew how to treat friends and enemies. Though he had nothing but the men with him, Clark conjured up a large army he said he had prepared to bring west. He offered the chiefs the red belt of war or the white belt of peace and seemed uncaring as to their choice. Indian decisions were not hastily made. Clark gave them some provisions and rum to sustain them while they held council. He graciously told the Indians he would not harm them while they were his guests.

Many of the whites in attendance had sweaty palms as Clark tongue-lashed the Indian braves. To demonstrate he was not concerned, Clark did not stay at the fort but occupied a nearby house. The Indians were awed by his courage, not aware that Clark had fifty

Rangers concealed in the house. He staged a dance, and throughout the night, the Indians heard music and laughter.

Indians thought losing a war offered little profit and tended to gravitate to the winning side. Clark came away with the support of Indian tribes for hundreds of miles. His morale was lifted by the news that American forces under Gen. Lachlan McIntosh intended to leave Fort Pitt to attack Detroit.

As Clark celebrated his victories, Henry Hamilton set about undoing them. On August 6, 1778, forest messengers brought word of the American success to Hamilton in Detroit. Reports were dispatched to Governor Carleton in Quebec and Lord Germain in England. Frederick Haldimand, who had replaced Carleton as governor, urged prompt effort to recover the Illinois territory. Hamilton sent messages to his subordinate posts and war belts to Indian tribes encouraging them to rally to drive out the Americans. He organized militia companies, readied boats, and stocked supplies. On October 2, 1778, Lt. Gov. Henry Hamilton assembled his Indians and danced the war dance with them.

Hamilton's objective was Vincennes, but a third of the North American continent was at stake. The expedition left Detroit on October 7 with 162 white men and 70 Indians. More Indians joined the force en route, bringing its total to about 600 men supported by light artillery. The Indians included Huron, Ottawa, Chippewa, and Wabash. The whites were a mixed lot, including 3 officers and 30 men of the British Regular Army plus English and French militia officers and men.

Forced by circumstance and haste, Hamilton had recruited Frenchmen who did not feel great loyalty to England. Travel was difficult, and food included raccoon, turkey, and bear that were shot along the way. Hamilton stopped at various points to persuade the Miami, Shawnee, Cherokee, and Wyandot Indians to forego their new friendship with Clark and support the English. Again, Hamilton danced the war dance and gave gifts, urging the Indians to take up the hatchet. Some Indians changed sides; others would not. Hamilton was an effective diplomat as he brought together tribes that frequently warred against each other. Each day brought strange occurrences. An eclipse had Indians firing their weapons in the air to frighten away the manitou that was eating the moon. The Shawnee chief White Fish had an eye shot out by another Indian who was shooting at a turkey. Hamilton needed the Shawnee and was pleased that the only complaint White Fish had was that he lost his eye to a friend, not an enemy. The Shawnee stayed.[1] Hamilton was delighted to learn that only Captain Helm and another American were at Vincennes supervising French militia. Hamilton captured Helm's scouts and prevented messengers from getting through to Clark.

Hamilton's force reached Vincennes on December 17, 1778, and saw the American flag flying over the fort. Establishing a battle line with a 6-pounder cannon positioned to fire on the fort gate, Hamilton called on Captain Helm to surrender. The French militia promptly deserted the American cause. Helm, having only one other American with him, surrendered. Hamilton set about rebuilding the fort into an excellent defensive position.

Hamilton learned that his principal adversary was a man named George Rogers Clark. Knowing that most men stayed indoors in the harsh winter, Hamilton sent a raiding party of forty Indians and French to hunt Clark in his winter quarters. He gave them strict orders to bring back Clark as a prisoner. Heavy rains flooded the countryside, and the weather was turning ever colder. Hamilton decided to delay his recapture of Kaskaskia until spring.

At Kaskaskia, Clark learned that General McIntosh had not made a serious move on Detroit and that Hamilton had left his headquarters with a strong force. No information was coming from Vincennes, which meant the likelihood of its fall. Clark dispatched scouts to cover every trail on the 200 miles between Kaskaskia and Vincennes. The rains continued, with flooding throughout the land. Indians preferred not to fight in such weather. Clark reasoned that if Hamilton had Vincennes, he would stay there until spring.

Hamilton's patrol managed to put Clark in its gunsights as he traveled to Cahokia to discuss the situation with Captain Bowman, but Clark had a strong escort that would have prevented the American leader from being taken prisoner. The Indians passed up an opportunity to kill Clark and watched quietly as their quarry passed by.

Clark now knew that all his effort was in danger of coming unraveled. The momentum of war was now with Hamilton and the only way to get it back was to attack. From Kaskaskia, on February 23, 1779, Clark sent the following letter to Virginia's governor, Patrick Henry.

Dear Sir

As it is near twelve Months Since I have received the last Intelligence from you I almost Despair of any Relief of this Cuntry.

Being Sensible that without Rheinforcement (which I at present harly right to Expect) that I should be obliged to give up the Cuntrey to Mr. Hamilton. I am resolved to take advantage of the present Situation and risque the whole on a single Battle and Shall set out in a few Days with all the force I can Raise amounting only to one hundred and seventy and take only those with me that I know will Die by me.

If I fall through in this Expedition the whole cuntrey is lost and I believe Kentucky also. But great things have been Done by a few men well Conducted. Perhaps we may be fortunate. I have this consolation. I know that my party will never Quit me and Sensible that I shall be excused by you when you know my Reasons. I know the case is Desperate. If I was sure of a Reinforcement I should not attempt it.

I am Sir with the
greatest Respect your
Very Hbl. Servt.
GR Clark[2]

No one on this march was forced to go. The men who followed George Rogers Clark were volunteers. They were men who recognized that more than their lives were at stake. This enterprise would decide who would control the west. It would determine the safety and the welfare of their families and friends. It would shape the future.

They marched as four companies on February 5, 1779, taking with them pack horses to carry supplies. Included in the equipment were over two dozen flags of varying description. Ahead of them lay 240 miles of trackless waste, much of it under water or mired in mud. The rivers and streams were swollen, and the icy winds of winter howled about them. They continued for nine hours, but progress was slow and only three miles were covered. Their camp was shaped as a square with each of the companies occupying one corner and the baggage and pack horses in the middle. Three days later, they crossed a large, level plain that was under water. Despite the hardship, they maintained their high spirits. Along the way, they killed bison and feasted on the flesh. On February 13, they reached the branches of the Little Wabash River. The branches of the river had flooded into a single stream, three feet deep at the shallowest and five miles wide. Clark had canoes built to ferry men and supplies across. The other side was also under water, and a scaffolding was built to hold the supplies. As the days passed, the exhausted men found strength to laugh at the sight of their little drummer boy floating over water areas on his drum.

They crossed the River Embarras and searched a riverside farm for boats that would carry them across the swollen waters of the Wabash. On February 18, they heard the sound of the morning gun being fired from Vincennes. They were short of food now, but too close to Vincennes to fire weapons. Morale was dropping among the hungry men. To kill their gaunt pack horses would only increase their difficulty. Two days passed without food, but no boats had been found.

On the twentieth, they were making canoes when scouts captured a boat with five Frenchmen. The prisoners told them no one was aware of their coming. On February 21, they used two makeshift canoes to take the men and equipment across the Wabash. This required leaving the pack horses behind. Clark formed his ragged band on a small hill, but still faced three miles of travel over flooded land where water was often shoulder high. At six foot in height, Clark could negotiate deeper water than many of his men. Those who were in the worst straits were carried in the canoes. Clark kept a running commentary of encouragement. He joked and cajoled them, frequently saying that dry land was just ahead. It became a form of humor to the desperate men. They could hear the morning and evening guns fired by the unsuspecting Hamilton and knew that while they froze and hungered, the enemy was warm and well fed in their fort.

On February 23, they were within eyesight of Vincennes. Hunger and exhaustion were forgotten. Clark's men came from families who had lived and suffered under the terror of Indian attack. Many had lost loved ones to the tomahawk and scalping knife or burning at the stake. They knew that British policy was to encourage and reward the Indians for killing Americans of any sex or age. Now the time of retribution was at hand, and they were the instrument of revenge.

Knowing he was likely outnumbered and his enemy in a fortified position with cannon, Clark chose not to attack. He determined to weaken the enemy by desertion. Keeping his men out of sight, Clark sent a letter to the French inhabitants of Vincennes that he was going to attack with overwhelming force. When darkness fell, he moved his men among the houses of the settlement. To those peering out at shadows, it seemed he had a vast army. Just as Clark reasoned, the townspeople deserted Hamilton with the same alacrity with which they had joined him.

Clark continued his deception. As daylight came, the flags that the Rangers carried were broken out and mounted on poles. They were carried back and forth behind a small hill. From Vincennes, only the flags were visible. To Hamilton and his officers, it appeared they were faced by a force of 500 to 1,000 men. As darkness fell, the Rangers closed on the fort, ignoring cannon fire which passed harmlessly overhead. Moving his men to within 200 yards of the fort walls, Clark had them dig in. He sent parties of marksmen to entrench themselves within 30 yards of the fort. The British cannon were mounted on the walls of the fort and could not depress sufficiently to fire on the Rangers. As dawn broke, the British opened their gun ports and attempted to employ their cannon and small-arms fire. They wounded one Ranger, but their action exposed them to the deadly fire of the marksmen, and the British paid a bloody price. They quickly closed their gun ports.

None of Hamilton's men could show himself without being a target. The defenders hunkered down in the fort while Hamilton watched his French and Indian allies grow restless and lose heart. The Rangers obtained food from the French inhabitants of the town and settled down to a hearty meal. Members of the French militia in the town promptly changed sides for the third time and delivered a much-needed store of powder to Clark.

Clark sent a demand for unconditional surrender within thirty minutes to Hamilton. Hamilton sent a message out by his prisoner Captain Helm that he would like a three-day truce. Clark rejected the truce and repeated his demand. He was concerned that Indian reinforcements for Hamilton might be on the way and pressed for prompt surrender.

The English in the fort were willing to fight to the death and gave three cheers for the king, but the French had been loyal to England only because they were conquered. They could see that seventy-five of their fellow Frenchmen from Vincennes had joined Clark, and they did not wish to fight other French. The Indians did not fight to die but to kill. Hamilton saw his force breaking apart before his eyes.

In the quiet, a sudden sound of gunfire resounded from the edge of the forest. It was a successful Indian raiding party returning to Vincennes with bloody scalps and prisoners. They were announcing their return in the customary fashion. Clark sent Capt. John Williams's company out to greet the new arrivals, shouting and singing welcome. The Rangers were dressed in woodsman garb common to both sides. By the time the raiders recognized that these were Americans, it was too late—only one Indian escaped.

Five Indians were killed and seven taken prisoner. The two white captives were freed and the raiders taken before the fort where they could be seen by its garrison. Here it was discovered that two of the war party were Frenchmen dressed and painted as Indians. Townspeople pleaded for their lives, and Clark reluctantly spared them. Another raider was the son of an Indian chief who once spared a Ranger's life. He was also spared.

Clark condemned the four remaining Indians to death by the tomahawk which they had used so freely. It was a terrifying scene, one whose message was not lost on the watching garrison. To be executioner was a job not wanting for volunteers. Some sources claim that Clark allowed the Ranger who had lost the most relatives to the Indians the privilege. Others believe that Clark himself wielded the hatchet. The four kneeling Indians began to sing their death song. Their skulls were split one after another. An Ottawa chief named Macutte Mong was not killed when the hatchet imbedded itself in his skull; he wrenched it free and handed it back to his executioner. Two more blows, followed by a rope around the neck and a toss into the river finished him.[3]

Hamilton was a man who did not mind how many people his orders caused to be butchered as long as he did not see it. He was horrified by what he witnessed. When the two men met, Clark's hands were bloody, either from the execution or an intent to terrorize. Clark washed the blood from his hands in rainwater as an aghast Hamilton looked on. Hamilton described Clark as "still reeking from the human sacrifice in which he acted as high priest."[4] The two commanders argued, accusing each other of murder. Hamilton protested that he would not surrender unconditionally. Clark was vehement that he would press his attack. He again bluffed, telling Hamilton that cannon would be on the scene in a few hours that would tear the walls of the fort apart. By now, Clark knew that Hamilton had no one to depend on except approximately thirty-five British soldiers. Hamilton knew it also. Clark had created the mood he sought. He now offered Hamilton the right to march out of the fort under arms, with fixed bayonets and knapsacks before he laid them down. It was a sham offer, but the desperate Hamilton seized upon it and surrendered.

On the morning of February 25, 1779, the British flag came down and the American flag was raised over what was now called Fort Patrick Henry. Clark was surprised to see that the fort had twelve cannon and sufficient supplies for a long siege. Despite Hamilton's protests, Clark put all those who could be identified as having been part of Indian raiding parties in irons.

Clark learned that a supply party was en route to Hamilton and sent Captain Helm and Rangers to intercept it. A vast amount of Indian trade goods and officers' comforts were captured and distributed among the Rangers. Included in the loot were official letters to Hamilton and bottles of his favorite wine. He complained that Clark never offered him a glass of his beverage.

Clark sent Hamilton seven officers and eighteen regular soldiers as prisoners of war to Virginia; the rest he paroled. If Hamilton expected mercy in Virginia, he was soon disillusioned. Though he complained greatly that he was not a hair buyer, he was the instrument of British policy.

On arrival in Virginia, Hamilton came under the jurisdiction of the new governor, Thomas Jefferson. Hamilton; his assistant, Captain Lamonthe; and Philip Dejean, the justice of peace for Detroit, were brought to Williamsburg, where Jefferson and the Virginia council decided their punishment. Jefferson took a lenient position on prisoners of war but felt this case involved the murdering of innocent women and children. He consulted with George Washington and Richard Henry Lee, and they agreed that this case was different. Jefferson felt that the "dictates of humanity" required action, and retaliation in this case became "an act of benevolence." Over many protests, Jefferson put Henry Hamilton in close confinement in the Williamsburg jail. He would remain locked up until March 1781, when he was freed to return to British control.

The astounding accomplishment of George Rogers Clark created a sudden and temporary wave of adulation. Virginia voted him a sword and promised reward to the troops. Clark saw his mission as unfulfilled until he had taken Detroit. He believed correctly that Detroit was a plum ripe for picking. Though he had only 200 men, he began planning another daring mission.

The frontier was in an uproar. The Indians were cowed. The French at Detroit were ready to shed English rule, and the English commandant at Detroit was begging Governor Haldimand at Quebec for assistance.

A force of 500 men under Colonel Montgomery was reported to be on its way from Virginia. Clark's former Capt. John Bowman was reportedly coming with 300 Kentucky Rangers. Success was the mother of failure. Instead of joining with his former commander, Bowman led his men in an attack on the Shawnee town of Chilicothe, a nest of Indian raiders. The result was spotty. Part of the Indian town was burned and a famed war chief killed, but the Rangers were driven off. Colonel Montgomery's force got sidetracked in actions against less important Indian towns and arrived late with only 150 men.

The British used this time to greatly strengthen Detroit, reestablish relations with the Indians, and control their French citizens. Governor Jefferson was a friend and admirer of Clark, but Virginia was short of cash. Jefferson's eyes were on Detroit, but they were clouded by problems closer to Williamsburg. In a March 19, 1780, letter to Clark, Jefferson wrote, "Many reasons have occurred lately for declining the expedition against Detroit. Want of men, want of money, scarcity of provisions, are of themselves sufficient."[5] Jefferson indicated there were other reasons, probably political, but did not reveal them. Clark did not receive the support he needed and had earned. The moment of opportunity passed and would haunt him for the rest of his life.

With the aid of Indian allies, the British sent a force under Capt. Henry Bird against St. Louis and Cahokia. Clark led a Ranger force to Cahokia and drove off the intruders, but Bird was successful in carrying off many prisoners. In January 1781, Clark was in Virginia pleading with authorities for support in the conquest of Detroit. His pleas went unheard. Virginia was invaded by a British force under Benedict Arnold. Clark put together a band of 240 Rangers and ambushed the invaders along the James River. Virginia commissioned him a brigadier general, and he hastened west to organize his Detroit campaign.

In late August 1781, Col. Archibald Lochry and a band of 100 experienced Rangers from western Pennsylvania attempted to reinforce Clark, but their intentions had been betrayed to the British. Near the mouth of the Great Miami River, they were ambushed by a British and Indian force. This war party was led by the Mohawk war chief Joseph Brant, who had been involved in the infamous Cherry Valley Massacre. Lochery, four of his officers, and thirty-six Rangers were killed and the rest taken prisoner. Western Pennsylvania lost many of its best frontiersmen, and Clark was left without a key element of support. Virginia authorities withdrew their support of the Detroit campaign.

Clark returned to Louisville and began building a fort at the falls of the Ohio and a gunboat to patrol the river. He called his fortification Fort Nelson. Clark was burned out. He could not pay the bills military activity generated with the words of encouragement that were his only recompense. Clark was despondent that men in power did not share his vision. He began to drink heavily. In August 1782, British Capt. William Caldwell led a force of Canadian Rangers southward, recruiting Indians as he came. Clark took 1,000 men across the Ohio River and wreaked havoc on the Indians on the Great Miami River. He destroyed their villages and crops, leaving them more interested in survival than war.

The arduous service and the drink were taking their toll. Clark was financially ruined. He asked to be relieved of command, and his wish was granted. By 1783, he was writing Virginia Governor Harrison asking for some clothes. Officers of the Continental Line were being given land and bounties by the new nation. Clark chaired a group of state officers who were asking for equal treatment. What Clark received was a notice that Virginia was no longer interested in carrying on offensive war against the Indians in the west. Clark was thanked for his work and dismissed. Clark and other men, such as Simon Kenton and Daniel Boone, who had built the west, found that land they had won was claimed by those who had money for lawyers. The great men of the frontier were reduced to poverty and died in that state.

Some non-monetary recognition was granted when, in October 1783, a town was established across the Ohio from Louisville. It was named Clarksville, and Clark was made one of its trustees. A grant of land was given Clark and his men, but it was in territory fiercely contested by the Indians. The British maintained a constant dialogue with—and supply of—the Indians to incite trouble on the frontier. Clark was concerned about 1,500 Wabash Indian warriors who were seeking war. They dared the Americans to come to the Wabash River, and they, the Shawnee, and other tribes sent raiding parties deep among the settlements. The war cry, the tomahawk, and the scalping knife spread terror across the frontier. In 1786, Clark led another large force against the Indians, but drink and disillusion had robbed him of his spirit and command presence. Some of his men distrusted him, and 300 of them exercised their volunteer status by returning home.

Though Detroit eluded Clark, his accomplishment would prove the death blow to British intentions to secure the American west. The British were unable to regain their lost territory in the Illinois country, and all of the area west to the Mississippi and north to the Great Lakes was ceded to the United States at the Treaty of Paris in 1783. Clark and Ranger Richard Butler were frequently engaged in meetings with the Shawnee and other Indians to establish a treaty that in 1786 gave the United States sovereignty over former British-controlled land.

Finding solace in a bottle harmed this great warrior. Clark's friend Thomas Jefferson lamented his decline, writing, "No man alive rated him higher than I did, and would again, were he to become again what I knew him."[6] The Spanish were interested in having more people in Spanish Louisiana west of the Mississippi and approached Clark to found a settlement. Getting nothing from the America he fought for, Clark considered moving west of the Mississippi. He told the Spanish he would move if they would agree to political and religious freedom in the settlement. They were not willing to do so.

Desperate for funds, Clark became involved in a French plot conceived by Genet, the French minister to the United States. Genet plotted to draw the United States into the French war against Britain and Spain. The intent was to raise Kentuckians to take Spanish holdings. France had greatly helped the Americans in the Revolution, and many Americans felt an obligation. Clark was commissioned as a major general by the French in 1793 to lead this expedition. Determined to ruin Clark and supplant him as leader in the west was James Wilkinson.

Wilkinson sought to implant the belief that Clark was attempting to sunder Kentucky from control of the United States to give to Spain or to France. The eastward mails were heavy with accusations against Clark. Clark had seized the goods of some Spanish merchants who he felt were illegally trading at Vincennes and sold these to fund supplies for his men. Wilkinson used this against him. Clark was accused of taking personal property and of inciting unnecessary war against the Indians. Accusations continued that Clark was always drunk and illegally raising troops. It was made to appear that a committee had been formed condemning Clark, but beneath it all was James Wilkinson. Clark had no idea who was destroying him, but Congress was so taken in that they ordered troops to forcibly drive Clark and his men from Vincennes even though neither Clark nor his men were there.[7]

The Frenchman Genet made a mistake when he publicly attacked President Washington for his position of neutrality. Washington had him recalled to France. His association with Genet, combined with Wilkinson's schemes, ended Clark's influence, and his career withered.

Yesterday's hero, George Rogers Clark became a lonely, forgotten man. He never married and lived in a hovel on Corn Island. He suffered a stroke, and later, his right leg was amputated. In 1809, his sister took him to live with her near Louisville, where, after a long illness, he died on February 13, 1819.

In terms of territory gained, what George Rogers Clark gave his nation surpasses the accomplishment of all other American Rangers. Many credit him with adding what became the states of Illinois, Indiana, and Michigan to the United States; others add Wisconsin and the preservation of Kentucky to his exploits. He did all this with a few dedicated and determined men, a head full of vision and audacity, and a heart of courage. His leadership took the fledgling United States west from the Appalachians to the Mississippi. Thanks in large part to George Rogers Clark, when Spain secretly ceded the vast land known as Louisiana back to France in 1800, the Americans were well positioned for Jefferson to make the Louisiana Purchase.

CHAPTER 12

Blood on the Border

In three years of border warfare during the American Revolution, one tribe alone—the Seneca—took more than 1,000 scalps, including 299 from women and 29 from children. These were sent to the governor of Canada, who sent them to King George III of England.[1]

Most of the Rangers of the frontier who fought against these raiders are long forgotten. They suffered great hardship and fought desperate battles that are unknown to history. The exploits of a few have come down to us. Though their warfare knew no bounds, their reputations are best remembered in their primary areas of ranging: Sam Brady from Pittsburgh to Lake Erie, Lou Wetzel in present-day West Virginia, Simon Kenton in Ohio, and Daniel Boone in Kentucky.

Sam Brady was the son of a noted frontiersman named John Brady, who fought with Henri Bouquet in Pontiac's War. In the Revolution, Sam Brady was a captain in the 12th Pennsylvania Continental Line and badly wounded at the Battle of Brandywine. His twenty-year-old son James was killed and scalped by Indians in 1778, and his father died under Indian tomahawks the following year. Sam Brady had enlisted in 1775 and had seen much of the war in the east in fights at Boston; Long Island, where his gallantry resulted in a lieutenancy; White Plains; Trenton; Princeton; Brandywine; and Germantown. He fought his way clear of the Paoli Massacre and was assigned to Fort Pitt, where Brady teamed up with a young Delaware Indian named Nanowland.

In June 1779, Brady and Nanowland left Fort Pitt with eighteen Rangers in Indian garb and war paint. They proceeded north toward Seneca country and intercepted a war party of seven Indians. These raiders had killed and scalped a soldier, a woman, and four children and taken two other children captive. Brady's Rangers killed the Indian leader and several of his men and took two wounded Indians prisoner. They freed the captives and recovered six horses, all plunder, and weapons.

Tradition has it that on another occasion, Brady and two other Rangers found a man whose home had just been burned and his wife, her sister, and five children taken. They tracked the unsuspecting war party and found it consisted of thirteen Indians. Knowing they could not engage in a gunfight with that number and win, the four frontiersmen waited until the Indians were asleep, then crawled from man to man and killed them with knife and tomahawk.

Brady and Lew Weitzel spoke the Shawnee and Delaware Indian tongues fluently. In 1782, they were assigned an intelligence-gathering mission. Posing as Indians, they slipped into an Indian council at Sandusky, New York. Wisely they had pinpointed the Indian horse herd and selected horses of obvious merit. They listened for a while but were under the suspicious gaze of an old Indian chief. Knowing they could not continue the ruse, the two Rangers suddenly killed this chief and another. Using the shock to their advantage, they ran for the horses and, after a harrowing flight, came home safe.

Many of the famed colonial and Revolutionary War Rangers were at some time captured by the Indians. These include Stark, Boone, Wetzel, Kenton, and Brady. They survived while many others died under torture or were burned at the stake. Brady escaped captivity by loosening his rawhide bonds. As he was led to the stake for a burning, he broke free, tore a baby from its mothers arms, and threw it in the fire. The natural reaction of the mother and the Indians was to seek to save the child. This gave Brady a head start. He was pursued for more than 100 miles, was wounded, and hid among the lilies breathing through a reed. Thinking he had drowned, the Indians gave up the chase.

Lewis Wetzel was born in 1764, most likely near Lancaster, Pennsylvania. He was the second of five sons. When Wetzel was eight years old, his family removed to the area of present-day Wheeling, West Virginia. With his brothers, Martin, Jacob, John, and George, Lewis Wetzel was quickly introduced to the hard and dangerous life of the frontier. By age thirteen, Wetzel was an Indian fighter. Wetzel's youngest brother, George, was killed, and Lewis and Jacob were taken prisoner by Indians. They escaped, but the experience left Lewis Wetzel with a hatred for Indians that lasted through his life. Tall with long black hair and eyes like daggers, Wetzel trained himself to be a merciless killer. He was a fast runner with great endurance. He knew the woods and was a supreme marksman who could reload on the run. He could not read or write, but his skill in woods lore and Indian fighting was such that he was a hero to the frontier.

A dark and foreboding warrior, Wetzel's primary social contact was as a skilled fiddler at frontier dances. When he was in the area, the settlers had a confidence and determination that a company of regulars would not have given them. He never spared an Indian. Even those who helped him and those who came in peace died at his hand. This created problems for Wetzel with the authorities, but the people of the frontier thought of their loved ones who had been shot, tomahawked, and scalped. These people would not allow a prosecution of Lewis Wetzel.

Simon Kenton was only sixteen when he ran away from home in Virginia and fled west across the Allegheny Mountains,. He thought he had killed a man who had once given him a sound thrashing. There were many men using assumed names on the frontier. Traveling through Fort Pitt and down the Ohio, Kenton took the name of Simon Butler. He became a trapper and hunter on the Ohio frontier.

Serving as a Ranger scout during Lord Dunmore's War, Kenton grew to be a powerful figure on the frontier, a man known and trusted by George Rogers Clark and Daniel Boone, by Indian chief Logan and the renegade Simon Girty. In time he learned that his opponent had survived the beating, and he resumed the name Simon Kenton. After many narrow escapes, Kenton was run down by mounted Indians and taken prisoner. As a great warrior, Kenton's long and painful death would provide great entertainment. He was brutally beaten and had an arm broken, but Girty and Logan were able to prolong the execution, and Kenton finally made his escape. He accompanied George Rogers Clark's expeditions to capture Kaskaskia and Vincennes. Kenton took part in three expeditions against the Indians at Chillicothe. He fought against the best Indian warriors including the White Indian Blue Jacket and Tecumseh.

When Kenton killed a deer or an Indian, he did not rush from hiding, but instead waited patiently until he knew Indians had not heard the shot. In the breathless cold of winter, Simon Kenton would take a position from which he could observe or ambush. Using flint and steel, he would build a small, smokeless fire, then cover the coals with earth. Wrapping himself in a buffalo robe, which trapped heat from the warmed ground, Kenton would sit upon this spot of heated earth for hours, waiting patiently until his quarry came into his sights.

He won with his rifle and made tomahawk-marked claims to large tracts of land. These were taken from him by men who knew how to use the law. Though given a small pension and some land, Kenton lived most of his later years in poverty. He died at age eighty-one, having built the foundation of prosperity for many who never knew his name.

Daniel Boone was born in 1734 near Reading, Pennsylvania. He was the sixth son of his parents. In 1750, his family followed the great path of migration that led from central Pennsylvania down the Shennendoah Valley to the Yadkin River country of North Carolina. Along with Dan Morgan, Boone served as a wagoner on Braddock's ill-fated expedition of 1755. When the bloody rout began, Boone and a companion named Finley cut the harness on their horses and rode for their lives. Finley, who had been through the Cumberland Gap to Kentucky, encouraged Boone to accompany him to the west and described a rich land where a man without means could make his fortune. Kentucky was Indian territory, more a rich hunting ground then a place of permanent residence for the tribes. Boone was a married man, a blacksmith who farmed when necessary, but his principal avocation was as a hunter. Bringing in meat for his family and the settlements and much-valued deerskins for barter or sale were his means of livelihood. The west offered the opportunity for land. His initial trip with Finley convinced him that his future was on the frontier.

As an agent for the Transylvania Company, Boone began to lead settlers to the new land. He and his men opened the famed migration route called the Wilderness Trail, then established the community of Boonesborough. Reacting to this invasion of their lands, the Indians began to send raiding parties against the settlers. The raids were so frequent and terrifying that Kentucky would be known as "the dark and bloody land." Boone would lose a young son and a brother to the scalping knife.

The Rangers of the frontier had to combine food gathering with war. Boone was always at his best when ranging the forest. One of his

Daniel Boone.
LIBRARY OF CONGRESS

most famous exploits was when a war party took Boone's fourteen-year-old daughter, Jemima; Fanny Calloway, age fourteen; and Betsey Calloway, age sixteen. The raiding party of Cherokee and Shawnee was traveling on foot. Reasoning the direction of travel, one group of frontiersmen rode horseback to circle around the Indians and set an ambush. Boone led another small band in foot pursuit. The children were of frontier stock and did all they could by breaking branches and making heavy footprints to leave a trail. The Rangers had to follow with caution. When war parties were attacked, they promptly tomahawked their captives. After traveling thirty-five miles, the Indians believed they had outdistanced pursuit and relaxed by a stream, killing some game and making a fire. With the exception of one armed guard, they carelessly left their weapons lying about while they rested and prepared to eat.

In heavy woodland and thick underbrush, Boone and his men were about twenty-five yards from the Indians when the Rangers and the Indians saw each other. The Rangers opened fire. John Floyd shot the Indian guard, and Boone shot another. Leaving the girls, their weapons, and supplies, the Indians ran into the thick brush and escaped. Blood trails showed that some would not go far. The girls told the Rangers that the Indians had said war parties were moving to other settlements. Boone and his friends broke off the pursuit to provide early warning.

In February 1778, Daniel Boone was captured by Shawnee Indians and taken to Detroit, where he met Henry Hamilton. The British officer unsuccessfully tried to get Boone to become a Tory. Boone was then returned to the Indian town of Chillicothe. He escaped by taking a horse. Frequently riding in stream beds to conceal his tracks, Boone made it to safety, covering over 150 miles in four days.

Boone's skills as a hunter, trapper, and surveyor were widely known. He achieved fame in his lifetime, but that did not protect him from those who knew the law. Boone had land claims of between 50,000 and 100,000 acres, but most of it was taken from him. Kentucky treated him poorly, and he removed to Spanish Missouri. He died on September 26, 1820, at age seventy-six.

CHAPTER 13

War in the South

American efforts had been primarily directed at fending off British attacks in the populated northeast. As the rebel conditions improved, so did interest in the south. This would be the last theater of the Revolutionary War. The British were now fighting France, Holland, and Spain, and their European and far-flung territories were under threat. A significant force had been committed to secure the colonies, and parliament felt the generals had enough military power to do the job. The south had a great number of Loyalists who supported British arms. In the south, the British were dealing with inefficient American generals and had reason to feel confident.

Command of the British forces in the south rested with Charles Cornwallis, an aristocrat who had many saving graces as a man. War is a risky business, and Cornwallis made blunders at the second Battle of Trenton in the north and in the southern campaign. Despite this, Charles Cornwallis was an aggressive campaigner who went in search of fights and was a dangerous adversary. In America, Cornwallis was second in command to Sir Henry Clinton who was a more passive commander. It was not a friendly relationship, and Cornwallis bypassed his commander to push approval for his strategy with parliament. Cornwallis had the services of two outstanding warriors in the Ranger mode: Banastre Tarleton and Patrick Ferguson.

In early battles, American regulars led by weak generals fared badly. The American hope and opportunity in the south frequently rested on militia. The best of these were Rangers who could conduct hit-and-run raids and keep the British harassed with bee-sting tactics. These resulted in the need to defend everywhere, a costly process that was wearing down the British Army.

To retaliate, the British sought to create a situation in which Americans fought Americans. Southern Tory units had more opportunity to fight for King George III in the south than British commanders gave them in the north. Throughout the thirteen colonies, the hatred between Loyalists and patriots made the Revolution a war of murder and pillage like no other Americans have fought. This hatred and persecution of one American by another reached their highest dimension in the south. There were depredations by both sides that would have kept war crimes tribunals overworked in modern times. Both sides hung men with or without courts-martial. When Tory leader Capt. Nathan Read was sentenced to hang, he was sufficiently respected that he was offered freedom if he would join the patriots. He declined, and though he was praised, he was hung.[1]

One of the primary executioners on the patriot side was a militia colonel named Benjamin Cleveland. He was so heavy that his men called him "Round About." He was much bothered by a Tory leader named Harrison who had stolen his animals and burned his fences. Harrison had also hung Cleveland's overseer, Jack Doss, from a dogwood tree using a grape vine as rope. When Cleveland and his men captured Harrison, the Tory knew he was in trouble. Cleveland took him to the same dogwood where Harrison had hung Doss and put the Tory on a log with a noose around his neck. Harrison pleaded peacetime friendship. He begged for his life on the grounds that he had invented a perpetual-motion machine that the world would lose. Cleveland listened to this, but when Harrison asked, "Where is your conscience?" he had enough. "Where are my horses and cattle . . . my barn and fences? Where is poor Jack Doss?" growled Cleveland, then concluded by telling one of his men to "butt him off the log—I'll show him perpetual motion."[2]

Influenced by the relatively open terrain in which they operated, the Rangers of the south frequently operated on horseback. Familiarity with the mountains and the woods and swamps of the low country facilitated their employment of hit-and-run tactics with varying success. The three best-known Ranger leaders in the south were Andrew Pickens, Thomas Sumter, and Francis Marion. They would be joined by the redoubtable Dan Morgan of Saratoga fame, Light Horse Harry Lee, Richard Caswell and William Richardson Davie in North Carolina, and Elijah Clarke, who campaigned along the Georgia border.

In February 1776, former British governor Josiah Martin of North Carolina was seeking to rally all those who supported the king. His intent was to establish a strong British base in the colony from which

Lord Charles Cornwallis.
NATIONAL ARCHIVES

the regulars could extend their power The Tory assembly point was set at Brunswick near Cape Fear. Close to present-day Fayetteville, Donald McDonald, a Tory and noted Scottish warrior who had fought at Culloden, gave the call to arms. His colonel was Donald McCleod, and as the names indicate, this was a gathering of Scottish Highlanders. Some 1,700 of them came, many wearing kilts. They carried muskets, rifles, and broadswords and marched to the skirl of bagpipes.

To oppose them and prevent their coming to the coast were an equal number of patriots, 800 of whom were North Carolina Rangers under Richard Caswell. The others were a mixed lot of Rangers, continentals, and militia. The Continentals under Col. James Moore possessed five pieces of artillery.

The patriot force also numbered many men who were of Scottish origin. Some historians have viewed the ensuing engagement as a settling of old scores between Highland and Lowland Scots. McDonald and his men tried to bypass the patriot force but were blocked in a series of maneuvers. The Tory Highlanders then resolved to go east by way of Moore's Creek Bridge, eighteen miles north of Wilmington.

Patriot militia reached Moore's Creek first. Arriving on February 25, they began to entrench themselves on the east side of the creek opposite from the enemy. The next day, Caswell's 800 Rangers came in and began preparing an earthwork on the west side of the creek. When this was partially completed, Caswell changed his mind and moved his men to join the other patriots. They lifted the planks from the bridge and, according to Tory reports, greased the supporting stringers. Behind schedule and having been blocked several times, McDonald and his leaders determined to cut their way through.

Capt. John Campbell led eighty Scottish volunteers in an effort to cross the skeleton of the bridge. They planned to fire one volley, then put aside their muskets and rifles and use the broadsword. To the sound of the pipes, Campbell shouted, "King George and the Broadswords," and began to cross the stringers.[3] They tried to stick the points of their swords into the wooden beams to give them footing, but they were under heavy fire from the onset. The greased beams added to their difficulty, Some fell in the water, and others were shot into it. Captain Campbell and a few of his men made it to the patriot side only to be killed.

With the Tory vanguard shattered, the Rangers and other patriot forces quickly relaid the bridge planking and came after their retreating foe. Lieutenant Slocum had found a ford and led a small force by that route to attack the Tories in the rear. Only thirty of the Highlanders were killed at the bridge crossing, but another thirty died in the aftermath.[4] Among these was Colonel McCleod. Donald McDonald was elderly and had been ill that morning. The loss of McCleod completed a deficit of leadership. Struck front and rear, the Tory force collapsed. McDonald and 849 men were taken captive. More than 1,800 muskets and rifles, 150 swords, wagons, and money were collected from the battlefield and nearby Tories. The patriots had two men wounded; one would later die of his wounds.

Moore's Creek was a small battle with large effects. Deprived of reinforcements, the regular British force departed from North Carolina. The Tory effort to put the colony in support of the king was thrown into disarray.

Andrew Pickens was born in Paxton Township near present-day Harrisburg, Pennsylvania, in 1739. His Scotch-Irish family became part of the great migration that traveled the natural highways of the

Cumberland and Shenendoah Valleys. They lived for a while in Virginia, then pressed on to the Carolinas, where they settled on 800 acres of land near Waxhaw Creek, South Carolina. Andrew Pickens was slender and of medium height and had the quick, flowing movements of an athlete. He was a Presbyterian Indian fighter whose young life was a blend of religion and rifle. Pickens was a very successful and happy man when the war began. He would see his home burned and a brother, Capt. Joseph Pickens, killed in action against the Tories. Another brother, John Pickens, was taken by the Cherokee Indians, who were allied to the English. When they found out he was Andrew's brother, the Indians tortured and scalped John and burned him at the stake.[5] On a number of occasions, Andrew Pickens wife, Rebecca, had to flee from Tory raiders. One of their children died, possibly as a result of these hardships.

When the Revolutionary War began, Andrew Pickens had considerable experience as an Indian fighter. He was a farmer, justice of the peace, and captain of a militia company living on Long Cane Creek with his wife and four children. As neighbors began to choose sides, Pickens stood for independence. Parties of patriots and Tories began to challenge each other. On November 19, 1775, 600 Americans, including Pickens, were confronted by 1,800 Tories. The patriots retreated into a stockaded village called Ninety-Six because it was believed to be ninety-six miles from Fort Prince George. The opponents skirmished for two days before arranging a truce that separated them. For two years, Pickens participated in various battles and was promoted to colonel.

In June 1778, the Americans were on the attack against the British. Pickens raised a force of 500 South Carolina militia. The American commander, Gen. Robert Howe, ordered Pickens to follow the retreating enemy. Accompanying Pickens was Col. Elijah Clarke, an uneducated woodsman, but of such physical courage that he was the leader of 300 Georgia frontiersmen. The Americans were ambushed, and Clarke was shot through the hip. He was soon recruiting men and leading Georgia Rangers.

A skilled and audacious North Carolina Tory leader named Boyd had raised a force of 700 men and was ravaging the Georgia countryside in a wave of destruction that included murder. Pickens, with 350 Carolina and Georgia Rangers, was tracking Boyd, who was en route to join British Lt. Col. Archibald Campbell's force at Augusta, Georgia. At Kettle Creek, Georgia, on February 14, 1779, Pickens caught up with Boyd and his men while the Tories were grazing their horses and killing cattle. The fight was sharp and lasted several hours, but Boyd died of wounds, and his force was defeated, losing 150 men killed, wounded, or captured. Five of the prisoners were found guilty of depredations and hanged. Pickens's victory gave the Americans of the back country confidence that they could win. It greatly enhanced recruiting for the patriot forces and harmed Tory efforts.

When the British captured Charleston in 1780, they gained temporary control of South Carolina. This was a time of horror as Tory raiders looted, raped, and murdered throughout the countryside. Marion and Sumter fought on, but Pickens and his men were captured. Lucky to escape the noose, Pickens was paroled and returned to his home, where he kept his word that he would not fight.

When his farm was stripped and his home burned by James Dunlap of the Queen's Rangers, an angry Pickens renounced his parole and returned to the war. The Tory Dunlap began raiding the countryside, and Pickens sent Clarke and James McCall after him. McCall blocked Dunlap from crossing a bridge. The Tory party barricaded itself in a mill and was attacked by Clarke. Knowing that mercy would not be forthcoming the Tories fought hard but at length were compelled to surrender. Of the seventy-five Tories, thirty-five were dead and most of the remainder wounded. Dunlap was summarily executed. Pickens was outraged by the killing. He started an investigation, but nothing came of it as there was no sympathy for Tory raiders among the men.

Clarke would lead the Georgia contingent of Rangers throughout the war, serving primarily under Pickens's command. He later cooperated with Pickens in actions against the Cherokee and Creek Indians. He was wounded three times.

Thomas Sumter was born on August 14, 1734, near Charlottesville, Virginia. As a youth, he was active and demonstrated impetuous traits that would follow him through his life. During the French and Indian War, he participated in both Braddock's and Forbes's expeditions. He fought the Cherokee in 1762 and was imprisoned for debt in Virginia. Breaking out of jail, Sumter fled to South Carolina, where he married well and become financially solvent. Sumter became a captain of mounted Rangers under William Thompson and progressed in rank until he was a lieutenant colonel. He was promoted colonel, but in 1778, he resigned his South Carolina commission. Sumter refused to support the king. On May 28, 1780, Capt. Charles Campbell of Tarleton's Legion was sent to capture him. Sumter was warned and escaped, but Campbell's men looted Sumter's home, carried his wife, Mary, into the yard, and burned the Sumter home.

There was no South Carlina government when, in June 1780, a band of Carolinians decided to elect a leader. After some debate, they voted for Thomas Sumter and appointed him brigadier general. With his usual enthusiasm and energy, Sumter set about organizing a unit of Rangers. He was recruiting in North Carolina when his men won their first fight. A British raiding party under Tarleton's Tory Capt. Christian Huck was terrorizing the area near present-day Rock Hill. On July 12, 1780, Sumter's Rangers under Colonel Bratton caught this force. Huck's men had just forced Bratton's wife to prepare food for them and were in a careless bivouac nearby. The Americans moved into position during the night and at daylight opened a withering fire on the unsuspecting British and Tories at point-blank range. Huck and most of his men were killed. Victory brought Sumter credit, volunteers and a large reward posted for his capture.

At Rocky Mount on August 1, Sumter and 600 men attacked British entrenchments. Without artillery, they were unable to break through though the results were inconclusive. Sumter moved twenty miles east and, five days later, attacked a British post at Hanging Rock. The British lost 200 men to Sumter's loss of 53. On August 18, Tarleton caught Sumter unprepared and sleeping at his camp near Fishing Creek. The dragoons swept down on the careless Rangers and killed or captured nearly all of them while liberating nearly 100 British prisoners. Sumter barely escaped, riding bareback on a wagon horse. Though soundly whipped, he was still full of fight.

On November 9, Sumter fought a meeting engagement with a British force at Fishdam Ford, twenty-five miles to the northwest of Winnsboro, South Carolina. Sumter came off the best in this action. The British now considered Sumter a serious threat and went to great lengths to have him kidnapped or murdered in his tent. A British major named Wymess asked Cornwallis for the mission. Guided by a

Banastre Tarleton.
NATIONAL ARCHIVES

traitor, Wymess mounted the men of his 63rd Regiment on horseback and rode to contact at night.

On November 9, Wymess succeeded in blundering into Sumter's outposts and was shot off his horse. His men continued the assault and, knowing Sumter's location, barely missed him. Nearly nude, with the British in hot pursuit, Sumter leaped from his blankets, jumped over a fence, ran through fields and a briar patch, and finally hid shivering with cold under a rock overhang. Despite the precipitous flight of their commander, the Americans gave the 63rd a whipping, killing seven British and taking Wymess and twenty-four others prisoner with horses and weapons. Sumter had a loss of four killed and ten wounded.

On November 20 at Blackstock's Hill, Sumter fought a gallant and successful fight against Tarleton. Though Sumter was shot in the chest and shoulder and badly wounded, he continued fighting until loss of blood caused him to turn over his command to Colonel

Twiggs. This officer fought well and completed Sumter's effort. Tarleton was driven from the field. When he tried to counterattack, the American Rangers had slipped away.

In 1781, Sumter decided to solve the problem of militia serving briefly and then going home to care for their families. He raised a state force of mounted Rangers that would remain on active duty. Unfortunately, Sumter did not have the funds to pay his new army. In a major miscalculation grudgingly approved by Governor Rutledge and General Greene, Sumter decided to pay the troops from plunder and the sale of slaves taken from Tories. Sumter got his state troops, but Sumter's Law, as it was known, increased the fighting spirit of the supporters of the king and gave Sumter the reputation of a plundering raider. He had lost much to the British, and throughout his military career, loot was an important factor in his operations.

Sumter kept a separate command and in July led what was called "the raid of the dog days." He intended to get his supplies by capturing the British post at Fort Granby but had to retreat before British reinforcements at Granby and at Belleville. He next made an impetuous attack on Fort Watson and was beaten off with loss.

A contemporary named Francis Marion was having better success. Marion was born in Berkeley County, South Carolina, in 1732. He was descended from French Huguenots who had fled religious persecution in 1685 to settle with others of their faith between Charleston and the Santee River. Francis was the youngest of six children, puny at birth and described as "not larger than a New England Lobster." He received an elementary education but would remain semi-illiterate. At the age of fifteen, he decided to be a sailor and signed on to a small West Indies schooner. When the vessel sank, the six-man crew escaped to an open boat. They lived by killing the schooner's dog, drinking its blood, and eating its flesh raw. Two of the men died, but on the seventh day, Marion and three others reached shore. The incident was significant to young Marion. Surviving the harrowing experience matured him and gave him confidence.

In 1756, as the French and Indian War was ending, the Cherokee Indians were thought to be preparing for the warpath. Marion joined a militia company and began attending their training. In 1761, when the war with the Cherokee did occur, Francis Marion was a first lieutenant in Capt. William Moultrie's company of infantry.

In Marion's first combat experience, he led thirty men in breaking an Indian ambush. Though twenty-one of his men were casualties, their efforts succeeded in permitting the militia to pass into Cherokee country and devastate it. Marion's actions drew high praise from his seniors.

In April 1775, fighting between the colonists and British forces flared at Lexington. The Continental Congress requested each colony raise troops. South Carolina was asked to furnish two regiments of infantry and one of cavalry. Marion was selected to be one of ten captains assigned to Moultrie's Second Regiment of South Carolina Infantry.

On February 22, 1776, Francis Marion was promoted to major. His regiment was heavily involved in the defense of Charleston, building a fort of Palmetto logs and sand on Sullivan's Island. On June 28, British warships opened fire on the makeshift fort. Though the British were firing solid shot at a range of 400 yards, their cannon balls sank harmlessly into the sand and palmetto wood. Preserving powder, Moultrie had ordered his American gunners to fire slowly and make each shot count. The wounded British fleet withdrew, and the Americans celebrated their victory. Francis Marion had commanded the left wing of the fort and again distinguished himself.

On November 23, 1776, Marion was promoted to lieutenant colonel of the 2nd Regiment of South Carolina. As Continentals, his regiment was part of the regular establishment of the fledgling republic. The 2nd Regiment occupied itself with the defense of Charleston. As the British were not attacking, men grew bored with garrison duty. Marion soldiered on, instilling discipline and pride of unit in the men. Those who reported for duty with a beard were dry shaved. Marion tolerated no laxity; he knew that soldiers would accept firm discipline provided it was equal and fair.

Marion thought it healthy to drink vinegar but would not touch whiskey. In March 1780, his fellow officers gave a party in which they locked the doors and proceeded to get drunk. Unable to leave the room, Marion jumped from a second floor window and broke his ankle in the process. Shortly thereafter, the British attacked Charleston, capturing the South Carolina Continental troops on May 12, 1780. Marion's friends took him away on a litter and he and his friends were the subject of an intense hunt by the British.

Roaming at will, the British and their Loyalist allies now terrorized the countryside. In the forefront was the British Legion, which was comprised of Loyalists primarily from New York and Philadelphia. They wore green jackets and black facings. Their colonel was Lord William Cathcart, but it was then the practice of the British that the colonel of a regiment seldom served with it, the title being primarily honorary. It was the lieutenant colonels and majors who led the troops. The British Legion was led by the dashing and ruthless cavalryman Lt. Col. Banastre Tarleton. This dragoon left the scar of his saber from Virginia through the Carolinas. Tarleton was an audacious and ruthless commander. Born August 21, 1754, he came from a family of means and became a lawyer in London. Life was too tame for this young blade, and sensing that war was coming, he purchased a commission. He was actively campaigning in America by 1776. At age twenty-four, he became major of the British Legion and made it over in his own name. Tarleton was a formidable adversary. He understood the importance of gathering accurate intelligence, then striking fast and hard. Tarleton mounted an infantryman and a dragoon two to a horse and pursued the 3rd Regiment of Virginia Continentals until he caught up with the Americans at the Waxhaws in South Carolina. Col. Abraham Buford, the American commander, ordered his men to hold their fire until the British were within thirty yards. That worked against infantry, but Tarleton's cavalry put spurs to their horses and were quickly on the Americans with drawn sabers. The Americans grounded their weapons and tried to surrender, but Carleton and his men slaughtered them. Tarleton's name became the curse and fear of the south. Tarleton enjoyed his notoriety. He had an abundant self-confidence that frequently crossed the line to arrogance.

With the British cause in ascendency, many of the local populace announced for the king, and Tories took vengeance on their neighbors. As a result of their depredations, a backlash was created and American militia grew in numbers. Marion had recruited about twenty men, both white and black, who, though poorly armed and equipped, were ready for a fight. As American forces began to assemble, Marion took command of the Williamsburg militia, giving him 100 men, a sufficient number to look for action.

On August 16, 1780, the British under Lord Cornwallis crushed American Continentals and militia under Generals Gates and Sumter at the Battle of Camden. Forgetting his men, "Granny" Gates fled the field using a horse famed for its speed. He made 60 miles to Charlotte the first day and galloped for two more days using a relay of horses over 120 miles to reach safety at Hillsboro, North Carolina.[6]

Gates ran as though the devil were after him, and he was. Banastre Tarlton's dragoons ruthlessly hunted the Americans, who were in a stampede. Marion's men had been on an expedition to burn boats the British could use. When he learned of the location of 150 American prisoners from the recent battle, Marion attacked, killing 24 of the enemy and freeing the prisoners. To his surprise, many of them insisted they were prisoners and wanted to remain so. Marion took them back, but only 60 rejoined their units. Most went home.

The problem of temporary soldiers was to plague Marion and all militia leaders throughout the war. Men went to serve for a battle or thirty days or sixty, and when their time was up, regardless of the military situation, they went home. There was no benevolent government looking out for their families. If crops were not planted, tended, and harvested, starvation was the result. The concept of independence was new and untested. Looking to protect their families and farms, some men switched sides to support the side having the most success.

The victorious British Army turned toward the Waxhaws and ravaged the countryside. Led by Tories who hunted or informed on their neighbors, they created an atmosphere of terror. Two young brothers were taken prisoner. The youngest at age thirteen had been serving as a messenger in the Ranger unit commanded by Col. William Richardson Davie. A British officer ordered the boy to clean his boots. When the lad refused, the officer struck him with his sword inflicting cuts on the head and hand. The young soldier was named Andrew Jackson. During the war, Jackson would lose his mother and brothers. In time, the British would pay a reckoning.

On September 28, 1780, at Black Mingo Creek northeast of Georgetown, Marion struck. He led his men in a thirty-mile ride crossing three rivers to make a night attack on a forty-six-man Tory outpost led by Captain Ball. In fifteen minutes of bloody fighting, the Americans broke the Loyalists and put them to rout. The spoils included a number of superb horses that were much needed. Marion took one and rode the horse he called "Ball" for the remainder of the war.

Fording the Black River near Kingstree, Marion made a night attack on a party of Loyalist recruits under Colonel Tynes and Captain Gaskins on October 7, 1781. Surprise was achieved as Marion's Rangers charged through the darkness on horseback. Gaskins was playing cards and died holding a winning hand. The rout was total, with eighty horses and much equipment taken. Twenty three Loyalists were captured, fourteen wounded, and three killed. Tynes escaped, but he was tracked by Captain Snipes and brought back as prisoner to Marion.

His victories brought Marion to the attention of British leaders, and they determined to eliminate him. General Cornwallis assigned the mission to Banastre Tarleton and his green dragoons. Tarleton had a force that Marion could not risk meeting head on. Wisely, Marion began a rapid withdrawal, with Tarleton in hot pursuit. The chase led through pinewoods and swamp. After twenty-six miles of arduous effort, Tarleton's horses and men were exhausted and stopped.

At that time, Tarleton received a message from Cornwallis that Thomas Sumter had dealt the British under Major Wemyss a blow at Fishdam Ford. Tarleton called off his fruitless chase of Marion, saying to his troops, "Come, my boys! Let us go back, and we will find the Gamecock, but as for this old fox, the devil himself could not catch him." A legend was born, the nickname of "The Fox" stuck on Marion, and in time he became "The Swamp Fox." Tarleton rode into the interior of South Carolina, expressing his frustration along the way by burning thirty houses. He punished a widow who had warned Marion by having her dead husband's body dug up, plundering her home, burning her barn, and destroying her livestock and grain.

Tarleton's rambunctious career may have ended had he continued his pursuit. Marion had found a superb position for ambush and was lying in wait for the Green Dragoon. Leading a militia that came and went as support of their families allowed, Marion held fast in eastern South Carolina. His force was not sufficient to deliver the knife thrust to the heart, but he could and did bleed the enemy from a multitude of cuts. Along the Black, Santee, and Lynches Rivers, the hooves of Marion's horses echoed on the still night air. Local Tories knew the British could not protect them. To draw Marion to them, the British sent a force of 200 Hessians and militia to occupy the town of Kingstree. Marion did not have the force to evict them, but his reputation had now grown to the point that the British commander Major McLeroth took no chances and withdrew. Marion burrowed into a hideaway on Snow's Island, a slightly elevated patch of land some five miles long by two miles wide and well protected by swamps and rivers. Marion watched his Rangers melt away to care for their families and wondered when the long-promised American army would move south.

Marion's ace horseman, Col. Peter Horry, led his Rangers on a raid, but en route encountered a clever Tory housewife. While Horry was questioning her husband, she encouraged the soldiers to fill their canteens with apple brandy. Before Horry could get to his objective, all the enlisted men of his command were drunk, giggling at orders, shouting, and falling from the saddle. Horry called off the raid, the only benefit being that their noisy passage through the countryside terrified the Tory inhabitants.

Calling out 700 militia horsemen, Marion clashed with veterans of the 64th Regiment under Major McLeroth. The two opposing commanders fell into an argument over the niceties of war. McLeroth complained that it was not proper for Marion to shoot British pickets. Marion protested that the British had no right to burn people's houses. McLeroth was one of the few British officers who would not obey orders to burn houses, but awaiting reinforcements and seeking to break contact, McLeroth passed on the point and cleverly gained time by challenging Marion to come out in the open and "fight like a man."

It was decided that both sides would chose their twenty best men to fight it out. As the American twenty advanced, McLeroth withdrew his men. Darkness was at hand, and the British left camp fires burning and slipped away, outfoxing the fox. This gallant Scottish officer was admired by local people for his kind treatment of American civilians and wounded soldiers. Many of Marion's men liked McLeroth to the point of not wanting to fight him. He was dismissed from the British Army because he would not follow Tarleton's example of depredations. Marion felt pursuing McLeroth was like pursuing a brother.

Marion now lay astride the British supply route, blocking roads and raiding coastal traffic. There had been little to cheer about. A succession of inept commanders had hurt the American cause in the south. Robert Howe lost Georgia and its key port of Savannah while Benjamin Lincoln had lost South Carolina and its port of Charleston. Horatio "Granny" Gates completed the job at Camden. Cornwallis reported more than 1,000 Americans killed and 800 captured, along with 7 cannons and 130 wagons. With the American army thoroughly whipped in the south, the British and their Tory allies felt supremely confident. The only thing that remained to oppose their forces were American Rangers. Cornwallis saw an opportunity to strike hard. He would take North Carolina and, while solidifying his control behind him, move into Virginia and link up with British forces in the north. The British marched north on two axes toward Waxhaws, with Cornwallis on the left side of the Wateree River and Tarleton on the right of it. Maj. Patrick Ferguson had moved into what had been Tryon County, North Carolina. He had a force of 800 Tories, including Rangers. Ferguson's mission would be to protect the rear and flank of the army.

Tarleton had with him his legion cavalry and a small force of attached light infantry. Still separated from Cornwallis, Tarleton began to make camp and prepared to destroy the plantation home of a Ranger captain named Wahab. Scouting the area was the superb North Carolina Ranger Col. William Davie. Born in England in 1756, Davie's family came to America when he was seven years old. As a young man, he graduated from Princeton. Davie had been studying for law in Salisbury North Carolina when the war began. He joined in Ranger operations, and because he had a flair for hit-and-run tactics, he rose in rank. On September 21, 1780, Davie approached Wahab's plantation. He had eighty Rangers on horseback and two dismounted companies of Ranger riflemen. These were under the command of Maj. George Davidson, a relative of militia Gen. William Lee Davidson. Wahab was part of the Americans force and presumably provided information on the terrain.

They could see Tarleton's horsemen in the saddle preparing to burn the house. Davie sent Major Davidson with his riflemen through a cornfield to the rear of the building to establish an ambush. As the flames licked Wahab's house, Davie led a mounted charge down the lane. Taken by surprise, Tarleton's raiders tried to escape. In so doing, they rode into the ambush Davie had set. Twelve of the British were killed; sixty more would later die of their wounds. Fifty saddled horses and numerous weapons were captured. This example of an impromptu ambush was accomplished at a cost of one American wounded. Unfortunately, Captain Wahab lost his home.[7] Davie took his winnings and promptly left the area before Cornwallis could respond.

Four days later, the audacious Davie put his small force across Cornwallis's line of march. He had Major Davidson's two dismounted companies, a small force of militia, and twenty men on horseback. Cornwallis had four regiments of British infantry, one of Irish volunteers, two Tory regiments, and Tarleton's Legion. Tarleton was ill with malaria, and his men were under Maj. George Hanger. Cornwallis also had four pieces of artillery in his train.

This was a bee taking on an elephant, but Davie was determined. He took his position on the road through the village of Charlotte, North Carolina, which was then a small community consisting of a courthouse and twenty houses. Davie put Major Davidson's Rangers and the militia behind fences along the road. His twenty mounted Rangers were put behind a stone wall near the courthouse.

Major Hanger commanded the British van. On seeing the Americans, Hanger deployed light infantry and advanced on line. The Rangers behind the fence line poured such a heavy volume of fire into them that the regulars broke. Neither Hanger nor Cornwallis could get them to advance. Hanger then sent his dragoons charging the twenty Rangers behind the stone wall. Shot up, they retreated and declined to return. Major Davidson's men and the Mecklenberg militia joined Davie behind the stone wall. General Cornwallis again personally exhorted his men to attack. Hanger, the Legion, and the British light infantry moved forward and this time succeeded in turning the Rangers' right flank. The Rangers had to retreat.

If Banastre Tarleton was the right arm of Cornwallis, Maj. Patrick Ferguson was the left. He was born to a wealthy family and entered military service at the age of fourteen. He had an active mind, and on seeing the success of the American long rifle, he set about making a better one. Ferguson designed a breech-loading rifle that fired a pointed bullet. It was an effective weapon. Ferguson raised a force of Tory Rangers in Halifax and operated in that fashion in the north. He was a dead shot who claimed to have once had Washington in his sights. Ferguson said he withheld fire as it was a back shot. He was a major in the 71st, but he was assigned as the inspector general of militia by Cornwallis. These duties included recruiting, training, and leading Tory units. He was a successful raider whose men burned and plundered the western districts. Not as ruthless as Tarleton, Ferguson was nonetheless feared and hated by the American patriots.

Ferguson also knew of these patriot leaders. With British arms in ascendancy, he sent a message to the over-the-mountain people carried by Samuel Phillips, an American prisoner. Ferguson wrote that "if they did not desist from their opposition to British Arms, and take protection under his standard, he would march his army over the mountains, hang their leaders, and lay their country waste with fire and sword."[8] This message angered the frontiersmen. They decided to eliminate Ferguson and his Tories. Shelby and Sevier began to recruit, and each of them brought in 240 Rangers. William Campbell added 400 Virginians. They met on September 25 at an assembly area at Sycamore Flats on the Watauga River. This is near present-day Elizabethton, Tennessee. On the twenty-sixth, they set out to cross over the mountains. On the eastern side, they were met by Charles McDowell with 160 Rangers and Col. "Round About" Cleveland with Major Joseph Winston, who added 360. There were the usual complaints from men who were accustomed to total independence and resisted discipline. A commander was needed. Charles McDowell was the senior officer, but he was not an active man. They wanted William Davie, but he was elsewhere, and sending for him would mean delay. After some discussion, Col. William Campbell was given command. He had brought the largest contingent, and since most of the colonels were from North Carolina, the selection of a Virginian prevented squabbles among them. More men from North and South Carolina joined, bringing Campbell's force to between 1,400 and 1,800 men.

Ferguson had 1,100 men. About 100 of these were members of the King's Rangers, the Queen's Rangers, or the New Jersey Volunteers. All of these were experienced fighters. The bulk of Ferguson's men were Tory militia armed primarily with the musket and the bayonet. Deserters brought Ferguson word of the patriot gathering, and he sent two Tory messengers to Cornwallis informing him of the situation. Patriot families en route were suspicious and closely pursued the messengers. Forced to travel by night, Ferguson's messengers did not reach Cornwallis in time.

Ferguson decided to fight a defensive battle and camped on an eminence called King's Mountain. Through spies, informers, and the ruse of sending a man posing as a Tory ahead, the Rangers pinpointed Ferguson's position. About 900 mounted Rangers rode to the attack. The rest did not have horses and followed on foot. Most Rangers carried the long rifle, a weapon the majority of them had used since childhood.

The thirty-six-year-old Ferguson had chosen his position well. King's Mountain was actually a hill of sixty feet. The sides were wooded and rocky and rose sharply to 500 feet, with level ground at the top. This flat averaged in width from 70 yards at its narrowest to about 125 yards wide in the area of the Tory camp. Ferguson's position was strong, and pickets were stationed to provide early warning.

It was about noon on Saturday, October 7, 1780, when the Rangers came to King's Mountain. The leaders made a reconnaissance. A Tory messenger carrying dispatches from Ferguson to Cornwallis was captured. George Watkins, a patriot who was a paroled prisoner, provided information on Ferguson's camp. Now well informed, Campbell and the other officers decided they could surround Ferguson's men. The patriots had marched throughout the night and the morning. They were tired but heartened at the prospect of battle.

Four columns moved abreast to a line of departure selected by the leaders. There each column would dismount, leave their horses under guard, and move to their assigned positions around the hill. Once dismounted they were within 400 yards of Ferguson's camp before he knew they were there. When his pickets saw the oncoming patriots, they opened fire, and Ferguson assembled his men for battle at the top of the hill. He was a good soldier and a man skilled in irregular warfare. His selection of terrain was ideal. His tactics were conventional and likely dictated by the training and weaponry of most of his men. Had the patriots tried to assault King's Mountain as a regular force of the period, Ferguson would likely have prevailed.

The patriots used Ranger tactics and infiltrated through the woods, taking maximum advantage of concealment and cover. Though the slopes were steep, there was little underbrush, and the trees and rocky outcrops offered excellent firing positions. Initially, the entire hill was surrounded, but as the battle progressed, the patriot lines were like a horseshoe laid upon the ground. From the right of the open end were positioned Campbell's men and to his right Sevier, then McDowell and Winston. Hambrick was at the closed top, and on his right were Cleveland, Lacey, Williams, and Shelby. Taken under fire first, Shelby made certain his men were in good firing position before replying. Campbell was attacking, shouting to his men, "Here they are, boys! Shout like hell and fight like devils." The accuracy and killing reach of the Ranger rifles began to take their toll. Ferguson's Tory Rangers fought bravely, but they carried the wrong weapons for this battle. They launched a bayonet attack against Shelby, whose men simply withdrew and took a toll of the attackers. As Ferguson's men launched a bayonet charge at one point in the line, the patriot Rangers on the other side moved up the hill.

Driven from the southeast end of the level area, Ferguson's men tried to rally in their camp site, firing from behind wagons. There was no shelter as the patriot Rangers were on all sides of them. Ferguson was mounted and rode to and fro gallantly trying to encourage his men. Men tried to hold up white cloths in surrender, and he tore those from them. Seeing that there was no hope, he and a few of his officers tried to break out. He was shot from the saddle and was later found to have seven bullet wounds in his body. Captain de Peyster then tried to rally the Tories, but it was no longer a battle.

More patriots were coming on the hill, firing into the Tories, who were huddled like animals in a pen. De Peyster tried to surrender, but despite the efforts of Campbell and Shelby, the killing continued. This included wounded who were shot as they begged for mercy. This was payback time. The battle and the slaughter lasted an hour and five minutes.

Ferguson's command was obliterated: 902 men lost, including 206 killed, 128 wounded, and 648 taken prisoner. Ferguson was dead, along with two militia colonels and three captains. Another colonel and a major died the next day. A Tory Ranger captain was also killed. On October 8, a Sunday, the victors left King's Mountain and moved to Gilbert Town. There a court-martial was convened, and thirty prisoners who were known to have committed depredations were tried. Twelve were convicted, and nine were hung.

This was a battle fought between Americans. There was only one British soldier in the fight, and that was Ferguson. The rest were

Americans who fought for king or independence. It is likely that Ferguson was the only regular in the battle; certainly, there were none on the patriot side.

Cornwallis abandoned his campaign in North Carolina and retreated south as fast as conditions would allow him. Ill and with fever, he moved to Winnsboro, South Carolina, down roads turned into swamps by pouring rain. His men were hungry, but there was no rest. They were constantly harassed by American Rangers.

CHAPTER 14

Turning the Tide

Having been markedly unsuccessful with their choice of commanders in the south, the Congress allowed George Washington to designate and supervise the one who would take up the challenge. Nathanael Greene, the man Washington selected, is considered by many historians the best American general of the war. An iron worker from Rhode Island of English Quaker descent, he was dismissed from his Quaker community because he attended a military parade. In 1774, Greene was an untrained private of militia; by 1775, he was a brigadier general. With the exception of a poor performance that resulted in disaster at Fort Washington in November of 1776, Greene performed well and steadily improved. Though not a great battlefield tactician, Greene understood the big-picture strategy better then most. He was a man of common sense, a patient communicator who tried to bring reasonable men together. He had a reasoned disdain for militia, justly believing that while regulars were no better or braver, the regulars were more practiced and more available for duty. Unfortunately, Greene had an injudicious pen. In a fit of passion, he wrote some intemperate remarks about militia, calling them "garnish of a table" He indicated that plundering was the only reason they came to the field and lumped Marion and Sumter in with them.

The only military support Greene brought south was a battle-tested mix of three companies of Continental infantry and three troops of cavalry under the command of a twenty-three-year-old Princeton-educated Virginia aristocrat named Henry Lee. "Light Horse Harry," as he came to be known, was on horseback by age four, and throughout his youth, he was highly trained in the use of the sword and pistol. He was a scholar-warrior who read Greek and Latin and considered Shakespeare light reading. Though not a brawler or a bully, Harry Lee was a dangerous man. His strength and skill with weapons were evident and well publicized by others. War gave Harry purpose, and an outlet for his energy. His wealth and station in life gave him prompt promotion. He started as a captain commanding a troop of horse in Col. Theodorick Bland's Virginia Light Dragoons, but he quickly managed to extract himself and his command to become an independent raider. Though he commanded both infantry and dragoons, Harry Lee is usually called a cavalryman. He specialized in reconnaissance and raiding.

Washington's army was in critical need of supplies that the British had in quantity. To supply their forces, the British relied on trains of wagons traveling in convoy. Harry Lee began raiding these wagon trains. The British responded by sending cavalry escorts. In these skirmishes Lee developed tactics of using surprise and shock action, avoiding the head-on charge, but striking from the flanks. He studied the methods of his British opponents, took the best of their techniques, and improved them with his own ideas. He would write in his *Memoirs* that he learned the most from the men he fought.

The supplies captured by Harry Lee's troops were critical to Washington's army. Washington formed a life-long affection for his young raider. Gen. Nathanael Greene admired Lee and wrote to Washington, "The captain's instinct is as sure and swift as that of the eagle that drops out of the skies to snatch its prey. No convoy within range of his horses is safe from his depredations."[1] Lee's success brought him promotion to major and the formation of a new organization, designated on October 21, 1780, as Lee's Partisan Corps. Lee made a practice of personally selecting his men. Two troops of Lee's mounted command included sons of patrician families and rifle-carrying and buckskin-clad frontiersmen. Forty Oneida Indians comprised the third troop. A scholar to the core, Lee had learned to speak the Indian tongue. Lee's men have been called "the most thoroughly disciplined and best equipped scouts and raiders in the Revolution."[2]

Col. Richard "Dickie" Butler, who had served as Morgan's second in command at Saratoga, now commanded a regiment of the Pennsylvania line. As General Washington sought to pin Clinton in New York, he ordered Butler and his men to raid the British. Lee and Butler wreaked havoc on Clinton's supply system.

Nathanael Greene.
NATIONAL ARCHIVES

In addition to raiding British supplies, Harry Lee's men performed valuable service in reconnaissance. Based on intelligence gathered by Lee's men, the new American light infantry force under Anthony Wayne was successful in taking the British bastion at Stony Point. Lee was so successful that he was authorized to plan his own raids, having them approved only by Washington.

A hallmark of Ranger operations is the ability to overcome adverse terrain and use the enemy's false sense of security to defeat him. At Paulus Hook in present-day Jersey City, Lee went under the guns of a British fleet and near the 10,000 British soldiers on the island of Manhattan to capture a post the British thought secure as it was surrounded by water and a salt marsh. This was a hit-and-run night raid with the Americans attacking at 0300 hours.

Lee used a prefabricated bridge built in sections, crossed the Hackensack River, and caught the sleeping defenders by surprise. The Americans could not sustain the position or destroy all the British cannon and supplies, but they bayoneted 50 British and captured 158 men and a large quantity of supplies. Lee's force had two men killed and two wounded. Lee had with him a contingent of Virginians, one of whom was a major who claimed seniority and challenged Lee's right to command the expedition. Lee had been given command by Washington and would not give it up. He lied about his date of rank, which, along with false accusations that he had botched the operation, resulted in jealous officers demanding his courts-martial. With Washington's backing, Lee's career was saved.

In addition to his raids, Harry Lee became Washington's spymaster. He organized an intelligence network of spies and informers that infiltrated British General Clinton's lines and kept Washington well informed.

In the years to come, Harry Lee would father a son named Robert E. Lee but waste the fortunes of two wealthy wives on foolish business practices. He would become governor of Virginia, a U.S. Congressman, and commander of Washington's army that quelled the Whiskey Rebellion. He would be an avowed enemy of Thomas Jefferson, who in a letter to Washington described Harry Lee as "a miserable tergiversator."[3] Lee would be savagely beaten by an American mob and die broke and separated from his family. All that was in the future. For the present, Harry Lee, with 100 horsemen and 180 infantry, had come south to write his name in bold print in the history of the American Revolution.

As the new commander in the south, Maj. Gen. Nathanael Greene had little to work with. Most of his army was clad in rags, lacking weapons, food, and medical supplies. Disease was rampant in the ranks. Greene had to build an army in the south before he could use it. To Greene's discontent, much of what remained of the southern army was militia. One of the good things that Gates had done was ask for and receive the services of Ranger Dan Morgan.

Meanwhile, Francis Marion withdrew to his lair on Snow's Island and set about recruiting. To serve was a hard choice for men. Joining Marion meant leaving families to the depredations of Tory raiders. Tory commanders were ruthlessly carrying out a policy that Cornwallis condoned. Homes were looted and burned, crops destroyed, wives and children were mistreated and left destitute. The ruthless Banastre

Lighthorse Harry Lee.
NATIONAL ARCHIVES

Tarleton had a Quaker boy who displeased him shot. He hung another boy and forced his smaller brother to join the British ranks. Tarleton saw rape as a British privilege.

In December 1780, Marion was promoted to brigadier general and given additional militia forces to round out his brigade. He converted some of his infantry to cavalry and, faced with a shortage of arms, had blacksmiths make swords out of saws. His area of operations extended from the Little Peedee to the Santee River. Horry's Mounted Rangers had a confused skirmish with the British Queen's Rangers. Horry was unhorsed and in danger of capture when the gallant Sergeant McDonald dismounted, gave Horry his horse, then slipped into the swamps to escape the oncoming enemy.

In mid-December 1781, Greene and Morgan were at Charlotte, North Carolina. Greene dispatched Morgan's Virginia militia and Lt. Col. William Washington's regiment of dragoons to threaten the British left flank and added South Carolina militia to this force to establish control to the west while Greene marched east to Cheraw on the Great Pee Dee River, where he could rejuvenate his main

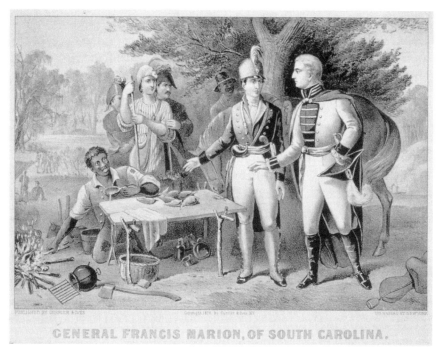

Francis Marion offers to share his meal with a British officer. LIBRARY OF CONGRESS

force, threaten British interests in the east, and block Cornwallis from having an open path to North Carolina and Virginia. Though necessary, it split the American commands beyond supporting distance. Morgan marched, and as he did, his forces grew to include 190 North Carolina Rangers under Maj. Joseph McDowell and 120 South Carolina Rangers under Maj. George Davidson.

In response, on January 1, 1781, Cornwallis sent Tarleton west to protect the British base at Ninety-Six and attack Morgan. Tarleton was to destroy Morgan's force or drive him back across the Broad River. Cornwallis would march northwest between Morgan and Greene with the bulk of his army. If Morgan retreated over the Broad River, Cornwallis would be in position to cut off Morgan and trap him between the two British forces. There was also the possibility of drawing Greene to battle. His route would have enabled him to support Tarleton.

Cornwallis sent Col. Nisbet Balfour against Marion, but the Swamp Fox slipped away, leaving Col. Peter Horry's Rangers to probe the enemy's movements. Horry's men again battled a detachment of the

Queen's Rangers, the green-jacketed Tory regiment that Robert Rogers had founded. Now under the command of Lt. Col. John Graves Simcoe, these American supporters of the king were hated with a passion usually reserved for Tarleton. Horry's Rangers fell upon the outnumbered Loyalists and drove them into Georgetown, where they were reinforced by more Tories under Major Ganey. Horry's men routed these as well. Sergeant McDonald engaged Major Ganey, who, when deserted by his men, attempted to flee. Ganey galloped his horse for two miles with McDonald in hot pursuit. Coming close, McDonald thrust the bayonet of his carbine through the back and chest of Ganey. The bayonet dislodged from the weapon and remained stuck up to the hilt in the Tory officer. Incredibly, Ganey escaped and survived.

Marion sent his men among the inhabitants surrounding Georgetown, shutting off the garrison supply route and seizing a valuable supply of salt, which he distributed to local people, earning their praise.

Cornwallis began his movement but was informed that Marion was being reinforced by the legion of the dashing Light Horse Harry Lee. Cornwallis decided to wait until an expected reinforcement of 4,000 men under General Leslie landed at Charleston. Changing his plan, Cornwallis temporarily stopped his move north. He sent additional troops and supplies to Tarleton, giving his young firebrand infantry, cavalry, and artillery consisting of two 3-pounder cannon commonly called "Grasshoppers" because of the shape of their carriages. Tarleton now had a combined-arms force totaling 1,200 men.

As Tarleton moved north to close with the Americans, Morgan was assembling American Continental and militia forces. Pickens's Rangers were Morgan's eyes and ears, forming a screen to the front of the Americans and keeping Morgan informed of Tarleton's progress. Morgan wrote to General Green on January 4, 1781: "Sensible of the Importance of Guarding against Surprises, I have used every precaution on the Head. I have had Men, who were recommended as every way calculated for the Business continually watching the motions of the Enemy so that unless they deceive me, I am in no danger of being surprised."[4] American reinforcements continued to arrive. Ranger Morgan withdrew before the British, carefully briefing his men that he wanted to draw Tarleton's Legion farther from the main British force. His public and private thoughts may have differed. Morgan was less inclined to battle with Tarleton. He recommended a campaign in Georgia to Greene and fretted over the capability of his militia. He was in bad circumstance for forage. Accustomed to the foot forces in the north, he condemned the practice of southern militia keeping their horses with them. He did not know these men well and worried whether they would desert him. Morgan had recently come down from the north and was new to the command of southern militia.

The aggressive Tarleton did not intend to give Morgan time. The British dragoon cleverly made a pretense of camping for the night, then moved after darkness to put him closer to the Americans. His ruse enabled him to get close. On learning of the enemy approach, Morgan's men quickly interrupted breakfast, broke camp, and retreated. Tarleton's men dined on Morgan's rations but were unable to close with the Old Wagoner. Pickens's Rangers kept between him and Morgan and took several prisoners from Tarleton's advance patrols of Tories.

Men from the Carolinas, Georgia, and Virginia were arriving in Morgan's camp. Many of the Americans who were coming to Morgan had suffered personal loss to Tarleton's men or knew someone who did. If Morgan had his doubts about his militia, they were also doubting him. They were cursing him for retreating. Some were local men who knew the terrain well and recommended a large animal pasturing ground called the Cowpens as a good place to make a stand. A disadvantage of this ground was that the Broad River would be five miles to Morgan's rear. Tarleton was ruthless. To lose at Cowpens would have fleeing Americans hemmed in by the river and slaughtered by the British dragoons.

The ground had its disadvantage to defense. It was somewhat undulating, open terrain with sparse trees and little underbrush. The freedom of movement available favored the use of cavalry, and Tarleton had three times the number of horsemen that Morgan had. There was a series of slightly rising grounds that culminated in two slight elevations. The flanks were relatively open to Tarleton, but his nature was so aggressive that Morgan expected the attack would be frontal.

Morgan made a thorough reconnaissance of the ground and decided that given Tarleton's hot pursuit, Cowpens was the spot to fight. His exact words are in dispute, but Morgan made it clear he intended to win or die at Cowpens. He thoroughly briefed his officers. With good security posted, he made certain his men had plenty of ammunition and were well fed and rested. He had veteran Continentals who had faced British steel before, and Morgan was a citizen-soldier at home with militia.

Scouts kept Morgan well informed. He knew that Tarleton would have a difficult and tiring twelve-mile approach march to get to Cowpens. Morgan believed that Tarleton's arrogance would cause him to immediately attack.

Morgan sent Georgia and North Carolina Rangers 150 yards forward to provide early warning of Tarleton's approach and to delay his advance; they would execute a fighting withdrawal drifting to the flanks to clear the line of fire for the next line, which was the militia under Pickens, which would begin the battle dismounted. Their horses were tethered to the rear of the battlefield. Their rifles had a more effective range then muskets of Tarleton's infantry. At Cowpens, Morgan intended to hit Tarleton hard with the rifles, reduce the British force, then extract the riflemen before Tarleton could close with the bayonet. Behind Pickens's line, Morgan established a third line that consisted primarily of 500 Maryland and Delaware Continentals. These were well-trained regular troops, uniformed, disciplined, experienced with the bayonet.

Morgan intentionally left gaps between his Continental units. He ordered Pickens to have his men deliver two volleys, then withdraw through the gaps before Tarleton could be on them with the bayonet. Morgan and his staff would be waiting there to reposition them. The Continentals would then have a clear field of fire against Tarleton's depleted force. Morgan was concerned about artillery: Tarleton had two 3-pounders, and Morgan had none.

Tarleton also had an advantage in cavalry. Morgan had William Washington with eighty white-coated dragoons and forty-five mounted Rangers under McCall, but Tarleton had twice that force on horseback, and they, like the rest of Tarleton's Legion, were fierce fighters. Morgan could do nothing about his lack of artillery, but he positioned his cavalry at a rear hill that allowed them to be close at hand and to support either flank. What Morgan established was a classic defense in depth that made the best use of the strengths of the force he had

Turning the Tide   225

Col. William Washington at Cowpens. NATIONAL ARCHIVES

available. Morgan displayed a key element of leadership by making certain that not just officers but all of his troops understood the plan.

Taking no chance that Morgan would escape, Tarleton allowed his tired men minimal rest, and at about 2 A.M. on January 17, 1781, he rousted them from their rest and began his twelve-mile approach march. The British soon learned that much of the route was difficult and tiring. It was five hours of hard marching before they could come to the attack.

American Rangers kept Morgan informed of Tarleton's movements and harassed the British by sniping and setting forest fires. Tarleton put fifty horsemen to the front who could rapidly close with Rangers as they reloaded. Some of the Rangers were sabered, but they emptied fifteen saddles. Fighting from behind trees, the Rangers employed a buddy system of two or three men, thus allowing for one rifle to be ready to fire while others reloaded. Considerably outnumbered and withdrawing, they took sufficient toll of the British column that Tarleton began to deploy his force on line.

In place of using his horsemen as a single powerful fist, Tarleton divided them into three elements. He held the Legion cavalry of 200 at the rear but posted fifty mounted dragoons on each flank, where they provided flank security and could be used in a single or double envelopment of Morgan's line. It was not an unreasonable move, but it reduced the power of his mounted arm.

Thus, from right to left, Tarleton had fifty dragoons, his light infantry, the Legion, the inexperienced 7th Regiment, and another fifty dragoons. His two pieces of artillery were forward and on line, one placed in the center, the other on the left. Behind these, ready to exploit the attack was cavalry and the Highland 71st Regiment. Brimming with confidence and without hesitation, Tarleton attacked.

The American scouts and skirmishers had taken their toll and withdrawn to Pickens's line. Now Andrew Pickens and his officers steadied their riflemen, cautioning them to wait while the wave of British rolled toward them. At less than 100 yards, the first volley cut the British like rows of corn. The rifles of the Rangers took an especially high toll of officers. This loss threw Tarleton's ranks into disorder. According to Colonel Howard, who commanded the Continentals, it was at this point "that the battle was gained."[5]

The highly disciplined British recoiled then, bending as though in a windstorm. They hurried forward, hoping to close with the bayonet before the riflemen could reload. They were not successful, and a second withering volley tore into their ranks.

Morgan had come forward to observe Pickens's reception of the enemy. When he saw they were steady, he removed to his next line and encouraged his regulars. Following their orders, Pickens's line now began to withdraw behind the bayonet-equipped Continentals. The British could not clearly see the line of regulars behind Pickens. It appeared the American line was breaking. The British infantry surged forward cheering. As the Americans on the left began to withdraw, Tarleton saw an opportunity to flank Morgan's position. He ordered the fifty dragoons from his right flank to ride the withdrawing men down, thus striking at Morgan's left. Tarleton also ordered his infantry reserve, the 1st Battalion of the 71st Highlanders, to attack on Morgan's right, instructing them to pass to the left of the 7th Regiment before firing. The fifty dragoons he had positioned on his left flank would participate in the attack on Morgan's right.

Tarleton was now executing a frontal attack combined with a double envelopment of Morgan's position. He still had his Legion cavalry in reserve to exploit an opportunity at any of the three critical points of the battlefield—Morgan's front or either of his flanks.

Any Ranger who survived Indian warfare knew how to reload on the run. On Morgan's left, Pickens men moved quickly, reloading while trying to break clear. But the English horsemen were among them quickly with swinging sabers. Without bayonets and in the process of reloading, the Americans were in a desperate circumstance. Some were ridden down or suffered terrible wounds from the long knives; others were able to fight back. Colonel Thomas Brandon was seen to kill three of Tarleton's riders with his sword. Other Rangers were able to take shelter among a stand of trees and, from this position, delivered accurate rifle fire that dropped dragoons from their saddles. Morgan galloped to the scene and shouted to the men to hold firm.

From his reserve position at the rear, William Washington saw the circumstance of Pickens's men and, without instruction from Morgan, ordered his white-coated dragoons to draw sabers and charge. Though Tarleton had a significant advantage in the number of horsemen, his decision to separate them into three locations meant that at the point of Washington's attack, the Americans had better than a two-to-one advantage.

The American horsemen hit Tarleton's dragoons like a thunderbolt, putting them to flight. This allowed Pickens's men to complete their movement and again become a unified fighting force. Washington had the presence of mind to withdraw his horsemen back to their reserve positions.

Battle smoke, a skillful use of a reverse slope, and a tree line behind the reserve position had provided partial concealment of Morgan's line of regulars. Tarleton's charging infantry were visibly shocked to see the silent line of Continentals. These were commanded by the gallant Lt. Col. John Eager Howard, a future governor of Maryland and United States senator. The British line paused, the surviving officers putting order into their ranks, then coming on in a three-battalion front. With Pickens's men now behind them, the American regulars closed to a solid line of three battalions firing volleys by company. A ripple of fire went down the line from right to left.

At close range, the British and American lines poured a horrendous fire into each other for a time that some participants thought was five minutes and others felt was thirty. It was sufficient to slaughter men on both sides.

Though in a hot engagement, Howard could see the 71st Highlanders coming in to attack his right flank. Howard ordered the company on his right flank to face to the right to meet the attack. The order was misunderstood, and the company began to march to the rear. Seeing this, the next company in line assumed they were to withdraw and began marching off. Company after company filed off.

Howard was justifiably amazed at this turn of events but kept his composure. He quickly saw that angling the right of his line was to his advantage against Tarleton's Highlanders. Morgan was aghast. He quickly rode to Howard and angrily demanded to know if Howard was retreating. Howard responded, "Do men who march like that look like they are beaten?" Morgan acknowledged this truth and told Howard he would ride back and halt the marching men, selecting a new line of battle for the right flank. Tarleton saw the withdrawal and thought the moment of victory was at hand. He urged his men forward and brought his 200-man Legion Cavalry forward to deal the crushing blow.

Thinking the Americans were beaten, Tarleton's men broke ranks and charged forward. From his hilltop position in reserve, Washington had seen Tarleton's second force of fifty dragoons charging Morgan's right flank. Again without waiting for orders, Washington swept down from his hill, and again having a decided numerical advantage at the point of action, his horsemen routed these dragoons. Washington also saw what appeared to be a red-coated mob running forward and recognized that Tarleton's officers had lost control of their men. He sent a messenger forward to Morgan saying, "They're coming on like a mob. Give them one fire and I'll charge them." Pickens's Rangers had now made a complete circuit of the rear of the line and were also in position to deliver fire into Tarleton's Highlanders.

Screaming their battle cries, the Highlanders and the 7th Regiment had closed to between fifteen and thirty yards of the American line. At that range, Howard faced his men toward the enemy and gave the order to fire. The Americans had fixed bayonets. The enemy was so close that no attempt was made to use aimed fire. Many Americans fired from the hip with their bayonets immediately ready for use.

The fire tore Tarleton's line apart by both lead and shock. Howard ordered a charge and the Americans surged forward behind the sharp points of their bayonets. Immediately after the American fire, Washington's horsemen charged into the British left flank.

The 7th Regiment and the Legion Infantry collapsed while the Highlanders tried to continue the fight. Washington led his horseman in an attack to seize Tarleton's two guns. The British artillerymen would not surrender and fought until every man was dead or wounded.

Pickens's Rangers saw the effect of Howard's blow and followed in, delivering accurate rifle fire into the reeling Highlanders. The brave soldiers in kilts tried to execute a fighting withdrawal, but they were broken up into small pockets of resistance and surrounded by Continentals, Rangers, and American dragoons. Those British who could were throwing down their weapons and fleeing the battlefield. As they had been given orders not to take any American prisoners, Tarleton's men were justifiably fearful that they would be slaughtered. Many begged for their lives, pleading that they were not responsible for their orders. American leaders were not inclined to end the battle with a slaughter of prisoners, and Howard and Pickens ordered their men to cease the killing. Major McArthur, the commander of the 71st Highlanders, surrendered his sword to Pickens, as did the others. Pickens later wrote, "I believe every officer of that regiment delivered his sword into my hand."[6]

Though much of Tarleton's cavalry was not engaged, they saw the disaster occurring to their front and panicked. Tarleton tried to reform his horsemen, but only 14 officers and 40 men rallied to him. More than 200 British cavalrymen were in flight. Leading his small group, Tarleton tried to save his guns in a a brief but vicious fight. There was a momentary and inconclusive personal clash between Banastre Tarleton and William Washington. Tarleton broke the engagement and rode southeast trying to gather his men. He then sought to make contact with General Cornwallis, who was twenty-five miles distant. Many of the Rangers mounted their horses and, with Washington's dragoons, rode in pursuit. Tarleton was pressed too hard to do an effective job of destroying his supplies. He had the added embarrassment of losing many of his supply wagons, his personal baggage, that of his men, and hundreds of weapons. The British lost 700 of their 1,100-man force, with 100 dead and 600 taken prisoner; 229 of these were wounded and 400 unwounded. Thirty-nine British officers were dead. The American loss was 12 killed and 60 wounded.

Cowpens was a tidy battle. Morgan's arrangements were a classic defense in depth utilizing the potential of each element of his force to its maximum. He made a thorough reconnaissance of his battleground and used the terrain wisely. He made certain that his men were well fed and supplied and rested. He went among his soldiers, giving them inspiration. Morgan had good intelligence and kept himself informed of the enemy strength and movement. Morgan arranged his defense to provide early warning and capitalize on the advantage in range and accuracy his rifles had over British muskets. Through his scouts and skirmishers and those on Pickens's line, Morgan was able to hit the enemy before they could hit him. His Rangers and militia took a heavy toll of the oncoming British, concentrating on officers. Loss of control hurt Tarleton badly.

Morgan recognized that rifle-equipped men could not stand against the bayonet. When they had hurt the enemy, Morgan withdrew his riflemen behind his bayonet-bearing Continentals. Behind them, superbly positioned to assist any part of the line, were Washington's dragoons and McCall's mounted South Carolina and Georgia Rangers. Thus, Tarleton's advance was punished throughout the battle area as it was drawn against successive lines. Morgan did a superb job in making certain his men knew the plan of action. Of great importance was that Morgan made a prompt assessment of the victory and took immediate action to preserve it.

Dan Morgan, the mouthy, hot-headed freight hauler of 1755, had learned much about war in twenty-six years. His Ranger experience gained in the French and Indian War, Pontiac's War, Dunmore's War, and Quebec and Saratoga served the American cause well. Morgan had become a general.

Tarleton was thrashed, but he remained resilient and, immediately upon joining Cornwallis, set about rebuilding his force. General Leslie and his 2,500 reinforcements joined Cornwallis on the day Tarleton returned. Cornwallis was only twenty-five miles from Cowpens and still had an angle of approach that would put him between Morgan and Greene. Within six hours of the Battle of Cowpens, Cornwallis was informed of the result by men who had fled the battlefield. By moving fast, he could interdict a movement north by Morgan or bring one or both of the American commanders to battle. It was unlikely they could join forces, but even if they succeeded, the British would outnumber the Americans. Cornwallis thought that Morgan would dally on the scene of his victory or perhaps move against the British post at Ninty-Six.

When the shooting stopped, Morgan was hampered with battlefield wounded from both sides and hundreds of prisoners. He wisely saw his predicament and moved fast. He detached Pickens and his horse-equipped Rangers and put them to arranging for care of the wounded and burying the dead. Taking those prisoners capable of marching and all the British supplies he could use, including tents and muskets, Morgan was on the march within two hours of the end of the fight. His direction was north, and Morgan did not stop for a brief rest until he had the Broad River between him and Cornwallis. On January 19, three days after the Battle of Cowpens, Cornwallis moved northwest, marching under the vain hope that he would trap Morgan against a river Morgan had already crossed.

Morgan was marching fast into North Carolina, covering more than 100 miles of difficult terrain and crossing the Catawba River. He paused there to rest and send off his prisoners. Pickens's men soon came riding in. Greene learned that Cornwallis was determined to pursue Morgan into North Carolina. The British general had ordered the destruction of tents and most wagons—anything that would slow the march. Greene saw the opportunity to starve the army of Cornwallis by drawing him deeper into the countryside. Greene decided to reunite his army and gave orders that set men moving on a tortuous march through bitter cold and ice-filled streams. Though the men lacked tents and blankets and clothing was minimal, they kept faith in their cause. After a harrowing ride through enemy-infested country, Greene joined Morgan.

After an arduous search, the young firebrand Harry Lee had made contact with the introspective, middle-aged Francis Marion. Lee liked Marion. For his part, Marion was interested to know that Lee's men wore green uniforms—the same color uniforms worn by Banastre Tarleton.

Marion had a fascination bordering on obsession with the town of Georgetown on the coast. It was an important British depot with ammunition, muskets, clothing, and salt. It was also a frequent nesting ground of the hated Queen's Rangers. Marion and Lee decided to cooperate in the attack. They struck the town on January 24, 1781. Marion had information that Georgetown was lightly guarded by sixty recuperating men. In fact, 200 British troops had been moved into Georgetown. This was not sufficient force to deter Marion and Lee. They knew where the British commander's quarters were and where the troops were billeted. They knew where the fort was and its defenses.

It was decided that Lee's men would be dismounted and move by boat to land under cover of darkness on the undefended Georgetown waterfront. At the same time, all those troops who were on horseback would charge from the landward side, and the British would be crushed between them.

To a point, all went according to plan. The landing was made at the waterfront, and the charge was made from the land. The British commander, Colonel Campbell, was taken prisoner in his quarters by Lee's men. Campbell's adjutant, Major Irvine, and a Major Crookshanks were found at a tavern by Marion's men. Irvine saw them coming and fired a pistol at them, then raised his hands to surrender. Lt. James Creyer had once been given 500 lashes and recognized Irvine as the man who had ordered the beating. As Irvine raised his hands, Creyer drove his bayonet into the British officer's chest. Crookshanks was nevertheless taken alive.

The Americans hurried forward to close with the enemy, but the British soldiers and Tories did not engage. They withdrew into the fortified barracks and a well-armed fort. A consultation between Marion and Lee revealed that neither of the great raiders had anticipated this development. They had no cannon to use on the walls of the fort. They lacked scaling ladders and battering rams. Rather than see their men butchered in a fruitless attack, the embarrassed leaders decided to draw off. In reports to General Greene, they put on a bold face, making the abortive attack seem a success. They had learned to work together, though Lee was a better penman and had a tendency to highlight his name in reports. Marion rued his lack of cannon, knowing that artillery would have brought Georgetown to surrender.

While Lee and Marion were meeting misfortune at Georgetown, Dan Morgan was meeting the same. On January 24, Morgan wrote a letter to General Greene telling the commander, "After my late success and my sanguine expectations to do some thing clever this campaign must inform you that I shall be oblig'd to give over the persuite, by reason of an old pain returning upon me, that laid me up for four month last winter and spring. It is a ciatick pain in my hip."[7] Morgan was very ill and in great pain, shaking from head to foot and enduring piles so painful that he could not sit his horse. He was out of the campaign.

As February 1781 opened, Cornwallis had 3,000 men in hot pursuit of the Americans. He crossed the Catawba River northwest of Charlotte, North Carolina, brushing aside local defense forces as he marched. Greene continued to pull away, drawing Cornwallis after him. Greene contemplated fighting in North Carolina and saw promising terrain near Guilford Court House. He felt he did not have sufficient force and continued his withdrawal northward. Behind him, he left a picked force of 700 men under Col. Otho Williams. These men fought a brilliant delaying action, destroying boats and bridges and harassing the British advance.

By mid-February, Greene had crossed the Dan River, the border between North Carolina and Virginia. Despite the terrible conditions under which four men shared a single blanket, volunteers were arriving in large numbers. Harry Lee and Pickens were now with Greene. The British had the larger force in the Carolinas but were far from their base of supplies. North Carolina contained a strong Loyalist contingent, and Cornwallis looked forward to receiving assistance from local Tories. Banastre Tarleton was sent on an active recruiting campaign, and the dragoon leader was not sympathetic to those who refused him. It was British policy that those who refused service to the king could lose all they possessed. Under Tarleton, they were fortunate if they lost only their homes and food. Through active recruiting, Tarleton now had 200 cavalry and 400 infantry supported by cannon in his command. Even this force was expected to grow. Four hundred Tory volunteers were assembled under a Colonel Pyle who was leading them to join Tarleton.

Hearing that Tories were swelling the British ranks, General Greene ordered his Rangers southward across the Dan River to disrupt the recruitment. Andrew Pickens and Harry Lee would act in concert. Preliminary to movement, Pickens sent scouts across the river. They learned that Tarleton was in the area recruiting and was separated from Cornwallis.

Lee and Pickens led their men across the Dan River and went in pursuit of Tarleton. Burning ruins were Tarleton's footprints, and the patriot leaders found local men who were eager to talk. They learned of the farmhouse where the British raider intended to camp and attacked only to come up empty handed. Tarleton had eaten a meal there but decided to move an additional six miles. Two officers of Tarleton's staff still remained at the farmhouse and were taken prisoner.

Tarleton's men wore green jackets, and so did Harry Lee's. To temporarily confuse the enemy, the Americans marched with Lee's horsemen in front and Pickens's following. The only identifying mark of Pickens's men was a green sprig torn from a bush or tree and stuck in the hatband.[8] At the head of the column, Lee encountered two young Tory horsemen who assumed the green jackets belonged to Tarleton's men. Lee posed as Tarleton, and the young riders told him they were part of Colonel Pyle's reinforcements, which were on the road a short distance ahead.

Lee told one of the Tories to remain with him as a guide and sent the other back to Colonel Pyle. He requested that the Tory leader line up his men along the side of the road. This would enable a review and congratulations of Pyle's men.

Lee sent a messenger to Pickens requesting the Carolinian to circle to the left of where Pyle's men were located. The intent was to close on both sides of the Tories and capture them. Lee's horsemen trotted forward and passed in front of the unsuspecting Tories, then wheeled in line to face them as though in salute. Colonel Pyle was reaching to shake Lee's hand when gunfire erupted. Some of the Tories were experienced woodsmen who heard or saw the movement of Pickens's Rangers as they closed through the woods and fired. Tories fired on Capt. Joseph Eggleston's troop of Lee's force.[9] The effect was immediate and devastating for Pyle's men. Lee's men drew sabers and cut the confused and terrified Tories down. They cried that they were friends and tried to run from the long knives that hacked them, but to no avail. They ran into Pickens's rifles and were shot down. It was butchery, not battle. More than 100 Tories were slaughtered. Colonel Pyle and most of the rest were wounded, bearing terrible cuts. Lee would write in his memoirs that it was "sickening." The Americans had a few men slightly scratched and one horse killed.

To Pickens and Lee, the event was but a stepping stone. Tarleton was the quarry they sought. The fighting British raider soon learned of the massacre of Pyle's men and stayed clear. Now a battle between the Americans and British was not likely until Greene and Cornwallis, the two senior commanders, chose. As reinforcements came in, General Greene crossed the Dan River into North Carolina. He established a screening force under Col. Otho Williams and ordered Harry Lee to join Williams.

Williams's men were ordered to move about, creating a confusion about American intent. Tarleton tried to shadow American movements to learn what they planned. Cornwallis was exhausting his supplies, and the slaughter of Pyle's men had cooled Tory efforts. He needed to bring Greene to a decisive battle. On April 14, 1781, Greene moved his army to the vicinity of Guilford Court House. As he knew from his previous visit, the ground was excellent for defense. The major drawback was that the best places to form lines were too distant from each other to be mutually supporting.

Greene was now ready for battle. He had received strong reinforcement and had 1,500 Continentals, but many of these were not experienced. The rest of his 4,400 men were militia, and much of those were untrained men enlisted for six weeks. Cornwallis could muster 2,000 men. He was not at great disadvantage as his men were battle hardened.

Greene in large part followed Morgan's defense-in-depth plan of successive lines with the militia in front to fire several volleys. They were to take a toll of the British, then withdraw to allow a second line of militia and then the third line of Continentals to take up the action. The flanks of the militia line were held by experienced militia, including Ranger riflemen buttressed by Washington's horsemen on the American right and Harry Lee's men on the American left. Greene reasoned that his battlefield was of such depth that he could not keep a reserve. Every unit he had was committed to a line of battle. Greene had no intention of fighting a winner-take-all battle. Taking the long view, he saw that it was necessary only for him to keep sapping the British strength.

March 15, 1781, dawned chill and clear. Seeking battle, Cornwallis made a twelve-mile approach march with Tarleton scouting to his front. Greene had Harry Lee and his horsemen patrolling well forward, and the green-jacketed British and Americans soon clashed. Lee's men withdrew, and as Tarleton came on, the Americans turned and drove Tarleton back upon the main body of Cornwallis. There they fought a brisk fight before withdrawing. Cornwallis marched on through a defile, then found Greene's lines in position to receive him. It must have been a pretty sight as the British and Hessian soldiers debouched from the defile and, moving at double quick, spread left to form the line of battle. To the music of fife and drum, the British line advanced over a quarter mile of open ground. Marching in ordered ranks, they moved into the fire of more than 1,000 rifles and muskets.

The North Carolina militia in the center of Greene's forward line were untrained citizen-soldiers whose instructions were not clear to them. They held to deliver the two fires as instructed. Their shots took a toll, but the British charge after the second fire put them to flight.

As the British charged in the center, they were taken under enfilade fire on both flanks from Lynch's Virginia Rangers and Kirkwood's light infantry on the American right and Campbell's and Lee's dismounted cavalry on the American left. This fire passed down the British line and took a terrible toll. Cornwallis swung units left and right to meet these fires frontally while other units moved into the center and continued the attack. The fighting was vicious as the British came up against the American second line of Virginians. These men delivered a heavy fire and repulsed several bayonet charges. Part of the British line swung past them and attacked the third American line. Across the battlefield, the Americans were fighting a steady delaying action, bleeding the oncoming British regulars. As the British tore into the third line, that of the regulars, they came upon the men of the 5th Maryland, who were in their first battle. The sight of British grenadiers and the 2nd Battalion of the Guards under Colonel Stuart coming at them with the bayonet terrified the Marylander regulars, and they ran for their lives, losing several guns at that part of the line.

Lt. Col. William Washington never needed an order to fight. On his own initiative, he rounded up several companies of mounted

Rangers and led these and his dragoons to the attack. Shooting and cutting, they rode through the British, killing Colonel Stuart. The battle was now a give and take of blood. Sensing that defeat was at hand, Cornwallis gave an order that would haunt him for the rest of his life. He directed his artillery to fire grape shot over the heads of his men into the Americans. He was an experienced soldier and knew that this was like firing gigantic shotguns. The balls would scatter to kill and maim British as well as Americans. Major General O'Hara, whom Cornwallis would leave to surrender his army at Yorktown, begged his commander not to do this, but Cornwallis insisted. The result was that the two armies drew apart and lay like two wounded and exhausted animals panting at each other.

Greene took calculated risks with but did not gamble his army. Col. John Green's proven regiment of Virginia Continentals had not yet been bloodied in the battle. This regiment was ordered to cover the withdrawal of the American army. It proved its mettle by fighting a skillful delaying action. The British force was too badly hurt to press on.

Guilford Courthouse was a pyrrhic victory for Cornwallis, who lost 532 men—approximately one quarter of his force. The fight cost the British so heavily that Cornwallis lost his grip on the south. Seeking to link up with other British troops, he headed north on roads that would lead to Yorktown, Virginia, and surrender. Now the British that remained in the south were under Lord Rawdon, who had little under his control but Augusta, Charleston, Georgetown, and Ninty-Six.

The Americans had suffered 78 men killed and 185 wounded. Greene had retreated rather than risk his army and seized the opportunity to march into South Carolina, where the only Americans actively fighting were Rangers. The opportunity was now at hand to drive the British from the south. Greene ordered Marion to take Georgetown and Pickens to take Augusta while he went after Ninty-Six.

While all this was taking place, other events had occurred. Back in late January, as Lee's Legion had marched away, Marion sent his men on raids capturing and burning British supplies. He was the junior brigadier, and General Greene had ordered him to cooperate with General Sumter. Marion sulked. He did not like serving under the flamboyant Sumter, who was audacious to the point of rashness. When it came to working with Sumter, the normally fast-moving Marion dragged his feet. Attacking without proper reconnaissance on February 28, Sumter went after the British position at Fort Watson on the east bank of the Santee. He was defeated. The British were determined to run him out of the country, and Sumter retreated to the north.

Marion was on his own with no American support and was being hunted by Lt. Col. John Watson, commander of the famed British 3rd Regiment of Foot. Because of the color of their uniform facings, these soldiers were known as the Buffs. Watson set out with 500 men, a mix of regulars and Tories. Reasoning that the enemy expected him to withdraw, Marion took the offensive and laid an ambush. Watson was not caught napping. He had Loyalist horsemen under Major Harrison scouting to his front and flanks. Marion attacked these scouts with Horry's mounted Rangers. There was a furious fight, with the American prevailing. Captain Conyers killed Major Harrison in hand-to-hand combat. Watson moved his main body to support his scouts, and Marion withdrew.

Doggedly, Watson continued the pursuit, with Marion drawing him on by staying just out of reach. The British moved toward Kingstree, the door to the heartland of American resistance. Marion now sent a picked force of seventy men under Major James around the British to seize a critical bridge. James performed brilliantly. He removed planking from the bridge, put sharpshooters behind the abutments, and supported them on the flanks. He knew the British had artillery, but their ground was higher, and they could not depress their guns to fire on his men. Marion arrived with the main body and took station some distance to the rear. A body of water only fifty yards wide separated the ragged Americans from the British and Tories. Time and again, Watson's men tried to cross, only to be shot down. The courageous Sergeant McDonald again distinguished himself, wounding an officer of the Buffs at a distance of 300 yards.

Angry communication passed between Marion and the British commanders regarding what each perceived as violations of the rules of war. The British had hung some of Marion's men they believed had violated their parole after capture. They had taken prisoner an American officer who was carrying a flag of truce, claiming he was a parole violator. A spirited correspondence passed between Marion and the British commanders without satisfactory conclusion. Marion was not ready to hang British prisoners but sent his men to shoot their sentinels. This was a heinous act in the eyes of the British, and they bitterly complained. Marion allowed Watson's wounded to pass after acrimonious accusations by both. Watson felt the practice of burning the houses of your enemy was "right and is customary in all countries."

When a British officer was sent under flag of truce to Marion, he was seized in retaliation. There was an outcry at this perceived injustice from the British, which Marion ignored. He now had a safeguard against the hanging of his officer.

Now in unfriendly territory, unable to get support from other British forces, Watson and his troops were in great difficulty. Pursued and sniped at, the Buffs and Tories moved, often at the double quick, across fifteen miles of pine land. Encumbered with dead and baggage, they could not break free. Hammered front and rear, Watson left his dead, dumped his artillery underwater, loaded his wounded on wagons, and fled to safety in Georgetown. This was not warfare in the accepted tradition. Watson was shocked at the conduct of Marion and huffed, "They will not sleep and fight like gentlemen, but like savages are eternally firing and whooping around us at night and by day waylaying and popping as us from behind every tree!"

Now it was Marion's turn to be embarrassed. While in hot pursuit of Watson, he had left his den unprotected. Tory raiders under Col. Welbore Doyle raided Snow's Island, destroyed Marion's supplies, burned his buildings, and freed his captive British officer. Doyle executed a superb hit-and-run raid. Marion broke off his pursuit of Watson's men to attempt to save his camp. The best he could achieve was a successful skirmish against the Tory rear guard. Marion's difficulties were compounded by his men leaving to help their families. The British and their Tory allies had burned about 100 homes. Women and children were destitute and needed the assistance of their husbands and fathers. Reduced to seventy men and two rounds of ammunition per man, Marion endured a time of discontent. He sent Horry's Ranger horsemen after Doyle, who quickly withdrew sixty miles west to Camden. Marion wondered why Doyle did this, but the reason was hidden in the fog of war.

Marion considered a withdrawal to North Carolina. The war clouds were gray and gloomy when a famished John Baker rode an exhausted horse into camp. While Baker wolfed food, Marion hurried to him and learned to his delight that Light Horse Harry Lee was on the way. It was not long before the sound of distant drums could be heard.

Now the reason for Doyle's withdrawal became clear. Captain Conyers rode in bearing a letter from General Greene that told of the battle at Guilford Courthouse. Greene was now advancing the American army into South Carolina. He was calling on all local forces to arise. Lee liked Marion and asked that they be permitted to fight together. Greene approved, and Marion's face lighted with joy at the sight of Lee's superbly drilled and equipped men. He called on his men, and about 500 responded, eager for revenge.

Against the advice of Lee, Marion was now determined to capture Fort Watson, a British fortification located southeast of the juncture of the Congaree and Wateree rivers. Marion was at his best at raids and ambush, not at siege warfare. Fortunately, the British garrison did not have artillery. For eight days, the affair dragged on. Marion had men killed and wounded without result. His men were disgusted and leaving. He asked for an artillery piece, but the officer bringing it became lost and wandered off on the wrong road. As so often happens in the military, the success of a commander hinged upon the quick thinking of a subordinate. Using a suggestion of Maj. Hezekiah Mahan, Marion had a log tower built during darkness, placing it close to the walls of the fort.

When dawn came, the British garrison found themselves under deadly fire from the rifles of American soldiers who overlooked their position. The American rifles had greater range, and the riflemen were protected by logs the British muskets could not penetrate. With the British unable to defend themselves, other Americans were pulling down the British outworks. Behind them could be seen Lee's infantry standing, ready to attack. Seeing their cause as hopeless, the garrison surrendered.

Marion was now in position to raise havoc with British communications and resupply between the coast and interior. Lord Rawdon's forces were scattered throughout South Carolina and Georgia. A junction of Greene's army and the force of Marion and Lee would give the

Americans a numerically superior force. With this in mind, Rawdon moved to attack Greene at Hobkirk's Hill. The Americans were forced to withdraw to Camden, but the British loss hurt Rawdon. He could not continue the attack and withdrew toward Charleston.

Though he was successful, it was not a happy time for the Swamp Fox. The American army he had so long hoped for was now on the scene, but Marion found his independence taken from him. He must now take orders from General Greene. Hampered by slow communication with Greene, waiting for orders while his bored men left him, Marion saw golden opportunities slipping away. British plans were changing. Cornwallis was moving his army to Virginia, and the remaining British forces were separated and trying to unite. Awaiting slow-moving reinforcements, Marion lost a chance to ambush Watson and the Buffs. Disgusted, he considered resignation.

Affairs were worse for the British, who burned their long-held inland base of Camden, South Carolina, and marched for Charleston on the coast. They hoped to maintain their inland presence with a series of forts, but these were soon under attack—by Marion at Fort Motte and Sumter at Orangeburg and Fort Granby. Successful at Fort Motte, Marion shadowed the British while Greene's army moved to invest the British post at Ninety-Six. Marion learned that Georgetown was lightly defended, and he could fulfill his orders. He sent Greene a message that he was attacking the town. Georgetown fell, with its garrison withdrawing to British ships while Marion leveled the fort. Light Horse Harry Lee had joined with Andrew Pickens and Elijah Clarke to capture Fort Cornwallis and Fort Grierson at Augusta, Georgia.

Fort Cornwallis was held by Lt. Col. Thomas Brown, commander of the Florida Rangers. This was the wealthy Georgia plantation owner who had mocked the rebellion. He had been tarred and feathered and forced to recant. Burning with hatred, Brown escaped and raised a body of raiders whose depredations were equal to or exceeded those of Tarleton. Brown was a forceful and skilled commander difficult to kill or capture. Near Fort Cornwallis was Fort Grierson, named for another Tory leader who was equally hated. The latter fort was weaker, so the Americans attacked it first. Lee positioned his men between Fort Grierson and Fort Cornwallis to prevent Brown from coming to the aid of his compatriot. Brown tried but was driven back by Lee. Fort Grierson was attacked by Pickens's Rangers, who swarmed over the walls using scaling ladders. Inside they fought a ferocious hand-to-hand battle with the defenders. Many of the men locked in a struggle to the death had grown up with each other, had once been neighbors, or had been friends. Beaten down, the Tory Rangers tried to escape or surrender. Grierson tried to lead part of his men in escape to Fort Cornwallis. They were ambushed by Elijah Clarke, whose men killed thirty Tories. Pickens's Rangers leaped on those who tried to surrender with tomahawk, knife, and rifle butt or shot them where they stood. It was a massacre, and Pickens could not or would not control his men.

Grierson and a few of his men made it to Fort Cornwallis only to find it was under attack. Thomas Brown was fighting a skillful defense, sallying forth when the opportunity presented and blowing up houses that would have allowed the patriots to get close to his fortifications. Harry Lee had some cannon with him, and faced with having his walls blown down, Brown finally surrendered. A soldier rode up to the house where Grierson was being held and fired through an open door, killing the Tory colonel. Pickens posted a large reward for the murder, but no one wanted to collect it. Brown was in considerable danger as the mood was to court-martial and hang him. On learning of Brown's capture and possible hanging, the British sent word that six American prisoners would be hung in retaliation. Brown would again see action for the British, but their cause was in decline. At the end of the war, his 5,000-acre plantation and belongings were confiscated. Thomas Brown was left to the mercy of the king he supported. He went to the Bahamas, was given some land on St. Vincent, and died there in 1825.

The exhausted British and Tories gathered at Monck's Corner. Both sides knew that 2,000 British troops had arrived at Charleston. As senior American officer present in the area, Brig. Gen. Thomas Sumter decided to attack. Marion was opposed to this as he and Lee knew the British were well positioned. Sumter would not be deterred, and in the ensuing battle, the Americans were trounced, with Marion losing a number of men. He vowed he would never again fight under Sumter. Despite this British success, they were reduced to controlling only the Charleston area. With Marion among them, key leaders of South Carolina met in legislature with Marion and established American civil government. John Matthews was selected as governor of South Carolina. One of the first to suffer from civilian control was Thomas Sumter. The new leadership rejected his infamous "law" of plundering. An angry Sumter took this as a slight on his character and resigned, leaving Marion the senior militia general in the South Carolina.

The British dealt harshly with captured American soldiers. When they hung an American major, Marion retaliated by luring a force of British dragoons into an ambush near the Edisto. The Americans fired three volleys into the confused British force and cut down 100 of them.

As September 1781 opened, Greene united American Continentals and militia and moved to attack the British main force at Eutaw Springs on the Santee River. His health broken by campaigning, Lord Rawdon had turned over his command to Lt. Col. Alexander Stewart (or Stuart) and sailed for home. Lord Rawdon's vessel was captured by a French warship, and Rawdon was interned. Stewart tried to learn what Greene was doing but was much harassed in gathering intelligence by Americans ambushing his scouts. Stewart wrote to Cornwallis: "They rendered it impossible by waylaying the bye-paths and passes through the different swamps."[10] British forces now totaled 2,000 men; Greene had about 2,400.

On September 8, Greene was in an approach march of seven miles to Eutaw Springs. Stewart had sent a large and unarmed working detail to dig sweet potatoes. Two deserters from Greene's army came into Stewart's lines and told him Greene was coming. Such desertions were not uncommon in this war. Americans were in British ranks and British were in American ranks in such numbers that Greene remarked, "At the close of the war, we fought the enemy with British soldiers and they fought us with those of America."[11] Stewart sent 200 cavalry forward. Lead scouts for the Americans saw them coming, and Harry Lee established an ambush by placing his dismounted cavalry across the road while those on horseback concealed themselves in the trees on either side. The British saw the men on foot and charged. Losing forty men, they retreated as fast as they had come.

Greene moved to the attack. It had now become a standard defense to put the militia in the first line with the Continentals behind them and a mounted reserve or flank guard. Now Greene decided to use the same tactic in the offense.

Pickens's and Marion's men formed the left and right of Greene's front line. In the center, Greene posted North Carolina militia. These were recently recruited, had little training and no combat experience, and were commanded by a foreigner, the Marquis Francis de Malmedy. A volunteer who had been a lieutenant in the French Army, Malmedy had been appointed a brigadier general in the Rhode Island militia. When that expired, he was given a Continental commission as a colonel. Malmedy whined to General Washington that this was a slight to him and received a curt reply. His reputation was that he had abandoned his post at the siege of Charleston.[12] At Eutaw Springs, Malmedy was the wrong man commanding the wrong troops.

Though he had limited artillery, Greene placed two of his 3-pounder "grasshoppers" with the North Carolina militia. Slightly to the rear and to the flanks of his first line, Greene posted Lee on the right near Marion and Henderson, with South Carolina horsemen on the left near Pickens. In his second line, Greene placed his Maryland, Virginia, and North Carolina Continentals with two 6-pounders. In reserve, he held Washington's dragoons and Kirkwood's Delaware Continentals.

The British were drawn up in a single line that comprised the 3rd Regiment (Buffs) on the British right; Cruger's green-coated Tories, who were experienced fighters, in the center; the 63rd and 64th Regiments on the left; and Coffin's cavalry in reserve.

Distant from the Buffs on the right flank, near Eutaw Creek, Stewart cleverly placed Major Majoribanks with the flank companies of light infantry and grenadiers. These 300 men were concealed in a thicket in excellent position to prevent a flanking movement by the Americans or to launch an attack into Greene's left flank as the Americans advanced. The British had 2,000 men. Behind the British line were their tents and baggage and, to the right rear of that, a two-story brick house.

The Rangers' mission at Eutaw Springs was to spearhead the attacks. They advanced into the British line delivering seventeen volleys of massed rifle fire. Though ripped by British cannon and under fire from the entire British line, they pressed on. What Greene expected of these men is unclear. They were without bayonets and closing on soldiers who had them. Greene would later write to Steuben, "Such conduct would have graced the veterans of the great king of Prussia."[13]

The experienced British, who knew full well the disadvantage of the rifle, fixed bayonets and sent the 63rd and 64th Regiments charging into the Americans. They struck Malmedy's raw North Carolina militia, who had only fired an average of three times and were hesitant. Now these militia broke, exposing the flanks of Pickens and Marion. Lee and Henderson were also attacked, and the American line began to fall back. Greene promptly committed the North Carolina Continentals and followed them with the regulars from Maryland and Virginia. These came forward with fixed bayonets. The fighting was furious. Lieutenant Colonel Henderson of the South Carolinia State Troops was wounded, and Lt. Col. Richard Campbell, commander of the Virginia Continentals, was killed. Amid shot and shell, officers fought each other with swords and pistols.

Volley fire and hand-to-hand combat with cold steel and the butts of rifles and muskets brought the British attack to a standstill and reversed it. The American attack regained momentum, and the British began a fighting withdrawal. In the British rear echelon, personnel panicked and fled. Stewart could not prevent this, but he sent men under Tory Major Sheridan to occupy the brick house. From the upper floors, these men would have excellent firing positions.

From his concealed position on the American left flank, Major Majoribanks poured a hot fire into the oncoming Americans. Pickens was shot from his horse. The musket ball fired at his chest had been deflected by the buckle of his sword belt. The impact was so great that the buckle had been driven into his breast. Pickens would live but never quite recover from the effects of the wound. Greene dispatched Washington with his horsemen to eliminate this threat. Majoribanks's thicket was too dense for mounted troops, and Washington tried to flank the thicket. Majoribanks had foreseen this threat and put accurate fire on the Americans. Half of Washington's men were killed or wounded, and many of his officers were down when Washington had his horse shot out from under him. Entangled in his stirrups and unable to get free, he was bayoneted by one of Majoribanks men. The soldier was preparing for a killing thrust when a British officer ordered Washington taken as a prisoner. The South

Carolina horsemen now under Wade Hampton made another attack on Majoribanks and were repulsed. Greene threw in Kirkwood's Delaware Continentals, one of the best units in the American army. They entered the thicket and drove Majoribanks men rearward.

Victory was in American hands. Majoribanks was striving desperately to hold a position. Stewart was behind the British camp trying to rally his fleeing men. The opportunity existed to cut off the British under Sheridan before they could fortify the brick house. All things seemed favorable, but Greene had an army of destitute men who had not been paid in two years. Even his regulars had little in the way of clothing. On the approach march to Eutaw Springs, food had been in such short supply that frogs found in adjoining swamps had been a principal part of their diet.

Now the Virginia and Maryland Continentals and Pickens's and Marion's troops found themselves in the well-stocked British camp. They found hams and barrels of beef, flour and wheat bread, clothing to cover their nakedness, and boots for their feet. There were also barrels of rum and the wine that was frequently a part of a British officer's baggage. Discipline vanished as the men gorged themselves. Some poured liquor down their throats and were quickly drunk. The officers tried to restore order, but the hungry, poverty-stricken troops would not leave the largesse they had received from the British.

Not all the Americans were so engaged. Sheridan's men were hotly pursued to the brick house by Lee's dismounted horsemen and Kirkwood's Delaware Continentals. The pursuit was so hot that the British slammed the door, leaving a number of their own outside begging for entrance. From the windows of the house, Sheridan's men now opened a hot fire on the Americans who were caught in the open. The only way they could get free was to seize a British prisoner and use him as a human shield. Captain Manning, the commander of Lee's foot soldiers, laid hands on a British officer who, likely in fear of his life, began to recite his pedigree: "I am Sir Henry Barre, deputy adjutant general of the British Army, captain of the 52nd Regiment, secretary of the commandant at Charleston, etc., etc." Manning assured the British gentleman that he was now a prisoner and "the very man I was looking for." He then put Sir Henry between himself and British musket balls as he withdrew to safety.[14]

Major Majoribanks led his men forward and captured American guns Greene sent forward to shell the house. Lt. Col. John Eager Howard, who fought with great valor at Cowpens, led a company of Maryland Continentals who had missed the looting against Majoribanks. Howard was wounded and the attack withered.

By now, Stewart had regained control of his men and formed them into a line of battle. Greene, dismayed by the loss of control of his men, ordered a withdrawal. Majoribanks attacked the Americans as did the British cavalry under Coffin. Both were repulsed, and the brave Majoribanks was mortally wounded.

Both armies were exhausted. Greene had 554 casualties, including 61 officers killed or wounded. Pickens, Washington, and Howard were among the wounded. Stewart was wounded and lost 682 men. Greene was saddened by the breakdown in discipline that cost the Americans a significant victory, but he knew what his hungry unclad men had endured.

Stewart retreated quickly, destroying baggage and throwing 1,000 muskets in the water. Greene pursued but could not catch up. His army was wounded and suffered from hunger and disease; malaria roamed the ranks. During the Revolutionary War, when the militia had enough of the suffering they endured, they went home.

When the American regulars had enough, they mutinied. The Pennsylvania Line, the New Jersey Line, and Continentals from New England had all refused orders, with their commanders' reaction becoming increasingly violent. Now when there was no salt, the Maryland Continentals had enough and threatened mutiny. Timothy Griffen of South Carolina made the mistake of loudly telling other soldiers not to accept their lot. In short order, he was knocked down by an officer, arrested, court-martialed, and shot by a firing squad in front of Greene's army. This had a quieting effect on the ranks.

Pickens was laid up with his wound, and Marion and Lee participated in a brief pursuit of Stewart. There was discontent in the American camp. Greene wrote a letter to Washington complaining about militia and asking for more of everything. He asked Harry Lee to carry the letter, knowing that Washington had high regard for Lee. Washington had Cornwallis penned up at Yorktown and already had his commanders. Harry Lee was forced to sit and observe. He saw that

Washington's army now had supplies and comforts that the men in the southern army never saw. When Greene sent his report on the Battle of Eutaw Springs, he did not mention Harry Lee among officers worthy of praise. Lee was furious and wrote a frigid letter to Greene requesting permission to resign.

Marion was again faced with his men going home to look after their families. He did what raiding he could with a small force. He was also unhappy with Greene. Some months before, Marion had sent one of his officers, Capt. John Postell, to escort some British prisoners being paroled to Georgetown. The British had seized Captain Postell and held him captive. Marion was livid with rage and made strong effort to get his man back. In disregard of instructions, he tried to make a private arrangement with the British. They refused as they considered Postell a man who had broken a previous parole. Marion had asked Greene to use captive British officers as trading material for Postell, but Greene took no action. An angry Marion set about capturing British officers whom he could use to trade for his man.

Like Lee, Marion felt his efforts were not appreciated. Lee had seen the discontent of the Swamp Fox and asked Greene to do something that would lift Marion's spirits. Greene wrote Marion, "To fight the enemy with a prospect of victory is nothing, but to fight with intrepidity under the constant impression of a defeat and to inspire irregular troops to do it is a talent peculiar to yourself." This raised Marion's morale, but Greene was being duplicitous. The general told Joseph Reed of Pennsylvania that while Sumter and Marion had done good work, the only reason they came to the field was for plunder and their efforts seemed to be directed at keeping the war alive.

Marion also had a battle within his command that threatened to tear his units apart. In desperate times, American officers had buried their differences. With victory in their grasp, ambition took precedence over cause. Marion's key subordinates Col. Peter Horry and Col. Hezekiah Mahan were at odds with each other over seniority. Horry was Marion's friend and was clearly senior with seven years of courageous service; for eighteen months, he had been Marion's fist. Mahan was also Marion's friend—younger, daring, and a better horseman—but he refused Horry's orders. Both men were valuable, yet they could no longer work together.

Marion decided to dismount Horry's command, making Horry commander of his foot soldiers. Horry's horses, saddles, and swords would go to Mahan, who would command the horsemen. Mahan felt he had triumphed. The decision deeply hurt the gallant Horry, who broke his friendship with Marion and left the service. Shortly thereafter, Mahan was captured by Tories and signed his parole not to fight again. Escaping, Mahan managed to take the document with him and felt he did not have to honor it. Marion said it had been signed in good faith and must be lived up to. He would not allow Mahan to resume his command.

Cornwallis surrendered to General Washington on October 19, 1781. In the slow communications of the time, the British Parliament did not learn of this until November 25. Fighting would continue for a year in win-some, lose-some fashion.

In late November, a detachment of Marion's men under Mahan took the British outpost at Fair Lawn, South Carolina. At the beginning of December, General Greene took Fort Dorchester. British morale was crumbling. Greene had only 400 men, but the British thought he had considerably more and fled. As 1782 dawned, Gen. Anthony Wayne brought another American army to the south and beat a Creek Indian force. In March, the British war government fell, and in April, Holland recognized the new United States. On June 4, in the Ohio territory, British and Indians beat an American force under Col. William Crawford, who was captured, then tortured and murdered by Indians. At Blue Lick Springs, also in Ohio, Americans under Maj. Hugh McGary were led into an ambush by McGary's rash action. More than seventy were killed, most of whom were skilled frontiersmen.

On August 29, 1782, Marion's men won a skirmish against the British at Fair Lawn, South Carolina. The final battle was at John's Island, South Carolina, on November 4, 1782. The American commander, William Wilmot, a Continental officer, won the battle but lost his life. He is believed to be the last man killed in action in the Revolutionary War.

As the war in South Carolina ground down, the British began to evacuate their forces. For Tories, it was a time of despair. They paid the price of the losing side. North and south, they fled to the seacoast to make their escape on English ships, leaving all behind them.

Marion was not a vengeful man. He held out the hand of friendship to those Americans who had fought against him and did not risk the death of more of his men in action against a beaten foe. He informed General Greene that "my Brigade is composed of citizens, enough of whose blood has already been shed." On December 14, 1782, the British sailed from Charleston. The South Carolinians went home to repair their farms; among them was Francis Marion. He was unpaid, and his home and outbuildings were destroyed, stock stolen, and furniture smashed.

CHAPTER 15

Post-Revolution Fights and the War of 1812

In 1785, when the fighting with Great Britain had ceased, a friend said to Benjamin Franklin, "We have won independence." Franklin wisely responded, "Say rather 'we have won the Revolution.' The war for independence has yet to be fought."[1] At the close of the Revolutionary War, what passed as the United States was still a collection of former colonies that had temporarily put aside their quarrels.

A nation had not yet been formed, and the British well knew the Americans lacked power. Engaged in a great war with France, Britain was short of men for its navy. British warships stopped American shipping and impressed American seamen at will, claiming they were deserters from the Royal Navy. With territory and a rich fur trade at stake and spurred by American Loyalists who had been forced to flee to Canada, the British adopted a policy of arming and supplying Indian tribes who would raid along the northern frontier. In 1791, an American expedition under Arthur St. Clair was sent to Ohio to curb the actions of the Maumee Indians. The 2,000 Americans were decisively beaten and lost half their number. Most of the small regular army of the United States was lost.

Having tasted humiliation, the Congress authorized the establishment of a force of 5,000 men, known as the Legion of the United States. In command was the able and experienced Gen. Anthony Wayne. In the Revolutionary War, Wayne had molded his Pennsylvania brigade into the best of the Continental units and was appointed by Washington to command the light infantry corps. Unlike the rash St. Clair, Wayne refused to be hurried. He disciplined, trained, and organized his legion for two years until they were molded into an efficient fighting force. When he moved, the eyes and ears of his organization were Rangers who scouted his front and flanks. The confident

Indians sought to ambush the Americans in Ohio at a spot where a tornado had cut a swath of destruction through the forest. The location was known as Fallen Timbers. Here the Indians had butchered St. Clair's men and hoped to do the same to Wayne and his legion. Alerted by his Rangers to the enemy's location, Wayne ordered his men to fix bayonets and routed the Indians in a decisive victory.

Those who were for it called the War of 1812 America's second war for independence; those opposed named it for the president they despised—Mr. Madison's War. As the provocations were mostly on the seas, it is probable that an American navy of reasonable size would have prevented the larger conflict. The United States declared war on Great Britain on June 18, 1812, and President Madison declared the war at an end on February 17, 1815.

While flames flickered on the American frontier, Europe was ablaze. In 1812, the English were anxiously consulting dispatches, holding their breath while their mortal enemy, the French Emperor Napoleon Bonaparte, led an army of 600,000 into Russia and returned to France leaving most of those men to perish in the freezing cold and snows of a Russian winter. Though it would be 1814 before the combined might of Britain, Russia, Prussia, Austria, Sweden, and Portugal could defeat Napoleon, the English felt sufficiently strong to treat their onetime colonies with disdain. British warships stopped American merchant ships on the high seas; ostensibly, they were looking for British sailors who had taken out American naturalization papers, but in their haste and arrogance, they often took American sailors and impressed them into service. The French were angered at the United States as promises had been made that in return for French help in the Revolutionary War, the Americans would in turn assist the French. This promise was broken, and the French seized American shipping.

Though strong ships and free trade were critical to the economy of the United States, Presidents Jefferson and Madison saw America as an agrarian society and failed to build a sufficient navy. Jefferson's coastal navy of gunboats was no match for the British fleets. Despite this, hot-tongued American politicians led by a group then called War Hawks eagerly embraced war. Some Americans wanted to fight the British and French simultaneously while they were fighting each other. The country was not prepared for war. Fortunately for the fledgling United States, cooler heads prevailed.

When war with England was imminent in January 1812, Congress had authorized the raising of six volunteer companies of mounted Rangers from Kentucky for frontier service, and an additional company was added in July 1812. In 1813, ten additional Ranger companies were formed to patrol the frontier from Michigan to Louisiana.

In June 1812, the war began with soaring American hopes. Gen. William Hull, governor of the Michigan Territory, invaded Canada. Many Canadians were American Loyalists who had been stripped of their homes and property by the victorious patriots of the Revolutionary War. The Loyalists despised the United States and would fight against it. Despite this, victory for the United States seemed assured. The population of the United States was six million while Canada could claim less than half a million white inhabitants. A general of reasonable ability might have prevailed, but William Hull was a man who could not control his imagination. Worried about the safety of his supply lines, Hull quickly abandoned the offensive and took refuge at Detroit.

Maj. Gen. Isaac Brock, governor general of Canada, was a soldier. Though vastly outnumbered, Brock allowed a false plan to be captured by the Americans. Hull read that thousands of Indians were nearby ready to help the Canadians. Brock also dressed his militia in the red coats of regulars. Thinking that he was outnumbered and that the more than 700 women and children in Detroit would be slaughtered by Indians, Hull lost his nerve. In August 1812, without resistance, Hull surrendered Detroit—including the 2,188-man American force, 39 pieces of artillery, and more than 3,000 rifles and muskets—to a small force of British and Canadians. Many of Hull's men wept with rage at being denied the opportunity to fight.

The high command of the Americans was inept. The political leaders of the fledgling United States had little concept of how to organize, train, and equip an army. They frequently mistook corpulence and rhetoric for ability. In command of the American army from 1800 to 1812 was Gen. James Wilkenson, whom a courageous young captain named Winfield Scott openly described as "a traitor, liar, and scoundrel."

At the dawn of the year 1813, most of the American army was a mob, indifferently armed and headed by a knave. Bumbling northward, Wilkenson launched a two-pronged invasion toward Montreal. A minuscule British force sent one wing of the American army into flight by posting buglers at different points and having them sound the charge. Wilkenson and his 8,000 men were thrashed by 800 British, Canadians, and Indians.

At sea, the sixteen vessels of the U.S. Navy faced the 600-ship British juggernaut that included 120 ships of the line and 116 frigates. The U.S. Navy had an outstanding officer corps and men who knew how to build fine warships. The U.S. Navy gave a good account of itself, avoiding the powerful but slow ships of the line and taking on British frigates that the Americans outgunned. American privateers raised havoc with the British merchant fleet. In the last eighteen months of the war, they captured 1,000 British ships. Though its reputation suffered, the power of the British fleet allowed them to blockade and strike where they chose.

While the big armies clashed in Europe, one of the greatest of Indian generals made his presence felt on the American frontier. He was a Shawnee named Tecumseh. He believed, as Pontiac had in 1763, that the Indian tribes must put aside their centuries of intertribal warfare and competition and come together to resist the encroaching whites. Tecumseh went among the tribes and incited them to war. To his detriment, Tecumseh practiced an Indian version of nepotism. His brother Tenskwatawa had a desire for fame, but lacking Tecumseh's military genius, he became a prophet. He awed the Indians by making powerful medicine that he said would protect them from the white man's bullets.

The Americans of the northwest were determined to correct the humiliation of Hull's surrender. The frontier citizens of Kentucky took action by electing William Henry Harrison, hero of the Battle of Tippecanoe, as major general of Kentucky militia. President Madison then appointed Harrison commander in chief of all Rangers, regulars, volunteers, and militia. This put men of Kentucky, Ohio, Indiana, Pennsylvania, and Virginia under his command. With nearly 10,000 men, the thirty-nine-year-old Harrison had the force he needed. Using 6,500 men in three columns, Harrison moved on Detroit. A column under the inept General Winchester was trapped and practically annihilated by Indians near the Raisin River. Breaking into casks of liquor, the Indians became drunk and enraged. They burned the makeshift hospital containing American wounded. While screaming men died, the Indians tomahawked any who tried to crawl free. From then on, "Remember the Raisin River" became the cry of grim-faced Americans as they killed Indians of any age or sex.

The loss of Winchester's men forced Harrison temporarily onto the defensive. American spirits soared when on August 1, 1813, Tecumseh's Indians and General Procter's regulars attacked Fort Stephenson on the Sandusky River. Twenty-three-year-old American Maj. George Croghan was in command of the fort. He had only 160 men and one old cannon, but his men were Kentucky Rangers. Though considerably outnumbered, Croghan and his Rangers stung the attackers so badly that they hurriedly retreated.

Tecumseh's years of effort to recruit other tribes were bearing fruit. Supplied with powder and bullets by the Spaniards in Florida, 2,000 Creek Indians went on the warpath. They painted their naked bodies black and red and gained the name "Red Sticks" from the red-painted war clubs they carried. On August 30, the Indians attacked Fort Mims, which was located about thirty-five miles north of Mobile on the east bank of the Alabama River. The American commander, Maj. Daniel Beasley, refused to believe the Red Sticks would attack. He left the gates of the fort open, threatened to court-martial subordinate officers who warned him.

Several hundred warriors sprinted through the open gate, tomahawked Beasley, and began the slaughter. Those who were not killed on the open ground were burned to death when the buildings were fired. Approximately 400 people were butchered or burned. The slaughter set a rage burning across the United States. Americans in the south redoubled their efforts to organize for war.

With no help from the government in Washington, Harrison recruited in Kentucky and gathered a force of 4,500 men to regain Detroit and push into Canada. Among these volunteers were 1,000 mounted Rangers from the Kentucky frontier, armed with rifle, knife, and tomahawk.

Using Oliver Hazard Perry's victorious little fleet of ships on Lake Erie, Harrison transported his army over water to seize Detroit while his mounted Rangers made a 100-mile ride around the western side of the lake. Detroit was regained. British General Procter, with 400 regulars of the 41st Foot and Tecumseh's 1,000 Indians, withdrew into Canada. Harrison pushed northeast after them, following a road that ran along the Thames River. Warships of Perry's fleet went into the river until the high banks of the Thames closed in on them, making the vessels subject to Indian sniping.

General Procter kept retreating into Canada. The British leader was being ridiculed by Tecumseh for refusing battle, but Procter was searching for the best defensive terrain. Near Chatham, Proctor found suitable ground. He told Tecumseh, "Here we will defeat Harrison or leave our bones."

Procter's left flank was protected by the Thames River with its steep banks. On his right flank was a large swamp that would inhibit movement. Chippewa Indians were concealed just inside this swamp in position to attack the flank of an attacking force. The ground to Procter's front was open woodland with little undergrowth. In the center of Procter's position was a small swamp. Procter arranged his forces to both sides of this natural obstacle. British infantry was positioned in two lines thirty yards apart between the small swamp and the river. Procter's single cannon covered the road with fire. Tecumseh and his warriors defended the ground on the right between the two swamps.

On October 5, 1813, Harrison moved to the attack. He posted Joseph Desha's troops on the American right in position to deal with any Indian attack from the large swamp. Colonel Trotter's brigade of infantry was positioned to make a frontal attack; to their front was Col. Richard M. Johnson and his 400 mounted Rangers. Harrison planned to allow the infantry to pass through Rangers, but on learning the British were drawn up in open order, he decided on a last-minute change. Knowing that Kentucky backwoodsmen were accustomed to riding at speed through woods, Harrison decided to commit Johnson's Rangers in a mounted charge through the open woodland.

On surveying the terrain, Col. Richard Johnson determined his frontage was too narrow to support the charge of 400 men. He divided his force. His brother, Lt. Col. James Johnson, would lead 200 men to attack the British troops while Richard Johnson turned left to cross the swamp and attack Tecumseh's Indians in their left flank. At the sound of a bugle, James Johnson's mounted Rangers trotted toward the enemy positions. They encountered heavy fire but were now close enough to spur their mounts. James Johnson and his men hit the British line like a thunderbolt, smashing through both lines they turned left and right, capturing Procter's cannon before it could fire. Of Procter's 800 soldiers, only 50 men and 1 lieutenant escaped. Procter had vowed to beat Harrison or leave his bones. He chose to leap into his carriage and lead his staff in flight. He had to move fast. Major Payne of the Rangers was on his trail. Procter fled sixty-five miles in twenty-four hours. The Rangers got his sword, carriage, and papers, but Procter escaped.

Meanwhile, Col. Richard Johnson had led his force in the attack on the Indians. He knew that the small swamp would impede movement and that Tecumseh was a skilled and courageous warrior. In an act of sacrifice, Richard Johnson called for twenty volunteers. He would lead these men against the Indians, accepting their massed fires. While the Indians were in the act of reloading, the remainder of his force would fall upon them. Despite knowing that to volunteer meant almost certain death, men stepped forward.

Unable to resist the target, hundreds of Indians emptied their weapons at the small group of approaching Rangers. Practically all of the frontiersmen fell riddled with bullets. The woods and underbrush were thick in this part of the battlefield. Johnson's men dismounted and came forward on foot, firing then meeting the Indians with rifle butt, knife, and tomahawk. No mercy was shown.

Colonel Johnson had been shot four times; his horse was hit and struggling. As Johnson dismounted, a large Indian rushed at him firing a musket. Johnson's left hand was shattered by the bullet. The Indian then ran forward brandishing his tomahawk. As the blade was raised overhead for the strike, Johnson drew a pistol and fired. The impact of the bullet hurled the Indian backward in death. Johnson reeled from his five wounds while his men rushed to his aid.

Tecumseh died fighting in Johnson's immediate area. Some sources claim that the Indian killed by Col. Richard Johnson was Tecumseh, but Johnson did not make the claim or accept it until he was an old man.

The American infantry under Major Thompson now struck into the Indian position. The blow broke Indian resistance. They fled the battlefield after losing fifty dead and the great leader that welded them together. The Americans had fifteen men killed. The British-Canadian-Indian alliance was smashed, and the door to Canada was open. Jubilation swept America. Seeing Harrison's popularity as a political threat to the administration, Secretary of War Armstrong removed Harrison from command, and the American initiative died. As in the Revolutionary War, blunders of great magnitude had prevented the uniting of North America into one country. Disgusted with politicians, Harrison became one, later using his battles as a stepping stone to become the ninth president of the United States.

The year 1814 brought gloom to the American camp. In April 1814, Napoleon was overthrown. Fourteen thousand veteran British troops were freed for use in the United States. Seeking to teach a lesson to their former colonies, the British planned to send a three-pronged invasion force. One army would enter New York by way of Lake Champlain, a second would enter the Chesapeake Bay and strike the Washington-Baltimore area, and a third would seize New Orleans. These attacks would be supported by the weight of the British navy, which would strangle the Americans with a tight blockade and raise havoc with raids on the American coast.

The Americans had learned from the years of war. In 1812, most American generals were in their sixties; by 1814, the majority were were vigorous men in their thirties. Winfield Scott was now a brigadier general. He and Maj. Gen. Jacob Brown commanded the Americans in the Niagara area. They did not wait for the oncoming British onslaught but attacked into Canada.

On July 5, 1814, along the Chippewa River, British Gen. Phineas Riall expected to make short work of the American militia. Surprised as well-uniformed troops moved in close formation to meet him, he cried out, "Those are regulars, by God." At seventy yards, the two forces halted and exchange massed volleys in the traditional manner. The result was a decisive American victory and a credit to the new American regular army.

On July 25, 1814, with 2,600 men, General Brown fought a five-hour battle with 3,000 British at the village of Lundy's Lane. This was a stiff fight that ended in a draw. Commodore Chauncey, the American naval commander on Lake Ontario, did not properly support General Brown, thus jeopardizing a continuance of the strategy. The Americans marched back to their side of the border.

In August 1814, the first of the three-pronged British attacks struck home. About 4,000 British troops sailed into the Chesapeake Bay under the command of Gen. Robert Ross, supported by Rear Adm. Sir George Cockburn's fleet of four ships of the line, twenty frigates, and twenty transports. The British planned to raid Washington and Baltimore and destroy American gunboats on the Patuxent River. The Americans were under the command of Gen. William Winder, an officer whose primary military experience was as a prisoner of war. He was, however, a blood relative of the governor of Maryland. Armed with these credentials and 6,400 men who were mostly militia, Winder set forth. The government was in a panic. Each state was interested only in its own safety. All was confusion. Winder fell into a ditch and was injured.

Americans from various sources gathered at Bladensburg, a little town on the east bank of a branch of the Potomac River. Blowing up the Navy Yard bridge behind them, President Madison, Secretary of War Armstrong, and Secretary of State Monroe came into camp and contributed greatly to the confusion, giving contradictory orders, positioning units incorrectly, and, in the case of the president, narrowly avoiding blundering into British hands. The badly shaken Winder managed to position his troops on a ridge where they could not support other Americans.

The British regulars came on at the double-quick, advancing through Bladensburg, crossing its bridge, and striking the Maryland militia. The battle that followed saw three engagements in half an hour. The Americans in the ranks fought well until the experienced British flanked them; then improper positioning of the Americans prevented them from properly supporting each other. During the action, some American units fled while others fought gamely. The laurels for courage went to the American sailors and marines who, having burned their gunboats, fought on line. Three times they hurled back the British regulars who were charging them. The American sailors counter attacked with cutlass against bayonet shouting nautical battle cries of "Away Boarders" and "Board 'em." With their wounded commander, Joshua Barney, captured, the sailors and marines withdrew in good order. They were the last Americans to leave the field. The Americans had lost 100 men; the British lost five times that number.

The road to the United States capital was open, and on August 24–25, 1814, the British moved to Washington and set about burning its buildings—the White House, the capitol building, most of the public buildings, an arsenal, a newspaper, and some private homes. The arsenal firing was carelessly done, and a magazine exploded, injuring nearly 100 British.

The first of the three-pronged British attack seemed to be going well. Now came the second thrust. Gen. Sir George Prevost led 11,000 British veteran troops, supported by four warships, twelve gunboats, and ninety guns in an attack southward on Lake Champlain. Seizure of the Hudson River Valley would split New England from the rest of the United States. Some New Englanders, angered at the way the war was going, were talking about secession from the United States. To oppose this powerful force, the Americans had 3,300 regulars and militia under Gen. Alexander Macomb. The objective was control of the vital waterway. To protect against British movement on Lake Champlain, the Americans had four warships and ten gunboats totaling eighty-six guns. Though evenly matched in numbers and firepower, there was an important difference between the two fleets. The British had guns designed to fire at long range while the Americans were equipped with carronades, guns that were of shorter range but threw a heavier weight of metal. American Capt. Thomas Macdonough was only thirty years old but was an experienced sailor. He anchored his fleet in a narrow strech of water, forcing any enemy who wished to fight him to come to close quarters. On September 11, near Plattsburg, New York, the armies and navies met. The British fleet attacked and a furious battle raged for two and a half hours. Macdonough drove his flagship at that of the British and captured it. Soon the entire British fleet surrendered. Significant portions of the British land force, lost their way, and blundered about in the forest. General Prevost decided that without having control of the water, he could not control the land. He marched his men back to Canada. One point of the trident was broken.

On September 12, it was Baltimore's turn. The fourth largest city in the United States, Baltimore was seaport home to a number of successful American privateers. Admiral Cockburn had threatened to burn out "the nest of pirates." The defense of Baltimore was under the command of Gen. Samuel Smith, a no-nonsense commander who worked his 13,000 regulars and militia to prepare a stout defense. A small force of Rangers was sent forward to delay the enemy with accurate rifle fire. The British infantry pressed them, overlapping the Ranger position, bringing on a running firefight. The British commander Gen. Robert Ross rode forward to make a reconnaissance and was shot and mortally wounded by Ranger marksmen. Each point the British attacked cost them dearly. The British fleet anchored near Fort McHenry and pounded it for twenty-five hours. The guns of the fort could not reach their tormentors, but the Americans would not surrender. From the deck of a small boat, a Washington lawyer watched the terrible bombardment and was inspired to write words that when set to the music of an old drinking song would become the national anthem of the United States. Baltimore would not be taken. On September 14, the British marched to their ships and sailed away for Jamaica.

Despite repulsing the British, the burning of the nation's capital became the prime conversation. The mood of the American public was one of shame and anger. Secretary of War Armstrong was hunted by a mob in Baltimore and hastily resigned. Members of the administration were booed and jeered in public. In New England, action began in several states to secede from the union. The United States was in danger of unraveling. A significant land victory was needed.

Enter Andrew Jackson, now a major general. His body still carried the scars from the sword cuts received when he refused to polish his British captor's boots during the Revolution. He later became both student and school teacher, learning his subject the day before he taught it. In December 1784, Jackson left Charleston for Salisbury, North Carolina, to study law and make his reputation. His law studies suffered, but he gained a reputation as the biggest hell-raiser in the area.

He was tall for the times, standing six feet, one inch. Penetrating blue eyes and abundant red hair bespoke a dominant personality. Somewhere along the line he had learned he could intimidate many people by acting out a mouth-foaming rage. It was an act he could turn on and off, but it served him well throughout his life. When he wanted to, Andrew Jackson could frighten people.

When the War of 1812 broke out, Jackson used his political influence to get elected as a major general in the Tennessee militia. The margin of victory was one vote. Jackson set about organizing a fighting force of Tennessee frontiersmen. In charge of some 670 mounted men was Col. John Coffee. Colonels Hart and Benton each commanded an infantry regiment. With 2,000 troops, Jackson needed a war. He decided to go after the Spanish in Florida. The Madison administration gave tacit approval as the Spanish were giving aid to the British. When he had traveled 500 miles toward his objective, Jackson was ordered to disregard his mission, disband his army, and return home. Without support or supplies from his government, Jackson brought his men home.

The Red Sticks of the Creek nation went on the warpath, began burning and killing, and committed the massacre at Fort Mims. With John Coffee's horsemen in the van, Jackson led a force into Creek territory. He was relentless in breaking them, destroying their crops, and burning their villages. In Pontiac's War of 1763, Henri Bouquet had defeated the Indians using tactics devised by the great Carthaginian general Hannibal in smashing the Roman legions at Cannae. Now on November 3, 1813, John Coffee would use them again. At a place called Tallushatchee, he sent a small party of men forward to lure the Indians to attack. Not grounded in Roman history, the savage Red Sticks rushed to attack. The bait force withdrew, and the Indians followed in headlong charge while Coffee's men stayed hidden in position along their flanks. Suddenly, a wall of flame and lead struck the Indians. "We shot them like dogs," said Davy Crockett. Coffee reported, "Not one of the warriors escaped to tell the news." More than 180 Red Stick warriors died.

With no survivors, the practical experience of Hannibal's procedures eluded the Creek Indians. Six days later, Andrew Jackson used the same tactics to lure 300 more Red Sticks to their doom, while Jackson lost fifteen.

On March 27, 1814, Jackson attacked the fortified Indian base at the Horse Shoe Bend of the Tallapoosa River. The Indians felt secure behind breastworks but had dozens of canoes with which to flee if necessary. Attacking the fortifications with his main force, Jackson sent Coffee's troops to ambush those who tried to escape by water.

Nearly 800 Indians were counted dead, including 200 whose bodies were floating in the river. Other Indians died of wounds in the forest.

Jackson was a hero and was appointed a major general in the regular army. Having broken the powerful Creeks, he took the victor's spoils. The Creeks were forced to cede twenty-three million acres, comprising much of present-day Alabama and part of Georgia, to the United States. The Americans could establish forts, roads, and trading posts down to the Gulf of Mexico.

As the British had armed and supported the Indians in the north, the Spanish did so in the south. The Spanish base of Pensacola was openly being used by the British. Jackson wanted the Spanish out of Florida. War with Spain was not a priority of the United States government, but Jackson had his own priorities. When a British and Indian force used Pensacola for an unsuccessful attempt to seize the American post on Mobile Bay, Jackson seized the Spanish town. He drove the British back to their ships and destroyed the port and garrison facilities. The politicians were left to answer Spain's frustration.

The British planned to punish the American south. The Americans knew the attack was coming but were uncertain if it would be at Mobile or New Orleans. Jackson's informants told him of British sails sighted and intrigues that indicated the blow would fall on New Orleans. While he went to New Orleans to judge for himself, Jackson sent Coffee's Tennessee and Mississippi Rangers to cover Baton Rouge. Formerly French, New Orleans had only been American eleven years, but Jackson got on well with the Creole population. Now convinced that the British would attack New Orleans, Jackson booted out the governor and legislature and ran New Orleans by martial law. John Coffee and 900 men force marched from Baton Rouge.

Jackson had long treasured the support and friendship of William Carroll, a young frontiersman from Pennsylvania. Carroll brought in 1,000 more Tennessee woods men. From Kentucky and Louisiana came 2,000 militia. Seven hundred regulars of the 7th and 44th Infantry and some artillery and marines arrived. There were about 600 free blacks in the city. Defying a howl of outrage from citizens who feared armed blacks, Jackson sought and received black volunteers and formed them into their own regiment.

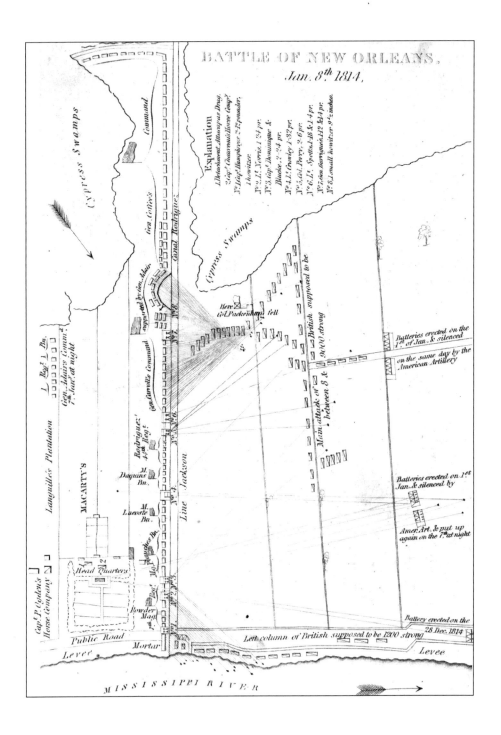

Capping this unusual collection of fighting men was a band of citizens called pirates. This well-armed group was under a former blacksmith named Jean Lafitte. A man much misunderstood in American history, Lafitte was not a pirate in the traditional sense of capturing ships, crews, and cargo. Lafitte would be better described as a master smuggler. He thought the collection of government dues on cargo was unjust and did not pay those fees. The result was that he brought cargo to New Orleans that he could sell for a profit but could be purchased at a much lower price. Denied revenue, the government hated him. The plantation owners bought his goods and were quite satisfied with this arrangement. Lafitte's ships and men would brook no interference in their trade. They were heavily armed and skilled gunners.

The British knew Jean Lafitte's worth and sought to gain his support. Despised by the United States government, Lafitte still considered himself a loyal American. He kept the Americans informed of British intentions. This prevented the British from achieving surprise.

Jackson needed every man he could get. Against his force of 5,000, a great British fleet of fifty ships was bringing 7,000 veteran soldiers of the Napoleonic Wars. These were men who had burned the American capital and attempted to seize Baltimore; they were reinforced by troops from Jamaica. The fleet sailed from Jamaica on November 26, arriving at the Gulf Coast on December 9. This was a confident army. Expecting little resistance, many of the officers had their wives with them. To their surprise, the British found they had to fight just to land their troops. American gunboats waged a spirited battle and inflicted stinging losses before being beaten aside.

The city of New Orleans sits beside the broad Mississippi River about 100 miles inland from the mouth of the great river on the Gulf of Mexico. In 1815, it was surrounded by great oaks draped in the parasitic Spanish moss. Swamps and bayous, the latter being accessible to small boats, offered avenues of approach for British attack. Knowing his must be a defensive battle, Jackson ordered the bayou approaches blocked with felled trees, but the effort was not properly supervised. A British advance force of 1,600 men under General Kean entered through Bayou Bienvenue and was in excellent position to seize the city. Local inhabitants convinced the British general that Jackson had

18,000 men waiting. Fortunately for Jackson, the British delayed. Jackson took the initiative and made a night attack on Kean's force. Though the battle was indecisive, the Americans suffered fewer casualties then the British. Coffee's Rangers ran night patrols into the British lines, depriving the British of sleep. In the darkness, the Rangers were particularly effective using tomahawks and long knifes for close-in fighting.

The British were under the command of Lt. Gen. Sir Edward Pakenham. The brother-in-law of the Duke of Wellington, Pakenham was thirty-seven and had been a soldier since age sixteen. He had proved his courage in many fights. Seeking battle, Pakenham moved his main body through Bayou Bienvenue. Jackson had the choice of ground and chose well. To Jackson's front was a dry mill race, ten feet wide and four feet deep. This obstruction ran from the east bank of the Mississippi River three quarters of a mile to a cypress swamp. Behind the mill race, Jackson built a rampart about five feet high. In some places, it was twenty feet thick. The installation of random bales of cotton would prove effective at stopping British bullets. Behind the mill race, Jackson prepared two other defensive lines.

On December 24, 1814, while Jackson and Pakenham prepared for battle, documents were being signed in Ghent, Belgium, ending the war. News traveled slowly across the Atlantic. At New Orleans, the war continued. Christmas was a happy time for the British forces. They had good food and equipment and were well trained. Despite receiving reinforcments of 2,000 to 3,000 men, by New Year's Day, the British force was hungry and exhausted and had suffered heavy casualties. They knew there would be no quick victory.

That Americans knew how to fight on land and water was evident. The little schooner *Carolina* rained fire on British positions and caused heavy casualties before a specially placed battery set her on fire. The *Louisiana*, another American schooner, would later hamper the British advance. The gunners of the *Carolina* and Lafitte's ships put guns in position to enfilade the British lines as they came forward into Jackson's position. A killing ground was established.

British and American artillery rained shells upon each other, with both positions wreathed in clouds of gun smoke. When the firing ceased, the American artillery, some of which was served by trained pirate gunners, was found to have lost one piece with two others damaged. As the smoke over the British position lifted, the American lines erupted in cheers. The British artillery positions were pounded into a shapeless mass of broken metal, flesh, and earth.

Jackson's force totaled 5,000. Maintaining a reserve and with various locations to be defended, he could afford but 2,200 on the line facing Pakenham. About 800 of Jackson's men were regular army, but most were new recruits. Jackson recognized he must defend both banks of the Mississippi. He wisely positioned 800 militia under General Morgan on the opposite bank.

On Jackson's right was the Mississippi River; on his left was a large cypress swamp. On the right flank, Jackson had various small units and men of the 7th Regiment, then the black volunteers under Colonel Lacoste; next in line was the 44th Regiment. Next in position was Carroll's Rangers and the extreme left of the line was held by Coffee's Rangers. The Ranger position covered two thirds of the American line. In battle, Coffee's men would be standing in the waters of the swamp. In preparation, they had constructed small rafts and tied them to trees. On these rafts, they slept and kept their equipment dry. Interspersed in the American positions were batteries of artillery that were well served. American cannon placed in redoubts forward of the main line could enfilade the line of British troops as they came forward.

Pakenham decided he would send a force across the Mississippi and seize the opposite shore in order to enfilade Jackson's line. Simultaneously, he would launch a frontal assault concentrating on the left of Jackson's position. The effort to seize the opposite shore encountered difficulties. An insufficient number of boats were at hand to transport the attacking force at one time. The British misjudged the current of the river and were carried downstream, forcing them to march a mile and a half to attack. Meanwhile, Jackson had sent another 400 men to reinforce the opposite shore. Pakenham's flanking maneuver was a failure.

In darkness and a thick morning fog, Pakenham moved his troops across the openness of the plain. As dawn came, the sun began to burn away the morning fog. The decisive battle opened at six o'clock on January 8, 1815, and would last until noon. Pakenham pressed his attack, moving forward in three columns. One would serve as a diversion. The second, under General Keane, would attack on the American right. They would flank the American position and seize artillery that could enfilade Pakenham's attack. The third column of British veterans, under General Gibbs, included men of the 44th, 21st, and 4th Regiments. Attacking in that order, they would serve as the main thrust, moving along and through the cypress swamp to attack the American fortification on the left. The 44th would carry fascines to fill the ditches to the front of the American position and scaling ladders to climb the walls. A West Indian regiment would attack through the swamp.

The three British regiments moved in echelon along the swamp while the one from the West Indies attempted to penetrate it. The West Indians were met by the deadly rifle fire, tomahawks, and knives of Coffee's Rangers and died in swamp muck. The British regiments coming in echelon were initially hit by accurate cannon fire. Shot and shell tore great gaps in the British ranks and turned the separate regiments into one body, bending forward under a storm of metal. Incredibly, it was discovered that the 44th did not have the fascines and scaling ladders to enable the British to cross the protective ditch.

All along the line, the disciplined British felt the fury of American fire. Engaged by Carroll and Coffee's Rangers on the left, the ordered British rows of infantry were cut down like wheat. The uniforms of British officers made them conspicuous targets, and they died in large numbers. The British faced a wall of fire that one British officer compared to "a row of flaming furnaces." Generals Gibbs and Keane were shot down; General Pakenham had his arm shattered and a horse shot from under him, but the brave officer mounted another horse and continued forward. The red lines of British beat upon the American position and broke as the tide on a rocky shore. They hesitated, then fell back, then ran for their lives. Their officers could not stop them.

As the British regulars fled, the American lines erupted in momentary cheers. The exultation of victory was soon stilled by the horror of the scene as the battle smoke drifted clear. From the broken mass of bodies that lay before the Americans came the groans and shrieks of the wounded, the piteous cries for aid and water. To Jack-

Post-Revolution Fights and the War of 1812 269

son, it seemed like a rising of the dead as 500 British who had lain prone among their 2,057 dead comrades rose to surrender. The American loss was thirteen men.

This decisive victory came at a time when there was little pride in being an American. The union itself was in question. Across the country, men and women raised their heads and cheered. Benjamin Franklin would have understood. Now America was truly independent.

CHAPTER 16

The Birth of Texas

While the seventeenth-century colonial wars between France and Britain raged east of the Mississippi, the Spanish sought to expand their control of the west. Moving northward from their secure base in Mexico, they established a foothold in what would become California, New Mexico, and Texas. They came with sword and cross, enslaving the native people to work their crops and ranches and forcing them to worship in the manner of the Spanish. The Pueblo Indians whom the Spanish met were essentially an agricultural people. Not warlike, these Indians were easy prey. The Spanish established fortified missions, little more than prisons to their captive Indians. From Los Angeles to Santa Fe to San Antonio, the Spanish established a route of communication and trade. They navigated over trackless wastes of desert by building stone cairns about the height of a man. In these piles of stone, they left an aperture. Looking through this small opening, the next cairn could be seen in the distance. These navigational aids are still found in the desert areas of the Old Spanish Trail.

Seeking to throw off Spanish enslavement, Mission Indians revolted in 1680. They slaughtered the priests and overseers and attempted to break free. Some had learned the benefits of a horse culture and used the knowledge to escape captivity on a Spanish horse. Some horses were lost or stolen. In the decade that followed, the Spanish brutally put down the revolt, but the knowledge of the horse spread among the Indians.

In their movement northward, the Spanish encountered a different type of Indian, warriors who would die before they would be enslaved. These Indians were the true rulers of the southwest. Some were local tribes such as the fierce Karankawa. They were coastal Indians who lived by the Gulf of Mexico. In 1827, a young adventurer named Noah Smithwick came west from Tennessee and encountered these Indians. He described them as covering their bodies with alligator grease and dirt and claimed the Karankawa were "the most savage looking people I ever saw." These Indians were a tall people, skilled bowmen and watermen whose diet featured fish and alligators. They haunted boat traffic along the shores and practiced cannibalism on their victims.[1]

The Karankawa were frequently in conflict with their neighbors, the Tonkawas. The few white people in Texas called the Karankawa the "Cronks" and the Tonkawas the "Tonks."[2] Both tribes were a source of frequent concern to the few white settlers.

The name "Texas" came from a Caddo Indian word describing the union of their people as "friends," but Texas was born, nurtured, and matured in conflict. A triangle of war developed in Texas between the Indian, the Mexican, and the American. Each of these participants sought advantage and security for themselves. They came into conflict, and hatred and cruelty grew into what became a war of extermination.

In northeast Texas lived Indians who had been forced from their original homelands by whites or other Indian tribes. Now a settled people who farmed and had towns, these Indians included the Cherokee, Delaware, and Shawnee. By the 1600s, a new force had entered the western arena. The Spanish called them Apache, the word meaning "enemy." Their origins were in the far north; their language was akin to that spoken by tribes in Alaska and Canada. As they migrated southward, they left behind them a trail of bloodshed. All whites and other Indians were enemies to the Apache, who came to occupy east and west Texas. They destroyed the Pueblo Indians that had escaped the Spanish, penned the Spaniards in their missions, and drove other tribes from the great hunting grounds that teemed with buffalo and antelope.

Neither the Spanish nor local Indians could defeat the Apache, but another band of Indian warriors did. Until they met the horse, these Indians were a rag-tag, poverty-stricken group of wanderers from the area of present-day Wyoming. They were identified in the sign language of the plains by the symbol for a snake moving backwards. The Spanish used the Ute Indian word, calling this tribe Comanche.

They came down from their mountains and became a people of the horse, a people of plains. They took the knowledge of horsemanship from the Spanish, a knowledge of halters, bits, and saddles, and adapted these with materials made of buffalo skins. A Comanche child could ride before it could walk. Using a rawhide loop as stirrup, they could slide to the side of their horses and present a fleeting target, yet they could accurately unleash arrows while at a gallop. Armed with lance and bow, the Comanche may well have been what some American army officers thought them—the finest light cavalry the world has known. It was said that a white man could ride a horse until it dropped; an Indian could get that horse up and ride it for another fifty miles. If the Indian was a Comanche, he could use the horse for a 200-mile raid. Raids of several hundred miles were frequently made by these roving warriors.

Centered in the area from the Brazos to the Colorado Rivers, the Comanche rode forth and drove the Apache from east Texas, forcing them to the west and south. The Apache then occupied the area along the Rio Grande and raided into Mexico.[3] The Comanche now possessed the finest hunting grounds in Texas.

In 1763, the British successfully ended French aspirations east of the Mississippi. The British then lost their prize in the American Revolution. The land west of the great river was still claimed by European powers. Spain returned the vast domain called Louisiana to the French only to see a cash-hungry Napoleon Bonaparte sell it to the United States under President Thomas Jefferson. Jefferson believed the purchased land included Texas. The sale of Louisiana disrupted Spanish interests in Texas and made them wary about the future.

In Mexico, Spanish authorities saw the restless Americans moving westward toward them. Exhausted by wars and extravagance, once-mighty Spain was in decline. Those responsible for the frontier were hard pressed to defend it from Indian raids. Though American immigrants were not the most desirable answer, if they swore allegiance to Spain and adopted the Catholic faith, they could serve to absorb much of the ferocity of the Apache and Comanche.

In 1820, an American named Moses Austin arrived in San Antonio with a proposition for the Spanish governor. Though born in Connecticut, Austin had moved west and developed business interests in

The Birth of Texas

Spanish territory in Missouri. There he had become a Spanish citizen. The sale of Louisiana and a financial depression had ruined Austin's financial holdings, but he saw new opportunity in Texas. He brought with him an offer to bring 300 American families. After some hesitation, the Spanish governor agreed. Moses Austin returned to the east and began organizing his project. Moses Austin did not live to see his dream become reality. He died in June 1821 and left the task of settlement to his remarkable son, Stephen F. Austin.

By the time the winter of 1821 was in the offing, some of the Americans had arrived in Texas. Stephen Austin had already experienced being taken captive by the Comanche. The Americans were new to the Comanche, more of a curiosity than a foe. The Comanche band was content to rob Austin and let him go. The newly arrived Americans were not all as fortunate, and the small contingent survived by bribery and appeasement. In particular, the Karankawa Indians were hostile and began to raid the newcomers.

The difficulties of the American immigrants were compounded by a change in government. In 1821, Spanish rule was overthrown, and Mexico became a nation. As with the people of the United States, they had wearied of a repressive, distant ruler. Unlike the Americans, the Mexicans lacked a leadership dedicated to the rights of man.

The Mexicans believed they inherited Spanish claims, including Texas. However, they did not provide a defense for the new arrivals; this was left to the Americans to accomplish for themselves. The situation that existed in Texas was as it had existed in the east in the 1600s. A frontier defense force was needed to protect against Indian raids. As more American immigrants arrived, temporary defensive units began to be formed. In 1823, Stephen F. Austin offered to pay from his own funds for ten men who would serve as "Rangers." This is the first known application of the word to a military force in Texas.

While bringing in new settlers and building his recruiting base, Austin managed to hold the Comanche at bay with diplomacy and gifts. The Mexicans were not so skilled or fortunate and were suffering greatly from Comanche attacks. The coastal Karankawa Indians and the Tonkawas were the primary adversaries for the Americans. Fortunately for Austin's settlers, most of the Indian tribes despised each other. Austin hoped to gain assistance from the Cherokee, Delaware, and Shawnee, but he was overruled by Mexican authorities who said he must wait until they could provide assistance. Knowing the Mexican penchant for delay, Austin in 1826 called a conference of militia leaders. They decided to keep a full time force of "twenty to thirty Rangers in service all the time."[4]

CHAPTER 17

The Triangle of War

The Indian, the Mexican, and the American now faced each other in a life or death struggle in Texas. Each was driven by self-interest. Each saw their cause as just. Each brought strengths and flaws to the contest.

The Indian warrior was a child of nature. He cared nothing about the elaborate charades his opponents built about so called civilities of war. The Indian raided and captured or destroyed. Prisons and prison camps were unknown in his culture. Prisoners who could not be ransomed or assimilated into the tribe were killed. Torture was a form of entertainment. Rape and mutilation and some cannibalism were practiced. The horror captives endured brought an unrelenting hatred from their American and Mexican opponents. Men were staked out on the plains with their entrails opened to the birds and insects. Fires were built upon their genitals or skulls. White and Mexican women captives were raped by warrior after warrior and mutilated by Indian women. Women who were freed after years of captivity often came home demented. Courage was prized, but the Indian did not seek pitched battles and would withdraw rather than accept heavy casualties.

The Mexicans were a people of passion. There were numerous examples of courage among officers in the middle ranks. The rot was at the top. Mexican horsemanship was superb, and they were skilled with lance, knife, and rope. The tactic of a mounted Mexican throwing a rope around an opponent's neck and dragging him to death behind a galloping horse was feared and hated by the Americans. They had few successes against the Comanche, who took horses, women, and loot from the Mexican at will. The Mexican became adept at guile. The Mexicans used agreements as an instrument of war, luring the opposition to their deaths by treachery.

The immigrant from America comprised the third point of the triangle. In the relentless march from the Atlantic shore, those who followed the frontier were a hardy people willing and able to fight. It was the only hope of survival. The Americans considered themselves a superior culture and a free-born people. They intended this land to be their own. They made accommodations until they had sufficient strength to gain their desires. They promised fealty to both the Spanish and Mexican government but would not accept the accompanying corruption and went their own way. They mouthed conversion to the Roman Catholic faith, which the Spanish and Mexican governments required, yet many continued to practice their Protestant beliefs. They resented any authority they did not establish. While independent, the Americans had a discipline for unified action their opponents lacked. They were willing to fight prolonged battles. The Americans were not skilled horsemen as the Indian and the Mexican were, but they were quick to learn. Initially, both the Indian and the Mexican had superior weapons. The lance, bow, and rope were better offensive weapons on the open plains than the single-shot long rifle or pistol carried by the Americans. The most successful tactic used by the Americans was to find defensive ground and use their remarkable accuracy at long range to kill their opponents. American weapons took time to reload. The Indians sought to draw fire then execute a charge before the Americans could ready another shot. Experienced Indian fighters knew that some men must hold their fire to receive the charge. In time, better weapons would give the Americans the edge.

These new settlers were well aware that Thomas Jefferson felt Texas was included in the Louisiana purchase, but Mexico did not agree. In 1825, the United States had offered to purchase Texas to the Rio Grande.[1] The Mexicans had no intention of selling Texas, but time was on the side of the growing power of the Americans.

In 1826, a group of American settlers at Nacogdoches revolted against Mexican rule. It was an isolated affair, not coordinated with or supported by other Americans in Texas. The revolt was put down, but the Mexicans harbored deep suspicions and endeavored to demonstrate that Texas belonged to them. Immigration of Americans to Texas was banned. Troops were sent and garrisons established. The Americans recognized that the troops were not there to protect them from the frequent Indian raids, but to hold them under Mexican authority. Looking out for their own interests, the Americans organized additional Ranger units and began their own search for Indian raiders. Chafing under Mexican restriction, the American immigrants took the example of their forefathers and began to organize committees of security and correspondence.

In Mexico, a thirty-eight-year-old general named Santa Anna seized control of the government and established a dictatorship. He gave added power to the Roman Catholic Church and thereby gained their support. He abolished the constitution which Mexico had adopted after freeing itself from Spain. He dismissed the existing legislatures and packed new ones with his own men. The heavy-handed rule of Santa Anna brought revolt in various parts of Mexico. These were quickly and ruthlessly crushed. Santa Anna now turned his attention to Texas and laid plans to bring the Americans to heel. Troops were sent to collect taxes, and a fight between Americans and Mexican troops at Gonzales was the spark that ignited a rebellion.

War was now a certainty. In October 1835, delegates from the various communities met in convention to establish their defense. On October 17, Daniel Parker put forth a resolution creating a corps of Texas Rangers.[2] This resolution and others concerning the formation of a Texas military resulted in the establishment of a Texas regular army of 1,200 men, a militia, and corps of Rangers. There were to be three Ranger companies, each consisting of fifty-six men and commanded by a captain. The companies would normally operate independently, but if the need arose, they would come together as a Ranger battalion. In that event, they would be commanded by a major. R. M. Williamson was selected to be the major commanding, and the companies were led by William Arlington, Isaac Burton, and John Tumlinson. The Rangers were required to furnish their own horses and arms. No uniform, guidon, or standard was prescribed. They were a rapid-reaction force required to be always ready.

Now that war was at hand, its objective became to break free of Mexican rule and establish the Republic of Texas. Many recognized the new republic was a temporary measure. They knew this vast land larger than France did not have the markets or the resources to stand alone. The ties to the United States were strong, and that young giant of nations was eagerly following events in Texas.

During the brief revolution that followed, the Rangers were primarily used to keep a watchful eye on the Indians. Wisely, the Texans made every effort to placate the Indians and avoid a two-front war. They did not need to encourage the Comanche to attack the Mexicans—raiding Mexico was a Comanche inheritance. The Mexicans eagerly sought the assistance of the Indians and promised them goods and land if they would attack the Texans. Had the war been prolonged, the Indians may have been a factor. On a short-term basis, they were content to accept whatever bribe was offered by Mexican or Texan.

In early 1835, an Indian raiding party appeared along the Colorado River. They killed one man and took horses. A locally organized Ranger unit went in pursuit, but the Indians they killed were not from the raiding tribe. The result was to inflame tensions on the frontier. In July, another skirmish began with an attack on an Indian village being repulsed. The Indians then pursued the whites until Col. John Moore came to the rescue with three companies of Rangers. The Indians departed the scene.[3]

Capt. Isaac Burton and twenty Rangers had the mission of scouting the coastline of the Gulf of Mexico. On June 3, 1835, they saw a vessel in the Bay of Copano. Burton kept most of his men in concealment while a few of the Rangers signaled the vessel to send a boat ashore. Whatever ruse was used resulted in five Mexicans being captured. Sixteen Rangers crowded into the boat and proceeded to capture the vessel. They found it to be loaded with supplies for the Mexican army. Two other ships came in, and Burton forced the Mexican captain he had captured to lure the officers of these ships on board his vessel. The result was the taking of three ships loaded with military supplies much needed by the Texans. Burton's Rangers were greeted joyfully when they sailed into the port of Velasco.[4] In January 1836, Capt. John J. Tumlinson was ordered to lead sixty mounted Rangers to a location at the headwaters of Brushy Creek, thirty miles north of Austin. Their mission was to build a blockhouse that could be used as a base of operations in the area.

Noah Smithwick was among those men who enlisted in Tumlinson's company for one year. The Rangers assembled at Hornsby's Station on the Colorado River some ten miles below Austin. Noah

Smithwick later related in his memoir *Evolution of a State* that the men were cooking their evening meal when an exhausted white woman stumbled into their camp. She was in desperate shape, her body cut and bleeding, her words rambling and words initially incoherent. When somewhat restored, she told the Rangers that she was a married woman by the name of Sarah Hibbons. She had been traveling by wagon with her husband, two children, and her brother en route to their home on the Guadalupe River. At an isolated spot, they were attacked by Comanche. The Indians killed the two men and took Mrs. Hibbons and the children prisoner. One of the children was a baby whose cries displeased the Comanche, and one of them crushed the baby's skull by swinging it against a tree.

The Indians then moved on, taking Mrs. Hibbon and her other child, who was three years old. In the vicinity of Austin, they crossed a river, and soon after, a cold, fierce storm descended upon them. The Indians took shelter among trees, wrapped themselves in their buffalo robes, and went to sleep. They felt confident that the woman would not leave her child and left her untied. Sarah Hibbons was a frontier woman and had been attentive to their direction of travel. She believed they had crossed the Colorado River, and there were white settlements somewhere in the area. Her only hope for her child and herself was to reach assistance. As the Indians slept, she left the child behind and hurried back to the the river. She had the good sense to hide her tracks by walking in the frigid waters. Leaving the water, she found her route hindered by thick brush and briars that tore her clothes and body. Her journey was fearful and arduous. It took twenty-four hours for Sarah Hibbons to cover ten miles. Her strength of will was matched by the good fortune of meeting the Rangers. After a brief rest, Sarah Hibbon's had the presence of mind to fully describe the Indians, their location, and the mules the Indians were using to transport the child.

Ranger Reuben Hornsby knew the area well. Finishing their meal, the Rangers mounted their horses and rode by night. When they neared their objective, they paused, taking no chance of losing the trail in the darkness. At first light, they were back in the saddle and Ranger scouts soon found the trail. Secure in their belief that they were undetected, the Comanche had spent the previous day in a fruitless search for Sarah Hibbons. When the Rangers came upon them in mid-morning, they were preparing to break camp. Leaving everything behind but their weapons, the Indians ran for the brush.

Ranger Noah Smithwick described his experience as follows:

> I was riding a fleet horse, which becoming excited, carried me right in among the fleeing savages, one of whom jumped behind a tree and fired on me with a musket, fortunately missing his aim. Unable to control my horse I jumped off him and gave chase to my assailant on foot, knowing his gun was empty. I fired on him and had the satisfaction of seeing him fall. My blood was up and leaving him for dead, I ran on loading my rifle as I ran, hoping to bring down another. A limb knocked my hat off and one of my comrades catching a glimpse of me flying bareheaded through the brake on foot, mistook me for a Comanche and raised his gun to check my flight; but another Ranger dashed the gun aside in time to save me. The brave I shot, lay flat on the ground and loaded his gun, which he discharged at Captain Tumlinson, narrowly missing him and killing his horse; when Conrad Rohrer ran up and snatching the gun from the Indian's hand dealt him a blow on the head with it, crushing his skull.[5]

The Indians fled into deep brush where it was not wise to follow them. Ranger Conrad Rohrer raised his rifle to fire at a target atop a mule only to have the weapon misfire. He tried again and again—the weapon failed to function. He was about to make a third attempt when another Ranger stopped him. The target was the little Hibbon boy, wrapped in a buffalo robe and tied by the Indians on top of the mule. Any Indian who made it to the brush was able to escape. The Comanche vanished. The Rangers reunited the little boy with his mother and got the Indian horses and their small accumulation of plunder. His fellow Rangers reasoned that the Indian Smithwick shot would have died of the wound and awarded the scalp of the dead Indian to Noah Smithwick. The Comanche war chief who led the raid must have experienced humiliation. For a Comanche to have his horses taken was a disgrace.

The Triangle of War

On February 23, 1836, Mexican cavalry led Santa Anna's troops into San Antonio. Waiting for them in the compound of an old Spanish church were a small band of resolute men who were about to write a page in American history. These defenders were led by Lt. Col. William Barrett Travis of the newly created Texas Regular Army. With Travis were 150 men, including the famous former United States congressman and bear hunter David Crockett and knife fighter Jim Bowie. When Crockett had been defeated in an election for Congress, he told his constituents to go to hell; he was going to Texas. Bowie had killed several men with the ten-inch knife he designed and had that one decorated for show. Ranger and blacksmith Noah Smithwick wrote that wanting a knife for practical purposes, Bowie gave Smithwick the order. The enterprising Ranger kept the pattern and sold a number of the knives.

The church that the Texians chose to fortify was named San Jose y Santiago del Alamo de Parras and likely dated from 1758. In 1836, it was commonly called the Alamo. It was built in the Spanish mission style with a church and a series of single-story adobe houses connected by a wall designed to keep captive Indians within and hinder the attacks of raiding tribes.

The enclosed space was too large for the Texians to establish a true perimeter defense. They reinforced the walls at some places and used palisades to fill in gaps. They had eighteen serviceable cannon and built ramps and gun platforms, placing the cannon to cover each side of the compound. In their haste to take up their positions, they had neglected to lay in a store of food. It seemed a miracle of God that ninety bushels of corn were found within the compound and thirty head of cattle were driven in. Travis shared joint command with Bowie. Likely from typhoid fever, Bowie was ill, as were some other members of the garrison. As the Mexicans closed the loop around the Alamo, high fever kept this strong leader confined to a bed, unable to participate in the defense. Travis had enough fighting spirit for all and sent out repeated messengers asking for assistance. His appeal went beyond a request to fellow Texians. Travis made his request for military aid to all Americans.

For a variety of reasons, including politics, lethargy, cowardice, and drunkenness, the large numbers of reinforcements which the men at the Alamo needed did not arrive. Only one group of men answered the desperate call. Located seventy miles from the Alamo, volunteers from the community of Gonzales had formed a twenty-two-man Ranger company. When Capt. Albert Martin of Gonzales brought the message from Travis, these Rangers rode to his support. Other volunteers joined them en route, bringing the total number of reinforcements to thirty-two. Infiltrating by night through the Mexican army, the Rangers rode into the Alamo, arriving in the early-morning darkness of March 1, 1836. None of these men would live to ride out. The men of the Alamo had refused to surrender, and Santa Anna had ordered his men to take no prisoners.

By March 6, the Alamo defenders were exhausted. Repeated demonstrations and attacks by the Mexicans and night sorties to disrupt Mexican gains had wearied the small force. It is likely that many were asleep at their positions when Santa Anna's men attacked through the darkness carrying the scaling ladders that took them over the walls. Heavily outnumbered, the Texians lost the fight for the walls and tried to fight from within the buildings. The Mexicans used captured cannon to destroy these and flush out the defenders, some of whom now raised their hands. Travis had died in the fight for the wall, and Bowie was murdered in his sick bed. When Crockett fell is unknown, but many believe he was butchered on the orders of Santa Anna after surrender. There was no mercy shown by the Mexicans. Texians were shot or bayoneted. Several groups of Americans were driven out of or sought to escape the Alamo compound. They were pinned beneath the lances of Mexican horsemen. None of the Texians who fought that last fight at the Alamo survived. Santa Anna had their bodies piled and burned. They fought as one and their ashes were mingled as one. They became part of the earth of Texas.

Though they paid the butcher's bill with their lives, the defenders of the Alamo bought Texas twelve days of preparedness and inflicted 1,600 dead and 500 wounded on Santa Anna's army.[6] A thousand Mexican troops were sent to attack two fifty-man contingents of Texians. They caught the first group at San Patricio and killed all but two who managed to flee. Twenty miles away, the second group of Texians was surrounded by Mexican lancers at a place known as Sweet Water. The majority of the Texians were promptly killed, and the captives were not spared. The Mexicans tied the feet of a doctor by the name of Grant to the rear legs of a wild mustang and his hands to the animal's tail. Grant was kicked to death by the animal. At Refugio, thirty-four Texians were taken prisoner and executed. Near Goliad, on March 30, 1836, the Mexicans captured Col. James Fannin and 331 of his men. Many of these were American volunteers from Alabama, Georgia, Kentucky, and Louisiana. Under orders from Santa Anna, the prisoners were divided into three groups, then shot. Some of the bodies were burned; others were devoured by wild animals. Santa Anna sent his troops onward with orders to exterminate any Americans they encountered. Terrified refugees fled before them.

Sam Houston led the Texas forces. He had counseled the building and training of an army until Santa Anna could be brought far from his base of supply and fragmented by the effort to control a vast land. Houston had both political and military experience. He had been governor of Tennessee and came up through the ranks to be commissioned in the United States Army. Houston fought well in actions against the Creek Indians and had strong political connections with his friend and former commander Andrew Jackson. His policy of delay, while Texas bled and burned, was not well received. Subordinate commanders, such as Travis and Fannin, disobeyed his orders to withdraw. Worried about the safety of their families, men deserted Houston's ranks. In the American Revolution, only a small percentage of men were willing to put their lives at risk for freedom. So it was in Texas. Thousands of men who could have served did not. Houston had only 1,000 men, but they were determined to fight.

A Ranger known as "Deaf" Smith captured a Mexican messenger who was carrying dispatches that revealed Santa Anna's plans. Smith, whose first name was Erastus, was born in New York and first came to Texas at age thirty. He became a superb scout though illness had taken his hearing. Armed with the information from Smith, Houston took position near San Jacinto. Staking everything on one battle, Houston was looking for a means to draw Santa Anna to him. He put his small force with a river and bayou at its back. If he lost, his army would be slaughtered.

Santa Anna had split his forces and was marching with 800 men; additional forces, while not immediately available, could reinforce his troops. Learning of the unlikely location of Houston's army, Santa Anna moved to pen the Texians into a killing ground. On April 20,

1836, he felt the trap was complete. Closing within less than a mile of Houston's men, Santa Anna paused his army, threw up hasty barriers of wood and saddle, and waited for more of his army to join.

To the disgust of his men, Houston also waited. He was not dug in and did not have a strong defensive position. His army was not in a defensive mood. An additional 400 Mexican troops arrived to join Santa Anna, and Houston's army was now outnumbered. Around noon of the twenty-first, Houston had a meeting of his officers. It was agreed to attack the Mexicans on the morning of the twenty-second, but the troops were tired of waiting and clamored for an immediate attack. Thus, at 3 P.M. on April 22, 1836, the army of Texas set forth in vengeance.

Houston formed his troops on line, a thin line of more than 900 men that would move shoulder to shoulder. Houston rode his horse to the front and made a few remarks that most men could not hear and did not need to. Drawing his sword, he signaled his men to advance. Santa Anna had cannon, but so did the Texians. The city of Cincinnati, Ohio, had given Houston's army two small field pieces called the Twin Sisters. These two cannon had made their presence known to the Mexicans in a previous skirmish. Santa Anna had chosen to take position behind a rise of ground, thus protecting himself from direct fire by these guns. The rise of ground hindered observation of the Texian position, but Santa Anna was not concerned.

Lulled by his previous success, Santa Anna did not allow the thought of being attacked to interrupt his leisure. He thought the Texian army would huddle in fear until he chose to attack and destroy them. As a result of this heady arrogance, he did not have patrols, outposts or pickets in front of his position. Many of his men were sleeping while the sun was high. The troops had stacked arms, and those who were not sleeping were occupied with the gambling, idle conversation, and routine chores of a soldier.

By the time the Mexicans saw the Texians coming, it was too late for defense. The two cannon blew apart the saddle and brush barrier, and the Texians were on the Mexicans with hatchets, rifles, and knives. The battle was short, the killing was long. Filling the air with the cry "Remember the Alamo," the Texians slaughtered the terrified Mexicans. Santa Anna's well-trained and disciplined soldiers were shot down as they milled about in confusion. Many were driven into the water and were shot there or drowned. Santa Anna fled, but his force was destroyed. Six hundred and thirty Mexicans were killed and with few exceptions, the rest were taken prisoner. The Texians lost two men killed in the fight; another six died of wounds, and eighteen were wounded. Houston had several horses shot from under him, and his ankle was shattered by a shot.

Santa Anna ran, first on horseback, then on foot. He was captured by a Texian mounted patrol who did not recognize him. When he was brought in, the Mexican prisoners cried out in recognition, and the dictator was taken before Sam Houston. Santa Anna protested his innocence in the murder of American prisoners, but Houston cut his protests short. It is likely that all the Texians wanted Santa Anna dead. Sam Houston understood that he could better control Mexican actions by keeping their ruler alive. Under Houston's directions, Santa Anna ordered a withdrawal of his remaining troops and agreed to end the fighting. On May 14, 1836, he signed the treaties that made the giant land of Texas free of domination by the government of Mexico. Santa Anna was sent east and met President Andrew Jackson. In 1837, Santa Anna was put on an American warship and sent home to Mexico.

CHAPTER 18

Texas Independence

There was still the threat of Mexican invasion, and both the British and the French were looking with hunger at this giant land. The eyes of Texas were looking east to the United States, and the eyes of the United States were on Texas. Sam Houston was badly hurt by his wound but recovered in time to be the first president of Texas elected by the people. They modeled the constitution of the new republic on that of the United States. The majority of whites in Texas clearly saw themselves as American Texians. Houston sought annexation of Texas by the United States and the establishment of peaceful relations with the Indians. Houston's desire for peace with the Indians did not find favor with many Texians. Houston had lived among the Cherokee and must have enjoyed himself there. The Indians had given him the unflattering descriptive name of "Big Drunk."

Texas did not have the money to support a standing army, but Indian raids were an ever-present danger. The people of Texas looked to the few men who patrolled the frontier for protection. This included Indian allies. The Lipan Apache and Tonkawa Indians had been enemies of the Comanche for generations. They were very effective in tracking raiding parties and scouting Comanche camps and often accompanied those who went in search of Indian raiders. The men who ranged the country were sometimes called spies, mounted volunteers, or mounted gunmen, but the name Ranger maintained its special significance.

In 1834, a Baptist frontier preacher named John Parker had taken his extended family of thirty members up the Brazos River into the area that is now Limestone County. They found a land rich in wildlife and prime for planting, but it was isolated from the assistance of other whites. Along the Navasota River, they built a stockade with cabins and named it Parker's Fort. They planted extensive corn fields whose care required men being out of sight of their fort. Most of the men were at work in these fields when, at 10 A.M. on May 19, 1836, a number of Comanche Indians rode up to fort. Traveling with them were some Kiowa and Caddo Indians. Old John Parker, the head of the family; Daniel Parker, who had proposed the formation of the Corps of Rangers; and Silas Parker, who had commanded a company, were among the six men who were with the women and children at the fort. Months of inactivity had a created a lull in security, and the gate to the fort stood open when the Indians arrived.

The Indians wanted water and a cow to butcher. Against the advice of the others, Daniel and Silas Parker went outside to seek to appease the Indians. When Daniel told the Indians he did not have a beef to give them, the Comanche drove their lances through him, then killed Silas. Two men named Frost tried to stop them at the gate but were cut down. The Indians poured into the fort. They lanced old John Parker, scalped him, and cut off his genitals. The women were captured and raped. Even John Parker's old wife, the grandmother of the clan, was stripped of her clothes, nailed to the ground by a lance, and sexually used. Five of the men were killed and two of the women would die of their wounds. As the Parker men came running from the fields, the Indians rode away. They took with them, Rachel Plummer and her little son, James, Elizabeth Kellog, and two small children, Cynthia Ann Parker, age nine, and her brother, John, age six. Tied with rawhide and beaten, the women were raped by any warrior who chose to use them. When the Indians dispersed, the captives were separated from each other.

Elizabeth Kellog was traded through several tribes and was purchased from captivity in December 1836 by Sam Houston. Rachel Plummer would never see her son again. She lived in hardship and terror for eighteen months with the Comanche and had a child by one of them. Through carelessness or malice, the Indians killed the child. At length, she was located at a New Mexico encampment and ransomed. She did not live long after her return. After six years of captivity, the two little boys were located and ransomed. Little John Parker had become a Comanche and could not adjust. He returned to the Indians. In time, he left them accompanied by a Mexican girl who had been captive and settled in Mexico.

For years, the search for Cynthia Ann Parker continued. She had been taken to a remote area by the Comanche, and they would not relinquish her. She was seen by an army officer when she was about seventeen, but the Indians threatened to kill him if he attempted to interfere. He said that she wept, would not speak, and ran from him. In time, she mated with Peta Nocono, a Comanche war chief.[1] The experience of the Parker family was routinely repeated on the American frontier. The savage butchery, the rape and torture of loved ones, the killing or disappearance of little children, engendered a hatred for the Indian that dictated a war of extermination. As the strength of the white settlers increased, their wrath exploded into a philosophy of "Kill them all."

In 1860, a Ranger force struck a Comanche Indian encampment near the Pease River in northwest Texas. The Rangers were in no mood to take prisoners. One was in pursuit of a woman with a small female child. When the chase ended, the woman glared at her captors with hatred. One of the Rangers identified her as a white woman. When Indian captives were returned, families tried desperately to be reunited. Isaac Parker, the uncle of Cynthia Ann, questioned this woman. She could not speak English but in Comanche described childhood recollections that seemed to fit. When he mentioned the name Cynthia Ann, she touched her chest and repeated the name.

The rescue of Cynthia Ann Parker by the Rangers did not have a happy ending. After twenty-four years as a Comanche, she could not cope with the life she had been born to. Her little girl died, and she began to reject food. In a weakened state, she died of the flu in 1870.[2]

There was much more to a Rangers life than hunting Indians. They had to provide their own horses, arms, and equipment, hunt for food and cook it, and make the deerskin clothes and moccasins they wore. Capt. Robert M. Coleman's Rangers were ordered to build a fort near Austin and another on the Leon River. The stockades and cabins were built and contained a form of wall to wall carpeting. Buffalo hides were nailed to the floors, fur side up.

On a spring evening in 1837, Ranger Noah Smithwick and his comrades were relaxing at the fort near Austin when someone noticed a campfire on the opposite side of the Colorado River. They reasoned it might be Indians. Lt. Nicholas Wren took fifteen of the best mounted men and crossed the river. They moved as quietly as possible to the vicinity of where the fire had been seen and waited for dawn. There were no guards posted. In the dim light, the Rangers could see sleeping forms, but could not be certain they were Indians. Whoever it was had a large number of horses and mules and were very careless about guarding them. As light came, one of the sleepers came out of his buffalo-hide blankets and rose to greet the sun. The Rangers saw clearly that he was a Comanche warrior. In the darkness, some of the Rangers had crawled so close to the Indians that they were in the line of fire. They attempted to withdraw but were heard by the warrior, who yelled the alarm. Ranger Joe Weeks killed the Indian who was shouting, but the rest quickly used the dim light and brush to disappear. One Indian paused long enough to get off a shot that killed Ranger Martin.

The Rangers took the horses and mules back to the fort, but they in turn mounted a careless guard. The Indians mounted a quick retaliatory raid and got away with part of the herd. The Rangers tracked this group but lost the tracks after three days search. Horses were a much prized booty of Indian raids. The Comanche would steal horses; the Rangers would pursue and sometimes get them back; the Indians would then steal some from the Rangers, who would again pursue and get some horses back. It was not done for entertainment. Dismounted men in the vast land of Texas were at a disadvantage. It was better to have the enemy on foot.

Comanche raiders made off with a large number of horses from near the Colorado River. On October 13, 1837, a small force under Captain Eastland and Lt. A. B. Van Benthusen was sent in pursuit. The two officers determined to enhance their search by splitting into two groups. Van Benthusen rode off with eighteen men and near the headwaters of the Trinity River encountered a large number of Indians. Van Benthusen ordered his men to dismount in a wooded defensive position. They were soon surrounded by the Indians. The fighting continued for over two hours and was at ranges often less than twenty yards. Four of Van Benthusen's men were casualties when a fortunate shot brought down the war chief who led the Comanche. There were times when that would have ended the battle, but after a few minutes of regrouping, these Indians came on again, now led by another war chief. They set the woods on fire, building a circle of flame around Van Benthusen's small party. Faced with a situation of attack or burn, Van Benthusen led his men in a charge, breaking the circles at the loss of six more men. Tiring of the battle, the Indians rode off. Left on foot and encumbered by wounded, it took Van Benthusen seventeen days to walk back to safety.[3]

The new Republic of Texas was plagued by a shortage of money. Defense was often left to locally organized Ranger units. Struggling to keep a government controlled defense force. On December 10, 1836, the Texas Congress passed legislation establishing pay rates for Rangers. A Ranger captain would be paid $75 a month. The basic rank was a rifleman, who earned $25 a month. Texas had little money but plenty of land. Good service could result in a Ranger being rewarded with acreage.[4]

Mirabeau Bonaparte Lamar was a hot-headed Georgian who led Sam Houston's sixty-man cavalry at the Battle of San Jocund. Lamar was vice president of the Republic of Texas, and he hated its president, Sam Houston. When Houston left office in 1838, he was prevented by the Texas Constitution from succeeding himself, and Lamar became the president in December 1838. From the outset, he was determined to reverse the policies of Sam Houston. Lamar felt Texas should be prepared to go it alone. He had no interest in peace with the Indians and intended to destroy them. If the Mexicans would not recognize the claims of Texas, then the Mexicans would be crushed. In his inaugural address, Lamar said, "If peace can be obtained only by the sword, let the sword do its work."[5] Lamar appealed to Texas pride, and Texians responded. Now the battle for the land began in earnest. Lamar was a winner-take-all leader and set about accomplishing his goal through military force.

As the Texians had pushed westward, they increasingly came within raiding distance of the Comanche, who took full advantage of this new-found source of supply. To combat the Comanche, Lamar put together a military force that included a regular army of Texas, home guard militia, and the militia volunteers with frontier skills who formed the aggressive Rangers. Increasingly, the whites took the war to the Indians, with the Comanche being hunted in the south and west. Lamar did not discriminate in his hatred for Indians and in time would drive out the Cherokee, Creeks, Delaware, Shawnee, Seminole, and other Indians of east Texas. It is likely that only some were involved in depredations, but all suffered displacement. These were a settled people who deserved a better fate.

The men who served as Rangers came as volunteers serving for a year. If circumstances required them to leave, they could do so, provided they found a suitable replacement. By 1838, Noah Smithwick had served his own tour and, in addition, had filled the spaces of two other Rangers. For each year of service, a Ranger was given a certificate entitling him to 1,280 acres of Texas. There was so much land available that the certificates were thought to be of little value. Ranger Smithwick traded a land certificate for a horse, which the Indians stole from him within a week.[6]

In late January 1839, Col. John H. Moore led sixty-three white Rangers and Indian scouts outward from near LaGrange along the Colorado River. The ubiquitous Noah Smithwick was a Ranger officer on this expedition. The mission was to search out and destroy Comanche encampments. On February 13, Indian scouts reported they had located a Comanche camp in the San Saba Valley on Spring Creek. The Rangers made a night move that brought them close to the Indians, then dismounted and readied themselves to attack at first light. The Comanche were taken by surprise as the Rangers broke into their habitations and began shooting any thing that moved. Moore thought the smoke and fire obscured the targets and eliminated his ability to control the shooting of his men. He felt it best to withdraw at the height of success. A number of his men had difficulty with this reasoning. The resilient Indians promptly managed to get behind the Rangers and captured half of their horses. One Ranger died of wounds; the rest, including the wounded, faced a difficult passage home.

Moore learned something from his Spring Creek expedition. In October 1840, his Rangers tracked a Comanche band that included more than 100 warriors to a camp along the Colorado River. Again the Indians had failed to mount an effective guard. The Indian camp was in the bend of the river, leaving them with water on three sides and the Rangers attacking from the fourth. The Rangers of this period were armed with the single-shot long rifle. It was cumbersome to use from horseback. This time, the Rangers used the horses for mobility. Charging the Comanche camp on horseback, they dismounted when they were in the camp and could bring their firepower to bear. Most of the Comanche tried to flee to the river. They were shot on the banks and in the water, some drowned, some made it across the river, but the Rangers had their horses at hand and pursued them over the open prairie. The Comanche lost 500 horses. The horses could be replaced by theft, a dead Comanche was a different circumstance. Nearly 130 Comanche were killed—a disaster to their nation.

Lamar saw the future Texas extending to the Pacific Ocean. He wanted the Mexicans to accept the Rio Grande River as the common border and felt the Mexican inhabitants of New Mexico would want to join a Republic of Texas that was on the rise. An expeditionary force of 300 men was sent on a 1,300-mile journey across the high plains to take Santa Fe and welcome New Mexico into the fold. It was a disaster. The harsh, waterless terrain, the burning sun, and Indians who burned captives took a heavy toll. Those who survived were promptly taken captive by the Mexican Army. They were brutally treated on a march to prison in Mexico.

The Comanche were feeling the pressure of Lamar's Indian policy and decided to seek a peace that would end the Ranger raids. On January 9, 1840, three Comanche chiefs came to San Antonio as representatives of their people. They related to Texas Ranger Henry Karnes that their people had held a meeting and decided to end the fighting. Ranger Karnes told them the peace could not be considered until the Comanche returned all their white captives. The Indians said that had already been agreed to among themselves. Karnes and the Indians decided that in twenty days the captives would be brought in and treaty arrangements begun. Karnes reported the meeting to Texas Secretary of War Albert Sidney Johnston, who later served as a general in the Confederate army. Karnes did not trust the Indians and recommended a strong military force be on hand when the meeting took place and that Indians be held hostage for the return of the white captives. Johnston sent Lt. Col. William S. Fisher of the 1st Texas Infantry and several companies of troops to provide security.

On March 19, the Comanche treaty party of more than sixty people arrived in San Antonio. Included in the Indian representatives were a number of chiefs, twelve of whom were invited to participate in discussions at a former building of the Spanish government known as the Council House. The Texians could see that the Comanche had brought only one white captive with them, and the sight of the young girl that was being returned had the Texians seething with anger. Her name was Matilda Lockhart. She was fifteen and had been a captive of the Comanche for two years. The Indians had brutally mistreated this young girl. The flesh had been burned from her nose and the hair from her head. The soles of her feet had been burned so that she could not escape. Though her body showed the burns, cuts, and bruises of torture, Matilda Lockhart had an unbroken spirit. She told the Texians that the Indians had other prisoners but planned to bring them forth one at a time and use them to negotiate to advantage.

When asked where the other captives were, the Indian spokesman lied that the girl was the only white captive they had, that the rest were with other tribes. He ended his remark with the haughty statement, "How do you like the answer?" The Texians did not like the answer. Fisher ordered a company of soldiers into the room and had others surround the Council House. Fisher told the chiefs they were prisoners and would be kept until their women and children went back to the tribe and returned with the other white captives. The Comanche promptly drew knives and one stabbed a soldier. Gunfire erupted, and fighting began inside and outside of the Council House. Most of the chiefs died fighting, with at least thirty-five of their party killed. Nearly all of the other Indians were captured. Seven Texians were killed and eight wounded.

One of the female Indian captives was sent back to the tribe to relate what happened and bring back the white captives. The Comanche filled the air with lament and rage. They no longer wanted a treaty. They wanted revenge. The Texians expected trouble and assembled volunteer units to meet the threat. Days passed, then weeks, then months, and yet the Indians did not attack. A false sense of security began to permeate the settlements. The volunteers had work to do and went home to their families. The Texians suspected the Mexicans were trying influence the Comanche to attack, but they did not know the Mexicans were supplying the Indians and encouraging them to delay until the blow would come as surprise.

Six months had passed when a great force of Comanche estimated at between 600 and 1,000 people moved toward the coastal settlements of the Gulf of Mexico. They moved as a nation, complete with women and children, their horse herds, and all their possessions. On August 5, 1840, their outriding scouts killed a man and wounded another. The incident alerted Ranger units, which began to assemble and move in pursuit. Those on the trail included experienced Ranger leaders Ben McCullough with twenty-four men and John J. Tumlinson with a company of more than seventy. They were joined by another Ranger company under Adam Zumwalt.

Around the community of Victoria, the Indians killed thirteen people and captured nearly 2,000 horses. Victoria was well defended, so the Comanche moved on to the port town of Linnville. It was Saturday, August 8, 1840; the unsuspecting residents of Linnville looked out in the morning light and saw dust coming toward the town. The Comanche were coming at a gallop, and the townspeople were not prepared to defend themselves. Seized by panic, the citizens of Linnville fled to the water. Only providence saved most of them. A large lighter was moored by the water. They were able to scramble into that and head for deep water. Not every one escaped. The Comanche killed five men and took two women and a child captive. They then proceeded to loot the town, taking whatever they desired. They were much attracted to the clothing of the whites. Comanche warriors outfitted themselves in shirts, boots, and stovepipe hats. They draped themselves in bolts of cloth and tied bright-colored ribbons in their horses manes and tails.

Satisfied with their raid and encumbered by their loot and the great horse herd, the Comanche headed back for the interior. By now, frontier Ranger units were springing to arms and horse, and the Texians were on the Indians' trail. Tumlinson and McCullough caught up with one part of the Comanche raiding party. The Rangers were heavily outnumbered, and Tumlinson resisted McCullough's call for an attack. The Indians killed one Ranger and got away.

The battle experience of the Rangers enabled them to accurately predict the route the Indians would take. Other Ranger units under Lafayette Ward and Matthew Caldwell sought to cut the Indian line of march. They were joined by Capt. James Bird and his company. Ben McCullough and three other Rangers had made a grueling ride to get around the Indian column. They came in eager to fight. A militia leader name Felix Huston arrived, and as he was a general, he was given command. He did not have the skill or daring of a Ranger captain and was hesitant.

A rider brought in word that Col. Edward Burleson was a few miles off, coming at a gallop with eighty-seven more Rangers and thirteen

Indian scouts. While waiting for Burleson to arrive, the Rangers concealed themselves in brush along a waterway known as Plum Creek, twenty-seven miles to the southeast of Austin. It was August 12, 1840. Waiting in ambush were an assemblage of the finest frontiersmen in Texas. These Rangers were experienced Indian fighters under proven leaders. They were all under the command of an uncertain general.

In the distance, a line appeared slowly moving diagonally across the front of the Ranger position. One witness said it appeared to be seven miles long. Burleson and his men rode in, and the Ranger companies sprang to the saddle and rode out to meet the Comanche. Immediately, the air was filled with the battle cries of the Indian warriors. A large number of them turned their horses to meet the Rangers. They rode with incredible grace and skill, putting on a breathtaking display with their beribboned steeds adorned with the cloth and ribbon taken from Linnville.

General Huston was a man of courage, but his lack of experience gave him pause. The Rangers moved forward slowly while the Indians galloped to and fro to their front. The Ranger captains were not deceived by the Indian display of horsemanship. They could see the long line of Indians escorting the horse herd and loot getting farther away. The delay tactic of the Indians was succeeding. The Comanche would ride hard at the Rangers, covering themselves with shields made of Buffalo hide. The shields could take the sting from a bullet, so Rangers waited until the Comanche turned to ride away, then dropped them. A magnificently caparisoned war chief rode toward the Rangers, taunting them. A well-aimed shot finished him. Ben McCullough and the other Ranger captains were pressuring General Huston to attack, and he now gave the order.

The Rangers touched their spurs to the flanks of their horses and charged into the Indians. They killed as they passed through the defensive screen and fell upon the guards of the horse herd and the Comanche column. The Comanche abandoned the horses and their loot and fled. They were hotly pursued. Upwards of eighty Indians were killed. The Indians had struck down some of their prisoners at the start of the attack. Three of the four taken at Linnville were rescued.

The Battle of Plum Creek changed the tactics of the Comanche. In the future, they would avoid the large-scale commitment of force that generated swift and massive retaliation. Now the Comanche would travel in small war parties covering a wider area. They hoped this would force the defenders to disperse their strength. Many fights remained for the future, but it is likely that Comanche war chiefs looked in the direction of the rising sun and felt despair. It was no longer their sun. It now belonged to a great wave of people who were coming to crush them.

CHAPTER 19

Ranger Jack Hays and the Colts

One of the Rangers who took part in the Battle of Plum Creek was a young man named John Coffee Hays. His fellow Rangers knew him as Jack. He was born near Nashville, Tennessee, on January 28, 1817. His family had good connections. Both his father and his grandfather had served under Andrew Jackson, who had purchased the land for his famed estate, the Hermitage, from Jack Hays's grandfather. Jack Hays received his middle name from another man the family knew as a friend, Gen. John Coffee, who led Jackson's horsemen and served as a mounted Ranger. Jack Hays was a small boy when his father died, and he was raised by an uncle. He grew up in good circumstances and combined the graces of education and civility with boundless energy, high character, and a passion for action. Men who met Jack Hays without knowing him were taken aback by his boyish appearance. Ranger Samuel Reid described Hays as "a delicate looking young man."

His uncle wanted Jack Hays to go to the U.S. Military Academy at West Point, but that type of regimented discipline did not appeal to this young warrior looking for immediate action. He decided to head for Texas and become a surveyor. He arrived sometime in late 1837 or early 1838, and while beginning to establish a good business reputation, he became a Texas Ranger, fighting under the command of Henry Karnes and Deaf Smith. His ability was so clearly evident that in 1841, Texas President Mirabeau Lamar appointed Jack to be captain of one of three newly forming Ranger companies.

At a time when the U.S. Army was using the lash to beat men to obedience, Jack Hays led his Rangers by example and inspiration. One of his Lipan Apache Indian scouts, the war chief named Flacco, once remarked, "Blue Wing and I . . . no fraid to go to hell together. Captain Jack great brave no fraid go to hell by himself."[1] No other type of leadership would have succeeded with the men Jack Hays led.

They were free born, and many were successful and educated men. Rangers Benjamin Highsmith and Samuel Reid, writing of their Ranger comrades before and during the Mexican War, noted that conversations around the campfire often included literature and history.

On his first mission as captain, Jack Hays led his Rangers to Laredo. Riding boldly into town, the Rangers cowed the Mexican garrison. They then rounded up the Mexican horses and took them, thus defying the Mexican soldiers to resist. The horses were taken from the town, then brought back and returned to their owners. Jack Hays told the Mexicans that he had no desire to harm them or take their property. He wanted the Mexicans to understand that any depredations they performed on the Texians would result in devastation for the Mexican people of Laredo. No one was killed on either side, but the point was made.

For fifteen years, the principal weapon the Rangers had used in fighting Indians and Mexicans was the long rifle. Though accurate, it fired a single shot and was unwieldy when used from the back of a horse. When Jack Hays took command of his Ranger company, he was carrying a new and revolutionary weapon. It was a .36-caliber cap-and-ball pistol that carried five rounds in a cylinder that could be loaded from the front. At each shot, the barrel would revolve, putting the next round in firing position; thus, the pistol became known as a five-shooter. Holsters were not in wide usage. The five-shooter was intended to be carried in the pocket or thrust under a belt. The trigger was not protected with a trigger guard. It was recessed until the weapon was cocked; then the trigger dropped into position. There were problems. The weapon had to be broken into three parts to be reloaded, the caliber was light, and a trigger guard was needed. Still, this was the ideal weapon for a horseman.

Ranger Sam Reid wrote of a story about Hays that has carried down through time. According to its source, during a fight in the early 1840s, Jack Hays was cut off from his men by the Comanche. Unable to break free, he drove his horse to the top of a place called Enchanted Hill and dismounted, taking cover as the Indians surrounded him. They were determined to take him alive for torture. Each time the Indians came close, Hays rose and pointed his rifle at them. They knew his reputation as a marksman, and none wanted to be the first to die. Hays did not fire but used the threat to hold them at bay. As the more venturesome Comanche closed to kill him, Hays took a toll of them with rifle and pistol. The Indians reasoned that the only way they would get Jack Hays was an all-out charge accepting casualties. As they began the effort that would have ended the life of Jack Hays, his Rangers succeeded in breaking through to save him.

Jack Hays had an excellent Indian scout in the Lipan Indian war chief Flacco. This enemy of the Comanche in turn had ten subordinates to look for sign. Though these Indian comrades were invaluable, Jack Hays was himself one of the best trackers in the west. He could read numbers and direction in the slightest disturbance of the earth.

When the Indians took shelter in the brush, Hays would have his men surround the area on horseback, and then he would lead a few dismounted men into the thick cover. Though suitable for hiding, the brush was not a convenient place for the Indian to use lance or bow and arrow. Colt's pistol was the ideal weapon for such close-quarter action.

When Mirabeau Lamar's term as president of the Republic of Texas expired, his old foe Sam Houston resumed the office. The aggressive, expansionist, red-ink budget policies of Lamar had done much to advance the frontier and reduce Indian raids, but these policies had beggared the treasury. Texas was broke. Sam Houston immediately set about trying to build peaceful relation with both the Indians and the Mexicans. Houston's policy, announced through his secretary of state, was to buy friendship with the Indians in what amounted to little more then bribes. No troops would be maintained except a few Rangers on the frontier.

Neither the Indians nor the Mexicans were agreeable to a live-and-let-live policy. A propensity to raid was in the genes of the Comanche. The Mexicans had no intention of forgetting their claim to the vast area Santa Anna had signed away. They were not cowed by the possibility of intervention by the United States. Many Texians did not support Houston. Some were actively engaged in helping Mexicans along the Rio Grande River who were rebelling against their government.

In March 1842, the Mexicans made a shambles of Houston's conciliatory policies. An army commanded by Gen. Rafael Vasquez marched into Texas. There was not sufficient strength to repel them. Jack Hays and his Rangers numbered only about 100, and the best they could do was scout the Mexicans and provide early warning to the settlements that lay in their path. Thanks to the Rangers, the citizens of San Antonio were able to evacuate prior to the occupation of their town.

Without money to pay them, Houston was forced to disband the Rangers. Only Hays and a few men were kept as scouts. The few Rangers were hard pressed to cover the borders from both the Indians and the Mexicans. In September, a 1,200-man Mexican army under Gen. Adrian Woll invaded Texas. They were briefly held at bay by a small force of Texas militia who sent out word they needed assistance. The fifty Texians who responded were surrounded in the open. Their marksmanship cost Woll sixty men, and he resorted to artillery to defeat the Texians. When the survivors surrendered, Woll's cavalry butchered them. Woll occupied San Antonio. This time, there was no early warning, and some of the town fathers were captured, shackled, and taken south. Hays and his few Rangers annoyed Woll on his withdrawal. The Rangers got among Woll's artillerymen and killed a number. General Woll offered a reward of 500 silver dollars for Jack Hays's head.[2]

Though short of ammunition, the Texians raised a volunteer mob of 750 men and briefly occupied the Mexican town of Laredo. General Somervell was ostensibly in charge, but exercised ineffective control. There was looting and rape. Seeing he could not control these people, Somervell decided to withdraw. About 300 men were determined to punish the Mexicans and ignored the order to return to Texas. They rode below the Rio Grande to the isolated Mexican town of Mier, which they occupied. They soon found themselves surrounded by a large Mexican force. House-to-house fighting began. The Texians cut holes in the adobe to get from the interior of the houses to the roof tops. There they took a heavy toll of the Mexicans. A Ranger named McMullen said, "We saw the terrible havoc that our rifles had made. The tops of their houses were covered with the dead, and the gutters on the roofs streamed with their blood."[3]

The Texians who went to Mier were a pick-up collection of angry men who lacked organization. Though they included some militia and Rangers, including Sam Walker and Big Foot Wallace, they were not participating as part of those organizations and did not represent Texas. They had agreed to follow the orders of Col. Bill Fisher, but when he was wounded, there was no chain of command. As ammunition dwindled and casualties mounted, the men received what they claimed was an offer of humane treatment if they would surrender. They did and were promptly taken into Mexican custody and marched to the interior.

At Saltillo, the Texians, led by the burly Scot Ewen Cameron, overpowered their guards, took their weapons, and escaped. They captured Mexican soldiers, took their weapons, and released them. They then headed north through the desert toward Texas. The scorching sun, the trackless waste, and a lack of food and water drove men to despair and death. Nine men died or disappeared. Well-equipped Mexican lancers tracked, them and when the exhausted men discarded their weapons, the Mexicans moved in and captured them. Only four men made it through the desert and home to Texas.[4]

Santa Anna was back in control of Mexico. His desire to execute all the Texians was opposed by foreign ambassadors, so the Mexican dictator decided that men would be killed by drawing lot. There were 176 captives. A vessel containing that number of beans was put before the men. There were 159 white beans and 17 black. Each man was required to draw a bean, and any who drew black would be executed. Ranger Wallace saw that the black beans had been poured in last. He drove his hand to the bottom of the vessel and drew a white bean. Eighteen men were executed; seventeen had drawn black beans, and on orders from Santa Anna, the Mexicans later shot Ewen Cameron. Those who survived were marched from Mexico City to prison at Perote on the road to Vera Cruz.

In late February 1844, Jack Hays was authorized to form and command another Ranger company on the southwest frontier. His rolls included proven Rangers Ben McCullough, Sam Walker, and Mike Chevallie, who would later be a Ranger major and boon companion of Rip Ford. The men of this company were equipped with the five-shot Colts and were eager to use them in battle. Early on, the Rangers began to carry a spare loaded cylinder, giving each man the capability of ten shots at the ready. At the beginning of June 1844, Hays and fifteen Rangers were in camp at Walker's Creek fifty miles above Seguin. Ten Comanche rode close enough to be seen, and Hays ordered his men to saddle and ride after them. Though he followed these Comanche, Hays reasoned that the Indian intent was to draw the Rangers into ambush by a larger force. The Rangers rode slowly, taking no chances. To the Comanche, it appeared that they had a small number of enemy that could be easily dealt with. When they saw their ambush would not work, the remainder of the Indians rode into view and formed for battle, taunting the Rangers. It is likely the Comanche expected the Rangers would dismount at the most defensible terrain they could find and use their long rifles, alternating their fires so that some weapons were always available to meet the Indian charge.

On this momentous day new tactics were born. After using their rifles, Hays ordered his men to "charge and powder burn them!" Drawing their five-shooters, the Rangers engaged the Indians at close quarters. The Comanche had never faced this type of firepower. Hays's fifteen men carried the death-dealing capability of more than 150 riflemen. Though the Comanche fought bravely, they were whipped, leaving twenty dead on the field and an equal number estimated as wounded. In his report of the battle, Hays stated that this mounted fight covered three miles. Hays credited the victory to the five-shooting pistols and the courage of his men.

CHAPTER 20

Manifest Destiny

The Republic of Texas was financially broke and needed a savior. The United States government under James K. Polk wanted Texas with a border on the Rio Grande River. For the Mexicans, competition for land west of the Mississippi had been inherited from the Spanish. They had learned they could not control the unruly Texians, but they did not want a hungry giant living next to them. Mexico would fight to prevent Texas from being annexed by the great power marching west.

In 1844, Texas confused the issue by electing Dr. Anson Jones as its president. Jones was against annexation, or at least that was his public stance. On March 4, 1845, the Democratic Party saw their candidate, James K. Polk, sworn into office as the eleventh president of the United States. Polk was an unknown, a compromise candidate of an undecided political party. He had no military experience but was an expansionist clone of Andrew Jackson. Whatever his lack of experience, James K. Polk knew the mood of the public. The march westward was an American quest.

President Polk wanted Texas and offered to pay Mexico for it, but he was prepared to clear away the Mexican claims by force of arms if his offer was refused. In June 1845, Brig. Gen. Zachary Taylor was ordered to assemble 2,000 troops at Fort Jessup, Louisiana. Now, when Texas was annexed, the United States had troops in position to prevent Mexican interference. President Jones of Texas liked terms that included military support of the United States. In July 1845, Texas voted for annexation.

The U.S. Army had an authorized strength of 8,500 men, but only 5,000 were available for duty. It was an army of woefully understrength infantry units supported by understrength units of artillery. Though the horse had been used effectively in southern military operations in the 1700s, the American army of 1845 had no troops trained to fight from the back of a horse. The philosophy of the period was to use dra-

Winfield Scott.
LIBRARY OF CONGRESS

goons, mounted infantry that used the horse as transportation and then dismounted to fight. The army did not use Sam Colt's revolver.

Two American generals would figure prominently in the Mexican War, Zachary Taylor and Winfield Scott. Taylor was the Omar Bradley of the Mexican War, the good old country boy. They called him "Old Rough and Ready." He talked plain and practiced simplicity of uniform and camp life. He was a member of the Whig Party and wanted to be president of the United States.

Winfield Scott was the George Patton of this war. He had success during the War of 1812 and parlayed that into a promotion to general after six years of service. Scott was a showboat. His uniforms were gaudy; his camp life resembled that of an oriental potentate. He was devoted to the European style of warfare, studied the French and English practices, and then wrote the book that was adopted by the U.S. Army as its regulations. At the time of the Mexican War, he had the nickname of "Old Fuss and Feathers." Scott sought to develop an officer corps that resembled English nobility, even making wine tasting part of his officer-training program. Winfield Scott was a member of the Democratic Party and wanted to be president.

Taylor was first in the field. Early on, he had a letter from Jack Hays with the offer of a company of Texas Ranger.[1] Taylor was not fond of volunteers, but he accepted the Rangers to placate the new

Americans and keep them on the frontier with the Indians. Taylor's initial orders were not to go into Mexico and pick fights. President Polk knew his political opponents were waiting for a cause they could use to attack him. While he pressed Congress to vote him a large army, Polk was feeling his way through a tangle of domestic politics, but he allowed Taylor to advance toward the Rio Grande to assert the American claims to that border.

In April 1846, the American army moved southward. It was soon grouping like a blind giant. Lacking cavalry, Taylor did not have a reconnaissance element that could scout the Mexican forces. The U.S. Army had the strength to occupy or defend a spot on the ground, but keeping open a line of communication and supply was a different matter. Mexico was determined to keep the territory between the Nueces and the Rio Grande Rivers, and large numbers of their cavalry were present in and near the region. An army cannot exist without supply. On the coast of the Gulf of Mexico, several miles north of the Rio Grande, Zachary Taylor established a logistical base at Point Isabel. This provided deep-water access for ships.

Taylor left part of his force at Point Isabel under the command of Maj. Jacob Brown. The Mexicans were outraged. Each day, they watched the American flag being raised over land they had called their own for generations.[2]

After positioning Brown, Taylor then moved his army twenty five miles distant, placing them on the other side of the Rio Grande from the Mexican city of Matamoros and a Mexican army under General Arista. The armies were now eyeball to eyeball, but both sides were seeking to place the blame for starting the war on the other party. As the Americans now occupied the disputed territory, the Mexicans had little choice but to drive them out. The hot blood of General Arista was stirred by the incessant complaint of Mexican ranchers who saw their land in the hands of the Americans. Unable to resist the bait, Arista sent his skilled horseman over the Rio Grande and into action. In doing this, the Mexican general believed he was defending the territory of his nation. As the United States claimed the land north of the Rio Grande, President Polk and his officers viewed General Arista's action as an invasion of American soil.

Partisan Mexican horsemen known as *rancheros* wreaked havoc on supply trains. Now American soldiers felt the Mexican lariat snaking around their necks as they were yanked from their wagon seats or feet and dragged to their deaths behind fleet Mexican horses. Col. Thomas Cross, who was Taylor's quartermaster, was among the American soldiers taken and killed.[3] Dressed in wool uniforms unsuited to the heat and unaccustomed to the terrain, American soldiers suffered from the heat, were frequently lost, and could not identify where actions took place. Arista committed 1,500 of his lancers across the river and followed with his main army. On April 24, 1846, the Mexicans captured sixty of Taylor's dragoons. The Americans had the incident they wanted. Taylor informed Polk that the war had begun.

By now, Taylor recognized he did not know his enemy or the terrain. Taylor reluctantly asked Texas for two regiments of horsemen and two of infantry. Jack Hays was given command of one regiment of mounted riflemen, and George Wood had the other. Hays's men tended to be from the border areas. They had more combat experience. As Hays formed his four Ranger companies, he promptly sent them into action. Fortunately for General Taylor, he quickly had Sam Walker's unit in the field with him.

General Arista had superiority of numbers and planned to use the advantage to destroy the main body of the American forces. Recognizing that Taylor's force was split, Arista decided to ambush the American army. Arista would take the brushwood barricade the Americans laughingly called Fort Brown under fire, and when Taylor's army came into the open to rescue Brown, the Mexicans would use their superior numbers to take them in the flank and destroy them.

General Arista had hard-riding scouts that kept him informed of the American movements. General Taylor, who detested volunteers, suddenly found he was in desperate need of information on the enemy, and the only troops he had who could get it for him were Sam Walker's Rangers.

Capt. Sam Walker was still in his early thirties. His origins were in Maryland, and he had fought in the U.S. Army in the wars against the Seminole Indians. Walker came to Texas in 1842 and became a Ranger. His primary quality was courage, and his focus was on killing Mexicans. Sam Walker hated them. He was among the men captured at Mier. Though he had drawn a white bean and been spared, he had seen friends die and suffered the beatings and chain-gang environment of Mexican captivity. He would bring home information, but did not burden himself with prisoners. Walker and his seventy-seven man company of Rangers were the scouting link between the Americans at Fort Brown and Taylor's army. The recruitment of Walker's Rangers for a three-month enlistment had been accomplished rapidly, and not all the men were up to Walker's standards.

Arista threw out a screen of 1,500 lancers. Walker's Rangers had to penetrate that screen to learn the Mexicans' intentions. Leaving his recruits in camp, Walker took his most experienced Rangers and went into the teeth of the Mexican storm. In his absence, the lancers located his camp, and the Ranger recruits were soundly thrashed. New volunteers for the Rangers died before the skill of the Mexican with horse, lance, and rope.

Walker probed the Mexican army, shrewdly using General Arista's dispositions to determine the intent of the Mexican general. For the information to be useful, it had to be in the hands of the American commanders. Mexican troops were between Walker and General Taylor in such numbers that it would be untimely to try and ride around them. As the Rangers were not in uniform, it was difficult to distinguish them at a distance from the Mexican mounted irregulars who were part of Arista's force. The Rangers walked their horses toward an enemy camp appearing as a returning patrol. When close enough, the Rangers spurred their horses, gave a Texas yell, and charged through the startled Mexicans. They were clear before the Mexicans could respond.

Sam Walker and his Rangers got the needed information to both General Taylor and Major Brown. Armed with the location of his enemy, Taylor avoided ambush and marched his army to battle. Though heavily outnumbered, the American army beat General Arista's large Mexican force in battles at Palo Alto on May 8 and Resaca de la Palma on the ninth. Major Brown was killed in action. General Arista put the remnants of his battered army on a 160-mile march to Monterey.

General Taylor did not move his army in pursuit but accepted the laurels of his victory and waited for reinforcements. The importance of the Ranger action was well known throughout the army but little praised by Taylor. The general wanted Rangers leading the way through country unknown to him but was concerned that they were waging total war. General Taylor was getting reports of Ranger activities, and these did not match his orders regarding relations with the Mexicans.

The hatred the Rangers felt for the Mexican was real. Unlike Zachary Taylor and his army of the east, the men of Texas had seen friends and families tortured and butchered. Many had personal experience of the cruelty of their foes. "Remember the Alamo" had a real meaning to them. Some Rangers would kill a Mexican or an Indian of any age or sex without hesitation or individual provocation. It was their version of pacification.

Many of the men who fought for Texas had been born elsewhere, and Tennessee was a prime source. Ben McCullough was reared on the Tennessee frontier. His father, Alexander McCullough, had been an Indian fighter during the war with the Creeks. Ben's family were neighbors with Davie Crockett, and like Crockett, Ben McCullough was noted for hunting and killing the bears that ate the settlers' pigs. McCullough followed Crockett to Texas, where an illness prevented him from joining Crockett among the Tennessee dead at the Alamo. Recovering from his sickness, McCullough fought Mexicans at San Jacinto and Comanche at Plum Creek. He was on the expedition to Mier but left before Walker, Wallace, and their comrades were captured.

He established his camp near Matamoros in May 1846 and went in search of Ranger recruits from among the various volunteer organizations with Taylor. One of the men who responded was Samuel Reid, the adjutant of the 6th Louisiana Volunteers. Sam Reid was an example of the many intelligent and well-educated men who joined the Rangers. Reid kept a journal of his Ranger service and left a precious record of the events that followed. He described his introduction to the Ranger camp: "Men in groups with long beards and moustaches, dressed in every variety of garment, with one exception, the slouched hat the unmistakable uniform of the Texas Ranger, and a belt of pistols around their waists . . . a rougher looking set we never saw."[4]

On June 12, 1846, McCullough's Rangers received orders to track the route of withdrawal of the Mexican army, to determine if water holes existed and if wagons and artillery could pass the terrain. McCullough would take forty men on the mission. To deceive any watchers, McCullough began as though his Rangers were riding to Reynosa, but when out of sight, they turned left off the road and rode through the brushy terrain to gain the Linares road. This was the rough-country route taken by Arista's army in the hope of throwing off pursuit.

The Rangers camped for the night by the Linares road and put out sentinels. Fierce Mexican *rancheros* under a leader known as Blas Falcon were known to operate in the area. He was known as the murderer of the American Colonel Cross. In the early light of the following morning, the Rangers were saddling their horses when a number of Mexican riders came down the road. McCullough and a few Rangers who were mounted rode toward them.

A startled Mexican toward the front cried, "Qien vive?"

McCullough kept moving and answered, "Amigos."

"Nuestros amigos!" shouted the startled Mexican as he attempted to level his gun at McCullough. "Los malditos Americanos!"

The Ranger captain shouted, "Saddle up men and follow me!" and charged into the Mexicans.[5]

The *rancheros* broke and fled into the heavy brush of nearby chaparral. Six of the best mounted Rangers were in hot pursuit. The light was dim, the ground was treacherous, and several horses of the Rangers fell. One Ranger was seriously injured when he was thrown to the ground and fell on his knife. Some of the frightened Mexicans dismounted in the heavy brush and fled on foot, leaving behind horses and weapons.

The injured Ranger had to be sent back under escort, leaving McCullough with thirty-five men. This small band made forced marches at night following the equipment-strewn trail of Arista's beaten army. Bypassing a Mexican ranch or community at night, the Rangers would double back and return at first light.

There was only one map of the area available to the command. It had been found in the captured baggage of General Arista and given to McCullough by General Taylor. It was a very detailed map and in most cases accurate. Sixty miles from Linares, they were having difficulty finding water. Lieutenant McMullin led a small party an

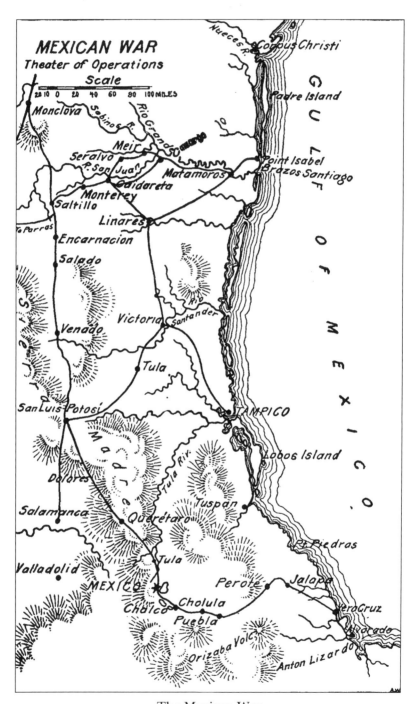

The Mexican War

additional thirty miles closer, but the only water hole they found was dry. There was no need to continue patrolling in the direction of Linares. McCullough had learned that Arista had left a stay behind force of 1,200 men but had taken the main body of his army to Monterey. The Ranger captain also noted that the route they were following did not have the water or sustenance to support the American army and decided to return to Taylor. The Rangers had learned that the Mexican General Canales was in the area recruiting. Canales was known as "The Chaparral Fox" and had ruthlessly killed many Texians. McCullough thought it was time someone killed this Mexican. Encouraging a Mexican to guide them, the Rangers set out through desolate country beset by a burning sun. It was a long ride. Canteens were empty and men and horse were in the torment of thirst. There was talk that the Mexican guide was betraying them. He was a worried man, knowing that his life depended on finding water. At length, a water hole was found. It had a stagnant look to it, but the men were desperate.

The Rangers spied a single rider coming in their direction and allowed him to come close. He was a mailman, the Mexican version of the pony express. McCullough and his officers searched the mail bags and took official correspondence that would be helpful to General Taylor. The frightened letter carrier was then allowed to proceed.

The Chaparral Fox was elusive, and McCullough did not forget his mission was to bring information to his commander. After a ten-day, 250-mile ride through desolation, the Rangers rode into Reynosa and provided the intelligence that kept the army from taking a road to ruin.

The citizens of Reynosa were not happy to see the Rangers. The town was a headquarters for the *rancheros*, and some of these known raiders openly swaggered the streets. The townspeople tricked Taylor's army into falsely thinking the Mexicans were coming to attack them, and Taylor's officers doubled the guards, tiring their men.

In the United States, opposition to the pursuit of the war had developed. President Polk's political opponents denounced the war as aggression. Polk was anxious to demonstrate that the American army was only defending its just borders. Orders were strict that the

Rangers must pay for any food that they secured. On learning of President Polk's orders, the Mexicans raised their prices to exorbitant levels. These same Mexicans were being raided by Comanche and Mexican bandits. They depended on the Rangers to protect them while holding out their hands for more money.

During July and August 1846, General Taylor brought his army together at Camargo on the Rio Grande River and began sending forces into the Mexican interior. The next objective was Monterey, 100 miles to the southwest. Ben McCullough was ill, and the company was briefly under the command of one of Taylor's officers, a Captain Duncan. He took the Rangers forward to seize the town of Cerralvo, and the lead elements of Taylor's army established themselves there.

General Taylor now had both Hays's and Wood's regiments of Rangers with his army, and from September 11 to 13, 1846, he began a deliberate march to Monterey. The main body of Rangers covered the flank of the army moving by parallel course.

McCullough recovered from his illness and was back in action. His was hunting Juan Seguin, a skilled fighter who was known to be headquartered at a Mexican town of about 1,500 people with the unlikely name of China. The Rangers arrived at China only to find that their quarry had fled a few hours before. The Mexicans were difficult to surprise as they had civilians constantly reporting on Taylor's army and an early-warning system that included women building smoky fires that could be seen for many miles.[6]

Ben McCullough's company continued to range forward. Near the town of Ramos, they found the trail of 200 Mexican lancers and followed them to Ramos. McCullough's total force consisted of forty men. He left most of them to create a dust cloud on the horizon and charged into Ramos with fifteen Rangers. Surprised and likely thinking they were attacked by a much larger force, the Mexicans took to the saddle and fled. The Rangers pursued them for six miles.[7] As the army of 6,000 men neared Monterey, Taylor ordered Hays's and Wood's Rangers to take the lead. McCullough's Rangers rejoined Hays, and Capt. Richard Gillespie's company took the lead. The Rangers led the army through a rich plain, a land of green, cultivated fields flanked by the Sierra Madre Mountains. To their front was the city of about 15,000 people. Protection included a great citadel that the Americans called the Black Fort and stone houses that had been fortified. The terrain to the front of the citadel was flat and open, and above its walls, the red, white, and green flag of Mexico stirred fitfully. Eager for battle, the Rangers rode onto the flat on September 19, 1846, and the Mexicans fired a cannon at them. Far from driving off the Rangers, the experience exhilarated them. Challenging each other to display their horsemanship, they galloped singly and in pairs toward the Mexican fortress. On the open plain, under Mexican gun sights, the Rangers now put on a dazzling display of horsemanship. They used many tricks they had learned from the Comanche and the Mexicans and added a dash of American ingenuity.

When wearied of the game, the Rangers joined Taylor's army in a wooded encampment of ancient trees called Walnut Grove. Ranger patrols went forward to determine the strength of Mexican positions in search of prisoners. Both the Rangers and their Mexican captives knew that a tight rope around the neck loosens the tongue. Based on these scouting reports from the Rangers and personal observation, Taylor had decided that the forts guarding the city on the east were formidable if attacked directly. Taylor opted to send a force around the city to cut the Saltillo road. This would prevent Mexican retreat or reinforcement and allow a better avenue of approach to the Mexican defenses. Taylor gave command of the operation to Gen. T. J. Worth, an officer who had a good fighting reputation. The two regiments of Rangers would be split. Hays's Rangers would lead the way for Worth while Wood's Rangers would remain with Taylor as a rapid-reaction force.

After a night of rain, the column moved on September 20, 1846. Throughout the day, the Rangers led Worth's men on a circuitous route around Monterey. Another night passed, and the attack continued. They encountered Mexican soldiers who attempted an ambush, but that was foiled when the Rangers saw the Mexicans moving into position.

Near San Jeronimo, they came upon an enemy force ready to do battle. It was a sight men would long remember. To the front of the Rangers were long lines of Mexican lancers with infantry in support. Below their colorful banners, their Mexican uniforms were a sea of color, their horses fitted with brilliant accoutrements. At their head, astride a spirited horse, was their valiant commander, Lieutenant Colonel Najera.

General Worth decided to take on the Mexicans with rifle fire. Ben McCullough was not given orders to dismount. He saw the enemy before him and ordered his Rangers to charge. The collision was horrific. Horses were overturned, and men went down among flailing hooves. These Mexican troops had a courageous leader and fought well. There were many hand-to-hand fights. When the Mexicans began to break and run, the Rangers leaped from their saddles and used aimed fire with their rifles to bring them down. Ben McCullough was fighting on horseback. When the Mexican horsemen fled, his steed was caught up in the herd instinct and took the Ranger captain with them. McCullough was hard pressed to get the head of his animal turned and fought his way back through the enemy without harm. The Mexican force was throughly defeated. Colonel Najera was killed and the battle area littered with more than 100 Mexican dead. The path was clear for General Worth to seize the Saltillo road.

Worth was not inclined to sit on his successes. The enemy was before him. The initial objectives were two hills, one named Federation and the other Independence. Worth decided to take Federation Hill first. It towered above them 380 feet high, its approaches covered with heavy brush. At the top could be seen the mouths of Mexican cannon, and officers looking through telescopes could see Mexicans swarming at the summit.

The attacking force consisted of 300 men, half of whom would be Rangers. General Worth assembled his assault force and ordered it to take the hill. Worth sent his men forward in three columns. Each of the attacking columns attacked with vigor. The Rangers moved along the Saltillo Road, then traveled single file, their movement concealed by corn and sugar cane. Their route required crossing a fast-moving, waist-deep stream. The Mexicans could see them in the water and opened fire, but the Rangers pressed on, gaining the concealment of the chaparral. There, they paused briefly to reorganize. Mexican reinforcements could be seen arriving on the hill, and snipers were being sent forward down the slopes to engage the Rangers. General Worth committed seven companies of infantry to the action, and the Mexicans turned their heaviest fire on the new arrivals who paused at the base of the hill. With their weapons dried, the Rangers now began to assault the Mexican position, pouring in a heavy volume of fire as they clambered up the steep and rocky slope. Seeing the Rangers take the lead, the infantry joined in a spirited assault, and it soon became a race to see who would be the first to drive the Mexicans from the hill.

The run through danger by the American columns was close, but it was Capt. Richard A. Gillespie and his men who won the race into the enemy emplacements by an eyelash. Federation Hill was gained. The Mexican artillerymen had overturned a 9-pounder cannon, hoping to disable it, but the Rangers and the 5th Infantry arrived before this could be accomplished. The enemy gun was soon back in action, firing upon the fleeing backs of the previous owners and on the enemy position at the bishop's palace. With the hill secure, an occupying force of infantry was left at the top, and the Rangers withdrew to care for their horses.

On the other side of Monterey, General Taylor supported Worth's attack by deploying his army and making a demonstration to reduce reinforcements being sent against General Worth. Wood's Rangers led the way when the army moved forward. The demonstration became a melee in the narrow streets at the outskirts of the city. Mexican cannon at the citadel supported their troops who were fighting from houses. The lanes were killing grounds, and Taylor's infantry and light artillery were hit hard. Many American officers were killed trying to lead their men in the face of the concentrated fire. Volunteer Regiments from Ohio, Mississippi, and Tennessee fought their way through frontal and enfilade fire. The Tennessee regiment had twenty-six killed and seventy-five wounded.[8] Despite heavy opposition and losses, the Americans penetrated the enemy emplacements and drove the Mexicans out.

For General Worth's command, Independence Hill and the bishop's palace were the next objectives. The men slept on their arms. Jack Hays drew in another Ranger unit—giving him seven Ranger companies—to make the attack on Independence Hill. Sam Walker was second in command, and the Ranger companies were led by Ben McCullough, James McCullough, Acklin, Ballowe, Herbert, Gillespie, and Green.

The objective was formidable, towering nearly 800 feet high. The Mexicans were on top with cannon and entrenchments. The slopes were steep and broken by rocky outcrops and thick brush that made a tough climb torturous. Many of the attackers thought it likely they were on a doomed mission. The Mexicans would have agreed. They thought their position was impregnable.

The assault force moved on foot in two columns beginning at three in the morning. It was a difficult climb, with men going searching for hand holds on rocks and brush while panting under the exertion of the effort. Superb noise discipline was maintained, and the Rangers were within 100 yards of the crest before they were discovered. A scattering of Mexican fire reached out for them, but the Rangers held their fire until they were within twenty yards. The fight for the top was at point-blank range. Capt. Richard Gillespie was mortally wounded at the head of his men. Gillespie was gut-shot and lived in terrible pain for almost a day before morphine was found and administered. He would be buried on the hill he fought for. A number of Rangers were wounded, and in addition to Gillespie, two others were killed. The Mexicans were literally shot off the hill. Their survivors fled, and the sun rose with the American flag at the summit of Independence Hill. The Rangers felt the glow of another victory.

In these victories, Mexican forces estimated that 1,500 men—well entrenched and supported by cannon—had been put to flight. Throughout the campaign, the Mexican Army outnumbered the Americans. They had occupied Monterey in strength, but anxious to control all parts of the city, they had split their forces, putting their men in redoubts. These strongpoints could not effectively support each other and could be attacked in succession and eliminated by the Americans. The separation of Mexican forces was especially harmful to their defense as pertained to Mexican artillery. There were a number of redoubts that contained one to four cannon, an insufficient amount to provide the firepower needed for a successful defense against the Americans. When they lost their guns, the Mexicans added to the strength of American artillery. The Mexican soldiers were fighting for their homeland, but they were often led at senior levels by corrupt, uncaring men and therefore lacked the fighting spirit of the Americans.

At tables in the bishop's palace of Monterey, the Mexican leadership plotted revenge; they wanted a battlefield victory that would keep the army from disintegrating. This eagerness made them care-

Samuel Walker.

less. When they saw American volunteers from Louisiana advancing, the Mexicans saw an opportunity. They formed their colorful forces, left the sheltering walls of the palace, and attacked.

The Louisiana troops retreated, drawing their enemy onward. Too late, the Mexicans saw the Rangers had closed on both of their flanks. The trap was sprung, and a hail of bullets tore into the Mexican ranks. They tried to flee behind the walls of the palace, but the Americans were close upon them. American artillery blasted open the palace gate, and the Mexicans were routed from their refuge. The men under General Worth's command now held the high ground, and the city and its remaining defenses lay beneath them exposed to their view. Taylor was attacking Monterey from the other side of the city, and Worth ordered his men to begin a house-to-house campaign to attack the Mexicans' front and rear and link up with Taylor's men.

The Rangers now proved their worth in urban fighting. Jack Hays was at the head of one column and Sam Walker led another as the Rangers fought their way into Monterey street by street, house by house. The Mexicans put up a fierce resistance. Ranger sharpshooters took to the rooftops and shot down any Mexican who tried to use the streets. Rangers under Sam Walker broke into a building that housed a company of Mexican infantry. These unfortunates tried to flee into the streets. The Rangers who had captured the post office had a clear field of fire and killed half of the Mexicans as they ran for cover. Ordered to withdraw so that artillery could be used, the Rangers refused to give up the streets and houses they had taken. They held their position under both enemy and friendly fire.

The victory was total, but when the Mexican commander, General Ampudia, asked for terms, Taylor granted such easy conditions that it made a mockery of the effort that been put forth to seize Monterey. The Mexican soldiers were permitted to keep arms and equipment and given a week to march away. The Americans would withdraw and not occupy the city until the Mexicans left. The Mexican flag at the citadel could be saluted by a Mexican artillery battery when it was lowered. Mexicans soldiers re-occupied the houses, took what they wanted, and then were allowed to march out with their faces openly set for revenge.

Disgusted with Taylor's peace, the Rangers made the most of their volunteer status. Many were serving beyond the time of their enlistments. The Comanche were raiding in Texas, and Ranger homes and families were exposed to Indian depredations. The Texians saddled up and rode home. Most were glad to be leaving General Taylor. The feeling was mutual. Taylor had no present need for the Rangers and was glad to see them go.

Many of Jack Hays's Rangers left the service, and he set about recruiting a second regiment. Selected as adjutant was John Salmon Ford. Born in South Carolina and raised in Tennessee, Ford was only twenty-one when he came to Texas in 1836. He was a doctor, a lawyer, and a newspaperman before he became a Ranger. He suffered from malaria and frequently performed his duties when ill. Ford's first Ranger experience was with Capt. William Kimbro's company operating against the Shawnee.

President James K. Polk and Gen. Zachary Taylor had an objective that went beyond victory on the battlefields of Mexico. Polk was a Democrat while Taylor was a member of the Whigs. Polk saw an ambition in this general that went beyond battle reputation; he saw a political rival. Five months passed as Polk used his role as commander in chief to emasculate Taylor's army and pass the laurels for victory in Mexico to Winfield Scott. The plan was to strip Taylor of much of his force and send those men to the Mexican coastal city of Vera Cruz.

Winfield Scott at
Vera Cruz, March 25, 1847.
NATIONAL ARCHIVES

There Scott would assemble an army and finish off the war by marching to Mexico City and forcing the Mexican government to its knees. Scott's army was not needed to secure American interests regarding the border with Mexico. Politics was being played with men's lives.

Taylor was informed that his generous peace terms to the Mexicans were not acceptable to President Polk; the war would continue. Taylor then resumed operations and advanced his force to Saltillo. Winfield Scott was Taylor's senior officer and ordered Taylor to send Scott the bulk of his troops and to return to Monterey and stay there. All the regular army units were taken from Taylor, who was left with the volunteer regiments.

Taylor was considerably disheartened. He considered resignation but decided to stay on with the forces at hand. Taylor ignored General Scott's instructions to return to Monterey and set about taking up a defensive position at Agua Nueva.

Both Taylor and Scott were finding that there was more to the Mexican enemy then colorful uniforms. Neither American general could come to grips with the hard-riding Mexican guerrillas. Small parties of Americans were ambushed and cut up. Couriers heard the soft sound of the lariat settling around their necks, then were jerked from their saddle and dragged to their deaths. As torn and bleeding bodies lay on the ground, they were repeatedly pierced by Mexican lances. Neither Taylor nor Scott understood the passionate violence of the frontier.

Among the American dead was a courier carrying the war plans of Winfield Scott. This prize was delivered to Santa Anna, who saw the opportunity to reverse the American tide of victories. Taylor was much weakened and could not be supported by Scott. Santa Anna had more than 15,000 men that he could throw against Taylor and, by crushing him, restore Mexican pride and inspire people to rise against the remaining Americans.

Taylor suspected that he might be attacked but was not aware that Santa Anna knew his strength. As Santa Anna marched his army to within striking distance, Taylor was desperate for information about the enemy. Thirty five miles of desert now separated the two armies. Santa Anna could see his objective clearly, but Taylor was enveloped in the fog of war.

Ben McCullough led a small band of Rangers into camp. Taylor immediately sent McCullough on reconnaissance to determine Mexican dispositions. Using their frontier knowledge and skills, Ben McCullough and sixteen of his Rangers penetrated the Mexican encampment. Operating boldly within the Mexican lines, they correctly estimated Santa Anna's strength and deduced his intent. Keeping only one man with him, McCullough sent Lieutenant Alston back to report to General Taylor, then continued to scout the Mexican Army. When finished, they slipped away, passing between the Mexican perimeter guards and outposts.

The information brought by the Rangers opened General Taylor's eyes to the weakness of his position. If Taylor were to effectively mount a defense, he must find a defensive position of great natural strength and use terrain to enhance his small numbers. Such terrain existed in a narrow gorge near Buena Vista.

The Battle of Buena Vista by H. R. Robinson, 1847. LIBRARY OF CONGRESS

After a hard ride, McCullough reported to Taylor. Based on Lieutenant Alston's report, the American army was already on the move. General Taylor did not waste time on compliments. He listened to the report, then rode to Buena Vista with his staff. Santa Anna had hard-riding scouts. The sudden move of Taylor's army was reported to him and was a spur to movement. The Mexican dictator hurried his army, confident that he was chasing a beaten foe. Because of the Rangers, the fog of war had been lifted from Taylor's eyes. He lay in wait for the oncoming Mexicans, with his army tucked in behind the Angostura Pass close to Buena Vista. There Taylor used terrain to influence Santa Anna's. The battle known as Buena Vista occurred on February 21–22. The Mexicans attacked with more courage than wisdom and paid a heavy price. Taylor's army tore the heart and soul out of Santa Anna's soldiers. Though additional battles would follow, Buena Vista was the mortal wound to Mexican hopes. With the Battle of Buena Vista won and war no longer on his horizon, Taylor requested that no more Texas Rangers be sent to him.

Meanwhile, in March 1847, Winfield Scott put his army ashore down south at Vera Cruz and went in pursuit of reputation. Scott did not have Texas Rangers with him, but he made good usage of some talented engineer officers who had an eye for terrain. Chief among these was an officer of considerable ability named Robert E. Lee. Scott had marched for Mexico City, which he captured on September 14. Santa Anna departed the capital, vowing resistance, and set about raising troops. Jack Hays and four companies of Rangers landed at Vera Cruz and were put to work hunting Mexican guerrillas. The principal objective was to eliminate a Colonel Zenobia who was headquartered thirty miles from Vera Cruz. The Rangers did not get Zenobia but killed several guerrillas. On finding blood-stained American clothing, the Rangers burned the magnificent ranch that had been Zenobia's home. They returned to the main army, having ridden sixty miles in one day.[9]

Santa Anna had left some troops and guns at Huamantla and was believed to be headquartered in the town. Gen. Joseph Lane decided to go after Santa Anna with 3,000 troops, and Sam Walker and his men would spearhead the attack. Huamantla proved to be a tough objective. Santa Anna had his army close by and committed them to a battle for the town. Mexican soldiers had fortified houses and were on the roofs. Their lancers charged down the narrow lanes. A bloody brawl erupted in the streets and houses. Again the Americans found themselves in gun fights at point-blank range or facing Mexican swords with their knives. The fighting was vicious with no quarter asked or given by either side. Step by step, the Mexicans were driven back and out of the town. Sam Walker was killed in this action, shot through the head and chest.

The Mexicans had surrounded an American force at Puebla, and the Rangers rode to the rescue and sent the Mexicans flying. The Ranger entry into Puebla was accompanied by a startling display of horsemanship. In the public square, the Mexicans watched in awe as Rangers galloped about, bending from their saddles to snatch sticks or handkerchiefs from the ground. One Ranger stood upright atop the saddle of his galloping horse waving both his pistols in the air. There were 580 of them, and their firepower was awesome.

Gen. Ethan Allen Hitchcock watched them ride in and wrote, "Hays's Rangers have come, their appearance never to be forgotten. Not any sort of uniforms, but well mounted and doubly well armed: each man has one or two Colt's revolvers besides ordinary pistols, a sword, and every man a rifle . . . The Mexicans are terribly afraid of them."

The war with Mexico ended with a peace treaty between Mexico and the United States signed on February 2, 1848. Toward the end of March, Hays's Rangers rode to Jalapa en route to Vera Cruz, where they would take a ship for Texas. While in Jalapa, they learned that Santa Anna had again been taken prisoner and was being exiled. The butcher of the Alamo and Goliad would be passing through Jalapa carrying a safe-conduct pass signed by Gen. Winfield Scott.

Hays ordered his men into a camp and gave them instructions to stay there while he went to see the former Mexican dictator. Hays should have known his men better. He was scarcely gone before a passion for killing arose in the men and voices were raised that this was an opportunity to finish the man who had brought so much grief to Texas. Rip Ford was the senior Ranger officer present, and he convinced the men that they should spare their enemy. They agreed on condition that they be allowed to see the man they hated.

The scene that followed was painted upon the minds of the men who participated. The carriage with Santa Anna, his wife, and daughter passed along the long line of stone-faced men. The hatred hung in the air. Santa Anna sat stiffly, his face frozen as seconds seemed like hours. No Ranger moved or made a sound until their enemy had passed from their view.

CHAPTER 21

Peace and War

War with Mexico was successfully concluded. Texas was now part of the United States. Its development hinged upon opening the territory to settlement and routes to California. The discovery of gold in California in 1849 created a stampede. It was in the interest of Texas to prove that a railroad could be constructed across the state. The ribbons of steel would link San Antonio to El Paso and then travel on to the California coast. The problem was that 600 miles of land lay between the two towns, and the Indians were the only ones who knew the terrain.

Jack Hays and some Rangers made the arduous ride but lacked an Indian guide and did not develop a suitable route. Hays then left for California in 1849 and remained there for the rest of his life, dying in 1883. In March 1849, another expedition went forth with Rip Ford and Maj. Robert Neighbors, the supervising agent for Indians in Texas. Neighbors had contact with the Comanche and arranged for guides. On this expedition, a variety of Indians including Choctaw, Comanche, Delaware, and Shawnee rode with the whites. Rip Ford learned much about rattlesnakes and Indians on this venture. The snakes were in profusion. Ford was fortunate when he stepped on one and was able to jump away before being bitten. He thought this a proof of his agility. Jim Shaw, a man more knowledgeable about the ability of the rattlesnake, informed Ford it was pure luck.

Though Texas was now part of the United States, many Texans wished it was not. The Comanche moon still shone on high, and the threat of raids by these great horsemen was constantly present. A "move them or kill them" mood prevailed among those who lived close to all Indians. That mood was not shared by the United States government. In Washington, there was strong sentiment that the Indians were wards of the government. Indian agents were dispatched to serve as liaison with the tribes, help them with some of their needs, and encourage them to follow the leadership of the Unites States government. Some of the men who served as Indian agents were self-serving; some were caring. All were powerless to end the difficulties between the Comanche and the Texians.

Texas politicians were inclined to ask much of the United States and, having had a taste of self rule, were indignant when they felt their requests were not properly met. They believed it was the duty of the United States to protect its citizens, but the troops sent to Texas could not do so, for they were mostly infantry and no match for the fast-riding Comanche. The Texas Rangers were in limbo. Money was scarce in Texas, and the United States had little interest in funding a collection of citizen-soldier volunteers.

In 1848, the Comanche began launching devastating raids in Texas. The United States Army was an ineffective response and Texians understood it would take men who understood border warfare to end the terror. Like the Quakers in Pennsylvania in the 1760s, the Washington politicians of the 1840s and 1850s tended to blame the victims and provided little assistance to those whose families were being slaughtered.

For ten years, the Comanches struck when and where they choose. The calls for the return of the Texas Rangers became more vocal. Sam Houston said that all the regular army could be taken out of Texas if the state had one regiment of Texas Rangers. A succession of governors took steps to put the Rangers back in the saddle. In 1858, Hardin F. Runnels became governor of Texas. He knew what he wanted and had the backing of the Texas legislature to get it. Runnels brought vigor to the Texas Rangers by placing them under the command of Hays's fomer adjutant John "Rip" Ford.

Runnels told Ford his mission was to follow any Indians who were a real or suspected threat and, if they proved to be enemy, to take action against them. Ford was to try to work in harmony with representatives of the federal government and their Indian agents, but when disagreement happened, the Ranger commander had the authority to act as he saw fit.[1] In the ultimate expression of civilian leadership, Runnels accepted responsibility for the actions of Ford.

Ford recruited experienced white frontiersmen to form the foundation of his force and combined the Indian and white Rangers into four elements that would scour the frontier. It was a lethal combination. Ford led a force of 200 men, about half of them Indians, north across the Red River and on to the Washita. There were no rules of engagement. The courageous Governor Runnels had given Ford the authority to hunt the Comanche in Texas or out of it. He could follow them to the ends of the earth if he chose. As anticipated, the Indian Rangers tracked Comanche hunters who unwittingly were leading them to the Indian camp.

On May 12, 1858, the Rangers struck a Comanche band estimated by Ford to contain 300 warriors. Some outlying Indian habitations had been destroyed, and the Comanche were alerted. The leader of this Comanche band was Chief Iron Jacket. Some ancient Spanish conquistador had lost his breastplate armor and likely his life on an expedition in search of gold. The shingled armor was now worn by Chief Iron Jacket, who had convinced himself that he was invulnerable to harm when garbed in metal.

Iron Jacket's horse was first shot out from under him; then the armor and the chief were penetrated by a half dozen bullets fired by both Indian and white Rangers. Another chief took over the Comanche leadership and suffered the same fate. The battle became a swirling contest of small fights. The Comanche hoped to isolate the reservation Indians. Rip Ford reported scenes of magnificent pageantry where warriors in full Indian regalia, riding spirited horses, demonstrated their horsemanship in challenge. They were seeking to draw the Ranger Indians away from their white comrades, isolate, and destroy them.

The fight lasted through most of the daylight hours, and the Rangers had two killed and two wounded. Eighteen Indian prisoners, primarily women and children, were taken captive. The Comanche went to great effort to carry off their dead but on this occasion could not do so. Ford believed his men had killed over seventy.

The fight on the Canadian River was significant as it proved the worth of a campaign to "follow them anywhere." The Comanche had looked upon the United States and Texas as two different tribes. They could talk peace with United States Indian agents and get benefits such as rifles to hunt game. These same rifles could be used to raid Texas. Then the mobile Comanche could clear the area and find safe haven beyond the borders of the Lone Star State.

Officers of the budget-depleted U.S. Army observed this action with great interest. The army had come west primarily as foot soldiers. They had dragoons, but these were infantry who used a horse to take them to the battlefield, then dismounted to fight. Step by step, the army was developing a cavalry arm. Seeing the Texas Rangers in action showed the army that only men who lived in and fought from the saddle could succeed against the Mexican raiders and the great Indian horsemen of the west.

Rangers Hays and Ford had demonstrated that horses whose diet included grain had superior staying power to those of the Indian who were sustained only on grass. The Rangers knew that beyond sixty yards a single Indian arrow could often be dodged. They knew to keep half their loaded weapons in reserve as a Comanche retreat would quickly become a charge. They sought to strike the enemy from behind and from the right of the mounted bowmen. Most Indians found it difficult to effectively use a bow in that direction. Ford believed in training, and his Rangers were drilled to ride and fight as a team.

American cavalry began a relentless pursuit of the Indians. On October 1, 1858, Brevet Major Van Dorn led a force primarily of cavalry and reservation Indians in a swift attack on a Comanche village. In the brief fight that lasted scarcely half an hour, the Indians took a beating, losing fifty warriors, their village, and their horses. It was no more, and probably less, of a victory than that achieved by Rip Ford's Rangers on the Canadian, but this had been achieved by horsemen of the U.S. Army, and the public-relations drums began to roll.

Life on the Indian reservations was hard. Some Indian agents sought to use their positions to enrich themselves and those who had the best interest of their charges at heart did not have the funds or support to make much difference. The southern Comanche had in large part been pacified to their ruin. The Caddos, Wacos, and Seminoles—indeed most of the Indians—had been warriors; they had no interest in planting corn and yearned for the life of their ancestors.

Many had lost their will to be independent and would not fight the whites again. There were some among them willing to work with the Comanche and Kiowa who roamed wild and free. The Comanche, who still raided the settlements, remembered that reservation Indians had caused them great harm. Indian raiders began to strike and kill and then leave a trail to the reservations.

Rip Ford was prepared to punish any reservation Indian who took part in the attacks. He would not harm any Indian not proven guilty but felt it was the job of the military to protect the reservations, not that of the Rangers. Soon whites began to kill reservation Indians. The compassionate Indian agent Robert S. Neighbors did all he could to assist his charges. He gathered them together and tried to improve their lives, but could not control the whites who thought the trails were real and these Indians were working in league with Comanche and Kiowa raiders. The Delaware, the Shawnee, and other reservation Indians were unjustly treated. At length, Neighbors was forced to lead his Indian charges away beyond the Red River, beyond the borders of Texas. Now any Indian found within the state could be freely hunted. Neighbors was distraught and bitter. When he returned to Texas, he was murdered.

Brownsville, Texas, had developed near the old Gulf Coast and Rio Grande location of Fort Brown established in prelude to the Mexican War. The whites who occupied the Brownsville area looked upon themselves as members of a superior and conquering culture. The many Mexicans who still lived in the area found that the rights of an American did not extend to them.

In this circumstance lived a proud and enterprising Mexican named Juan Cortinas. In July 1859, Cortinas was in Brownsville when he saw the white town marshall beating up a drunken Mexican. Cortinas tried to get the marshall to stop. Words were exchanged. Cortinas drew his weapon and wounded the lawman. He then rescued the inebriated Mexican and rode away with him. This action made Cortinas a folk hero to the Mexican populace, who began to assist him. Cortinas lived on his mother's ranch and freely traded insults with authorities who he believed mistreated Mexicans. Though Cortinas was indicted, the local law was unable to capture him. Emboldened by the failure of his enemies, Cortinas rallied nearly 100 supporters, occupied Brownsville, and set out to kill those he deemed guilty of outrages. All of the quarry were warned and escaped except a William Neale, who was shot while sleeping at his home.

There was no unit of the Texas Rangers or U.S. Army in the area, and the townspeople of Brownsville were terrified. An appeal was made to the Mexican leaders at nearby Matamoras. Knowing an American punitive force would inevitably arrive, the Matamoras authorities talked Cortinas into leaving Brownsville and sent Mexican soldiers to the aid of the Americans to be certain he did.

A posse managed to capture a man named Cabrera, a lieutenant of Cortinas, and carry him back to prison and trial at Brownsville. Cortinas demanded the release of his companion and threatened to burn the town if his demand was not met. The townspeople formed a home guard they called the Tigers and patrolled the streets. A mixed party of these American tigers and Mexicans totaling sixty men went after Cortinas, carrying along with them two cannon. The courage mustered in the bars of Brownsville did not sustain them in battle. When Cortinas ambushed the mixed force, the Tigers and their Mexican companions ran like rabbits for Brownsville, leaving their two guns behind.

Flush with success, the Mexican warrior isolated Brownsville, reading the incoming and outgoing mail before letting it pass on. He established himself as the champion of the oppressed Mexican and issued ringing proclamations that enhanced his recruiting. As his force grew, rumor ran rampant, and Cortinas seemed a larger-than-life figure who threatened eastern Texas. Governor Runnels sent Ranger Capt. William Tobin and a company of Rangers to capture Cortinas.

To the Mexican, Cortinas was an avenging angel who punished the "gringos." His people concealed his movements and kept him informed. Learning that thirty of the Texas Rangers were on a patrol, Cortinas lay in wait and defeated them. His men killed three Rangers and wounded four others. A Ranger who was taken prisoner was executed.[2] Tobin was an ambitious but ineffective Ranger leader.

The U.S. Army sent Maj. Samuel Heintzelman with 122 soldiers to aid the citizens of Brownsville. Alarmed by perceived threats to Corpus Christi, Governor Runnels ordered Rip Ford to take another Ranger force against Cortinas. In their lean years since the end of the Mexican War, the Rangers had fallen into the disastrous course of electing their leaders. Ford was senior officer, but Tobin now saw a chance to take command of all the Rangers on the campaign by winning an election against Ford. Major Heintzelman and his men were conducting as aggressive campaign against the Mexican opponent.

Heintzelman could fight Cortinas, but in order to succeed, he first needed to find and fix his opponent. That was a Ranger job. Captain Tobin was not doing well at ranging, but he was an easy-going officer, popular with the men.

Ford joined Heintzelman and established a good relationship with the soldier. It was learned that Cortinas was about 100 miles from Brownsville at a little community with the big name of Rio Grande City. The Mexican force of several hundred men and cannon also occupied the abandoned army encampment of Fort Ringgold. While the Americans made a rapid march to bring them into position to attack, Cortinas remained in a defensive posture with strong and alert outposts.

On the evening of December 26, the Americans had closed within twenty miles of Cortinas. Ford and Heintzelman reviewed their options and made a decision. The plan was for the Americans to move to contact, with the Rangers in the lead. The Rangers would use their superior mobility to pass to the flank of the Mexican position and to its rear. There they would establish a blocking position that would prevent the Mexican escape. Major Heintzelman and his men would attack Cortinas with artillery and infantry, thus pinning him between two fires. Ford would not have all the Rangers with him as Heintzelman kept Tobin and two companies. These he sent in advance of his right flank.

The attack was planned for daybreak, but with the dawn came a heavy fog that made movement difficult. The Rangers were unable to pass undetected around the Mexican outposts as the fog prevented them from finding a bypass route. Cortinas had talent as a commander. He disposed the main force of his troops and artillery in the center of his line covering the road. His left wing occupied a hill near the easily identified landmark of a cemetery, and his right protected the Rio Grande River flank.

Dismounting his battle-hardened Rangers, Ford established security and told the remainder of his men to rest. Accustomed to outdoor life, they quickly went to sleep on the ground, the reins of their horses wrapped about their wrists. Ford communicated to Heintzelman that he was unable to get behind the Mexicans and proposed new tactics. As the morning fog began to lift, Ford and his Rangers would attack down the road, driving in the Mexican outposts. Tobin would attack the hill near the cemetery while Heintzelman brought his slower-moving troops and artillery into position. Ford's Rangers would clear the line of fire, and the American artillery would tenderize the Mexican lines in preparation for the assault on the center.

Ford's Rangers were quickly awake and in the saddle. Rip Ford understood the importance of shock in battle. He wanted to hit the Mexicans with speed and force. The Rangers went through the Mexican outposts at a gallop and, with pistols blazing, hit the Mexican line, forcing the Mexicans into the small town. Cortinas tried to use his artillery, but the action quickly became hand-to-hand, with Mexicans shooting from roof tops and the Rangers passing from house to house clearing them out. The Mexicans fought well and attempted to deliver a counter attack by horsemen. The Rangers broke the attack, sending riderless Mexican horses galloping about the battlefield. Captain Tobin's men did render some support, but their leader was dilatory and did not attack the Mexican flank. Ford's Rangers took the Mexican guns, but as Tobin had not attacked them the Mexicans from cemetery hill were able to pitch into the battle and recapture them.

Driven steadily backward, the Mexicans decided to withdraw and save their artillery. In their hasty departure, they were not able to secure their camp equipment and supplies. Heintzelman's regulars did not have the mobility to actively participate in this fluid fight. They contented themselves with occupying the Mexican positions and capturing what supplies remained behind. Ford's Rangers continued the attack, and the Mexican withdrawal turned into a rout that continued for nearly ten miles. Again the Mexicans lost their artillery to the Rangers, and this time, they could not recover it. The battle ended with none of the Americans being killed. Seventeen Rangers were wounded, with Rip Ford among these. One cannon blast of Mexican grape shot had done most of the damage. Cortinas escaped, but the Mexican command was hit hard, with estimates running to 60 dead and 140 wounded. Hintzelman's regulars were more spectators than participants in the fight.

Both Ford and Tobin recognized that while the days of Juan Cortinas the general were at an end, the nights of Juan Cortinas the guerrilla were beginning. Both Rangers knew they would face another threat from their colorful foe. With the glow of victory in the air, Captain Tobin insisted that elections to determine the command of the Rangers were long overdue. Tobin was not lacking in personal courage, but his ambition exceeded his talent. He had no understanding of organization, could not or would not keep accounts, and let the men do as they wished when not in battle. Ford believed in discipline and tight control. Tobin won the election, and for some months, the Rangers were ineffective. There were complaints that they caused more damage to private property then Cortinas.

The Ranger opinion that Cortinas would not stop fighting was accurate. The Mexican chief established his headquarters at a Mexican ranch near La Bolsa, thirty-five miles up the Rio Grande River from Brownsville. From here, Cortinas launched his riders on raids into Texas, robbing ranches and taking horses. His reputation as a man fighting for the Mexican people was not dimmed by military defeat. Cortinas had the most precious gift a guerrilla can have, the support of his people. Thousands of eyes kept watch for him, and he was kept well informed.

The Cortinas raids had virtually shut down commercial river traffic on the Rio Grande. With the rout of the Mexicans at Rio Grande City, the Americans hoped free enterprise could resume. As an opening gambit, the steamboat *Ranchero* embarked on a mission of delivering several hundred thousand dollars of cargo downriver to the Gulf of Mexico. To succeed, the steamboat would need to pass through a narrow bend in the river near the Cortinas hideaway. Some American soldiers under a lieutenant named Langdon were put aboard the steamboat to ward off any Mexican raiders.

Though Ranger lines of command were still murky, Texas officials were disturbed by Captain Tobin's inept leadership. Reestablishing control, Texas officials began the process of dismissing Tobin and placing Rip Ford back in command of the Rangers. Ford's instructions were to take orders from the U.S. Army, which did not want to cross the Rio Grande itself.

On February 4, 1860, a party of Rangers saw some of Cortinas's Mexicans recrossing the Rio Grande near La Bolsa. The Mexicans were encumbered with stolen horses and loot, much of which they abandoned when taken under fire. Their Mexican comrades on the opposite riverbank supported them by fire. Some of Tobin's Rangers came up, and a firefight across 200 yards of river developed. It was at that untimely moment that the steamboat *Ranchero* huffed into view. A moving target attracts the eye, and the Mexicans immediately transferred their gunfire to the vessel.

Ranger Rip Ford and his men were on patrol with a U.S. Cavalry unit under the command of Capt. George Stoneman when a breathless rider came in with the news of the engagement. The Rangers were quickly in the saddle and en route to the action.

The steamboat had moved over to the American shore, and Lieutenant Langdon was active in defending her. Tobin's Rangers had with them the two cannon captured from Cortinas at Rio Grande City. Langdon put these into action and forced the Mexicans back from the riverbank.

Rip Ford arrived with his Rangers and assessed the situation. It was obvious to him that the *Ranchero* could not be protected if the Americans controlled only one side of the river. Ford decided to cross to the Mexican side and sent a courier to Major Heintzelman telling him the Rangers were going into Mexico. Ford's intention was to escort the steamboat on the Mexican side of the Rio Grande River, and he asked Heintzelman to do the same on the American shore.

Some of Tobin's Rangers did a reconnaissance patrol over the river but returned, saying that Cortinas seemed to have left the area. Rip Ford believed he could see Mexican defensive positions and decided to attack them.

With Lieutenant Langdon and the captured cannon on board the steamboat, Ford put forty-five Rangers on the *Ranchero* and steamed across the river in an amphibious assault on the Mexican shore. The landing was unopposed, but as the Rangers moved along the riverbank, they came under heavy fire. Yelling their wild battle cry, the Rangers attacked with pistols, delivering a hail of fire. Cortinas and his Mexicans outnumbered the Rangers at least seven to one, but the ferocity of the attack broke their spirit. The first to flee were those who had horses and could make the fastest escape. When the Mexicans on foot saw their horsemen departing in a cloud of dust, they ran. Cortinas had done all a leader could do to hold his men in battle. Ford ordered some of his best shots to bring down the Mexican leader, and they took Cortinas in their sights. Bullets clipped his hair, his clothes, and his saddle, but he came through unscathed. The last

Mexican to leave the battlefield, Cortinas emptied his pistol at the Rangers, shouted defiance, and galloped away.

While Cortinas and his Mexican riders were causing problems, there was still an Indian threat to be met. Hardin Runnels vacated the chair as governor of Texas in December 1859 when Sam Houston was elected to the office. Runnels had spent money the state did not have, but he used the Rangers to chastise the Comanche and drive them to the extent of their range. The horse warriors would not give up their penchant for raiding, though they had to ride much longer distances in smaller numbers and depend upon stealth, surprise, and a quick getaway for success. Runnels, harsh treatment of the reservation Indians met with less favor. Unscrupulous white settlers and the warring Comanche found it convenient to blame depredations on reservation Indians.

Governor Houston organized seven Rangers companies, varying in strength from twenty to fifty men. These he backed up with community militia units designed to quickly mobilize and come to action. Sam Houston recognized that the most potent military force in Texas was not the slow-moving U.S. Army of the period, but the Texas Rangers who could ride, had the firepower of the revolver, and knew the enemy and terrain. Assuming command of the U.S. Army in the Department of Texas was Col. Robert E. Lee, who was not an experienced Indian fighter. As he wore the uniform of the U.S. Army, Lee was also faced with the increasing hostility of those who wanted separation from the Union. For various reasons, many Texians felt it had been a mistake to join the United States. Forgetting how desperate their circumstance had been when they entered the union, many now felt the restrictions of life as part of a larger community. Texas did not always get what it wanted or needed from the United States government. The Texians felt that it was the duty of the federal government to provide protection from the marauding Indians and raiders such as Cortinas.

Slavery had been debated from the outset. Most of the settlers in Texas had come from the southern United States. They had lived with the concept of slaveholding throughout their lives, and few found fault in it. Their slaves accompanied them to the frontier, and many of these suffered under the scalping knife or ended up going from a white master to an Indian master. The Texians, who were accustomed to and favored slavery, were incensed at the threat northern politicians posed to an institution they considered their birthright.

As the sectional animosity between northern and southern states deteriorated into secession, Texians met in a state convention to determine their course of action. The delegates voted for separation. They recommended a vote be taken among the Texians to confirm their view. An ugly mood began to sweep the state.

Ben McCullough and Rip Ford were among the many Texas Rangers who cast their fortunes with the Confederate States of America. McCullough would be killed in action at the Battle of Pea Ridge in Arkansas. Among those Rangers who would not take up arms against the United States was Noah Smithwick, who wrote, "As the son of a revolutionary soldier, I could not raise my hand against the union he had fought to establish. I had fought to make Texas a member of the Union and I would not turn round and fight to undo my work."

Under a death threat, Noah Smithwick decided to leave Texas. He sold his property at a loss and made the long trek to California. Smithwick's nephew, who remained behind, was killed by secessionists.[3]

The immensity of the Civil War made a backwater of the struggle in Texas. The Indian depredations continued, primarily in northwest Texas. Those who thought the United States had been ineffective in defending the frontier found that the Confederate States of America had greater concerns than the Texas frontier. A state Ranger organization called the Frontier Regiment was formed. The regiment of 500 men was too small and its responsibility too large to be effective. The big war drew off experienced leaders and Rangers, and there was condemnation of those who stayed at home to fight Indians. Seeing their opportunity, the Comanche and Kiowa made 1863 and 1864 years of horror. Hundreds of Texians died, and many women and children were taken from their families.

Though the Texas Rangers would resume fighting Indians after the Civil War, the mission began to change from military operations to law enforcement. From 1823 to 1861, the citizen-soldier Texas Rangers had proved their worth in the triangle of war with the Indian and Mexican. The Rangers continued to be the cutting edge of the American frontier.

APPENDIX A

Robert Rogers's Rules for Rangers, 1757

I. All Rangers are to be subject to the rules and articles of war; to appear at roll-call every evening, on their own parade, equipped, each with a Firelock, sixty rounds of powder and ball, and a hatchet, at which time an officer from each company is to inspect the same, to see they are in order, so as to be ready on any emergency to march at a minute's warning; and before they are dismissed, the necessary guards are to be draughted, and scouts for the next day appointed.

II. Whenever you are ordered out to the enemies forts or frontiers for discoveries, if your number be small, march in a single file, keeping at such a distance from each other as to prevent one shot from killing two men, sending one man, or more, forward, and the like on each side, at the distance of twenty yards from the main body, if the ground you march over will admit of it, to give the signal to the officer of the approach of an enemy, and of their number, &c.

III. If you march over marshes or soft ground, change your position, and march abreast of each other to prevent the enemy from tracking you (as they would do if you marched in a single file) till you get over such ground, and then resume your former order, and march till it is quite dark before you encamp, which do, if possible, on a piece of ground which that may afford your centries the advantage of seeing or hearing the enemy some considerable distance, keeping one half of your whole party awake alternately through the night.

IV. Some time before you come to the place you would reconnoitre, make a stand, and send one or two men in whom you can confide, to look out the best ground for making your observations.

V. If you have the good fortune to take any prisoners, keep them separate, till they are examined, and in your return take a different route from that in which you went out, that you may the better discover any party in your rear, and have an opportunity, if their strength be superior to yours, to alter your course, or disperse, as circumstances may require.

VI. If you march in a large body of three or four hundred, with a design to attack the enemy, divide your party into three columns, each headed by a proper officer, and let those columns march in single files, the columns to the right and left keeping at twenty yards distance or more from that of the center, if the ground will admit, and let proper guards be kept in the front and rear, and suitable flanking parties at a due distance as before directed, with orders to halt on all eminences, to take a view of the surrounding ground, to prevent your being ambuscaded, and to notify the approach or retreat of the enemy, that proper dispositions may be made for attacking, defending, &c. And if the enemy approach in your front on level ground, form a front of your three columns or main body with the advanced guard, keeping out your flanking parties, as if you were marching under the command of trusty officers, to prevent the enemy from pressing hard on either of your wings, or surrounding you, which is the usual method of the savages, if their number will admit of it, and be careful likewise to support and strengthen your rear-guard.

VII. If you are obliged to receive the enemy's fire, fall, or squat down, till it is over; then rise and discharge at them. If their main body is equal to yours, extend yourselves occasionally; but if superior, be careful to support and strengthen your flanking parties, to make them equal to theirs, that if possible you may repulse them to their main body, in which case push upon them with the greatest resolution with equal force in each flank and in the center, observing to keep at a due distance from each other, and advance from tree to tree, with one half of the party before the other ten or twelve yards. If the enemy push upon you, let your front fire and fall down, and then let your rear advance thro' them and do the like, by which time those who before were in front will be ready to discharge again, and repeat the same alternately, as occasion shall require; by this means you will keep up such a constant fire, that the enemy will not be able easily to break your order, or gain your ground.

VIII. If you oblige the enemy to retreat, be careful, in your pursuit of them, to keep out your flanking parties, and prevent them from gaining eminences, or rising grounds, in which case they would perhaps be able to rally and repulse you in their turn.

IX. If you are obliged to retreat, let the front of your whole party fire and fall back, till the rear hath done the same, making for the best ground you can; by this means you will oblige the enemy to pursue you, if they do it at all, in the face of a constant fire.

X. If the enemy is so superior that you are in danger of being surrounded by them, let the whole body disperse, and every one take a different road to the place of rendezvous appointed for that evening, which must every morning be altered and fixed for the evening ensuing, in order to bring the whole party, or as many of them as possible, together, after any separation that may happen in the day; but if you should happen to be actually surrounded, form yourselves into a square, or if in the woods, a circle is best, and, if possible, make a stand till the darkness of the night favours your escape.

XI. If your rear is attacked, the main body and flankers must face about to the right or left, as occasion shall require, and form themselves to oppose the enemy, as before directed; and the same method must be observed, if attacked in either of your flanks, by which means you will always make a rear of one of your flank-guards.

XII. If you determine to rally after a retreat, in order to make a fresh stand against the enemy, by all means endeavour to do it on the most rising ground you come at, which will give you greatly the advantage in point of situation, and enable you to repulse superior numbers.

XIII. In general, when pushed upon by the enemy, reserve your fire till they approach very near, which will then put them into the greatest surprize and consternation, and give you an opportunity of rushing upon them with your hatchets and cutlasses to the better advantage.

XIV. When you encamp at night, fix your centries in such a manner as not to be relieved from the main body till morning, profound secrecy and silence being often of the last importance in these cases. Each centry therefore should consist of six men, two of whom must be constantly alert, and when relieved by their fellows, it should be done without noise; and in case those on duty see or hear any thing, which alarms them, they are not to speak, but one of them is silently to retreat, and acquaint the commanding officer thereof, that proper

Appendix A

dispositions may be made; and all occasional centries should be fixed in like manner.

XV. At the first dawn of day, awake your whole detachment; that being the time when the savages the savages chuse to fall upon their enemies, you should by all means be in readiness to receive them.

XVI. If the enemy should be discovered by your detachments in the morning, and their numbers are superior to yours, and a victory doubtful, you should not attack them till the evening, as then they will not know your numbers, and if you are repulsed, your retreat will be favoured by the darkness of the night.

XVII. Before you leave your encampment, send out small parties to scout round it, to see if there be any appearance or track of an enemy that might have been near you during the night.

XVIII. When you stop for refreshment, chuse some spring or rivulet if you can, and dispose your party so as not to be surprised, posting proper guards and centries at a due distance, and let a small party waylay the path you came in, lest the enemy should be pursuing.

XIX. If, in your return, you have to cross rivers, avoid the usual fords as much as possible, lest the enemy should have discovered, and be there expecting you.

XX. If you have to pass by lakes, keep at some distance from the edge of the water, lest, in case of an ambuscade or an attack from the enemy, when in that situation, your retreat should be cut off.

XXI. If the enemy pursue your rear, take a circle till you come to your own tracks, and there form an ambush to receive them, and give them the first fire.

XXII. When you return from a scout, and come near our forts, avoid the usual roads, and avenues thereto, lest the enemy should have headed you, and lay in ambush to receive you, when almost exhausted with fatigues.

XXIII. When you pursue any party that has been near our forts or encampments, follow not directly in their tracks, lest they should be discovered by their rear guards, who, at such a time, would be most alert; but endeavour, by a different route, to head and meet them in some narrow pass, or lay in ambush to receive them when and where they least expect it.

XXIV. If you are to embark in canoes, battoes, or otherwise, by water, chuse the evening for the time of your embarkation, as you will then have the whole night before you, to pass undiscovered by any parties of the enemy, on hills, or other places, which command a prospect of the lake or river you are upon.

XXV. In padling or rowing, give orders that the boat or canoe next the sternmost, wait for her, and the third for the second, and the fourth for the third, and so on, to prevent separation, and that you may be ready to assist each other on any emergency.

XXVI. Appoint one man in each boat to look out for fires, on the adjacent shores, from the numbers and size of which you may form some judgment of the number that kindled them, and whether you are able to attack them or not.

XXVII. If you find the enemy encamped near the banks of a river or lake, which you imagine they will attempt to cross for their security upon being attacked, leave a detachment of your party on the opposite shore to receive them, while, with the remainder, you surprize them, having them between you and the lake or river.

XXVIII. If you cannot satisfy yourself as to the enemy's number and strength, from their fire, &c. conceal your boats at some distance, and ascertain their number by a reconnoitering party, when they embark, or march, in the morning, marking the course they steer, &c. when you may pursue, ambush, and attack them, or let them pass, as prudence shall direct you. In general, however, that you may not be discovered by the enemy upon the lakes and rivers at a great distance, it is safest to lay by, with your boats and party concealed all day, without noise or shew; and to pursue your intended route by night; and whether you go by land or water, give out parole and countersigns, in order to know one another in the dark, and likewise appoint a station every man to repair to, in case of any accident that may separate you.

Such in general are the rules to be observed in the Ranging service; there are, however, a thousand occurrences and circumstances which may happen that will make it necessary in some measure to depart from them and to put other arts and stratagems in practice; in which cases every man's reason and judgment must be his guide, according to the particular situation and nature of things; and that he may do this to advantage, he should keep in mind a maxim never to be departed from by a commander, viz. to preserve a firmness and presence of mind on every occasion.

APPENDIX B

John Stark's Commission in the Rangers, July 23, 1756

By His Excellency James Abercrombie, Esq., Major General and Commander in Chief of All His Majesty's Forces in North America

To: John Stark, Gent.

Whereas it may be of great use to His Majesty's service in the operations now carrying on for recovering His right in America to have a number of Rangers employed in obtaining intelligence of the strength, situations, and motions of the enemy, as well as other services for which Rangers or men acquainted with the woods only are fit. I do therefore hereby constitute and appoint you, the said John Stark, to be First Lieutenant to that independent company of Rangers (whereof Robert Rogers is Captain) to be forewith ranked and employed in His Majesty's service as foresaid. You are therefore to use your best endeavors to keep the said company in good order and discipline, and I do hereby command them to obey you as their first lieutenant and you are to observe and follow such orders and directions from time to time as you shall receive from the commanders in chief, your captain, or any others your superior officers, according to the rules and discipline of war.

Given at Albany, the twenty-third day of July, one-thousand and seven-hundred and fifty-six.

By His Excellency's Command Peter DeWitt	James Abercrombie Major General

Notes

CHAPTER 1
1. *Minutes of the Provincial Council of Pennsylvania, from the Organization to the Termination of the Proprietary Government,* 10 vols. (Philadelphia, J. Severns, 1851–52), 4:698–737; Fred Anderson, *Crucible of War: The Seven Years' War and the Fate of Empire in British North America* (New York: Alfred A. Knopf, 2000), 18.
2. Philip L. Barbour, ed., *The Complete Works of Captain John Smith* (Chapel Hill, NC: University of North Carolina Press, 1986), 264.
3. Frederick E. Hoxie, ed., *Encyclopedia of North American Indians* (Boston: Houghton Mifflin Company, 1996), 572.
4. Robert Heinl, *Dictionary of Military and Naval Quotations* (Annapolis, MD: United States Naval Institute, 1966), 155.
5. *Indian Narratives* (Claremont, NH: Tracy and Brothers, 1854), 262, 264.
6. A. G. Bradley, ed., *Travels and Works of Captain John Smith* (Edinburgh, Scotland: John Grant, 1910), 558, 594, 604.

CHAPTER 2
1. George Percy, "A Trewe Relacyon," *Tyler's Quarterly Historical and Geneological Magazine* 3 (April 1922): 272.
2. John Ferling, *Struggle for a Continent: The Wars of Early American* (Arlington Heights, IL: Harlan Davidson, 1993), x.
3. Records of the Virginia Company of London.
4. Page Smith, *A New Age Now Begins: A People's History of the American Revolution,* 2 vols. (New York: McGraw-Hill, 1976), 1:18.
5. Charles Banks, *History of York, Maine* (Boston: Calkins Press, 1931), 91.
6. *Maryland Historical Magazine* 28 (June 1933): 180–85.
7. "Deposition of Hugh Cole at Plymouth Court, A.D. 1670." *Collections of the Massachusetts Historical Society for the year 1798* (Boston: Samuel Hall, 1798), 211.
8. Benjamin Church, *The History of Philip's War* (Boston: T. B. Wait and Son, 1827), 93.
9. Church, *History of Philip's War,* 125–26
10. David Brion Davis and Steven Mintz, *The Boisterous Sea of Liberty: A Documentary History of America from Discovery through the Civil War* (New York: Oxford University Press, 1998), 72.
11. Richard B. Morris, *Encyclopedia of American History* (New York: Harper, 1961), 39.
12. Church, *History of Philip's War,* 108–9.

CHAPTER 3
1. *William and Mary Quarterly* (January 1923): 8–9.

Notes

2. *William and Mary Quarterly* (October 1899): 167.
3. R. Ernest Dupuy and Trevor N. Dupuy, *The Encyclopedia of Military History* (New York: Harper & Row, 1970), 660.
4. *William and Mary Quarterly* (July 1923): 145–53.
5. John Abbott, *The History of Maine* (Portland, Maine: Brown Thurston Company, 1892), 128–29.
6. Banks, *History of York, Maine*, 296.
7. Ibid., 236.
8. Abbott, *History of Maine*, 321–26.
9. Howard Pekham, *The Colonial Wars, 1689–1762* (Chicago: University of Chicago Press, 1964), 93.
10. Oglethorpe to Newcastle, January 1742–43.
11. John Elting, "Further light on the Beginning of Gorham's Rangers," *Military Collector and Historian* (Fall 1960): 74–77).
12. Chandler Potter, *The Military History of the State of New-Hampshire, from Its Settlement, in 1623, to the Rebellion, in 1861* (Concord, NH: McFarland & Jenks, 1866), 93–95.

CHAPTER 4

1. James Thomas Flexner, *Lord of the Mohawks: A Biography of Sir William Johnson* (Boston: Little, Brown, 1979), 124–25.
2. Robert C. Alberts, *The Most Extraordinary Adventures of Major Robert Stobo* (Boston: Houghton Mifflin, 1965), 98–107.
3. *Report of the Commission to Locate the Site of the Frontier Forts of Pennsylvania* (Harrisburg, PA: C. M. Busch, 1896), 574–76.
4. Ibid., 61–62.
5. William Harrison Lowdermilk, *History of Cumberland (Maryland) from the Time of the Indian Town, Caiuctucuc, in 1728, up to the Present Day* (Washington, DC: J. Anglim, 1878), 160–61; Allan W. Eckert, *Wilderness Empire* (Boston: Little, Brown, 1969), 336.
6. Eckert, *Wilderness Empire*, 354.
7. George P. Donehoo, *Pennsylvania: A History* 7 vols. (New York: Lewis Historical Publishing Company, 1926), 2:753.
8. Israel D. Rupp, *The History and Topography of Dauphin, Cumberland, Franklin, Bedford, Adams, and Perry Counties* (Lancaster, PA: G. Hills, 1846), 563–64.
9. *Report of the Commission to Locate the Site of the Frontier Forts of Pennsylvania*, 76.
10. John R. Cuneo, *Robert Rogers of the Rangers*, 32.
11. Stanley Pargellis, ed., *Military Affairs in North America, 1748–1765: Selected Documents from the Cumberland Papers in Windsor Castle* (New York: Appleton-Century Company, 1936), 224.
12. Ibid., 269.
13. Rogers spelled the name "Spikeman," but "Speakman" is the correct spelling. Eckert, *Wilderness Empire*, 728.
14. Ibid., 127.
15. Robert Rogers, *Journals of Major Robert Rogers* (London: J. Millan, 1765), 61.
16. Donehoo, *Pennsylvania*, 2:815.
17. Rogers, *Journals*, 104–5.
18. Christopher Lloyd, *The Capture of Quebec* (New York: Macmillan, 1959), 88.
19. Ibid., 98–99.

CHAPTER 5
1. John C. Fitzpatrick, ed., *The Writings of George Washington from the Original Manuscript Sources, 1745–1799* 39 vols. (Washington, DC: U.S. Government Printing Office, 1931–44), 5:185.
2. Ibid., 184.

CHAPTER 6
1. Letter, Bouquet to Amherst, 26 July 1763.
2. Niles Anderson, *The Battle of Bushy Run* (Harrisburg, PA: Pennsylvania Historical and Museum Commission, 1975), 7.
3. *Report of the Commission to Locate the Site of the Frontier Forts of Pennsylvania*, 484.
4. Donehoo, *Pennsylvania*, 890.

CHAPTER 7
1. Thomas Purvis, *Revolutionary America, 1763 to 1800* (New York: Facts on File, 1995), 123
2. Winston Churchill, *A History of the English-Speaking Peoples*, 4 vols. (New York: Dodd, Mead, 1956–58), 2:256.
3. Robin May, *The British Army in North America, 1775–1783* (New York: Hippocrene Books, 1974), 6.
4. Joseph Galloway, *The Claim of the American Loyalists Reviewed and Maintained upon Incontrovertible Principles of Law and Justice* (London: G. and T. Wilkie, 1788).
5. Maine Historical Society, *Documentary History of the State of Maine* (Portland, Maine: Bailey and Noyes, 1869–1916), 304.
6. Christopher Ward, *The War of the Revolution*, 2 vols. (New York: Macmillan, 1952), 1:99.
7. Robert K. Wright, *The Continental Army* (Washington, DC: Center of Military History, U.S. Army, 1983), 23.
8. John K. Mahon and Romana Danysh, *Infantry* (Washington, DC: Office of the Chief of Military History, U.S. Army, 1972), 3.
9. Purvis, *Revolutionary America*, 123.
10. Harold L. Peterson. *The Book of the Continental Soldier* (Harrisburg, PA: Stackpole Company, 1968), 42.
11. Frederic A. Godcharles, *Chronicles of Central Pennsylvania* (New York: Lewis Historical Publishing Company, 1944), 25.

CHAPTER 9
1. Henry Steel Commager, ed., *Documents of American History* (New York: F. S. Crofts & Co., 1938), 45–47.
2. David Hackett Fischer, *Paul Revere's Ride* (New York: Oxford University Press), 209.
3. Craig L. Symonds, *A Battlefield Atlas of the American Revolution* (Annapolis, MD: Nautical & Aviation Publishing Company of America, 1986), 15.
4. Letters of Hugh, Earl Percy and Afterwards Duke of Northumberland, 1774–78.
5. William F. Livingston, *Israel Putnam: Pioneer, Ranger, and Major-General* (New York: G. P. Putnam's Sons, 1901), 222.
6. Ibid., 226.
7. Catherine Drinker Bowen, *John Adams and the American Revolution* (Boston: Little, Brown, 1950), 531.

8. Samuel Eliot Morison, *John Paul Jones: A Sailor's Biography* (Boston: Little, Brown, 1959), 103–4.

CHAPTER 10

1. Otis K. Rice, *The Allegheny Frontier: West Virginia Beginnings, 1730–1830* (Lexington, KY: University Press of Kentucky, 1970), 89.
2. Oscar H. Stroh, *Thompson's Battalion* (Harrisburg, PA: Graphic Services, 1976), 48; Hendricks journal.
3. James Thacher, *Military Journal of the American Revolution* (Hartford, CT: Hurlbut, Williams & Company, 1862).
4. Ibid.
5. *Philadelphia Evening Post*, 1775.
6. Stroh, *Thompsons's Battalion*, 48; Hendricks journal.
7. Simeon Thayer, *The Invasion of Canada in 1775* (Providence, RI: Knowles, Anthony & Co., 1867), 59–60
8. North Callahan, *Daniel Morgan, Ranger of the Revolution* (New York: Holt, Rinehart and Winston, 1961), 80
9. Stroh, *Thompson's Battalion*, 51; Hendricks journal.
10. Fitzpatrick, ed., *Writings of George Washington*, 178
11. Ibid., 178–79.
12. George H. Jepson, *Herrick's Rangers* (Bennington, VT: Hadwen, 1977), 23.
13. Ibid., 9–10.
14. Godcharles, *Chronicles of Central Pennsylvania*, 266

CHAPTER 11

1. John D. Barnhart, *Henry Hamilton and George Rogers Clark in the American Revolution* (Crawfordsville, IN: R. E. Banta, 1951), 54–55.
2. Papers of George Rogers Clark, U.S. Army Military History Institute.
3. Barnhart, *Henry Hamilton and George Rogers Clark*, 182–83
4. Ibid., 75.
5. Thomas Jefferson, *Papers* , 33 vols., ed. Julian Boyd (Princeton, NJ: Princeton University Press, 1950–2006), 3:317:
6. Ibid., 3:218
7. John E. Bakeless, *Background to Glory: The Life of George Rogers Clark* (Philadelphia: Lippincott, 1957), 335.

CHAPTER 12

1. Cyrus T. Brady, *Border Fights & Fighters: Stories of the Pioneers between the Alleghenies and the Mississippi and in the Texan Republic* (New York: McClure, Phillips & Co., 1902), 24.

CHAPTER 13

1. James D. Bailey, *Commanders at King's Mountain* (Gaffney, SC: E. H. De Camp, 1926), 26.
2. Ibid., 164–65.
3. Ward, *War of the Revolution* 2:664.
4. Michael Calvert, *A Dictionary of Battles* (New York: Mayflower Books, 1978), 181–82
5. Ibid., 104.

6. Mark M. Boatner, *Encyclopedia of the American Revolution* (New York: D. McKay Co., 1966), 415.
7. Chalmers G. Davidson, *Piedmont Partisan: The Life and Times of Brigadier-General William Lee Davidson* (Davidson, NC: Davidson College), 74; Ward, *War of the Revolution*, 2:738–39.
8. *Historical Statements Concerning the Battle of King's Mountain and the Battle of Cowpens, South Carolina* (Washington, DC: U.S. Government Printing Office, 1928), 18.

CHAPTER 14
1. Correspondence of Nathanael Greene.
2. Ward, *War of the Revolution*, 2:753.
3. Malone. *Jefferson and the Ordeal of Liberty* (Charlottesville, VA: University of Virginia Press, 2005), 269.
4. Richard K. Showman, ed., *The Papers of General Nathanael Greene*, 13 vols. (Chapel Hill, NC: University of North Carolina Press, 1976–2005), 7:51.
5. William Moultrie, *Memoirs of the American Revolution*, 2 vols. (New York: D. Longworth, 1802), 1:255.
6. Alice Noble Waring, *The Fighting Elder* (Columbia, SC: University of South Carolina Press, 1962), 49.
7. Showman, ed., *Papers of General Nathanael Greene*, 3:190–92.
8. Waring, *Fighting Elder*, 60.
9. Noel B. Gerson, *Light-Horse Harry: A Biography of Washington's Great Cavalryman, General Henry Lee* (Garden City, NY: Doubleday, 1966), 103.
10. Henry Lee, *Memoirs of the War in the Southern Department of the United States* (Philadelphia: Bradford and Inskeep, 1812), 604–5.
11. Ibid., 371–72.
12. Waring, *Fighting Elder*, 97.
13. William Johnson, *Sketches of the Life and Correspondence of Nathanael Greene*, 2 vols. (Charleston, SC: A. E. Miller, 1822), 2:230.
14. Boatner, *Encylopedia of the American Revolution*, 355.

CHAPTER 15
1. Benson J. Lossing, *The Pictorial Field-Book of the War of 1812* (New York: Harper & Brothers, 1868), 19.

CHAPTER 16
1. Noah Smithwick, *The Evolution of a State* (Austin, TX: Gammel Book Company, 1900), 3.
2. Ibid., 10.
3. Jean Louis Berlandier, *The Indians of Texas in 1830* (Washington, DC: Smithsonian Institution Press, 1969), fig. 13.
4. Walter P. Webb, *The Texas Rangers: A Century of Frontier Defense* (Boston: Houghton Mifflin, 1935), 21.

CHAPTER 17
1. Charles M. Robinson, *The Men Who Wear the Star: The Story of the Texas Rangers* (New York: Random House, 2000), 25.
2. Webb, *Texas Rangers*, 17–18.

3. Robinson, *Men Who Wear the Star*, 32.
4. Webb, *Texas Rangers*, 25; Henderson K. Yoakum, *History of Texas: From Its First Settlement in 1685 to Its Annexation to the United States in 1846*, 2 vols. (New York: Redfield, 1855), 2:180–81.
5. Southwick, *Evolution of a State*.
6. T. R. Fehrenbach, *Lone Star: A History of Texas and the Texans* (New York: Macmillan, 1968), 214–15.

CHAPTER 18
1. Fehrenbach, *Lone Star*, 449–51.
2. Robinson, *Men Who Wear the Star*, 119–20.
3. Webb, *Texas Rangers*, 43.
4. Robinson, *Men Who Wear the Star*, 48.
5. Fehrenbach, *Lone Star*, 255.
6. Smithwick, *Evolution of a State*, 151.

CHAPTER 19
1. Samuel C. Reid, *Scouting Expeditions of McCulloch's Texas Rangers* (Philadelphia: G. B. Zieber and Co., 1847), 112.
2. Fehrenbach, *Lone Star*, 479.
3. Reid, *Scouting Expeditions*, 30.
4. Webb, *Texas Rangers*, 7.

CHAPTER 20
1. Robinson, *Men Who Wear the Star*, 73.
2. Fehrenbach, *Lone Star*, 271.
3. Robinson, *Men Who Wear the Star*, 75.
4. Reid, *Scouting Expeditions*, 26.
5. Ibid., 44.
6. Ibid., 83.
7. Ibid., 128–29.
8. Ibid., 178.
9. John S. Ford, *Rip Ford's Texas* (Austin, TX: University of Texas Press, 1963), 67–68.

CHAPTER 21
1. Webb, *Texas Rangers*, 151.
2. Webb, *Texas Rangers*, 124.
3. Smithwick, *Evolution of a State*, 250–51.

Bibliography

COLONIAL WARS

Alberts, Robert C. *The Most Extraordinary Adventures of Major Robert Stobo.* Boston: Houghton Mifflin Co., 1965.
Anderson Fred. *Crucible of War.* New York: Alfred A. Knopf, 2000.
Arber, Edward. *Captain J. Smith Works, 1608–1631.* Birmingham, England: The English Scholar's Library, 1884.
Bearor, Bob. *The Battle on Snowshoes.* Bowie, MD: Heritage Books, 1997.
Boorstin, Daniel J. *The Americans: The Colonial Experience.* New York: Random House 1958.
Careless J. M. S. *Canada.* Toronto: Macmillan of Canada, 1970.
Church, Thomas. *The History of Philip's War.* Reprint. Bowie, MD: Heritage Books 1989.
Cuneo, John R. *Robert Rogers of the Rangers.* New York: Oxford University Press, 1959.
Eckert, Allan W. *Frontiersmen.* New York: Little, Brown, 1967
Faragher, John Mack. *The Encyclopedia of Colonial and Revolutionary America.* New York: Facts on File, 1990.
Josephy, Alvin M. *500 Nations: An Illustrated History of North American Indians.* New York: Alfred A. Knopf., 1994.
Kelley, Joseph J. *Pennsylvania: The Colonial Years, 1681–1776.* Garden City, NY: Doubleday, 1980
Lloyd, Christopher. *The Capture of Quebec.* New York: Macmillan, 1959.
Livingston, William Ferrand. *Israel Putnam: Pioneer, Ranger, and Major General.* New York: Putnam, 1901.
Loescher, Burt Garfield. *The History of Rogers's Rangers.* San Mateo, CA: Self-published, 1946.
Parkman Francis. *The Oregon Trail: The Conspiracy of Pontiac.* New York: Literary Classics of the United States, 1991.
Roby, Luther. *Reminiscences of the French War.* Concord, NH: Self-published, 1831.
Rogers, Robert. *Journals of Major Robert Rogers.* Reprint. New York: Corinth Books, 1961.
Schwartz, Seymour I. *The French and Indian War.* New York: Simon and Schuster, 1994.
Smith Page. *A New Age Now Begins.* New York: McGraw-Hill Book Company, 1976.
Todish, Timothy J. *America's First World War.* Grand Rapids, MI: Suagothel Productions, 1982.

Bibliography

REVOLUTIONARY WAR

Alden, John Richard. *General Gage in America.* Baton Rouge, LA: State University Press, 1948.
Babits, Lawrence E. *A Devil of a Whipping: The Battle of Cowpens.* Chapel Hill, NC: University of North Carolina Press, 1989.
Bailey, J. D. *Commanders at King's Mountain.* Greenville, SC: A Press, 1980
Balderston, Marion, and David Syrett, eds. *The Lost War Letters from British Officers during the American Revolution.* New York: Horizon Press, 1975.
Bakeless, John. *Background to Glory: The Life of George Rogers Clark.* Philadelphia: J. B. Lippincott Company, 1957.
———. *Daniel Boone.* New York: William Morrow, 1939.
Bakeless, Katherine and John. *Spies of the Revolution.* New York: Scholastic Book Services, 1962.
Barnhart John D., ed. *Henry Hamilton and George Rogers Clark in the American Revolution with the Unpublished Journal of Lieut. Gov. Henry Hamilton.* Crawfordsville, IN: R. E. Banta, 1951.
Bass, Robert D. *Gamecock.* New York: Holt, Rinehart and Winston, 1961
———. *Swamp Fox.* Orangeburg, SC: Sandlapper Publishing Co., 1959.
Berg, Fred Anderson. *Encyclopedia of Continental Army Units.* Harrisburg, PA: The Stackpole Company, 1972.
Boatner, Mark M. *Encyclopedia of the American Revolution.* New York: David McKay Company, 1966.
Bowen, Catherine Drinker. *John Adams and the American Revolution.* Boston: Little, Brown, 1950.
Boyd, Julian P., ed. *The Papers of Thomas Jefferson.* Princeton, NJ: Princeton University Press, 1951.
Brady, Cyrus Townsend. *Border Fights and Fighters.* New York: Doubleday, Page & Co., 1902.
Callahan, North. *Daniel Morgan: Ranger of the Revolution.* New York: Holt, Rinehart and Winston, 1961.
Carrington, Henry B. *Battles of the American Revolution.* New York: Arno Press, 1968.
Coakley, Robert W., and Conn Stetson. *The War of the American Revolution.* Washington, DC: Center of Military History, 1975.
Coleman, Kenneth. *The American Revolution in Georgia, 1763–1789.* Athens, GA: University of Georgia Press, 1958.
Commager, Henry Steele, and Richard B. Morris, eds. *The Spirit of Seventy-Six.* New York: Harper and Rowe, 1958.
Cullen, Maurice R. *Battle Road.* Old Greenwich, CT: The Chatham Press, 1970.
Darling, Anthony D. *Red Coat and Brown Bess.* Alexandria Bay, New York: Museum Restoration Service, 1971.
Davidson, Chalmers Gaston. *Piedmont Partisan.* Davidson, NC: Davidson College, 1951.
Davis, Burke. *The Cowpens–Guilford Courthouse Campaign.* Philadelphia: J. B. Lippencott Company, 1962.
Davis, David Brion, and Steven Mintz. *The Boisterous Sea of Liberty.* New York: Oxford University Press, 1998.
Derleth, August. *Vincennes Portal to the West.* Englewood Cliffs, NJ: Prentice-Hall, 1968.
Donehoo, George P., ed. *Pennsylvania: A History.* 3 vols. New York: Lewis Publishing Co., 1926.

Fischer, David Hackett. *Paul Revere's Ride.* New York: Oxford University Press, 1994.
Fleming, Thomas J. *Now We Are Enemies.* New York: St. Martin's Press, 1960.
Freeman, Douglas Southall. *Washington.* Abridged ed. New York: Charles Scribner's Sons, 1968.
Gerson, Noel B. *Light Horse Harry.* Garden City, NY: Doubleday, 1966.
Godcharles, Frederic A. *Chronicles of Central Pennsylvania.* New York: Lewis Historical Publishing Co., 1944.
Graham, James. *Life of General Daniel Morgan.* Reprint. Bloomingburg, NY: Zebroski Historical Services Publishing Company, 1993.
Hall-Quest, Olfa W. *Guardians of Liberty.* New York: E. P. Dutton, 1963.
Higginbotham, Don. *Daniel Morgan: Revolutionary Rifleman.* Chapel Hill, NC: University of North Carolina Press, 1961.
Karapalides, Harry J. *Dates of the American Revolution.* Shippensburg, PA: Burd Street Press, 1998.
Katcher, Philip. *King George's Army, 1775–1783.* Harrisburg, PA: Stackpole Company, 1973.
Ketchum, Richard M., ed. *The American Heritage Book of the Revolution.* New York: American Heritage Publishing Company, 1958.
Kidder, Frederic. *History of the First New Hampshire Regiment.* Albany, NY: Joel Munsell, 1868.
Malone, Dumas. *Jefferson and His Time.* 6 vols. Boston: Little, Brown, 1948.
May, Robin. *The British Army in North America, 1775–1783.* New York: Hippocrine Books, 1974.
Moore, Howard Parker. *A Life of General John Stark.* Boston: Spaulding Moss Company, 1949.
Morison, Samuel Eliot. *John Paul Jones.* Boston: Little, Brown, 1959.
Palmer, Frederick. *Clark of the Ohio.* New York: Dodd, Mead and Company, 1930.
Peterson, Harold L. *The Book of the Continental Soldier.* Harrisburg, PA: Stackpole Company, 1968.
Randall, Willard Stern. *Benedict Arnold: Patriot and Traitor.* New York: William Morrow, 1990.
Rankin, Hugh F. *The Swamp Fox.* New York: Thomas Crowell Company, 1973.
Showman, Richard K. *The Papers of Nathanael Greene.* 7 vols. Chapel Hill, NC: University of North Carolina Press, 1994.
Shy, John. *Toward Lexington.* Princeton, NJ: Princeton University Press, 1965.
Stark, Caleb. *Memoir and Official Correspondence of General John Stark.* Reprint. Boston: Gregg Press, 1972.
Stroh, Oscar H. *Thompson's Battalion.* Harrisburg, PA: Graphic Press, 1975.
Tarbox, Increase N. *Life of Israel Putnam.* Reprint. New York: Kennikat Press, 1970.
Thayer, Simeon. *Journal of Captain Simeon Thayer (Quebec Expedition).* Providence, RI: Knowles, Anthony and Co., 1867.
Tuchman, Barbara W. *The March of Folly.* New York: Alfred Knopf, 1984.
Wallace, Willard. M. *Traitorous Hero: The Life and Fortunes of Benedict Arnold.* New York: Harper and Brothers Publishers, 1954.
Ward, Christopher. *The War of the Revolution.* 2 vols. New York: The Macmillan Company, 1952.
Waring, Alice Noble. *The Fighting Elder.* Columbia, SC: University of South Carolina Press, 1962.

Bibliography

Wright, Robert K. *The Continental Army.* Washington, DC: Center of Military History, United States Army, 1989.

WAR OF 1812

Coles, Harry L. *The War of 1812.* Chicago: University of Chicago Press, 1965.
Gilleland, J. C. *History of the Late War between the United States and Great Britain.* Baltimore, MD: Schaeffer and Maund, 1818.
Johnson, Rossiter. *A History of the War of 1812–15.* New York: Dodd, Mead, 1882.
Lossing, Benson J. *The Pictorial Field Book of the War of 1812.* New York: Harper, 1869.
Quisenberry, A. C. *Kentucky in the War of 1812.* Frankfort, KY: State Historical Society, 1915.
Remini, Robert V. *Andrew Jackson.* New York: Twayne Publishers, 1966.
Sugden, John. *Tecumseh.* New York: Henry Holt, 1997.
Zaslow, Morris. *The Defended Border.* Toronto: Macmillan, 1964.

TEXAS RANGERS AND THE MEXICAN WAR

Fehrenbach, T. R. *Lone Star.* New York: American Legacy Press, 1983.
Nichols, Edward J. *Zach Taylor's Little Army.* New York: Doubleday, 1963.
Reid, Samuel C. *McCulloch's Texas Rangers.* Reprint. Freeport, New York: Books for Library Press, 1970.
Robinson, Charles M. *The Men Who Wear the Star.* New York: Random House, 2000.
Webb, Walter Prescott. *The Texas Rangers.* Austin, TX: University of Texas Press, 1965.
Wilcox, Cadmus. *History of the Mexican War.* Washington, DC: Church News Publishing, 1892.

Index

Page numbers in italics indicate illustrations.

Abercromby, James, 38, 64, 67
Adams, John, 110, 129
Adams, Samuel, 110
Agua Nueva, battle at, 319–20
Alamo, 281–82
Albany, attack on, 155–59
Allen, Ebenezer, 157
Allen, Ethan, 118–19, 157
American Continental Army, 104–5
American Revolution
    Albany, 155–59
    beginning of, 110–12
    Bennington, Battle of, 157–60
    Black Mingo Creek, 207–8
    Bloody Curve, 115
    Breed's Hill, Battle of, 120–28, *121*
    Brook's Hill, 115
    Bunker Hill, 120–28, *121*
    Camden, Battle of, 207
    Charlestown, 117, 120
    citizen-soldiers of, 108–9
    Cowpens, Battle of, 108, 223–30
    Crown Point capture, 119
    Dan River, battle near, 233–35
    Eutaw Springs, Battle of, 243–48
    events leading up to, 99–107
    firing at Lexington, 113
    Fort Cornwallis, 241–42
    Fort Grierson, 241–42
    Fort Watson, 240
    Georgetown, 231–32
    Guilford Court House, 235–37
    Harlem Heights, 148–50
    John's Island, Battle of, 249
    Kettle Creek, 201
    King's Mountain, 213–15
    Kip's Bay assault, 148
    Lechmere Point, 137
    Lexington Common, 116
    Meriam's Corner, 115
    Moore's Creek, 198–99
    Ninety-Six, village of, 200
    Paulus Hook, 218–19
    Ploughed Hill, 136
    Quebec invasion, 137–47, *139*, *144*
    Saratoga, Battle of, 108, 162–67
    Skenesborough, 118–19
    in the South, 196–215
    Ticonderoga, 118–19
    Wahab's plantation ambush, 210–11
Amherst, Jeffrey, 38, 64, 69–70, 93–94, 96
Andre, John, 169
Arlington, William, 277
Armstrong, John, 60–61, 97
Arnold, Benedict, *118*, 118–19
    Battle of Saratoga and, 163–67
    Quebec invasion and, 138–47
Austin, Moses, 272–73
Austin, Stephen F., 273–74

Baker, John, 240
Balfour, Nisbet, 221
Bamford, William, 152
Bancroft, Ebenezer, 124–25
Barnes, John, 119
Barney, Joshua, capture of, 259
Barrett, James, 113, 114
Bartelo, Francis, 36
Battle of the Snowshoes, 64–67
Baum, Frederich, 156–59
Beasley, Daniel, 255
Beaujeu, Captain, 44–46
Bedel, Thomas, 109
Bennington, Battle of, 157–60
Berkeley, William, 24
Berkeley Plantation Massacre, viii, 9
Bird, James, 294
Black Mingo Creek battle, 207–8
Boone, Daniel, 43, 174, 193–95, *194*

Index

Bouquet, Henri, 94–96, 97, 98
Bowie, Jim, 281, 282
Bowman, John, 186
Bowman, Joseph, 176
Braddock, Edward, 38, 40–47
Brady, Sam, 190–91
Brandon, Thomas, 227
Brant, Joseph, 53, *62*, 167
Breed's Hill, Battle of, 120–28, *121*
British Army, 99–100, 102
Brock, Isaac, 253
Brown, Jacob, 258, 305, 307
Brown, Stephen, 150
Brown, Thomas, 103, 241–42
Browne, Elizabeth "Betsy," 81
Buena Vista, Battle of, 320–21, *321*
Buford, Abraham, 206
Bunker Hill, 120–28, *121*
Burd, James, 49
Burgoyne, John, 155–59, *159*
  Battle of Saratoga and, 162–67
Burleson, Edward, 294
Burr, Aaron, 146, 148
Burton, Isaac, 277, 278
Butler, Richard "Dickie", 160, 163, 188, 217
Byrd, James, 68

Cahokia, 178–79
Caldwell, Matthew, 294
Camden, Battle of, 207
Cameron, Scot Ewen, 301
Campbell, Charles, 202
Campbell, John, 38, 58, 146, 199
Campbell, Richard, death of, 245
Campbell, William, 212–15
Canadian River, fight on the, 326
Canales, "The Chaparral Fox," 311
Captain Jack, 41
Carroll, William, 263
Cartier, Jacques, 22
Caswell, Richard, 197, 198
Cathcart, William, 206
Chambers, James, 131, 135
Champlain, Samuel, 23
Cherry Valley Massacre, 103
Chevallie, Mike, 301
Chief Iron Jacket, 326

Church, Benjamin, 16–21, 110–11
Civil War, 335
Claiborne, William, 14
Clapham, William, 36
Clark, George Rogers, 101, 135, 171–89
  at Cahokia, 178–79
  capture of Kaskaskia and, 175–78
  march against Vincennes, *172*, 179–85
  relieved of command, 187
  western route of, *174*
Clarke, Elijah, 197, 200
Cleveland, Benjamin "Round About," 197, 212
Clinton, Henry, 123
Coffee, John, 262, 263
Coleman, Robert M., 288
colonists, 1, 6–7, 23
Cornwallis, Charles, Lord, 196, *198*, 211, 215, 230–31, 233, 235–37, 249
Cornwallis, Edward, 36
Cortinas, Juan, 328–34
Cowpens, Battle of, 108, 223–30
Crary, Archibald, 149
Crawford, William, death of, 249
Crockett, David, 262, 281, 282
Croghan, George, 42, 255
Cross, Thomas, death of, 306
Cruise, Walter, 136
Curry, Abigail, 134

Dalyell, James, 90
Dan River, battle near, 233–35
Davidson, George, 210
Davie, William Richardson, 197, 207, 210–11
Dawes, William, 111
Dearborn, Henry, 161, 165
Defoe, Daniel, 1–2
DeLeyba, Fernando, 178
Desha, Joseph, 256
Doudel, Michael, 135–36
Douglas, George, 152
Doyle, Welbore, 239–40
Dumas, Jean Daniel, 46
Dunbar, Thomas, 48
Dunlap, James, 201
Dunmore's War, 134–35

Ecuyer, Simon, 93
Elder, John, 90–92
Endicott, John, 12
Eutaw Springs, Battle of, 243–48
Eyre, William, 50

Falcon, Blas, 309
Fallen Timbers, 252
Federation Hill, 314–15
Ferguson, Patrick, 196, 210, 211–12, 214
First Anglo-Powhatan War, 9–10
Fisher, William S., 292, 301
Forbes, John, 64, 68
Ford, John "Rip," 323, 324, 335
  Indian wars in Texas and, 325–34
  wounding of, 331
Ford, John Salmon, 318
Fort Beausejour, 41
Fort Carillon, battle for, 67, 69–70
Fort Cornwallis, 241–42
Fort Duquesne, battle for, 39, 40–48, 45, 68–69
Fort Frederic, battle for, 38–39, 49–58, 70
Fort Grierson, 241–42
Fort Loudoun, 98
Fort Lyman, battle for, 50, 52–53
Fort Mims, massacre at, 262
Fort Nelson, 187
Fort Pitt, battle for, 93–96
Fort Watson, battle for, 240
Fort William Henry, 50, 78–79
Franklin, Benjamin, 43
Fraser, Simon, 166
French Huguenots, 22
French and Indian War, 24, 38–77, *43*
  Battle of the Snowshoes, 64–67
  Fort Carillon, 67, 69–70
  Fort Duquesne, 40–48, 68–69
  Fort Frederic, 49–58, 70
  Fort Lyman, 52–53
  Kittanning raid, 59–61
  Lake George patrol, 61–63
  Quebec seizure, 75–77
  St. Lawrence river area settlements attacks, 70–74
  Virginia and Pennsylvania frontier attacks, 48–49

Fry, Joshua, 39
Frye, Eben, 154
Frye, Jonathan, 31–32

Gage, Thomas, 44, 67, 80–81, 110, 123
Gates, Horatio "Granny," 161–62, *162*, 207, 210
  Battle of Saratoga and, 162–67
Georgetown, battle of, 231–32
Gerrish, Samuel, 127
Gibault, Pierre, 177–78
Gillespie, Richard A., 312, 315, 316
Gist, Nathaniel, 109
Goffe, John, 36
Gorham, John, 21, 34–37
Gorham, Joseph, 34–37
Green, John, 237
Greene, Christopher, 140–41
Greene, Nathanael, 216, 217, *218*, 219, 233–37, 245
  Battle of Eutaw Springs and, 243–48
  in vicinity of Guilford Court House, 235–37
Griffen, Timothy, 247
Guelph, George, 102
Guilford Court House, battle at, 235–37

Hale, Nathan, 85, 150–52
Hamilton, Henry, 173–74
  capture of, 185
  at Vincennes, 179–85
Hampton, Wade, 246
Hancock, John, 110, 129
Hanger, George, 106, 211
Harlem Heights battle, 148–50
Harmon, Johnson, 28
Harrington, Jonathan, 113
Harris, George, 152
Harrison, William Henry, 254–58
Harrod, James, 174
Harrod, William, 176
Haviland, William, 64–67
Hays, John Coffee "Jack," 297–302, 324
  during Mexican War, 306–23
  Enchanted Hill incident, 298–99
  as tracker, 299
Hazen, Moses, 84
Heath, William, 117

Index

Heintzelman, Samuel, 329–34
Helm, Leonard, 176
Hendrick, William, 131, 140–47
Henry, John, 140
Henry, Patrick, 172
Herrick, Samuel, 157, 158
Hessians, attack on, 153–54
Hibbons, Sarah, incident, 279–80
Highsmith, Benjamin, 298
Hitchcock, Ethan Allen, 322
Hornsby, Reuben, 279
Horry, Peter, 209, 220, 248–49
Horse Shoe Bend, attack on Indian base at, 262–63
Houston, Sam, 283–85, 286, 299, 334
Howard, John Eager, 27–28, 247
Howe, George, 64
Howe, Robert, 200, 210
Huck, Christian, 202
Hull, William, 253
Huston, Felix, 294

Independence Hill, 314, 315–16
Indian reservations, life on, 327
Indian summer, term, 7
Indian wars, 24
    King Philip's, 9, 15–20
    Pequot, 9, 12–14
    Powhatan, 9–11
    in Texas 324–34
Indians, 3–4
    Abenaki, 26–30
    Apache, 271, 272
    cavalry pursuit of, 327
    Cherokee, 171, 271
    Chickasaw, 171
    Comanche, 271–72, 292–96, 325, 326
    Creek, 25–26, 255
    Delaware, 271
    Iroquois, 15, 23
    Karankawa, 270–71
    Lipan Apache, 286
    Maumee, 251
    Mission, 270
    Mohawk, 19
    Mohegan, 15
    Moravian, 91–92
    Narragansett, 12, 15, 18–19
    Ottawa, 88–89
    Paspehegh, 9–10
    Pequawket, 30–32
    Pequot, 12–14
    Powhatan, 9–11
    Pueblo, 270
    Red Sticks of the Creek, 262–63
    Shawnee, 171, 271
    Tarratine, 26
    Tonkawa, 271, 286
    Tuscarora, 25
    Wampanoag, 15
    war tactics of, 49
    Yamassee, 25–26

Jackson, Andrew, War of 1812 and, 261–69
Jaques, Benjamin, 29
Jefferson, Thomas, 185, 188
Jenkins, Robert, 32
John's Island, Battle of, 249
Johnson, James, 256–57
Johnson, Richard M., 256–57
Johnson, William, 40, 49–58, 81
Johnston, Albert Sidney, 292
Jones, Anson, 303
Jones, John Paul, 130

Karnes, Henry, 292
Kaskaskia, capture of, 175–78
Kellog, Elizabeth, 287
Kent Island confrontation, 14–15
Kenton, Simon, 173, 192–93
Kettle Creek, Georgia, battle of, 201
King George's War, 24, 34–37
King Philip, 15–20
King Philip's War, 9, 15–20
    casualties, 20
    Deerfield, 19
    Great Swamp Fight, 19–20
    South Kingston Fort, 18–19
King William's War, 20–21
King's Mountain, battle of, 213–15
Kittanning, raid on, 59–61
Knowlton, Thomas, 125, 148–50

La Peyroney, William, 40, 47
Ladd, David, 36
Lafitte, Jean, 265
Lamar, Mirabeau Bonaparte, 290

Lane, Joseph, 322
Langlade, Charles, 45
Lee, Henry "Light Horse Harry," 197, 216–19, *220*, 231–32, 233–37, 240–46
Lee, Robert E., 322, 334
LeFevre, Philip, 106
Legion of the United States, 251
Leitch, Andrew, 149, 150
Lexington Company, 112, 116
Lienard, Daniel, 44
Lincoln, Benjamin, 210
Linn, Benjamin, 174, 175
Linn, William, 176
Lochry, Archibald, 187
Lockhart, Matilda, 292–93
Logan, Benjamin, 174
Long Island, Battle of, 107
Lovewell, John, 30–31
Loyalist Americans, 101
Lyman, Phineas, 52

McClary, Andrew, 125, 128
McCleod, Donald, 198, 199
McCullough, Ben, 294, 301, 308–23, 335
McDonald, Donald, 198
Macdonough, Thomas, 260
McDowell, Charles, 212
McGary, Hugh, death of, 249
Macomb, Alexander, 260
Mahan, Hezekiah, 240, 248–49
Malmedy, Marquis Francis de, 244
Marion, Francis, 197, 204–5, 207–9, 219, 220, *221*
    American Revolution battles and, 237–50
    at Georgetown, 222, 231–32
Martin, Albert, 282
Mason, John, 13–14
Matthews, John, 243
Mercer, George, 40
Merchant, George, 106
Mexican War, 304–23
    Agua Nueva, 319–20
    Buena Vista, Battle of, 320–21, *321*
    Cerralvo, 312
    Federation Hill, 314–15
    Huamantla, 322
    Independence Hill, 314, 315–16
    Monterey, 312–13, 316–18
    Point Isabel, 305
    Puebla, 322–23
    Ramos, 312
    Reynosa, 311
    Rio Grande area, 305
    Saltillo Road, 314
    San Jeronimo, 313–14
    theater of operations, *310*
    Vera Cruz, 318–19, 321–22
    Walnut Grove, 313
Meylan, Martin, 106
militia, 6–8, 100, 104, 106
Miller, Henry, 135–36
Monckton, Robert, 40, 41
Monterey, battle at, 316–18
Montgomery, John, 176
Montgomery, Richard, Quebec invasion and, 138–46
Moor, John, 125
Moore, James, 198
Moore, John H., 278, 291–92
Moore, Samuel, 174, 175
Moore's Creek, battle of, 198–99
Morgan, Daniel, 43, 101, 105, 132–35, 160, 197, 219, 222–23, 228, 230, 231, 232–33
    Battle of Cowpens and, 223–30
    Battle of Saratoga and, 163–67
    capture of, 147
    Quebec invasion and, 140–47
Morton, Thomas, 12
Moulton, Jeremiah, 26–30
Munroe, Edmund, 84, 112–13
Munroe, Robert, 113
Murphy, Tim, 166

Neale, William, 328
Neighbors, Robert S., 324, 328
New Orleans, Battle of, 263–69, *264*
Newman, Tom, 112
Nixon, John, 149
Norridgewock, Maine, raid on, 26–30
Northwest Passage expedition, 83
Norton, Walter, 12

Index 357

Oglethorpe, John, 32–34
Oldham, John, 12
Otis, James, 110
Ourry, Lewis, 93

Paine, Thomas, 153
Pakenham, Edward, 266–69
Parker, Cynthia Ann, 287–88
Parker, Daniel, 277, 287
Parker, John, 112, 116, 286–87
Parker, Jonas, 113
Parker, Silas, 287
Parker's Fort, raid on, 286–87
Parkman, Francis, 86
Paulus Hook, battle at, 218–19
Pepperell, William, 35
Pequot War, 9
Percy, George, Paspehegh Indian village expedition, 9–10
Percy, Hugh, 116–18
Phillips, Samuel, 212
Pickens, Andrew, 197, 199–201, 226, 227, 233–37, 245
Pickering, Timothy, 117
Pitcairn, John, 111, 116
Pitt, William, 63–64, 69
Plattsburg, New York, battle near, 260
Plum Creek, Battle of, 295
Plummer, Rachel, 287
Polk, James K., 303, 318
Pomeroy, Seth, 128, 129
Pontiac, chief of the Ottawa, 88–89, 96, 97–98
Pontiac's War, 88–98
Postell, John, 248
Potter, Nathanial, 86
Prescott, Samuel, 112
Prescott, William, 120–28
Prevost, George, 260
Pulling, John, 112
Putnam, Israel, 53, 57–58, 59, 84, 120–28, 129, 148

Queach, Jeremy, 29
Quebec, invasion of, 75–77, 137–47, *139, 144*
Queen Anne's War, 24, 25

Rale, Sebastian, 27–30
Randell, Joseph, 96
Rangers, 101–7
  American Loyalist, 103
  Bedel's, 105
  Bedford County, 109
  birth of, 7–8
  Black Boys, 97
  Brady's, 190–91
  Butler's, 103–4
  earliest mention of, 7
  Gorham's, 36–37
  Green Mountain, 118–19
  Horry's Mounted, 220, 221–22
  Knowlton's, 109, 148–50
  life of, 288–89
  McCullough's, 308–23
  Marion's, 208
  New Hampshire, 109
  New York, 109, 119
  North Carolina, 109
  Paxtang, 90–92
  pay, 290
  Pennsylvania, 108
  Queen's American, 85
  rules for, 336–40
  Sam Walker's, 306–7
  Stark's commission in the, 341
  Texas, 273–74, 277, 325–34
  used in exploration, 26
  Whitcomb's, 105
Read, Nathan, 197
Reed, Joseph, 149, 248
Reid, Samuel, 298, 308
Revere, Paul, 112
Riall, Phineas, 258
Robbins, Jonathan, 32
Roberts, Kenneth, 86
Roesser, Matthew, 106
Rogers, Richard, 59
Rogers, Robert, 36, 53–56, 55, 64–67, 103, 110, 147, 152
  arrested for treason, 83
  counterfeiting conviction, 55
  Crown Point expedition and, 56–58
  defending Detroit, 90
  financial disaster of, 81–82
  on Lake George patrol, 61–63

life of, 79–87
literary works of, 82
Northwest Passage expedition, 83
Ranger rules, 80, 336–40
Ranger training, 79–80
St. Lawrence river area settlements attacks and, 70–74
wife of, 81
Rogers's Island, 64–65
Rohrer, Conrad, 280
Ross, James, 131
Ross, Robert, 259, 261
Runnels, Hardin F., 325, 334

Safford, Samuel, 160
St. Clair, Arthur, 251
Saratoga, Battle of, 108, 162–67
Sassamon, John, 16
Schuyler, Phillip, *158*, 161
Scott, Winfield, 253, 258, *304*
  during Mexican War, 304–23
  at Vera Cruz, *319*
Seguin, Juan, 312
Shaw, Jim, 324
Shirley, William, 38, 40
Simcoe, John Graves, 104, 222
Simpson, William, 136
slavery, 334–35
Smith, Charles, 169
Smith, Erastus "Deaf," 283
Smith, Francis, 111, 115–16
Smith, James, 45–46, 47, 97, 98
Smith, John, 7
Smith, Matthew, 131, 140–41
Smith, Samuel, 261
Smithwick, Noah, 271, 278–79, 280, 281, 288, 291, 335
Stark, Caleb, 125
Stark, John, 36, 53, 54, 56, *56*, 58, 78–79, 84, 101, 125–26, 147, 154–55, 169
  Battle of Bennington and, 157–60
  Commission in the Rangers, 341
  on Lake George patrol, 61–63
Steele, Archibald, 140
Stephenson, Hugh, 109, 132
Stevens, Ephraim, 154
Stewart, Alexander, 243

Stewart, Lazarus, 91
Stobo, Robert, 40
Stone, John, 12
Stoneman, George, 333
Sumter, Thomas, 197, 201–4, 237–38, 242, 243

Tarleton, Banastre, 196, 202–4, *203*, 206, 208, 210, 219–20, 223, 230, 233–37
  Battle of Cowpens and, 223–30
  Washington relationship, 229
Taylor, Zachary, 303, 304–23
Tecumseh, 254–57
Texas
  the Alamo, 281–82
  annexation of, 303
  birth of, 270–74
  Brownsville, 328–29
  independence of, 286–96
  Indian wars in, 324–34
  La Bolsa ranch, 332–34
  name origin, 271
  Plum Creek, Battle of, 295
  revolution, 275–85
  Rio Grande City, 330–31
  San Patricio, 282
  Sweet, Water, 282
Texas Regular Army, 281
Thames River, battle in area of, 256–58
Thompson, William, 109, 129, 202
Thorning, William, 115
Tobin, William, 329–34
Todd, John, 174
Travis, William Barrett, 281, 282
Treaty of Utrecht, 25
Truscott, Lucian, 87
Tumlinson, John J., 277, 278, 294

Underhill, John, 13
United States Army, birth of, 104
United States Navy, 254

Van Benthusen, A. B., 289
Vasquez, Rafael, 299–300
Vera Cruz, battle at, 318–19, 321–22
Vincennes, march against, 179–85

Index 359

Waggoner, Thomas, 40, 47
Wahab's plantation, ambush at, 210–11
Waldseemuller, Martin, 1
Walker, Samuel, 300, 301, 306–7, 315–18, *317*
Wallace, Big Foot, 300
War of 1812, 252–69
    Baltimore, 260–61
    Baton Rouge, 263
    Bladensburg, 259
    Chippewa River area, 258
    Fort Mims massacre, 255, 262
    Fort Stephenson, 255
    Horse Shoe Bend, 262–63
    Lake Champlain area, 260
    Lundy's Lane village, 258
    New Orleans, Battle of, 263–69, *264*
    Pensacola, 263
    Plattsburg, 260
    Thames River area, 256–58
War of Jenkins's Ear, 24, 32–34
War of the League of Augsburg, 20
Ward, Artemus, 129
Ward, Christopher, 104
Ward, Lafayette, 294
Warner, Seth, 119, 120, 157
Warren, Joseph, 111
Washington, George, 39, 42, 48, 68, 69, 84–85
    elected Commander in Chief, 129
    methods for keeping troops in line, 152

Washington, William, 224, 227, 236–37
    capture of, 245
    at Cowpens, *225*
    Tarleton relationship, 229
Watkins, George, 213
Watson, John, 238–39
Wayne, Anthony, 249, 251–52
weapons, 106–7, 298
Weeks, Joe, 289
Weitzel, Lewis, 191–92
Whitcomb, Benjamin, 167–68
White, Jacob, 108
Wilkenson, James, 253–54
Wilkinson, James, 188–89
Willet, Thomas, 15–16
Williams, Ephraim, 51, 52
Williams, Otho, 233, 235
Williamson, R. M., 277
Wilmot, William, death of, 249
Winder, William, 259
Winslow, John, 40, 41
Winslow, Josiah, 17, 26
Winston, Joseph, 212
Winthrop, John, 8
Wolfe, James, 64, 75–77
Woll, Adrian, 300
Wood, George, 306–23
Worth, T. J., 313
Wren, Nicholas, 288
Wyman, Seth, 31–32

Zumwalt, Adam, 294

Stackpole Military History Series

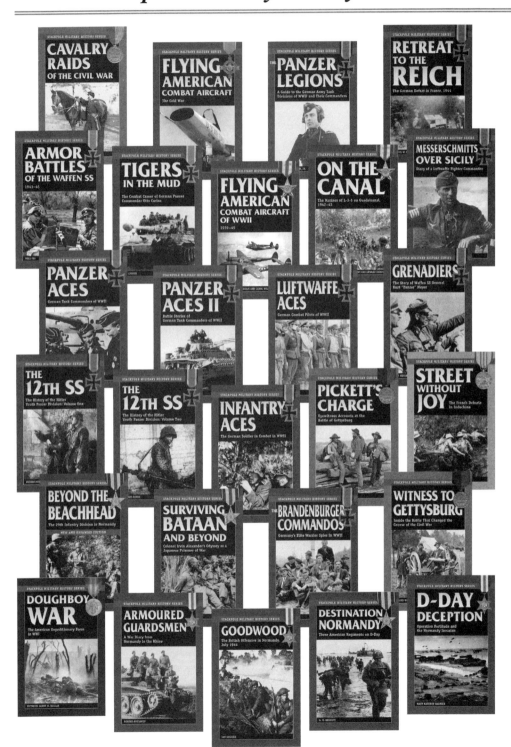

Real battles. Real soldiers. Real stories.

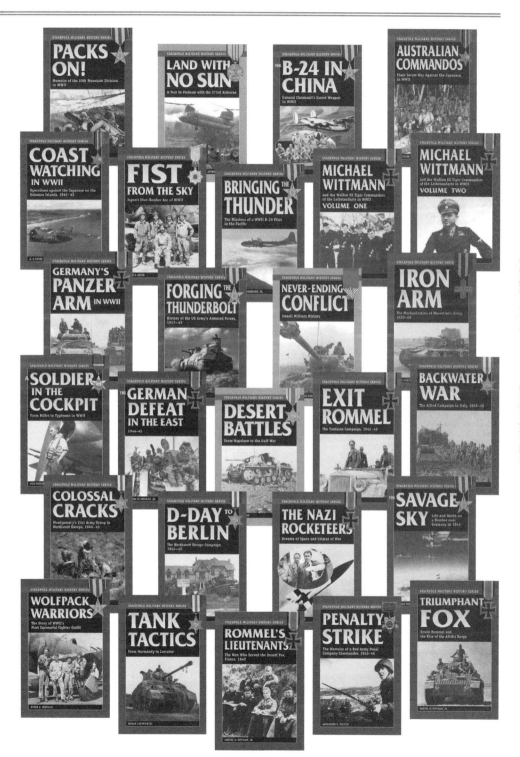

Stackpole Military History Series

Real battles. Real soldiers. Real stories.

Stackpole Military History Series

Real battles. Real soldiers. Real stories.

Stackpole Military History Series

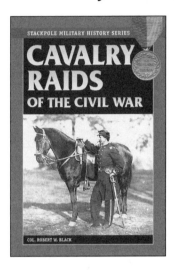

CAVALRY RAIDS OF THE CIVIL WAR
Robert W. Black

In war, the raid is the epitome of daring. Usually outnumbered, raiders launch surprise attacks behind enemy lines to take prisoners, destroy communications, and seize supplies—in short, to cause as much disruption and confusion as possible. During the Civil War, these men marauded on horseback, stunning their opponents with speed and mobility. From J. E. B. Stuart's 1862 ride around the Union army to James Wilson's crushing raids in Alabama and Georgia in 1865, both Union and Confederate raiders engaged in some of the most adventurous exploits of the war.

$17.95 • Paperback • 6 x 9 • 288 pages • 18 b/w photos

WWW.STACKPOLEBOOKS.COM
1-800-732-3669

Stackpole Military History Series

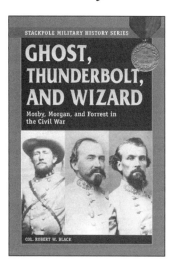

GHOST, THUNDERBOLT, AND WIZARD
MOSBY, MORGAN, AND FORREST IN THE CIVIL WAR
Col. Robert W. Black

Speed, boldness, and controversy marked the Civil War careers of this trio of Confederate cavalrymen. John Singleton Mosby teamed with J. E. B. Stuart to conduct the famous ride around McClellan's army in 1862. A year later, John Hunt Morgan led his gray raiders deep into Ohio, farther north than any other uniformed rebel force. Lacking military training, Nathan Bedford Forrest proved himself one of the war's best generals with his hit-and-run campaigns in Tennessee. Masters of scouting, raiding, and harassing the Union, Mosby, Morgan, and Forrest charged into history as pioneers of irregular warfare.

$19.95 • Paperback • 6 x 9 • 368 pages • 20 b/w photos

WWW.STACKPOLEBOOKS.COM
1-800-732-3669

Stackpole Military History Series

BEYOND THE BEACHHEAD
THE 29TH INFANTRY DIVISION IN NORMANDY
Joseph Balkoski

Previously untested in battle, the American 29th Infantry Division stormed Omaha Beach on D-Day and began a summer of bloody combat in the hedgerows of Normandy. Against a tenacious German foe, the division fought fiercely for every inch of ground and, at great cost, liberated the town of St. Lô. This new and expanded edition of Joseph Balkoski's classic follows the 29th through the final stages of the campaign and the brutal struggle for the town of Vire.

$19.95 • Paperback • 6 x 9 • 352 pages
36 b/w photos, 30 maps

WWW.STACKPOLEBOOKS.COM
1-800-732-3669

Stackpole Military History Series

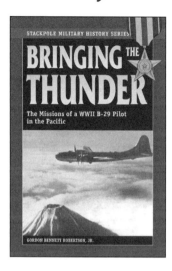

BRINGING THE THUNDER
THE MISSIONS OF A WWII B-29 PILOT IN THE PACIFIC
Gordon Bennett Robertson, Jr.

By March 1945, when Ben Robertson took to the skies above Japan in his B-29 Superfortress, the end of World War II in the Pacific seemed imminent. But although American forces were closing in on its home islands, Japan refused to surrender, and American B-29s were tasked with hammering Japan to its knees with devastating bomb runs. That meant flying low-altitude, nighttime incendiary raids under threat of flak, enemy fighters, mechanical malfunction, and fatigue. It may have been the beginning of the end, but just how soon the end would come—and whether Robertson and his crew would make it home—was far from certain.

$19.95 • Paperback • 6 x 9 • 304 pages • 36 b/w photos, 1 map

WWW.STACKPOLEBOOKS.COM
1-800-732-3669

Stackpole Military History Series

THE BRANDENBURGER COMMANDOS
GERMANY'S ELITE WARRIOR SPIES IN WORLD WAR II
Franz Kurowski

Before the German blitzkrieg stormed across Europe in 1939–40, a group of elite soldiers prepared the way by seizing bridges and other strategic targets ahead of the attack. In the following years, these warrior-spies, known as the Brandenburgers, operated behind enemy lines around the globe, from Russia and Yugoslavia to Egypt, Iraq, and India, often bending the rules of war while completing their daring covert missions.

$19.95 • Paperback • 6 x 9 • 384 pages • 114 b/w photos

WWW.STACKPOLEBOOKS.COM
1-800-732-3669

Stackpole Military History Series

INFANTRY ACES
THE GERMAN SOLDIER IN COMBAT IN WORLD WAR II
Franz Kurowski

This is an authentic account of German infantry aces—one paratrooper, two members of the Waffen-SS, and five Wehrmacht soldiers—who were thrust into the maelstrom of death and destruction that was World War II. Enduring countless horrors on the icy Eastern Front, in the deserts of Africa, and on other bloody fields, these rank-and-file soldiers took on enemy units alone, battled giant tanks, stormed hills, and rescued wounded comrades.

$19.95 • Paperback • 6 x 9 • 512 pages
43 b/w photos, 11 maps

WWW.STACKPOLEBOOKS.COM
1-800-732-3669

Stackpole Military History Series

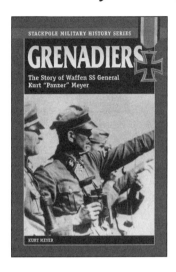

GRENADIERS
THE STORY OF WAFFEN SS GENERAL KURT "PANZER" MEYER
Kurt Meyer

Known for his bold and aggressive leadership, Kurt Meyer was one of the most highly decorated German soldiers of World War II. As commander of various units, from a motorcycle company to the Hitler Youth Panzer Division, he saw intense combat across Europe, from the invasion of Poland in 1939 to the 1944 campaign for Normandy, where he fell into Allied hands and was charged with war crimes.

$19.95 • Paperback • 6 x 9 • 448 pages • 93 b/w photos

WWW.STACKPOLEBOOKS.COM
1-800-732-3669

Stackpole Military History Series

TIGERS IN THE MUD
THE COMBAT CAREER OF GERMAN PANZER COMMANDER OTTO CARIUS

*Otto Carius,
translated by Robert J. Edwards*

World War II began with a metallic roar as the German Blitzkrieg raced across Europe, spearheaded by the most dreadful weapon of the twentieth century: the Panzer. Tank commander Otto Carius thrusts the reader into the thick of battle, replete with the blood, smoke, mud, and gunpowder so common to the elite German fighting units.

*$19.95 • Paperback • 6 x 9 • 368 pages
51 photos • 48 illustrations • 3 maps*

**WWW.STACKPOLEBOOKS.COM
1-800-732-3669**

Stackpole Military History Series

GUERRILLA WARFARE
IRREGULAR WARFARE IN THE TWENTIETH CENTURY
William Weir

Guerrilla Warfare covers a century of unconventional fighters at war, including the American hunt for Pancho Villa, Lawrence of Arabia's exploits during World War I, Mao versus Chiang in the Chinese Civil War, the showdown at Dien Bien Phu in 1954, France's long war in Algeria, the siege of Khe Sanh in the Vietnam War, the Afghan-Soviet War from 1979 to 1989, and more.

$16.95 • Paperback • 6 x 9 • 272 pages • 22 photos

**WWW.STACKPOLEBOOKS.COM
1-800-732-3669**

Stackpole Military History Series

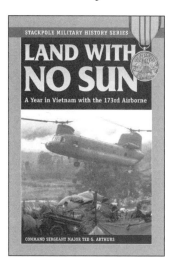

LAND WITH NO SUN
A YEAR IN VIETNAM WITH THE 173RD AIRBORNE
Command Sergeant Major Ted G. Arthurs

You know it's going to be hot when your brigade is referred to as a fireball unit. From May 1967 through May 1968, the Sky Soldiers of the 173rd Airborne were in the thick of it, humping eighty-pound rucksacks through triple-canopy jungle and chasing down the Viet Cong and North Vietnamese in the Central Highlands of South Vietnam. As sergeant major for a battalion of 800 men, it was Ted Arthurs's job to see them through this jungle hell and get them back home again.

$19.95 • Paperback • 6 x 9 • 416 pages • 60 b/w photos

WWW.STACKPOLEBOOKS.COM
1-800-732-3669

Also available from Stackpole Books

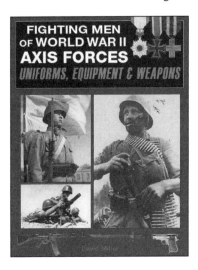 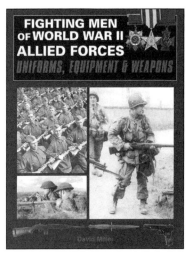

FIGHTING MEN OF WORLD WAR II
VOLUME 1: AXIS FORCES
VOLUME 2: ALLIED FORCES
David Miller

These comprehensive volumes present a full-color look at Axis and Allied soldiers in World War II, covering their weapons, equipment, clothing, rations, and more. The Axis volume includes Germany, Italy, and Japan while the Allied volume presents troops from the United States, Great Britain, and the Soviet Union. These books create a vivid picture of the daily life and battle conditions of the fighting men of the Second World War.

$49.95 • Hardcover • 9 x 12 • 384 pages • 600 color illustrations

WWW.STACKPOLEBOOKS.COM
1-800-732-3669